Criminal Justice Masterworks

Criminal Justice Masterworks
A History of Ideas about Crime, Law, Police, and Corrections

Robert Panzarella

Daniel Vona

John Jay College of Criminal Justice

CAROLINA ACADEMIC PRESS
Durham, North Carolina

Library of Congress Cataloging-in-Publication Data
Criminal justice masterworks : a history of ideas about crime, law, police, and corrections / [edited by] Robert Panzarella and Daniel O'Neal Vona.
    p. cm.
  ISBN 1-59460-229-8
  1. Criminal justice, Administration of--History. 2. Criminal justice, Administration of--Philosophy. 3. Criminology--History. 4. Criminal law--History. 5. Corrections--Philosophy--History. 6. Police administration--Philosophy--History. I. Panzarella, Robert. II. Vona, Daniel O'Neal. II. Title.

HV7405.C744 2006
364.09--dc22

                                                              2006014061

CAROLINA ACADEMIC PRESS
700 Kent Street
Durham, NC 27701
Telephone (919) 489-7486
Fax (919) 493-5668
www.cap-press.com

Printed in the United States of America

Contents

Acknowledgments

We wish to express out gratitude to Prof. Charles Lindner for a thorough and insightful review of the entire manuscript. We thank William J. Chambliss, Robert M. Fogelson, Herman Goldstein, and William A. Westley not only for their masterworks but also for their assistance in composing the introductions to their works. Most of all, we thank our students who have led us to new discoveries every time we ventured into these pages. However, when seeking those responsible for the flaws in this book, whether from ripping selections out of their contexts or from insipid introductions, the reader needs to look no further than the usual suspects—Panzarella and Vona.

Preface

Masterworks, the History of Ideas, and Critical Thinking

This selection of masterworks in the field of criminal justice was intended primarily for use as a capstone seminar for college undergraduates majoring in criminal justice studies. It is also useful as a brief survey of great writings in criminal justice for any advanced undergraduate or beginning graduate student or criminal justice professional. The editors' approach weaves together three strands of intellectual pursuit: an acquaintance with great writings on criminal justice, the perspective provided by a history of ideas, and the skills of critical thinking.

The selections provide a taste of classic works usually known to students only through textbook summaries, short excerpts, or references elsewhere. Although there are other anthologies which present selections from some of these same classics in the field of criminal justice, they offer only very short selections which are not sufficient to give the student a grasp of the work or a basis for critical analysis of it. The selections offered here are extensive enough to convey the main ideas, display the logical and empirical foundations of the works, and allow for critical thinking on the enduring fundamental issues in the field of criminal justice.

These masterworks in criminal justice are separated into four areas: criminology, legal studies, police studies, and correctional studies. One could add other areas, such as victimology or forensic science. However, this is not intended to be an exhaustive or even comprehensive survey of the field of criminal justice. It is only a sampling of some of the most prominent works in the most prominent traditional areas of criminal justice studies. Hopefully, it will give the reader a handle on some masterworks and some material for critical thinking about the most important issues in the field.

The selections are set in the context of the history of ideas. Political, economic and social events provide a distant background for these masterworks.

But their immediate background is the history of ideas, especially the ideas of the Age of Enlightenment and such subsequent ideas as biological, economic and social evolution, changing notions of society, and varying conceptions of human nature. A Historical Introduction summarizes the history of ideas of justice prior to the Age of Enlightenment and the key ideas of the Age of Enlightenment itself. Short introductions to the various selections provide information about the authors and the surfacing of their ideas in the intellectual currents of their times.

Masterworks can be read on either of two levels. To appreciate them on a fairly simple level, one could read them only for the purpose of discovering what their authors wrote. For example, one could read Beccaria to learn what his position was with regard to the death penalty. This would not be an especially challenging way to read, or teach, the masterworks. On a more sophisticated and more challenging level, one could read the masterworks as an exercise in critical thinking. On this level one would examine the specific arguments Beccaria presented in discussing the death penalty, what evidence he offered to support his arguments, and what assumptions he may have been making.

One of the hallmarks of a masterwork is that it sheds light on issues which remain urgent despite the passage of decades or even centuries. Masterworks encourage a critical analysis of ideas or practices which were significant at the time of their writing and remain significant today. The enduring relevance of masterworks invites critical thinking on contemporary issues in criminal justice. The introduction to each selection alerts the reader to some of the persisting issues related to each of the readings in this book.

The editors of this anthology believe that critical thinking requires at least three ingredients. First is a firm grip on an author's *ideas*. Ideas go beyond mere facts known then or now. Ideas consist of interpretations of the facts, the articulation of relationships between facts or events, and the implications of facts as perceived by the author. Sometimes the facts presented in a masterwork were discovered by the author; sometimes the facts were taken from research done by others. Particular facts may even have been wrong, yet an author's ideas may be valid on the basis of other facts to be found elsewhere. What is special about a masterwork is how the author has used diverse facts to generate new ideas. The selections have been deliberately chosen to highlight the new ideas expressed in the masterwork.

The second ingredient in critical thinking is an assessment of an author's ideas in terms of the evidence for the ideas presented by the author. The evidence presented to support an idea may be some form of reasoning, historical evidence, documents or records, analysis of texts, evidence from empirical research done by the author or cited by the author, case histories, or an author's personal observations or experiences. What constitutes acceptable evidence has been different at different moments in history and varies from one discipline to another. The type of evidence and kind of reasoning used in a law reading may be quite different from the type of evidence and kind of thinking used in a criminology reading from a social science study. No matter what the reader's own style of reasoning or taste in types of evidence, critical thinking requires the reader to know and judge the adequacy of an author's evidence and reasoning for each key idea. It is the presentation of the evidence along with the ideas which makes critical thinking possible. Thus the selections in this collection include whatever presentation of evidence for the ideas was included in a masterwork.

Finally, critical thinking calls for digging out the unstated assumptions underlying an author's ideas. Discovering assumptions may be the most challenging aspect of critical thinking. Assumptions are notions so basic that an author takes them for granted, and so does the reader usually. The assumptions are common beliefs which are such an integral part of a culture that they are seldom held up for inspection and rarely challenged. For example, in a culture where it is generally agreed and therefore assumed that a legal system is a system of justice, it is rare for someone to demand an explanation of how a legal system can be called "justice." The assumptions made by authors, and often by readers too, are assumptions about human nature, about the causes of behavior, about society, about the necessity or adequacy of institutions or systems, about the effectiveness of common practices, and so on. Often the author of a masterwork has challenged basic assumptions of the world in which they lived, and it requires as much fresh thinking now for a reader to challenge assumptions of the author and of the world in which we live. The introductions to the selections do not deprive a reader of the opportunity to discover an author's assumptions. But the introductions do point a finger in the direction of some of the assumptions which may underlie the main ideas in a masterwork.

It is, then, with these three impulses that the reader should proceed: an appetite for some great works in the field of criminal justice, an eye on the history of ideas, and an urge to do some critical thinking.

Historical Introduction:
Criminal Justice and the Age of Enlightenment

The study of modern European and American ideas about crime and justice begins with the radical new ideas of the Age of Enlightenment. But to grasp how radical these new ideas were it is necessary to understand how people thought about crime and justice in earlier times. Ordinarily ideas evolve over the course of many centuries or even thousands of years. However, the Age of Enlightenment was a period of only about two hundred years, roughly the seventeenth and eighteenth centuries. It was essentially the time when Europeans began to take a strictly rational approach to everything, relying on reason rather than religion and tradition. It was an intellectual revolution because instead of adding to earlier ideas, it was a time when earlier ideas were rejected to a large extent and replaced with a whole new way of looking at everything. The new way emphasized reason.

Changing Concepts of Crime and Justice

Primitive societies consisted of small tribes or clans. In a society which lived by hunting and gathering food, a clan might consist of about thirty people with a patriarch or matriarch. With the introduction of farming a greater number of people could live in one place, and then there might be a more formal leader or a council of elders. People knew what was right and what was wrong from custom. There were no formal laws, and there were no lawmakers. There was only the ordinary way of living in the clan. The first "laws" in any sense were the decisions made by deciding disputes. Disputes within a clan or tribe were usually settled by the head of the clan or by a group of elders.

If there was an act of violence between individuals from different tribes or clans, it was likely to trigger a blood feud. Justice was a clan matter, not an individual matter. If a person from clan A killed a person from clan B, then somebody from clan B would revenge the act by killing someone from clan A. It was not necessary to kill the individual who committed the crime. The crime could be avenged by anybody from clan B killing anybody from clan A. In society based on separate clans, doing vengeance was the greatest of all virtues. The mark of a hero in ancient sagas, such as the tale of Beowulf, was his readiness to take vengeance for his clan, knowing full well that by doing so he probably condemned himself to become the next to die in the cycle of vengeance. Such was the custom and unwritten law of many ancient societies. Different clans lived in separate places, which put some natural limits on blood feuds until the distances between them were reduced by population increases and the development of agriculture.

Justice meant vengeance for a wrong. This idea of justice was refined with the maxim, "An eye for an eye, and a tooth for a tooth." This was a more refined sense of justice than an unspecified demand for unlimited vengeance. This maxim was intended to keep the violence of vengeance from escalating. It meant, "Only one eye for one eye, and only one tooth for one tooth." Excessive vengeance itself became a wrong. Equal retribution was justice; excessive retribution was injustice. This was a more advanced concept of justice.

A revolution in the idea of "justice" occurred when justice based on personal or clan revenge was outlawed entirely and replaced by punishment administered by government. This development may have been prompted by several factors. The practice of allowing people to get their own personal justice may have seemed inefficient because sometimes the innocent were not capable of getting their own revenge, and sometimes the revenge set off a chain reaction of people from different clans taking turns killing one another without any way to stop it. Also, as societies grew larger, personal revenge as justice may have become less necessary and less practical.

The concept of justice changed when clan responsibility began to be replaced by individual responsibility. The idea of the individual is itself an idea which has evolved very slowly and is still not fully accepted. In ancient societies people were seen by others, and by themselves, as part of their clan rather than as individuals. One's entire life was lived as a member of a clan. One's good or bad fortune was only a share in the good or bad fortune of the clan. One bore responsibility for whatever was done by any member of the clan. A person lived a whole lifetime within the same clan, and within the clan itself one's place was settled. A hallmark of the Renaissance in fourteenth and fifteenth century Italy was the development of a sense of individual self apart from one's identity as part of a group. Before the Renaissance a person was regarded as a Florentine or Venetian or Roman and only later as an individual. Even today some parents and teachers may punish all children for something done by only one member of the family or class, and in modern warfare whole villages may be destroyed because one or a few individuals have done something. Still, the idea of the individual and the corollary of individual responsibility have evolved notably since ancient times. The evolving sense of the individual redefines the meaning of justice.

Larger societies led to the development of government institutions, even such simple government as a king and the king's strong-arm men. The most ancient writings and depictions of kings portray them as protectors of their people. Kings were also portrayed as spokesmen for deities and sometimes as themselves deities. These notions about kings, fostered by kings themselves, promoted general acceptance of the ruler's authority and thus provided legitimacy for government to intervene in the affairs of individuals. Once the authority of kings was established, justice by means of personal revenge not only threatened to undermine public order but also to undermine the king's right to decide what is just. Still, at first it may have seemed strange to let some government official, a person not even involved in the matter, take over the role of avenger. But kings may have demanded this as a right, and people may have been ready to accept it or unable to resist it. No matter the explanation, the old act of justice—personal revenge for some wrong done—became a crime. Justice was redefined as some sort of punishment administered by government.

In addition to the ancient ideas of a king as protector of the people and as the deity's spokesperson, from ancient to modern times various other ideas have been promoted to give legitimacy to government interventions in personal affairs. A purely secular philosophical argument in favor of justice as decided by government can be found as early as the fourth century B.C. in Plato's *Crito*. In that dialogue Socrates explained to his old friend Crito that, having been found guilty at his trial and having refused the penalty of banishment from Athens, Socrates must accept death according to the laws of Athens. Although in this case, said Socrates, the law reflected the will of the foolish multitude instead of the judgment of a wise man, the laws provided for the well-being of all citizens on the whole. Socrates argued that the laws bestowed such great benefits, in general, that one must accept even the unwise law and the unwise verdict of a particular trial, such as his own. The benefits of a lawful society outweighed any particular mistakes.

In England in the Middle Ages the legal idea which was used to support government intervention instead of personal vengeance was the idea that all people were the personal property of the king. Once kings claimed sovereignty over all their subjects, no one could take it upon himself to damage the property of the king. Only the king himself could do injury to his own property. Hence, if a person had a complaint against another person, it was necessary to bring the accused person before the king, or a representative of the king, for trial and punishment. A matter could not be settled between two individuals themselves. In keeping with this doctrine, "crime" became an offense against society, not just against another person. Eventually this also led to the doctrine that something could be a crime against society even if no individual seemed to be a victim of it. Thus, loitering or gambling could become a crime. It was society, or at least the rules of society, which determined what was a crime and how it should be dealt with. In the Age of Enlightenment some of the older doctrines, such as the people being the property of the king, were challenged and some new rationales were formulated to give legitimacy to the notion that justice means trial and punishment by government for an offense against society.

In ancient writings one also finds a few suggestions that there could be justice without punishment. Some ancient religious traditions introduced the concepts of repentance and forgiveness. These traditions provided a basis for redefining justice as restoring peace and order instead of exacting revenge. From this point of view, the goal of reforming people could replace the goal of punishing them. Justice could be defined anew as restoring peace and order. But ideas can take ages to soak into a culture, they may follow a crooked path, and there is no guarantee that any particular idea will ever win general acceptance. Although the notion that people might reform themselves or be reformed by others was important in some ancient religions, it was not a part of the administration of justice. Repentance and preaching repentance to others could straighten out one's relationship to the deity but could not restore balance to the scales of justice in this world. Only retribution could do that. The need for retribution became a core concept in Christianity, especially in the fourth century doctrine developed by St. Anselm that only the death of the son of the deity could atone for mankind's offenses against the deity. Punishment could not be waived. Understandably, an earthly system of justice, following the divine model, could demand no less. Crimes had to be punished before repentance could count.

Religious traditions also fostered the development of the idea that people should be judged by their intentions as well as by their actions. Twelfth century Irish monks developed the doctrine that one's intentions were even more important than one's deeds. The important thing was not what a person did, either good or bad, but what a person intended. The doctrine of Irish monks was able to influence all of European society because Irish monks served as personal confessors to popes. The idea that intentions outweigh deeds was so popular by the fifteenth century that a disgusted Dante wrote in *The Inferno,* "The road to hell is paved with good intentions." Dante wanted to hold onto the older idea that people should be held responsible for their actions regardless of their intentions. But the idea that intentions count, and could count more than actual deeds, gradually worked its way into the administration of justice. Lack of clear, deliberate intention could mitigate criminal charges; for example, killing someone might not be a crime if it was not intended. On the other hand, intentions even without deeds, such as a conspiracy, could be crimes.

Ideas about the importance of people's intentions, together with the idea of justice as reforming individuals and restoring peace, found new voices in the Age of Enlightenment, particularly in the writings of Montesquieu (1689–1755), Jean Jacques Rousseau (1712–1778), and Cesare Beccaria (1738–1794). It was not on the basis of religion but on the basis of reason that Enlightenment thinkers thought it necessary to rethink the question, What is justice? They began with the premise that all governments and all laws are man-made and should be limited to what is reasonably necessary for the safety and happiness of people. The purpose of government was to provide for the greatest possible good of the greatest possible number of people.

The Enlightenment thinkers believed in "the pursuit of happiness." This phrase carried the idea that individuals should seek self-advancement and happiness by whatever means do not interfere with the happiness of others. It was a rejection of the religious idea that happiness is to be sought in an after-life. As far as crime was concerned, the important thing was a person's mental state. They questioned the need for punishment and whether punishment it-self could reform. Starting with the Age of Enlightenment, the idea of reform-ing offenders became more prevalent both in criminal justice theory and in practice.

Thus the concepts of crime and justice developed over thousands of years. This was probably due to increasing populations, the need to check the spread of personal vengeance, the development of more organized and pow-erful governments, the potent influence of religious ideas, and finally the ra-tional and humanitarian values of the Age of Enlightenment.

The Emergence of Law Codes and Commentaries

The first written law code was the Code of Hammurabi of Babylon about 2100 B.C. Hammurabi's Code was about 4,000 lines long, inscribed on a stone pillar erected in the marketplace. The Code contained laws about crimes, including sorcery, as well as laws about family issues, property rights and social order. It laid down the principle of "an eye for an eye, a tooth for a tooth." As an ancient ruler Hammurabi was more than a king. Ancient kings were the religious leaders of their societies. Whatever earthly power the king had was derived from the belief that the king was a visible representative of the deity, perhaps even a deity himself. The ancient world was a religious world. Events were controlled by deities, society and government were established by deities, and the conduct of individuals had to conform to the wills of the deities. The Code assumed that the conduct of individuals would be guided by the necessity to keep oaths sworn to the deities. Hence, at trials people were made to swear oaths that they would tell the truth. The people of ancient societies would dread the consequences of violating oaths to the deities.

The law code which Moses inscribed on stone for the Hebrews about three centuries later was the much simpler code of only ten commandments. The biblical narrative makes it clear that this code was prompted by the need to establish some uniform rules to bring order and govern a society which was verging towards chaos. But again it was considered a code which was the word of the deity. Moses was both the representative of the deity and the leader of the tribes of Israel. However this code of only ten commandments was so short and simple that before long a great many smaller, more specific laws were developed in order to apply the code to all aspects of life. In addition, over the centuries scholars wrote commentaries on the law and wrote about how the law was applied in particular cases, so that the ten simple commandments became only the bedrock of a mountain of written laws and commentaries covering all aspects of life. One of the ten basic laws was, Thou shalt not bear false witness. Again, those who might break the law learned to fear not only the vengeance of men but also the wrath of the deity.

In 593 B.C. Solon, the chief magistrate of Athens, composed the first written code of laws among the Greeks. Solon's code of laws was more like a constitution. It divided the people into distinct social classes based on their property, granted the rights of citizenship to all free people, and prohibited settling debts by selling a person into slavery. Although Solon's laws were not said to come from the deities, obeying the laws was seen as essential to keep from offending the deities. Even the government of Athens, where reason was so important, was considered a reflection of the wills of the deities. People who were accused of committing crimes but claimed to be innocent had to swear oaths of innocence, believing that false oaths would be punished severely by the deities.

In ancient Rome, about 500 B.C., a group of ten distinguished men was appointed to create a written law code based on existing customs. Their code was written on ten tablets and put on display in the marketplace. Another two tablets were added later. In Rome too, the authority of the deities as well as punishment by the authorities were the forces behind the laws. Every

Roman boy had to memorize the tables of the law. The Roman laws, spreading with the Roman Empire, infiltrated the laws and customs of the various peoples in the empire and became the basic law code for most of Europe. Like the Mosaic code, the Roman code grew as commentators recorded specific examples of how the laws were applied in various situations and how the laws were adapted to changing conditions. By the sixth century A.D. the Roman code had become so unwieldy that the Emperor Justinian ordered a comprehensive revision and compilation of the laws, which became known as the Justinian Code. However, with the fall of the Roman Empire, ancient local laws and customs reasserted themselves in the nations of Europe. It was not until the rediscovery of the Justinian law code in the eleventh century that Roman law was revived and overtook local laws in most of the countries of Europe.

Under ancient law codes not all people were equal. Solon's code was most explicit in dividing society into distinct social classes. All ancient codes assumed and cemented the idea that different classes of people had different duties and rights. For example, in the Roman Empire citizens of the City of Rome had more rights than anyone else. Hence there were practical advantages for someone born elsewhere to be granted Roman citizenship. But the system contained its own time bomb. Merchants throughout the empire would refuse to do business with citizens of Rome because these merchants did not have equal rights if a business matter ended up in court. Eventually Rome had to grant equal rights to all merchants, Roman or not. This was just the first step in the development of equal rights under law for everyone. Still, as late as the time of the French Revolution, it was common to have separate laws and separate courts for different classes of people in the same society.

The real importance of the development of a written law code was that the law could then be known to everyone, and therefore it had to be applied in the same manner to everyone. The existence of a written law code reduced the power of a king to make arbitrary decisions. However, kings themselves could still change the laws, and kings themselves stood above the laws, similar to the way parents might make rules for their children. It was thousands of years later, in the Age of Enlightenment, that the development of law codes reached its peak when even kings were made subject to a code of law.

Law codes were themselves transformed by the development of lawyers and courts. Written law codes made it possible for lawyers to develop as a profession separate from lawmakers. Before the twentieth century most people could not read or write. They became dependent on lawyers as far as law was concerned. Written law codes also made it possible for courts to multiply like franchises with a common set of rules and procedures. The written codes provided some uniformity throughout a kingdom, however large. With many courts and many lawyers, eventually law took on a life of its own separate from rulers. In the hands of judges and lawyers dealing with the problems of ordinary people, laws returned to their earliest origins in the common customs and morals of society as a whole. Lacking the authority and mystique of kings, judges, and lawyers had to justify their legal system by showing that it was an expression of accepted customs and values. Laws came to be seen as the rules of society, not merely the will of the king.

The development of Middle Eastern and European law codes suggests that codes of law developed and were put into writing due to societies becoming larger and more complex. Laws were accepted because they defined people's places in society and created consistency throughout a kingdom. Over time laws enabled even the lowest classes of people to be more secure and free from the whims of capricious rulers. In time, government with law evolved into government under law.

Trials and Punishments

The earliest trials consisted of an accused person and, when possible, the victim being brought before a ruler to determine if the accused was guilty and what punishment was appropriate. Among the Greeks and Romans magistrates were appointed to settle cases. A single magistrate or a group of magistrates together might conduct the trial. In the early days a citizen who did not trust the magistrates could have his trial brought before an assembly of all the people of Athens or Rome, although later these citizen "juries" were reduced to a group of fifty in Athens and to a varying number up to seventy-five in Rome. In Rome there was a final appeal to the emperor, as in the earliest days.

Witnesses and evidence might be presented at trials. But the principal feature of trials, and sometimes the only basis for a trial, was the swearing of oaths. If the accused wanted to claim innocence, he had to swear a formal oath that he was innocent. The accuser has to swear a formal oath that he was bringing true charges, not false accusations. The suspect had to get people who knew him to also swear oaths that they believed he was telling the truth in claiming to be innocent. The accuser got people to swear that he was telling the truth in making the accusations. Basically, whichever side got more people to swear oaths won the case. This procedure was not so strange in the ancient world where people grew up and lived together all their lives in small villages. The witnesses swearing oaths were well known to everyone in the village; they, together with the accused and the accuser, would continue to live in the village in almost every case. The system depended on the oath takers fearing the wrath of the deities as well as the retribution of their fellow citizens if their oaths were false.

Swearing of oaths remained the core of trials for noble people until well into the nineteenth century. But other kinds of trials were devised for ordinary people. At various times omens were used to get a judgment from the deities. In the Middle Ages, particularly in northern Europe, ordeals were developed, such as making a person walk on hot embers or dunking a person in a river with his hands tied behind his back, with the idea that the deity would not allow an innocent person to be harmed much by such ordeals. In practice most of a "trial" was the inquiry which took place beforehand to decide if an ordeal would be necessary. Also, historical records tell that people were often rescued from ordeals after only a few minutes; that was enough time to determine the deity's judgment in the case. Eventually trials began to depend mostly on confessions. But, since guilty people could not be expected to confess readily, torture was used to induce an individual to make a confession. However, one by one these various ways of getting at the truth proved unsatisfactory. The history of trials is a history of disillusionment. People lost confidence in various procedures one after another. Disillusionment paved the path from oaths and omens to ordeals and then to torture.

Contrary to what one might imagine, the most sadistic punishments were not generally found in primitive societies. In small primitive societies punishments tended to be mild. The punishments for serious crimes were mostly banishments and limited mutilations which marked the person as a criminal for everyone to see, as in the biblical story of Cain who was punished for murdering his brother by being marked in some way and made to wander over the face of the earth. However, banishment was almost a death sentence; it meant that the person had to survive alone in the wilderness or had to try to gain acceptance among some other people at a time when in many languages the word for "stranger" was the same as the word for "enemy." If the offender was not banished, punishment often consisted of shunning the offender or demanding some form of compensation. Perhaps the leniency of punishments in primitive societies was a consequence of everybody knowing everybody else, everybody living as a single small community, and nobody wanting to trigger a blood feud. Sadistic punishments were more characteristic of such societies as the Roman Empire, the empire of Alexander the

Great, and the societies of medieval Europe. Sadistic punishments tended to begin as an aspect of empires, which imposed cruel punishments on the conquered peoples. But eventually the same treatments were applied to the people of the homeland also. It was the sadistic punishments of European societies that prompted outcries against cruel punishments in the Age of Enlightenment.

Punishments for crimes have changed over the centuries. Punishment by banishment continued to more modern times, but the banishment might be to some dreadful place, such as the French penal colony on Devil's Island or the English penal colony in Australia. In ancient and medieval times the most common type of mutilation was branding, usually on the face. Sometimes part of an ear or nose would be cut off, or a hand as in Islamic law for hardcore thieves. Fines were common in Roman law. Being reduced to servitude or outright sold as a slave was a way to handle the crime of not paying debts. A criminal might be sentenced to some kind of harsh public service, such as being a rower on a galley or a forced laborer in mines or on roads, for a number of years.

Ancient and medieval treatments of criminals emphasized punishment because punishment was seen as a necessary and effective way to deal with crime and criminals. To start with, punishment satisfied the necessity for vengeance in order to balance the scales of justice. In addition, punishment was seen as a deterrent to turn other people away from crime. Finally, for those who believed that criminals should be reformed, punishment was seen as the most effective way to reform offenders. A strong belief in the efficacy of punishment enabled people to believe that punishment itself was a good thing. This belief was so deeply rooted in ancient and medieval religious traditions that even self punishment was viewed as a way of becoming a holier and better person. However, the philosophers of the Age of Enlightenment began to question the basic premise that a person can be made better by punishment.

Prisons were not used as a punishment in ancient times. A person might be held prisoner briefly before a trial. A person might also be held in a prison after a trial while awaiting punishment or banishment. But one would not be sentenced to prison as the punishment for a crime unless it was for nonpayment of a debt, with the expectation that some relative or friend would be induced to pay the debt and then the prisoner could be released. A prisoner was not clothed, fed, or kept warm at public expense. It was up to the prisoner's family or friends to bring food, clothes and any other necessities. From ancient times there were some people who brought food or clothing to prisoners as an act of charity. The only obligation of the authorities was to keep the person locked up. Prison conditions were horrendous until prison reform became an issue in the Age of Enlightenment.

The Ages of Renaissance, Discovery, and Enlightenment

The Age of Enlightenment was the culmination of the Renaissance and the Age of Discovery. The Renaissance, starting in Italy in the fourteenth century and spreading to northern Europe over the next two centuries, was the time when Europe rediscovered the ancient Greek and Roman cultures. Ideals of beauty were rediscovered in ancient sculpture and painting. Ideals of truth were rediscovered in the works of ancient philosophers, historians and scientists. The thinkers of the Renaissance were amazed that reason and experience alone, not Christian revelation, had produced such works as Plato's *Republic,* Aristotle's *Ethics,* Aristotle's studies of botany and Ptolemy's *Geography.* The invention of the printing press suddenly made these rare and nearly forgotten old works available to intellectuals throughout Europe. The result was a new faith in reason and an optimistic view of the capabilities of human nature. Part of this was a new view of nature as something governed by some sort of laws. These laws could be used to explain various events in nature, so that one no longer needed to explain events as acts of a deity. An earthquake or a stroke of lightning could be seen as a purely natural event rather than as an act of a deity punishing sinners.

The new Renaissance view of the world included a new view of human beings. Instead of thinking of human beings as bodies with souls infused directly by a deity, human beings were seen as simply another part of nature. When Copernicus and then Galileo published studies of astronomy and proposed the theories that the sun did not revolve around the earth and that man was not the center of the universe, the religious authorities correctly perceived that they were attacking the established Christian view of the world. The scientific studies of people like Copernicus and Galileo undermined the basic beliefs which were the foundation of society. Society could not remain the same if a purely natural view of the universe and of human nature replaced the Christian view of the world. Even ideas of the deity had to be made more rational and more compatible with the perceived laws of nature. Renaissance thinkers implied that genuine truth could be determined better by studies of nature instead of study of the Bible.

It was especially English scientists and philosophers, such as Isaac Newton and John Locke, who pushed the idea of laws of nature to the limits. Locke explained the human mind and the processes of thinking in terms of natural laws. He explained how physical sensations give rise to mental perceptions and how perceptions then combine into thoughts, following natural laws governing the connections between impressions. It was a law of the mind, for example, that two perceptions which often occur together, such as the brightness of the sun and the warmth of the air, would become associated with one another in the mind. The old view of the divinely infused soul as the distinguishing feature of a human being was replaced by a view of the human being as an entirely natural creature, part and parcel with the rest of nature and following natural laws like the rest of nature. Even the mind was a purely natural thing, following its own natural laws of sensory impressions and mental associations.

The Renaissance flowed into and mingled with the Age of Discovery. In the fifteenth and sixteenth centuries European navigators, inspired by the extraordinary tales of earlier merchant travelers like Marco Polo, pushed beyond the limits of the known world in quests for the gold of Africa and, later, for the spices of the Orient. Portuguese mariners pushed first down the coast of Africa and then around the Cape to India, where they connected to the trading routes from the Orient. The ancient Greek geographers Strabo and Ptolemy had pointed out that the earth is round, but seafaring adventurer Christopher Columbus believed (mistakenly) that it was smaller than Portuguese royal geographers had calculated, and hence Columbus thought that his little ships could make it all the way around to China by sailing west. The Portuguese said no to Columbus, but the Spanish authorities were willing, reluctantly, to sponsor his voyage on a low budget. When Columbus returned to Spain after his first voyage across the Atlantic, he still thought he had been to some islands and a peninsula of China. It was only on his second voyage that he realized it was a New World.

Columbus' voyages provoked not only a revolution in geography but also a revolution in ideas. By chance, Columbus' first voyage took him to islands of the northern Caribbean, where he encountered Taino Indians. The Tainos were extremely peaceful people whose traditions included sharing everything with others. They took their livelihood directly from the land and sea, which produced abundant food without much labor. The warm climate demanded only minimal clothing and shelter. Columbus' sailors were delighted that the natives gave them as presents anything the sailors took a fancy to, cheerfully brought food to them, built simple houses for them, did chores for them, and brought women to them as companions and helpers. When Columbus returned to Spain, his account of his first journey was published and read with wonder throughout Europe. People concluded that these Tainos were proof that all human beings were originally gentle and loving beings living in idyllic harmony with a bountiful nature. The tale of the innocent, happy savage was a direct challenge to the traditional Christian view accepted throughout Europe that human beings were born sinners, selfish, ignorant, and prone to violence as a result of original sin. It was not until later voyages that Columbus encountered the fierce Arawaks and the bellicose cannibalistic Caribs of the eastern Caribbean islands. But later voyages were not so well publicized and could not uproot the new belief that human nature was innocent, kind, and sociable unless corrupted by modern civilization.

The new belief in the innocent savage implied that human nature could be trusted. The complex societies and cultures of the New World signaled that people were not by nature ignorant although they might be uninformed about many things. A society could be built on the basis of natural reason and skills without any divine intervention. The lessons of the Renaissance about the ability of unaided human nature to create a great civilization were reinforced by the Age of Discovery.

Medieval social order was based on the idea that each person was born into a particular place in society, whether a noble or a craftsman or a serf, and everyone should stay in their place. Even in the same noble family, there was the firstborn son who would inherit everything and the other children who would get only the charity of the firstborn. The Spanish conquistadors of the New World were individuals with little or no social standing in Spain who embarked on their voyages to win the wealth and power they could not have in Spain. They took advantage of the ocean separating the New World from Spain to create for themselves a lifestyle with huge estates and compulsory native laborers. By their own efforts they made themselves the equals of the Old World aristocratic families, as did the later Englishmen with Caribbean sugar plantations. An Old World assumption that people were born into a particular station in life in accordance with the will of the deity and that people should stay in their proper places crumbled before the New World assertion that the individual could become whatever individual enterprise could attain.

The conquistadors' belief that they could seize, slaughter or subjugate the natives of the New World was based on the belief that the conquerors were spreading Christianity by whatever means were necessary. This rationale kept the Old World authorities from interfering with the conquest. Farther to the north in this New World the British, Dutch and French were basing their conquests on the principle that the natives had failed to develop the land whereas the Europeans had the skills and the means to develop the land and plant a higher civilization. This also defied Old World traditions about people staying in their place. The American colonists embodied a new belief in the rightness and proper rewards of individual industry as opposed to the traditional rights of hereditary estates and entitlements of nobility. Groups like the Puritans had made themselves unwelcome in the Old World by demanding that lower classes of people—but not the very lowest—be given rights previously reserved to upper classes. A new belief in the right of the individual to defy the established social order and seize any opportunity for self-advancement in the pursuit of happiness became the basis for a new social order in which people were created equal in some sense.

New Ideas about Government

During the French Revolution (1789–1799) the revolutionaries took over the churches and set up a statue of the goddess of reason in Notre Dame Cathedral in Paris. This act epitomized the Age of Enlightenment—the deity of the Enlightenment was a deity of reason. The Enlightenment challenged not only the basic institutions of European society but also the most fundamental beliefs and assumptions of society.

Seventeenth century Enlightenment thinkers, like the English philosopher Thomas Hobbes and the French philosopher Jean Jacques Rousseau, also began saying that society and government were the results of natural causes, not divinely ordained. If people formed a government it was because natural situations and basic human needs, such as the need for security, prompted people to develop forms of collective society and governments. Henceforward it became necessary for governments to explain themselves and to show what right they had to rule over people. It became a new faith that governments derived their powers from the people, not from a deity.

The Constitution of the United States, a product of the Age of Enlightenment, was conspicuous for making no mention at all of a deity. Although "In God We Trust" later appeared on American money and "under God" was added to the American "Pledge of Allegiance" in 1954, the ideas which were the foundation of the Constitution, as well as its text, began with, "We the People...." In theory, at least for the moment, the state was separated from religion.

The discovery of the New World presented a challenge to the system of government of the Old World. European countries were monarchies. Kings and queens were crowned in cathedrals to symbolize the belief that they were the representatives of the deity in ruling the earthly kingdoms. When the conquistadors discovered the Aztec, Mayan and Inca kingdoms, it provoked great debate among the theologians at the University of Salamanca in Spain. These theologians could not imagine anything happening which was not the will of the deity. Their conclusion was that the New World kings also must have been chosen by the deity even if those kings did not have the Christian revelation. This led to a new theory about a natural world and a natural society which was not Christian but was not evil. From that time on, even for Christians there could be a legitimate natural society separate from any particular church or religion.

The monarchs of Spain, Ferdinand and Isabella, ordered the conquistadors to show the New World kings all the respect due to royalty. They knew that if people were allowed to abuse one king, they would soon abuse another. However, the conquistadors, always mindful of the ocean between themselves and Spain, ignored the royal commands and slaughtered the New World kings for their gold and lands. Henceforward kings were no longer regarded as sacred. The English beheaded their King Charles I in 1649, although in 1660 they restored the monarchy by recognizing Charles II as King. However, the New World soon and permanently rejected kings. The American Revolution against the king of England also echoed back across the Atlantic in 1789, adding inspiration to the tumult of the French revolution.

A speech by King Louis XVI of France summarized the Old World view of government. The Parlement of Paris, a judicial and administrative body of the city, had attempted to block some new laws which the King had decided upon. Although these assemblies did not make laws, they were expected to approve laws before laws were put into effect. The King personally appeared before the Parlement and reminded them:

> It is in my person alone that sovereign power resides.... It is from me alone that my courts derive their authority; and the plenitude of this authority, which they exercise only in my name, remains always in me.... It is to me alone that legislative power belongs, without any dependence and without any division.... The whole public order emanates from me, and the rights and interests of the nation ... are necessarily joined with mine and rest only in my hands. (Doyle, 1989, p. 38.)

King Louis XVI had supported and supplied the American Revolution against the British, but he was not ready for such a change in France. In the course of the civil disorders of the French Revolution, King Louis XVI was eventually beheaded. All the members of his family were also killed, so that there could be no direct heir to the throne. Henceforth the power of rulers depended on the will of the people. Lawmaking also passed from kings to citizen lawmakers elected by the people. Soon afterwards Napoleon Bonaparte rose to power and had himself made emperor, and later in the nineteenth century a monarchy was reestablished in France for a time with the consent of the people. But European monarchies were no longer absolute. With limited functions left in the hands of the monarch, they became another form of democracy.

After the Enlightenment: Progress, Retreat, and Tolerance

A quick glance at the Renaissance, the Age of Discovery, and the Enlightenment might give the impression that there is an inevitable onward march of progress over the course of history. In the nineteenth century, after the Enlightenment, many people did believe in such a march of progress. But history is full of uncertainties, starts and stops, advances and retreats, and zigzags. On top of it all there are debates about what constitutes "progress," especially when one considers cultural and social changes as well as technological developments. The Renaissance, for example, held and advanced scientific technology but retreated 1,500 years and more to recover basic ideas about the nature of the universe, human nature, society, government, and the pursuit of earthly happiness. The centuries between the fall of Rome and the Renaissance were viewed as "the Dark Ages." Progress was found in a retreat to the ancient cultures of Greece and Rome before lurching forward in the Age of Discovery.

The Enlightenment thinkers of the seventeenth century tried to usher in an "age of reason." They believed that the human mind, working carefully with the raw material supplied by the senses, could know reality. They trusted the mind more than the senses. Logic was the best proof of anything. However, nineteenth century concepts of science played down reason as a means of finding the truth; the "scientific method" demanded objective evidence, not just reasoning, to support any conclusion. Not only could the senses be deceived, but the mind also was subject to misperceptions, biases, false conclusions, and even unconscious aberrations. The scientists of the nineteenth century were not alone in questioning the adequacy of reason. Popular philosophers abandoned reason for "idealism" and "romanticism." Idealism, recalling Plato, taught that the human mind can know only sense impressions and mental perceptions rather than reality itself. Romanticism elevated emotions above reason, emphasizing "knowing" through intuition and feeling. For melancholic beauty, the wealthy adorned their estates with imitation ancient ruins. For educated people the Enlightenment had provided mostly books of illuminating essays about the world, history and society. For the growing number of literate people the nineteenth century romantics provided a new kind of literature consisting of mostly novels of love and tales of horror, whatever aroused the emotions most. The Enlightenment was in retreat.

For religion the Enlightenment offered "deism" in place of the miracles and ancient dualism of supernatural powers of good and evil contending for the souls of humans. Deism was belief in a deity of reason who created an orderly universe governed by laws of nature. The laws of nature were so grounded in reason that a deity of reason would not interfere with natural laws. It would be unreasonable to do so.

The Enlightenment was upstaged in the nineteenth century by a revival of religious fundamentalism in Europe and America with a reaffirmation of some earlier beliefs about the deity, the devil, miracles, and justice in an afterlife. The first seven presidents of the United States were deists; all of them believed in a deity of reason and natural law, but none of them professed belief in traditional Christianity. Their speeches included only vague occasional allusions to Christianity, apparently for political reasons. They may have held a common Enlightenment opinion that traditional Christianity was necessary for uneducated common people, who would form a more stable society because of their belief in submission to authority in this life and justice to be achieved in an afterlife. But by the middle of the nineteenth century, religious revivalism was so strong that no one could aspire to political office in the United States without professing traditional Christian beliefs. Revival meetings, stirred by great preachers, attracted vast crowds, and traditional churches flourished in the nineteenth century. Faith rose up again and challenged reason.

The seeds of a new development in society and in ideas about human nature had been planted in the seventeenth century in the colony of Rhode Island. This colony had been founded by Roger Williams, an extremely religious man who had fled for his life from the Massachusetts colony. He had excellent connections with England's King Charles I; then with Oliver Cromwell, who had beheaded King Charles I; and after that with King Charles II, who had Cromwell's corpse removed from Westminster Abbey and beheaded. Williams gave up his family inheritance rather than submit to a simple court procedure to claim it, because he considered it a debasement of religion to swear on a Bible to tell the truth in court. He also considered it a debasement of religion that the colony of

Massachusetts was ruled as a theocracy by a committee of ten religious leaders. He wanted absolute separation of religion from government and politics. It especially annoyed the religious powers in Massachusetts that Williams had obtained a royal charter to set up a colony next to them in which there would be no government affiliated religion. It meant, as Williams had spelled out in his colony's charter, that people of every religion would be welcome and legally equal in his colony, including various Christian sects, Jews, Moslems (called "Turks" in those days), and, most offensive of all, atheists. Perhaps as a consequence of this official tolerance, his colony's charter was the only one to include a Bill of Rights. Williams' good connections in England enabled him to hold onto his colony and its charter despite the efforts of the Massachusetts group to have him imprisoned or executed and to annex his colony. In fact, his connections were good enough for him to tell the English rulers that they had no right to give land in America to anyone because it belonged to the natives of the place. His colony was the only one created by purchasing the land from the native tribes, among whom he was known as a great peace maker.

Roger Williams is credited as the inventor of the idea of "tolerance." His colony was the first place in the world to give equality to all faiths and even to atheism. He lived in a world where most people were convinced that being a true believer included believing that all other religions were false and should be stamped out. It was an accepted fact that if one is right, the others must be wrong, and any true believer would do all that one could to promote the right and oppose the wrong. But Williams thought that a person could be a true believer and still live peacefully in society with other people who had different beliefs.

A tolerant society prompted a new idea about the human mind and human nature. If different faiths could live peacefully side by side in society, different ideas could live peacefully side by side in the human mind. The mind itself could become tolerant. Contrary to Enlightenment notions about human beings as purely rational beings, a person could hold firmly to beliefs which appeared to be contradictory, believing in both a natural and a supernatural world and keeping the two separate from one another. Thus an individual could be both rational and faith-based at the same time. A person could be rational in some aspects of life and faith-based in other aspects of life. One need not exclude the other. A wall of separation between church and state found a parallel in the mind: a wall of separation between faith and reason.

The revival of religion which took place in the nineteenth century had major impacts on criminal justice. Religious convictions and religious organizations played supporting roles and sometimes leading roles in lawmaking, court decisions, correctional institutions, and correctional philosophies. Criminology, too, gave some acknowledgment to the role of churches in forming the law-abiding habits of citizens. Religious individuals and religious organizations led the way in developing humane penitentiaries and modern probation policies. Concepts of tolerance and individual rights informed not only lawmaking and court decisions but also philosophies and practices of policing. The Enlightenment thinkers generally assumed that human beings were the same everywhere, and so they did not give much thought to cultural diversity. However, the intensified contacts between cultures and the great population movements of the nineteenth and twentieth centuries have demanded a greater role for tolerance in the institutions of government, especially in criminal justice institutions.

The new-found tolerance of the nineteenth and twentieth centuries made it possible for the ideas of the Enlightenment to continue to exercise their influence despite the competing beliefs of reaffirmed traditional religions. The Age of Enlightenment had put on the table a new set of beliefs about human nature, society, government, and law. Some of the ideas of the Age of Enlightenment have become so widely accepted that they are now assumptions. It is taken for granted that ordinary people should choose their rulers and lawmakers. Where hereditary monarchs survive, what little power they may exercise is determined by citizens. The idea that people were born a certain way and that this determined their place in life has been replaced by the assumption that people have the right to become whatever they can. The idea that laws represent the will of a deity following the outlines of a revealed morality has been supplanted by the belief that laws are the products of human legislators and ought to be based on reason. The idea that all people should be equal as far as law is concerned is no longer debated. Since the Age of Enlightenment criminal justice has been viewed as an entirely natural, human creation which should be guided by reason and subject to the collective will of the people. Modern criminal justice writers seldom discuss these fundamental beliefs. The modern history of criminal justice begins with these basic ideas of the Age of Enlightenment.

Suggested Reading

Barnes, H.E. (1965). *An intellectual and cultural history of the western world,* 3rd edition. New York: Dover Publications, Inc. See especially Volume 2, *From the Renaissance through the eighteenth century.*

Doyle, W. (1989). *The Oxford history of the French revolution.* New York: Oxford University Press.

Montesquieu. (1973). *Persian letters* (C.J. Betts, Trans.). New York: Penguin Books. (Original work published 1721)

Plato. (1999). *Crito.* In *Great dialogues of Plato* (W.H.D. Rouse, Trans.). New York: Signet Classics.

Rembar, C. (1980). *The law of the land: The evolution of our legal system.* New York: Simon and Schuster.

Rice, E.F., Jr., & Grafton, A. (1994). *The foundations of early modern Europe 1460–1559,* 2nd ed. New York: W.W. Norton & Co.

Williamson, E. (1992). *The Penguin history of Latin America.* London: Penguin Books

❧ Part 1 ☙
Criminology Masterworks

Introduction to Criminology Masterworks

The Classical School said "reform the law."
The Positive School said "reform the man."
The environmental school would say "reform the environment."

(Jeffery, 1973, p. 498)

It is difficult to choose only a few masterworks in the field of criminology. The three selections chosen for this book are from the works of Cesare Beccaria, Cesare Lombroso, and Clifford R. Shaw and Henry D. McKay. Others could be added, but none of these could be subtracted from the list of giants in the field of criminology. These were chosen to represent three very different approaches to explaining the causes of criminal behavior.

The criminologist of the Enlightenment was Cesare Beccaria. The Age of Enlightenment demanded rational explanations even for things which might appear to be irrational. Old ideas of sin resulting from temptation by the devil and the corruption of human nature by the original sin of Adam and Eve in the garden of Eden were replaced by ideas of crime springing from the remnants of savagery in society and from irrational self-interest. Beccaria's theories became the foundation of the "classical school" of criminology, so called because it was the first systematic theory of crime and its prevention. Beccaria, true to the Enlightenment philosophy, saw crime as a product of irrationality. Believing that people are above all else rational beings, Beccaria was inclined to view crime as a result of irrational laws and punishments as well as irrational, nearsighted choices. If the laws themselves were rational, Beccaria believed, people would obey them. Hence, the key to crime control was to reform the laws, to have a rational explanation for every law, and to make punishments clear and certain rather than severe.

Several modern theories of crime claim to be descendents of Beccaria's theories. But these theories view crime as rational rather than irrational. Some of the modern theories concentrate on offenders' assessments of material, psychological and social rewards and deterrents associated with crime. Other modern theories view crime as a logical means to acquire goods which a lower-class person could not acquire by legitimate means. Rational decision making is also the foundation for modern theories of crime which focus on environmental features or routines of daily living which either block or facilitate the commission of crimes by offenders who assess situations carefully and plan their crimes in rational ways. The idea that crime is a rational activity is the working philosophy of most lawmakers and the general public. They are inclined to believe that criminals think before they act, weigh the consequences of their choices in a rational manner, and are guided by logical considerations of the certainty and severity of punishments. The modern legal system also assumes this rational view of criminal behavior motivated by self interest and resulting from free choices. Although these ideas about crime as a rational activity often claim to be descended from Beccaria's views, they are not. To Beccaria crime was not rational; it was irrational. Crime was the result of a legal system which was based on self-interest and emotions, not reason. It was a failure of reason to overcome momentary sensations and impulses. Still, Beccaria provided a platform for surveying all the theories of crime which have rational decision making, or the lack of it, as their foundation.

The historical reaction to the classical school of criminology was the "positivist" approaches to criminology. The positivists relied on natural and social sciences to explain behavior. Rather than seeing human behavior primarily as rational choices, they emphasized the biological, psychological and social determinants of behavior. Among the positivists Cesare Lombroso was outstanding for his biological, psychological and anthropological approaches to criminology. His views evolved over a long lifetime of research. He wrote on virtually all aspects of crime, including such diverse topics as trivial offenders, pathological criminals, white collar crime, organized crime, and even the effects of the weather on crime.

Lombroso's medical studies of criminals were limited mostly to anatomy. A century of advances in biological sciences now makes possible other kinds of studies. Modern criminologists who have an interest in biological causes of criminality examine physiology more than anatomy. They find, for example, that people prone to criminality often have low rates of heartbeat and brain wave activity. But the modern physiological studies face the same challenges as older anatomical studies. The biological factors are difficult to separate from environmental, social, psychological and other medical factors.

For the past half-century biological theories of behavior have not been popular with Americans, whose medicine cabinets reveal heavy reliance on chemicals to control physical and mental states but whose ideology generally rejects the notion that a person's behavior is biologically determined. The fundamental American belief that individuals can become whatever they choose and work for precludes emphasis on biological factors. Explanations for crime based on such biological factors as chromosomal abnormalities, premenstrual syndrome or attention deficit disorders are viewed as exceptional cases rather than as indications of general biological factors. A few recent criminologists have put forth the view, and some evidence, that biological factors may underlie certain personality traits associated with criminality, such as thrill seeking and poor impulse control.

Psychological theories of crime based on mental deficiencies, psychopathologies, maladjustments or character disorders were more popular in the first half of the twentieth century but for the last half century have tended to be relegated to special cases, such as serial killers, terrorists or arsonists. Like biological theories, psychological theories tend to isolate problems to individuals; they look away from problems in society which might cause crime. Anthropological theories likewise have not been acceptable to American criminologists except for specialized, small-scale applications such as juvenile gangs or organized crime cultures. Despite their general unpopularity, biological, psychological and anthropological theories continue to pop up in criminology. Lombroso was the pioneer in these fields.

Clifford R. Shaw and Henry D. McMay represent a sociological approach to criminology. Like Lombroso, they believed that criminology must concentrate on the study of criminals, not crimes. However, Shaw and McKay focused on juveniles, not adults. Also, they studied criminals in group contexts rather than as individuals. They acknowledged the lone criminal, but they believed that most criminals behave under the influence of groups. Their research looked at juvenile delinquents who were members of gangs, which was considered the most appropriate milieu for studying the causes of criminal behavior.

The sociological approach to crime is so widely accepted in the United States that criminology itself is generally regarded as a branch of sociology, not law, medicine, psychology or even anthropology. The sociological approach has taken diverse forms, such as Merton's theory of anomie and Sutherland's theory of differential association. Merton's theory of anomie suggested that criminal behavior occurred in the absence of clearly defined social norms due to breakdown of such social structures as the family. Sutherland's theory of differential association contended that criminal behavior was a result of a person identifying more closely with a criminal group than with a noncriminal group. The research of Shaw and McKay provided the foundation for many of these sociological theories. Sociological theories maintain that essentially criminal behavior, if not all behavior, is the result of interactions with other people. An advantage of sociological theories is that they provide more hope for crime prevention strategies and allow for crime prevention strategies at a group level instead of on a one-by-one individual basis. Ultimately the social value of any criminological theory depends in large measure on its ability to produce crime prevention strategies.

Suggested Reading

Butterfield, F. (1996). *All God's children.* New York: Avon Books.

Jeffery, C.R. (1973). The historical development of criminology. In H. Mannheim (Ed.), *Pioneers in criminology,* 2nd ed. Montclair, N.J.: Patterson Smith. Pp. 458–498.

Mannheim, H. (Ed.). (1973). *Pioneers in criminology,* 2nd ed. Montclair, NJ: Patterson Smith.

Martin, R., Mutchnick, R.J., & Austin, W.T. (1990). *Criminological thought: Pioneers past and present.* New York: Macmillan.

Rowe, D.C. (2002). *Biology and crime.* Los Angeles: Roxbury.

Vold, G.B., Bernard, T.J., & Snipes, J.B. (1998). *Theoretical criminology,* 4th ed. New York: Oxford University Press.

Introduction to
Cesare Beccaria

The city of Milan passed from Spanish to Austrian control in 1706, but the same noble families retained control over the affairs of the city. In Milan on March 15, 1738, Cesare Bonesana, future Marchese di Beccaria, was born into a world in which people knew their place and were expected to maintain it. The title of marquis was his to inherit. He was expected to be educated as a gentleman, inherit the family estate, expand it by marriage to a woman of nobility and property, and take a place in government as an official of some sort. A nervous and timid boy who had no enthusiasm for study, Cesare was sent to the Jesuit school at nearby Parma for eight years and after that to the University of Pavia to study law. This was standard education for his time and place. The study of law in those days was more like the study of government and political science. Cesare was an indifferent student, although at one time his favorite subject was classical literature and at another time it was mathematics. It was not unusual that he finished his studies at the age of twenty in a world where that was old enough to assume his station in life.

However, Cesare fell in love with sixteen-year-old Teresa di Blasco, a noble woman of Sicilian-Spanish descent who was unacceptable to his family because her family had lost most of its wealth. Encouraged by his friends the rakish Count Pietro Verri and his younger brother Allesandro Verri, Cesare insisted on marrying her. Exercising the legal powers of a father at that time, Cesare's father had him arrested, thinking that imprisonment would make him think seriously about the matter. But Cesare was sentenced to house arrest at home. Various nobles of the city intervened on both sides of the dispute. After three months Cesare was released and married the girl. His father provided a modest income for the couple but refused to receive the girl. About a year later the Verri brothers mediated a full reconciliation between Cesare and his father.

Among the nobility it was quite fashionable for groups of friends to meet regularly in the salon of a great house to discuss all that was new in art, literature, science, philosophy, economy, and world affairs. It provided the privacy necessary to express opinions which might not be acceptable to the authorities. The Verri brothers hosted such a salon, and they invited young Beccaria to join their circle. They tended to be more radical in their views than other aristocratic salons. Pietro Verri, about ten years older than Cesare, prompted Cesare to read the most influential French and English philosophers of the Enlightenment. The book which made the greatest impression on Beccaria was the French philosopher Montesquieu's *Persian Letters,* which had been published anonymously in a republic of The Netherlands in 1721. Disguised as fictional letters of a naive Persian ambassador writing home about European customs and receiving letters which reveal contrasting Persian customs, this book was a withering critique of European society, including the legal system.

Pietro Verri also encouraged Beccaria to write based on the discussions held in the Verri house. Beccaria wrote some articles for a literary journal published by this group of young nobles and a book on economic reform, *On Remedies for the Monetary Disorders of Milan in the Year 1762*. Then discussions turned to the legal system. Pietro Verri had compiled materials for a history of torture and Allesandro Verri held the post of Protector of Prisoners in Milan, an ombudsman for people in prison. The forty-seven short chapters of Beccaria's *On Crimes and Punishments* (1764) were summaries of almost daily discussions which took place in 1763—1764. Beccaria would compose segments, and Pietro Verri edited them extensively. Some people claimed that Pietro Verri was the real author of the book. Years later Pietro Verri acknowledged his major role in editing the book, but he insisted that it was the work of the Marquis Beccaria, who found writing to be very exhausting.

On Crimes and Punishments was radical. It was a condemnation of the prevailing legal system and commonly accepted ideas about justice. The book itself might have been viewed as a criminal attack upon the government and might have brought down on the author's head the dreaded machinery of law and the harsh punishments which the book derided. Years later explaining why some passages in the book were rather obscure, Beccaria said that fear had prompted him to be obscure in places. The decision was made to publish the book anonymously. The book was an instant sensation throughout Europe. It was translated into French and English and went through several printings in its first two years. It was welcomed as a blueprint for legal reform in Italian states, France, England, Prussia, Sweden, Spain, and Austria. Count Firmian, ruler of Milan in the name of the Austrian crown, defended the book even when the Catholic Church condemned it, and Beccaria was able to put his name on later editions of the book without fear of prosecution. Catherine the Great wanted Beccaria to go to Russia and personally oversee the reform of the laws. Even in the American colonies Beccaria was applauded. The Paris intelligentsia clamored for Beccaria. Reluctantly, in 1766 Beccaria agreed to visit the salons of Paris, the intellectual center of Europe, but only if accompanied by Allesandro Verri. Together they made the journey. After three or four weeks in Paris, however, the shy and homesick Beccaria could handle the admiring salons no more. He fled back to Milan, leaving Allesandro to make apologies.

Beccaria lived quietly devoted to his wife and two daughters. For two years he filled a position especially created for him as professor of political economy at the Palatine college in Milan. Thereafter he held mid-level government posts and served on some economic, educational, and legal reform commissions which made use of his knowledge but imposed no toilsome burdens. He had no great ambitions. On two occasions the King of Naples went to Beccaria's house to visit him, but Beccaria made himself absent. With nothing further coming from Beccaria, rumors circulated throughout Europe that he had been silenced by the authorities in Milan. But it was not true. He simply preferred a quiet life with his family and his books. When his wife died at the age of twenty-nine in 1774, Beccaria married again after three months and had a son by his second wife. Beccaria died of a stroke on November 28, 1794. Three years later, to demonstrate Milan's esteem for Beccaria, Pietro Verri urged the city to erect a statue of Beccaria. A statue of Beccaria can be seen today in a small plaza behind the cathedral.

Beccaria's *On Crimes and Punishments* is regarded as one of the great works of the Age of Enlightenment and often said to be the greatest work ever published in the field of criminal justice. It is closely linked to the writings of other philosophers of the Enlightenment. The basic premise was that all laws must be reasonable and necessary. The actual legal systems of the times were a complex maze of ancient Roman and medieval legal systems. In the same country were dozens of different courts with somewhat different laws and procedures for different segments of the society. What a person did was treated on the basis of who a person was. There was no equality before the law. The law itself was endlessly confusing and beyond the grasp of most people.

In Beccaria's time the difficulty of convicting people in criminal cases was often resolved through torture. When there were no witnesses or witnesses were uncertain or contradictory, the legal system could impose punishments with a feeling that justice was being done only if the person confessed. Persons who were believed to be guilty but were unwilling to admit it were often induced by torture or a threat of torture to confess. Torture to induce confessions was viewed as necessary and legitimate. This is not so incredible when one bears in mind that Americans today view as necessary and legitimate such tactics as police use of deception and trickery, psychological intimidations, lengthy detention under high bails, and coercible plea bargains to induce confessions in over ninety percent of cases. Beccaria was not expressing popular opinions. Beccaria was attacking the legal system's standard tactics for getting guilty pleas.

For a theory of society and government Beccaria accepted the ideas of the English philosophers John Locke and Thomas Hobbes and the French philosopher Jean Jacques Rousseau. With some variations, they expounded the theory that society is the result of a "social contract" worked out at an early stage of civilization. It was an antidote to the traditional idea that the existing form of government was an arrangement from the beginning of time for an orderly world ruled by kings whose power derived from a deity.

The social contract theory stated that primitive human beings lived separately in a sparsely populated world and were hostile competitors with one another for food and territory. As population increased, violent conflicts between humans increased until there was a state of constant warfare. At that point, to save themselves from mutual destruction, humans agreed upon a contract for mutual protection. Each individual would surrender some liberty in order to accommodate others, and in return all would be guaranteed security for themselves and their possessions. A sovereign would be appointed to administer the contract, and into the hands of the sovereign would be placed all of the liberty surrendered by individuals.

Beccaria accepted the idea of the social contract, although it has been challenged by later scholars. In his history of ancient law Henry S. Maine (1866) pointed out that the idea of a "contract" did not even exist in primitive society. In *The History of the French Revolution* (1836) Thomas Carlyle suggested the more cynical view that the social contract theory was a way of tricking people into thinking that the government they had was a government to which they had agreed. The idea that society is the result of a social contract has been called into question not only by legal historians who have noted that the notion of a contract did not exist in primitive societies but also by anthropologists who report that many primitive societies were matriarchal societies loosely organized on the basis of motherhood, the only certain relationship. Still, the idea of the social contract has persisted. The theory of the social contract was a way to say that a government, even a king, derives legitimate power from the people and is limited by what is necessary for the security of people in society. This is the idea which has survived despite any contradictory facts.

In Beccaria's time it was common for many localities, like the early American colonies, to be ruled by some sort of governor or "magistrate" who was sovereign in the area, made the local laws, and acted as the judge in all sorts of cases. However, another theme of the Enlightenment philosophers of government was the need for a separation of distinct government powers, expressed first in a discussion of the English system of government in Montesquieu's *The Spirit of the Laws*. The lawmaking power was considered the most important power and was assigned to some sort of legislator. In Beccaria's writing the ideal legislator was an individual wise philosopher who had studied human nature and had no vested interests in the laws. However, in the post-Enlightenment era the role of legislator has been assigned to an elected body of citizens, now referred to as a legislature rather than a legislator. In the Enlightenment philosophy of government, the executive power was proscribed from making the laws. The role of the executive was to carry out the will of the legislator or legislature. The executive power was also proscribed from making judgments in particular cases. Criminal offenses were seen as offenses against society, not just against individual people, so they had to be judged by someone other than the representative of the offended society, which was the executive. A duty of the executive was to bring charges against offenders. Then cases would be tried by an independent separate power, the courts, which would apply the laws to the cases.

The modern American reader could easily misunderstand the Enlightenment doctrine on the separation of powers. The modern American ideas of "separate but equal powers" and "checks and balances" are somewhat different, later historical developments. To the authors of the U.S. Constitution, the powers were not meant to be equal and were not a "checks and balances" arrangement. The "checks and balances" of the U.S. Constitution as understood when it was written were the checks and balances between large states and small states and between the federal government and the state governments. The source of all power and the true sovereign was the people, who invested their power in legislators, who in turn designated an executive (through the Electoral College in the U.S. system) and appointed a judiciary. The legislators as the foremost power were expected to set the course of the government, the executive or sovereign was to faithfully execute the will of the legislators, and the courts were to administer the civil and criminal laws.

In Beccaria's writing one finds two different bases for law and justice. One basis for law and justice is "human nature." Hence, Beccaria's ideal legislator was above all else a student of human nature. The second basis for law and justice was "the social contract." To Beccaria these two different foundations for law and justice were compatible since he viewed human nature as perfectly rational, and he viewed the social contract as a rational agreement among human beings. Beccaria accepted certain ideas about human nature from the English philosopher Thomas Hobbes. This included the view that human beings are by nature selfish and seek their own individual good, but they know that one must sometimes sacrifice immediate or lesser goods to achieve greater or long term goods. Also, conflicts arise between individuals, and then individuals make the rational decision to sacrifice some of their individual desires in order to find mutual peace and security. This is the "social contract."

However, in the post-Enlightenment era these two ideas of laws based on human nature and laws based on the social contract have split apart. In American historical traditions, the Declaration of Independence was based on the notion that government, law, and justice are based on a certain understanding of human nature. Hence, the Declaration was based on the premise that "All Men are created equal, that they are endowed by their Creator with certain unalienable Rights...." The Declaration of Independence was not well known and not revered by most Americans until after the Civil War. But, in contrast, the Constitution of the United States, composed by other hands, who were anxious to avoid a rift among the colonies over the issue of slavery, was developed as a social contract. It embodied an agreement between the government and individual citizens in which specific rights and obligations were assigned to each and which could be modified by procedures established in the contract itself. American politics from the Revolutionary War to the Civil War included an ongoing debate between the advocates of the Declaration of Independence, mostly abolitionists, versus advocates of the Constitution, with Abraham Lincoln as a mid-century spokesman for the Declaration, at least after his wartime proclamation of freedom for those slaves in the rebel states of the Confederacy. The Bill of Rights, which deliberately had not been made a part of the Constitution but instead added as a supplement, was ignored as unimportant until after the Civil War. In 1868 advocates of the Declaration added the Fourteenth Amendment to the Constitution, which revived the Bill of Rights and forced the States to respect at least "Constitutional Rights," a social contract version of some human rights.

Historically, European countries have developed the human rights tradition, which assumes that human nature is the same for all human beings, all human beings have the same rights, and government cannot modify these rights because it cannot change human nature. However, the United States has developed the social contract tradition in which majority agreement determines what rights and obligations people have, and majority agreement can modify people's rights and obligations. Hence, in the American system based on the social contract, people who live in different states can have different rights, citizens can have different rights from non-citizens, citizens or non-citizens can be classified in different groups with different rights, rights can be modified by government with some sort of majority consent, and human nature conveys no inalienable rights, not even the right to life. These contrasting bases for government, law, and justice are the cause of continuing conflict between the United States and European Union countries, exemplified in the American refusal to recognize a

World Court of Human Rights and the European Union refusal to extradite suspects to the United States in cases in which the United States has death penalties. Reading Beccaria with these philosophical and historical assumptions in mind can still prompt considerable reflection on the nature of government, law and justice.

Beccaria, like other Enlightenment philosophers, began with the conviction that human beings are "rational creatures." The meaning of this phrase was much stronger than it is today. As the eighteenth century English philosopher John Locke, among others, had explained in detail, the mind was governed by its own laws of nature just as inevitably as the movements of the planets or the seasons of the year were governed by laws of nature. The idea of human beings as rational creatures was that human beings were ruled, not merely guided, by reason. Reason was a compelling force. A human being followed reason as surely as a falling apple followed the law of gravity. Of course, the law of gravity could be blunted somewhat by a powerful wind or a mid-air collision with another object, and, similarly, reason could be blunted by strong emotions or defective physical senses which distorted reality. Beccaria shared the biases of his times that upper-class people inherited more sensitive senses and keener intellects, and that upper-class people have more accurate perception of reality and greater rationality than lower-class people. Aristocrats are gentle ladies and gentle men. But the fundamental principle was that, despite individual differences, all human beings are essentially alike and are compelled by reason. To the extent that there might be some sort of "free will," it would be free only to follow reason.

As an Enlightenment philosopher Beccaria depended mostly on reason in presenting his ideas. Occasionally he made references to some historical situation or to some other writer's work, but mostly he depended on logic to make his points. He believed that logic was better proof of something than history or other types of evidence which might be disputed. Although some of the topics he discussed, such as torture and the death penalty, are often dealt with in an emotional way by other writers, Beccaria's views were based strictly on logic. However, he did realize that the logical treatment of a topic had to include a logical consideration of how feelings and sensations influence people's behavior. It was on the basis of logic that he attacked the existing legal system, especially the vagaries of law, the inconsistencies of judges, the uncertainty of punishments, the illogical and ineffectual death penalty, and the uselessness of torture for extracting truthful confessions. It would be a misunderstanding of Beccaria to think that he opposed torture or the death penalty on emotional or "humanitarian" grounds. His opposition was based on reason. To understand

Beccaria a reader must put aside humanitarian considerations and grapple with Beccaria's reasoning.

Beccaria's *On Crimes and Punishments* dealt with issues still unresolved centuries later, although Enlightenment ideas have been accepted more in the twenty-first century European Union countries than in America. When reading Beccaria, the modern student of criminal justice may be prompted to reflect further on the cult-like obscurity of laws, class biases in legislation (e.g., cocaine versus heroin laws), laws based on political considerations (e.g., tough-on-crime laws passed in election years), laws prompted by lobbying of special interest groups (e.g., correction officer unions lobbying for longer sentences, medical and counseling businesses lobbying for mandatory treatment laws), the multiplicity of unequal and inconsistent American legal systems (federal, separate state systems, military, tribal and territorial legal systems) which allow prosecutors to choose to prosecute an offender under a more lenient or more punitive system, disparate charging and sentencing practices of prosecutors and judges, mandatory sentencing debates, coercive means for obtaining confessions, parole and other early release practices, and the continuing death penalty debate in the United States. Beccaria's issues are still the fundamental issues facing the criminal justice system.

References

Carlyle, T. (1837). *The French Revolution: A history.* New York: Random House.

Maine, H.S. (1866). *Ancient law: Its connection with the early history of society and its relation to modern ideas.* New York: E.P. Dutton & Co.

This selection consists of excerpts from Cesare Beccaria, *On crimes and punishments*. (Original work published 1764) This translation was made especially for this book. Notes in the text which were added by the editors have been placed in square brackets. Footnotes have been renumbered and put at the end of the selection.

Cesare Beccaria

On Crimes and Punishments

Introduction:
The Need to Apply Reason in Matters of Law and Justice

Men generally leave even the most important lawmaking either to ordinary common sense or to the discretion of persons who have a personal interest in opposing truly wise laws—that is, laws which promote the distribution of advantages throughout society. A wise lawmaker must resist the forces which tend to concentrate advantages in the hands of only a few, which would give all power and happiness to some people, but only weakness and misery to others. It is only after people have struggled through a thousand errors in matters most essential to life and liberty, after they have reached the limits of endurance, exhausted by the wrongs they have suffered, that people are ready to do something about the disorders that oppress them and to acknowledge the most obvious truths. These truths, precisely because of their simplicity, escape the attention of common minds which are accustomed not to analyzing things but to accepting things from unexamined traditions rather than from careful study.

If we glance at the pages of history, we will find that laws, which surely are, or ought to be, agreements of free men, have been for the most part a mere tool of the ambitions of some or have arisen from accidental and temporary needs. Never have laws been dictated by a dispassionate student of human nature who might, by taking into account the life of the multitude, compose laws with this single objective in mind: that the greatest happiness may be shared by the greatest number of people. Happy are those few nations which have not waited for the slow succession of coincidence and human events to force some little turn for the better after the limit of evil had been reached, but have facilitated continuous progress by means of good laws. Humanity owes a debt of gratitude to that philosopher[1] who, from the obscurity of his isolated study, had the courage to scatter among the multitude the first seeds, so long unfruitful, of useful truths.

The true relationships between sovereigns and their subjects, and between nations, have been discovered. Commerce has been reanimated by the widespread knowledge of philosophical truths diffused by the art of printing, and there has sprung up among nations a rivalry of industriousness that is most humane and truly worthy of rational beings. Such good things we owe to the productive enlightenment of this age. But very few persons have studied and fought against cruelty of punishments and inconsistencies of criminal procedures, a part of lawmaking that is as fundamental as it is widely neglected in all of Europe. Very few persons have undertaken to demolish the accumulated errors of centuries by returning to general principles, thus bringing to a halt, with the force that acknowledged truths possess, the relentless march of ill-directed power which has continually produced a long and undeniable history of the most cold-blooded barbarity. And yet the groans of the weak, sacrificed to cruel ignorance and to opulent indolence; the barbarous torments, multiplied with lavish and useless severity, for crimes either not proved or wholly imaginary; the filth and horrors of prison, intensified by that cruelest tormentor of the miserable, uncertainty—all these ought to have roused the public officials who guide the opinions of men....

2.
The Origin of a Sovereign's Right to Punish:
The Social Contract

No lasting advantage is to be hoped for from political principles if they are not founded upon the ineradicable sentiments of mankind. Any law that deviates from these sentiments will inevitably encounter resistance that is certain to prevail over it in the end—in the same way that any force, however small, if continuously applied, is certainly going to bring to a halt any object set in motion by even the most powerful impetus.

Let us consult the human heart[2] and we shall find there the basic principles of the true right of the sovereign to punish crimes. No man ever freely sacrificed a portion of his personal liberty merely on behalf of the common good. That chimera exists only in novels. If it were possible, every one of us would prefer that the rules and agreements binding others did not bind us. Every man tends to make himself the center of his whole world.

In primitive times the size of the human population was not great in itself. But continuous growth of the population surpassed by far what barren and uncultivated natural resources could provide for the satisfaction of ever increasing needs. This prompted the earliest savages to form communities. These first communities inevitably caused the formation of others to resist the first, and so the primitive state of warfare passed from individuals to nations.

Laws are the agreements under which independent and isolated men united to form a society. Weary of living in a constant state of war, and having a liberty made useless by the uncertainty of preserving it, they sacrificed a part of liberty so that they might enjoy the rest of it in peace and safety. The sum of all those portions of liberty sacrificed by each for his own good constitutes the sovereignty of a nation, and their legitimate depository and administrator is the sovereign ruler.

But merely to have established this deposit of liberty was not enough; it had to be defended against private usurpations by individuals, each of whom always tried not only to withdraw his own share but also to usurp for himself that of others. Some tangible incentives had to be introduced to prevent the despotic spirit, which is in every man, from plunging a society based on laws back into its original chaos. These tangible incentives are the punishments established against violators of the laws. I say "tangible incentives" because experience has shown that the multitude of people adopt no fixed principles of conduct and will not be released from the grip of that universal principle of decay which is seen to operate both in the physical and moral universe, except for incentives that directly strike the senses. These incentives, by dint of repeated presentation to the mind, counterbalance the powerful impressions of selfish drives which oppose the common good. Not eloquence, not speeches, not even the most sublime truths have sufficed, for any considerable length of time, to curb selfish drives excited by vivid impressions of present objects.

It was necessity that forced men to give up part of their personal liberty. Hence, it is certain that each man is willing to place in the public fund only the smallest possible portion of his liberty, no more than is necessary to induce others to defend it. The sum of these smallest possible portions of individual liberty put into the hands of the sovereign confers the right to punish. Any punishment that exceeds what individuals have handed over to the sovereign is abuse and not justice; it is fact but by no means right.

Punishments which exceed what is necessary for protection of the deposit of public security are by their very nature unjust. Punishments are increasingly more just as the safety which the sovereign secures for his subjects is the more sacred and inviolable, and as the liberty is greater.

3.
Logical Consequences of the Social Contract

The first consequence of these principles is that only the laws can decree punishments for crimes; authority for this can reside only with the legislator [the sovereign] who represents the entire society united by a social contract.

No judge, who is only a part of society, can inflict punishments of his own, with justice, upon another member of society. Any punishment that exceeds the limit fixed by the laws is a just punishment plus another punishment; a judge cannot, therefore, under any pretext of zeal or concern for the public good, add to the punishments already established for a citizen who breaks the law.

The second consequence is that the sovereign, who represents the whole society, can only establish the laws, which then bind all members. He cannot also be the judge of whether some individual has violated the social contract. A trial divides the nation into two parts, one represented by the sovereign, who asserts the violation of the contract, and the other by the accused, who denies it. There must be a neutral third party to judge the truth of the facts. There is need for a judge whose decisions should be final; there ought to be no appeal to the sovereign. A judge's decisions should consist of mere affirmations or denials of the alleged facts in a case.

The third consequence is this: Even if severe punishments may not be directly contrary to the public good and to the purpose of preventing crimes, still it may be possible to prove that severe punishments are useless. Useless severity would be contrary to those kindly virtues that spring from enlightened reason, for one would rather rule happy men than a herd of slaves among whom cruelty makes its endless rounds. Useless severity of punishments would be contrary to justice itself and to the very nature of the social contract.

4.
Interpretations of the Laws

A fourth consequence of the social contract is this: Judges in criminal cases cannot have the authority to interpret laws any way they want. The reason, again, is that they are not legislators. It is not from our ancestors that judges have received the laws, as if the laws were a family legacy or inheritance that leaves to posterity only the burden of obeying them. On the contrary, the laws come from the society now living, or from the sovereign representing it, who is the legitimate depository of whatever comes from the common will of all. Judges do not receive the laws as obligations from some ancient contract[3], which would be null and void to begin with because it would pretend to bind wills that did not then exist, and evil because it would reduce men from a social state to that of an animal herd. Rather, judges receive the laws as consequences of the explicit or implicit contract of allegiance which the united wills of living subjects have pledged to their sovereign, and as bonds necessary for restraining and regulating the internal

ferment of personal interests.⁴ This constitutes the natural and real authority
of the laws.

Who, then, is to be the legitimate interpreter of the laws? Is it to be the
sovereign, that is, the depository of the actual wills of all, or the judge,
whose sole duty is merely to examine whether a particular man has or has
not committed an unlawful act?

For every crime that comes before him, a judge is required only to complete a perfect syllogism⁵, in which the major premise must be the law; the
minor premise must be the action that conforms or does not conform to the
law; and the conclusion must be acquittal or conviction. If the judge was restricted in following the law, or if he wanted to compose even a single additional syllogism, the door would thereby be opened to uncertainty.

Nothing can be more dangerous than the popular axiom that it is necessary
to consider the spirit of a law. It is a dam that has burst and released a torrent
of opinions. The truth, which seems paradoxical to ordinary minds that are
struck more by trivial present disorders than by the dangerous but remote effects of false principles rooted in a nation, seems to me to be fully demonstrated. Our understandings and all our ideas are connected to one another;
the more complicated they are, the more numerous must be the logical paths
that lead to them and depart from them. Each man has his own point of view,
and, at each different time, a different one. Hence, the "spirit" of the law
would be the product of a judge's good or bad logic, of his good or bad digestion; it would depend on the strength of his emotions, on the weakness of the
accused, on the judge's connections with him, and on all those minute factors
that alter the appearance of an object in the fluctuating mind of man. Thus we
see the fate of a citizen subjected to frequent changes when passing through
different courts, and we see the lives of poor wretches becoming the victims of
false rationalizations or of the tempestuous moods of a judge who mistakes for
a legitimate interpretation some vague product of jumbled notions stirred up
in his mind. Thus we see the same crimes punished differently at different
times by the same court, as a result of having consulted not the constant fixed
voice of the law but rather the erring instability of interpretations.

The disorder that may arise from rigorous observance of the letter of a
penal law is hardly comparable to the disorders that arise from interpretations. The temporary inconvenience of following the letter of the law
prompts one to make the rather easy and needed correction in the words of
the law which are the source of uncertainty; following the letter of the law
curbs that fatal license of discussion which gives rise to arbitrary and corrupt
interpretations. When a fixed code of laws, which must be observed to the

letter, leaves no further duty to the judge than to examine the acts of citizens and to decide whether or not they conform to the law as written; when the standard of the just or the unjust, which is to be the norm of conduct for the ignorant as well as for the philosophic citizen, is not a matter of controversy but of fact; only then are citizens not subject to the petty tyrannies of the many, which are the more cruel as the distance between the oppressed and the oppressor is less, and which are far more fatal than the tyrannies of a single man.[6] The despotism of the many can be corrected only by the despotism of one. The cruelty of a single despot is proportioned not to his might but to the obstacles he encounters.

With a fixed written code of law citizens acquire a feeling of security for their own persons, which is both just, because a code of law is the product of human association, and also useful, because it enables people to calculate accurately the penalty of a misdeed. It is true, moreover, that with a fixed written code of law citizens acquire a spirit of independence, but not one that upsets the laws and resists the authorities; rather a spirit of independence which resists those who have dared to disguise their own weaknesses as virtues and who have succumbed to their own self-interested and capricious opinions.

These principles will displease those who have assumed for themselves a right to transmit to those below them the blows of tyranny that they have received from those above them. I would, indeed, be most fearful if the spirit of tyranny were in the least compatible with the spirit of literacy.

5.
Obscurity of the Laws

If the interpretation of laws is an evil, another evil, evidently, is the obscurity which makes interpretation necessary. This evil would be very great indeed where the laws are written in a language that is foreign to a people, forcing them to rely on a handful of men because they are unable to judge for themselves how their liberty or their limbs may fare—in a language that transforms a sacred and public book into something very like a private family possession. When the number of those who can understand the sacred code of laws and hold it in their hands increases, the frequency of crimes will be found to decrease, for undoubtedly ignorance and uncertainty of punishments add much to the eloquence of selfish desires. What are we to make of men, therefore, when we reflect that this very evil is the standard practice of a large part of cultured and enlightened Europe?

One consequence of this last reflection is that without writing a society can never acquire a fixed form of government with power that derives from the whole and not from only some parts, in which laws cannot be altered except by the general will, and therefore cannot be corrupted by private interests. Experience and reason have shown us that the certainty of human traditions diminishes the further removed they are from their source. If there exists no enduring record of the social contract, how could laws withstand the inevitable pressures of time and of selfish interests?

We can see how useful the art of printing is, which makes the public, and not some few individuals, the guardians of the sacred laws. And we can see how it has dispelled the benighted spirit of cabal and intrigue, which must soon vanish in the presence of enlightened studies and sciences outwardly despised but inwardly feared by schemers. This explains why we now see in Europe a diminishing of the atrocity of the crimes that afflicted our ancestors, who became tyrants and slaves by turns. Anyone acquainted with the history of the past two centuries and of our own time may observe how from the lap of luxury and softness have sprung the most pleasing virtues, humanity, benevolence, and toleration of human errors. He will see what were the real effects of the so-called simplicity and good faith of olden times: humanity groaning under stubborn superstitions; greed and private ambition staining with blood the golden treasure chests and thrones of kings; secret betrayals and public massacres; every nobleman a tyrant over the people; ministers of the gospel soiling with blood the hands that daily touch the God of mercy—these, surely, are not the work of this enlightened age which some people call corrupt.

12.
Torture

A cruelty consecrated by the practice of most nations is torture of the accused during his trial, either to make him confess the crime, or to clear up contradictory statements, or to discover accomplices, or to purge him of guilt in some metaphysical and incomprehensible way, or, finally, to discover other crimes of which he might be guilty but of which he is not accused.

No man can be called guilty before a judge has found him guilty, nor can society deprive him of public protection before it has been decided that he has in fact violated the conditions under which such protection was accorded him. What right is it, then, if not simply that of might, which empowers a judge to inflict punishment on a citizen while doubt still remains as to his guilt or innocence? Here is the dilemma, which is nothing new: the fact of the crime is either certain or uncertain; if guilt is certain, all that is due is the punishment established by the laws, and tortures are useless because the criminal's confession is useless; if guilt is uncertain, then one must not torture the innocent, for such, according to the laws, is a man whose crimes are not yet proved.

What is the social purpose of punishments? To instill fear in other men. But what justification can we find, then, for the secret and private tortures which the tyranny of custom practices on both the guilty and the innocent? It is important, indeed, to let no known crime pass unpunished. But it is useless to reveal the author of a crime that lies deeply buried in darkness. A wrong already committed, and for which there is no remedy, ought to be punished by society only because it might otherwise excite false hopes of impunity in others. If it be true that a greater number of men, whether because of fear or virtue, respect the laws rather than break them, then the risk of torturing an innocent person should be considered greater when, other things being equal, the probability is greater that a man has respected the laws rather than despised them.

But I say more: it tends to confuse all roles to require that a man be at the same time accuser and accused, and that pain be made the crucible of truth, as if the standard of truth lay in the muscles and sinews of a miserable wretch. The law that authorizes torture is a law that says: "Yes, resist pain! Nature has created in you an inextinguishable self-love. It has granted you an inalienable right of self-defense. However, I create in you an altogether contrary sentiment, a heroic hatred of yourself. I command you to accuse yourself, to speak the truth while your muscles are being torn and your bones disjointed."

This infamous crucible of truth is a surviving remnant of the ancient and barbarous legislation of a time when trials by fire and by boiling water, as well as the uncertain outcomes of duels, were called "judgments of God," as if the links of the eternal chain of cause and effect, which is in the mind of the First Cause, must at every moment be disordered and broken by frivolous human arrangements. The only difference between torture and trials by fire and boiling water is that the outcome seems to depend, in the case of torture, on the will of the accused, and in the case of trials by fire and boiling water, on purely physical and inescapable events. But this difference between ordeals and torture is only apparent, not real. One is as much free to tell the truth in the midst of convulsions and torments as one was free then to impede the effects of fire and boiling water.

Every act of our will is invariably proportioned to the force of the sensory impression which is its wellspring; and the sensory capacity of every man is limited. Thus the impression of pain may become so great that, filling the entire sensory capacity of the tortured person, it leaves him free only to choose what for the moment is the shortest way to escape from pain. The response of the accused is then as inevitable as the injuries from fire and boiling water. An innocent man, especially a sensitive one, will confess himself guilty when he believes that by so doing he can put an end to his torment. Every difference between guilt and innocence disappears because of the very means one pretends to be using to discover it. Torture is an infallible means, indeed, for absolving robust scoundrels and for condemning innocent persons who happen to be weak. Such are the fatal defects of this so-called criterion of truth, a criterion fit for a cannibal. The Romans, who were barbarous on many counts, reserved torture only for slaves, the victims of fierce and overly praised Roman manliness.

Of two men, equally innocent or equally guilty, the strong and fearless will be acquitted, the weak and timid condemned. The use of torture is based on a rigorous rationale such as this: "I, the judge, was supposed to find you guilty of such and such a crime. You, the strong, have been able to resist the pain, and I therefore absolve you. You, the weak, have yielded, and I therefore condemn you. I am aware that a confession wrenched forth by torments ought to be of no weight whatsoever, but I will torture you again if you do not reaffirm what you have confessed."

The effect of torture, therefore, is a matter of temperament and calculation that varies with each man according to his strength and physical sensitivity, so that, with this method, a mathematician could more readily than a judge resolve this problem: Given the muscular strength and nervous sensitivity of an innocent person, calculate the degree of pain that will make him confess himself guilty of a given crime. The examination of an accused person is undertaken to ascertain the truth. But if this truth is difficult to discover in the bearing, gesture, and countenance of a man at ease, its discovery will be much more difficult when the convulsions of pain have distorted all the signs by which truth usually reveals itself in the faces of most men in spite of themselves. Every violent act confuses and dissolves those little differences by means of which one may occasionally distinguish the true from the false.

A strange consequence that necessarily follows from the use of torture is that the innocent person is placed in a condition worse than the guilty, for if both are tortured, the circumstances are all against the innocent person. Either he confesses the crime and is condemned, or he is declared innocent and has suffered a punishment he did not deserve. The guilty man, on the contrary, finds himself in a favorable situation; if, as a consequence of having firmly resisted the torture, he is absolved as innocent, he will have escaped a greater punishment by enduring a lesser one. Thus the innocent can only lose, whereas the guilty may gain.

16.

The Death Penalty

The abundance of useless torments, which has never made men better, has prompted me to examine whether death is really useful and just in a well organized government.

What right can men claim to slaughter their fellow beings? Certainly not the rights which are the basis of sovereign power. Legitimate rights of the sovereign and the laws are nothing but the sum of the least portions of the private liberty of each person; these rights and laws represent the general will, which is the aggregate of individual wills. Was there ever a man who could have wished to leave to other men the choice of killing him? Is it conceivable that the least sacrifice of each person's liberty should include sacrifice of the greatest of all goods, life? And if that were the case, how could such a principle be reconciled with this other, that man is not entitled to take his own life? He would have to be, if he could surrender that right to others or to society as a whole.

The punishment of death, therefore, is not a right, for I have demonstrated that it cannot be such. Instead it is a war of a nation against a citizen whose destruction it judges to be necessary or useful. If, then, I can show that death is neither useful nor necessary, I shall have served the cause of humanity.

There are only two possible motives for believing that the death of a citizen is necessary. The first is when it is evident that, even if he has been deprived of liberty, he still has connections and power such as endanger the security of the nation—that is, when his existence can produce a dangerous revolution against the established form of government. The death of a citizen thus becomes necessary when a nation is recovering or losing its liberty, or in a time of anarchy, when disorders themselves take the place of laws.

However, while the laws reign peacefully in a form of government enjoying the consent of the entire nation, a nation well defended externally and internally by force, and by opinion, which is perhaps even more effective than force, where executive power is lodged with the true sovereign alone, where riches purchase pleasures and not authority, I see no necessity for destroying a citizen, except if his death were the only real way of restraining others from committing crimes. This is the second motive for believing that the death penalty may be just and necessary....

Yet it is not the intensity of punishment that has the greatest effect on the human spirit, but its duration, for our sensibility is more easily and more permanently affected by slight but repeated impressions than by a powerful but momentary event. The sway of habit is universal over every sentient being; just as man speaks and walks and satisfies his needs by habits, so likewise the ideas of morality come to be stamped upon the mind only by habits instilled by long and repeated impressions. It is not the terrible yet momentary spectacle of the death of a wretch, but the long and painful example of a man deprived of liberty, who, having become a beast of burden, repays with his labors the society he has offended, which is the strongest curb against crimes. The efficacious idea—efficacious because very often repeated to ourselves—that "I myself shall be reduced to so long and miserable a condition if I commit a similar misdeed" is far more powerful than the idea of death, which men envision always at an obscure distance....

The death penalty [carried out in a public place] becomes for the majority of people a spectacle and for some others an object of disdain mixed with compassion. These sentiments rather than the salutary fear which the laws are meant to inspire occupy the minds of the spectators. But in moderate and prolonged punishments the dominant sentiments are disdain and compassion, because these are the only emotions when there is no spectacle. The limit which the legislator ought to fix on the rigor of punishments should be determined by the point at which the sentiment of compassion begins to prevail over every other in the hearts of those who are the witnesses of punishment, which is inflicted for their sake rather than for the criminal's.

For a punishment to be just it should consist of only such gradations of intensity as suffice to deter men from committing crimes. Now, the person does not exist who, reflecting upon it, could choose for himself total and perpetual loss of personal liberty, no matter how advantageous a crime might seem to be. The intensity of the punishment of a life sentence of hard labor, in place of the death penalty, is punishment enough to deter any determined spirit. A life sentence is, let me add, an even greater punishment than death. Many men are able to look calmly and with firmness upon death— some from fanaticism, some from vanity, which almost always accompanies man even beyond the tomb, some from a final and desperate attempt either to live no longer or to escape their misery. But neither fanaticism nor vanity can survive among fetters or chains, under the rod, under the yoke, in a cage of iron, where the desperate wretch does not end his woes but merely begins them. Our spirit resists violence and extreme but momentary pains more easily than it does time and incessant weariness; the spirit can, so to speak, collect itself for a moment to withstand extreme but momentary pain, but the spirit cannot endure the long and constant weariness of a life sentence.

With the death penalty, every example given to the nation requires a new crime. With the penalty of a lifetime of hard labor a single crime supplies a lasting example. And if it be important that men frequently observe the power of the laws, penal executions ought not to be separated by long intervals; they, therefore, require frequent crimes. Thus, if this punishment is to be really useful, it somehow must not make the impression on men that it should; that is, it must deter crimes and not deter crimes at the same time.

To anyone raising the argument that perpetual hard labor is as painful as death and therefore equally cruel, I will reply that, adding up all the moments of unhappiness of hard labor, it may well be even more cruel; but these moments are drawn out over an entire lifetime, while the pain of death exerts its whole force in a moment. And precisely this is the advantage of penal servitude, that it inspires terror in the spectator more than in the sufferer, for the spectator considers the entire sum of unhappy moments, while the sufferer is distracted from the thought of future misery by that of the present moment. All evils are magnified in the imagination, and the sufferer finds compensations and consolations unknown and incredible to spectators who substitute their own sensibility for the callous spirit of a miserable wretch....

The death penalty cannot be useful, because of the example of barbarity it gives men. If the passions or the necessities of war have taught the shedding of human blood, the laws, moderators of the conduct of men, should not extend the beastly example, which becomes more vicious since the inflicting of legal death is attended with much study and formality. It seems to me absurd that the laws, which are an expression of the public will, which detest and punish homicide, should themselves commit it, and that to deter citizens from murder, they order a public one.

Which are the true and most useful laws? Those agreements and those conditions which everyone would propose and observe.... What are the sentiments of each and every man about the death penalty? Let us read their sentiments in the acts of indignation and contempt with which everyone regards the hangman, who is, after all, merely the innocent executor of the public will, a good citizen contributing to the public good, an instrument as necessary to the internal security of a people as valorous soldiers are to the external. What then is the origin of this contradiction? And why, in spite of reason, is this sentiment indelible in men? Because men, in the most secret recess of their spirits, in the part that more than any other still conserves their original nature, have always believed that one's own life ought to be in the power of no one, except only fateful necessity which rules the universe with its iron scepter....

If one were to cite against me the example of all the ages and of almost all the nations that have applied the death penalty to certain crimes, my reply would be that this example is reduced to nothing in the face of truth, against which there is no right to continue indefinitely; that the history of men leaves us with the sight of a vast sea of errors, among which, at great intervals, some rare and barely recognizable truths appear to float on the surface. Human sacrifices were once common to almost all nations, yet who will dare to defend them? That only a few societies, and for a short time only, have abstained from applying the death penalty, stands in my favor rather than against me, for that conforms with the usual lot of great truths, which are about as long lasting as a lightning flash in comparison with the long dark night which envelops mankind.

20.
The Certainty of Punishment. Mercy

One of the greatest curbs on crimes is not the cruelty of punishments but their inevitability, and, together with this, the vigilance of police and the sternness of an inexorable judge which, to be a useful virtue, must be accompanied by a mild legislation. The certainty of a punishment, even if it be moderate, will always make a stronger impression than the fear of some other punishment which is more terrible but combined with a hope of avoiding punishment. Even the least evils, when they are certain, always terrify men's minds; but hope, that heavenly gift which is often our sole consolation for everything, tends to keep the thought of greater evils remote from us, especially when hope's strength is increased by the idea of escaping punishment, an idea which avarice and weakness too often promote.

Sometimes a man is freed from punishment for a lesser crime when the offended party chooses to forgive—an act in accord with kindness and humanity but contrary to the public good—as if a private citizen, by an act of forgiveness, could eliminate the need for an example, in the same way that he could waive compensation for an injury. The right to inflict punishment is the right not of an individual but of all citizens, or of their sovereign. An individual can renounce his own portion of this right, but cannot annul the right of others.

As punishments become milder, clemency and pardon become less necessary. Happy the nation in which clemency and pardons might some day be considered evil! Clemency, the virtue which has sometimes been deemed a sufficient substitute in a sovereign for all the duties of the throne, should be excluded from perfect legislation, where the punishments are mild and the process of judgment regular and speedy. This truth will seem harsh to anyone living in the midst of the disorders of a criminal system where pardons and mercy are necessary to compensate for the absurdity of the laws and the severity of the sentences. Pardons and mercy, which are indeed the noblest prerogatives of the throne, the most desirable attributes of sovereignty, are also, however, on the part of the benevolent dispenser of public happiness, a tacit disapproval of the penal code which, laden with imperfections, has in its favor centuries of approval, the voluminous and imposing dowry of innumerable commentators, the weighty apparatus of endless formalities, and the allegiance of the most cunning and least formidable of the semi-learned.

But one ought to consider that clemency should be a virtue of the legislator and not of the executors of the laws, that it ought to shine in the code itself rather than in particular judgments. To make men see that crimes can be pardoned or that punishment is not their necessary consequence fosters a beguiling hope of pardon and creates a belief that, because sentences might be remitted, those sentences which are not remitted are acts of oppressive violence rather than justice. What is to be said, then, when the ruler grants pardons—that is, public security to a particular individual—and, with a personal act of unenlightened kindness, issues a public decree of pardon? Let the laws, therefore, be unbending, and let their executors be unbending in particular cases, but let the legislator be tender, indulgent, and humane. Let him, a wise architect, raise his building upon a foundation of self-love, and let the general interest be the result of the interest of each individual. Then the ruler shall not be compelled, by laws only partly applied and disorderly remedies, to constantly separate the public good from the good of individuals and to build the image of public well-being upon fear and distrust. Wise and compassionate philosopher, let him permit men, his brothers, to enjoy in peace that small portion of happiness which the grand system established by the First Cause, by That Which Is, allows them to enjoy in this corner of the universe.

Footnotes

[Footnotes in square brackets have been added by the editors. Footnote 3 is from the original.]

1. [Probably referring to Montesquieu.]

2. [In Beccaria's time the heart was the symbol of intelligence as well as emotions. Intelligence was considered the core of a human being, and the heart is near the center of the body.]

3. Each individual is indeed bound to society, but society is, in turn, bound to each individual by a contract which, of its very nature, places both parties under obligation. This obligation, which descends from the throne to the cottage, which binds equally the loftiest and lowest of men, signifies that it is in the interests of all that the pacts advantageous to the greatest number should be observed....

4. [The idea that laws should represent the will of the living society, not an inheritance from the past, was extended further by Thomas Jefferson in a letter to James Madison. Jefferson suggested that all laws should be repealed every twenty years and new laws should be enacted. Madison did not reply to this point in Jefferson's letter.]

5. [A syllogism is a form of logic with three steps:

    (1) a major premise, which is a general statement;

    (2) a minor premise, which is a particular fact; and

    (3) a conclusion.

For example:

    (1) Larceny is deliberately taking another person's property with the intention to keep it.

    (2) John deliberately took Edward's coat with the intention to keep it.

    (3) John committed the crime of larceny.

6. [The idea that the people of a nation could be considered the sovereign and that the people could be more tyrannical than an individual despot was a theme of later writers, such as James Madison in *The Federalist Papers* (see Nos. 48—51) and John Stuart Mill in *On Liberty*.]

Introduction to
Cesare Lombroso

Lombroso's parents were Sephardic Jews who emigrated from Spain, first to Tunisia and then to Italy. They were part of a well-to-do family of traders. The second of their five children, Ezechia Marco Lombroso, called Cesare, was born in Verona on November 6, 1835. The family was very pious and Cesare was expected to be a very religious person. Cesare was considered a "sensitive" child who reported having mystical visions. But in his teens in public high school in Verona Cesare became an atheist and a rebellious freethinker. At that point his parents removed him from school and educated him privately in the humanities.

Lombroso became interested in a wide variety of subjects. Among other things he wrote an extended essay on the history of the Roman Republic with emphasis on the nature of civilization, an essay on ancient agriculture, and a review of a book on ancient monuments and linguistic analysis by Paolo Marzolo. Marzolo asked to meet the learned book reviewer, and he was astonished that Lombroso was only sixteen years old. It was Marzolo, himself trained in medicine, who influenced Lombroso to begin the study of medicine at the University of Pavia in 1852. While in medical school, Lombroso corresponded with F.A. Maury, the author of a well known book about dreams. Ideas about dreams played an important role in the development of Lombroso's later theories about criminal behavior.

An unhappy love affair led Lombroso to leave Pavia for the University of Padova in 1854–55. He studied at the University of Vienna in 1855–56, where he first became interested in psychiatry. He returned to Pavia in 1857 and received his medical degree from the University of Pavia in 1858 with a doctoral dissertation on cretinism which was published the next year. He went on to earn a degree in surgery from the University of Genoa in 1859. During his years as a student Lombroso became increasingly opposed to the free-will philosophy accepted in Italian academic circles. He was more receptive to the ideas of the French, German and English philosophers, natural scientists and the early social scientists. These ideas emphasized materialism, evolution, and knowledge based on observations and experiments.

From 1859 to 1865 Lombroso distinguished himself as a volunteer serving in a medical corps in the Second Italian War for Independence. He wrote a prize winning text on *Wounds by Firearms*, and he made anthropological observations on some 3000 soldiers from various parts of Italy. One of his observations concerned the generally obscene tattoos commonly found on soldiers with disciplinary records. While serving in poverty stricken Calabria in southern Italy, Lombroso took note of the poor standards of health and hygiene. It alerted him to the influences of the environment and the economy. He also studied the mental patients in a hospital and delivered a series of lectures on mental diseases, which was published as a textbook in 1863. The next year he published the first of several works suggesting a connection between genius and insanity. Between 1861 and 1871 Lombroso also published several studies on pathologies of the brain.

Lombroso left the army in 1865 and became a professor of psychiatry at Pavia. In 1869 he married Nina De Benedetto, a twenty-two-year-old Jewish woman from Alexandria by whom he subsequently had two daughters. The following year, at age thirty-six, Lombroso was invited to direct a psychiatric hospital with criminal patients in Pesaro on the east coast of Italy. In the hospital Lombroso examined about four hundred criminals, collected their biographies and family histories, anthropological data, and psychological observations. It was at this time that Lombroso became very interested in criminality. In 1871 Lombroso published an article on cases of criminal insanity in Italy; in 1872 he published an anthropological study of 400 criminals from Venice; and in 1874 a work on criminal psychology. These led up to the publication of his most important work, *L'Uomo Delinquente (Criminal Man)*, published in 1876 and a few years later translated into several European languages and eventually into English in 1911.

Lombroso left Pesaro in 1876 to accept a professorship in legal medicine in Turin. In 1877 Lombroso published *Legal Medicine of the Corpse,* which was a pioneering work in forensic science. Lombroso created a laboratory of criminal anthropology and started a museum in which he deposited all the material he collected over the years and skulls he began to receive from all over the world. In 1878 he published a book on the influence of the weather on crime. In 1885 Lombroso published an article on the madness of the sixteenth century physician, philosopher and mathematician Cardano, who had a fascination with dreams. This was another work in which Lombroso wrote about the connection between genius and madness, which he said can be detected especially in dreams. He described Cardano's condition as a regressive metamorphosis, a sort of cerebral change which can awaken the instincts of primitive man. In 1886 Lombroso was appointed prison physician in Turin in addition to his professorial position, which enabled him to study more criminals. The same year he translated into Italian a book by a German philosopher and physiologist, Moleschott, who maintained that evil, including the evil done by people, is a natural part of the universe and that to understand everything is to forgive everything.

In 1886–87 Lombroso also became interested in hypnosis. At that time in Europe, especially in France, hypnosis was of great interest to psychiatrists as an almost miraculously effective way to treat certain illnesses, which today are categorized as psychosomatic. In 1888, after criticizing spiritualism which was quite popular throughout Europe at the time, Lombroso reluctantly accepted an invitation to meet a famous spiritual medium, Eusapia Palatino, in Naples. After attending spiritualistic sessions, in one of which he believed he heard the voice of his deceased mother, Lombroso took a somewhat less critical position on spiritualism. This surprised his scientific and social acquaintances because Lombroso was well known to be an enemy of irrationality. In 1890 he became Professor of Psychiatry. In 1893 Lombroso co-authored with his son-in-law Guglielmo Ferrero *The Female Offender*.

In 1897 Lombroso traveled to Moscow for a conference and arranged to meet the Russian novelist Tolstoy. Tolstoy was reluctant, fearing that Lombroso might declare him to be insane. They did meet, and Lombroso left their meeting convinced that Tolstoy was proof of the theory that madness and genius were connected.

Crime: Its Causes and Remedies was published in 1899. It was an expanded version of *Criminal Man*, which summed up all of Lombroso's studies of criminology, incorporating environmental, biological, psychological, anthropological and sociological dimensions of criminology, not to mention the meteorological studies and a wealth of historical observations. Following a medical model, Lombroso described a variety of different kinds of criminals which, like different kinds of diseases, had different causes and required different treatments, including some which seemed to be minor and required practically no treatment. The "born criminal" was the most biologically determined and least treatable type of criminal.

Based on his research and experience as a prison physician, Lombroso made extensive recommendations regarding prisons, probation and the treatment of young offenders. He particularly admired the new late nineteenth century American approaches to penology. According to Lombroso, the most savage and violent of criminals needed to be imprisoned for the safety of society, as a person with a disease might be quarantined, but should not be punished for behavior he could not control.

In 1906 Lombroso was named Professor of Criminal Anthropology at the University of Turin. Anthropology itself was a new science at the time; it focused mostly on exotic primitive peoples, documenting their strange rituals, frenzied dances, cosmetic body piercing and whole body tattooing. Lombroso was a pioneer in creating the more specialized field of criminal anthropology. Familiarity with anthropology made him aware of the differences between primitive societies and more advanced societies. It enabled him to make comparisons between criminals and primitive people.

Apart from his career as a doctor, psychiatrist and criminal anthropologist, Lombroso was an outstanding citizen. For many years he was a municipal councilor selected by one of the working class neighborhoods of Turin to represent them, although he did not give himself over to party politics. He was especially strong in advocating controls over the quality of grain; he believed that diseased grain which was being sold to the poor as a basic food was the cause of one of the most common illnesses of the time, pellagra. Opposed to revolution or class warfare and hardly an advocate of full equality, he did favor modest efforts at social reform. He spoke out against the greed of the upper class and economic destitution of poor tenant farmers. As a result, his once lucrative medical and psychiatric practice lost many upper-class patients.

Lombroso died on October 19, 1909, as a result of a heart condition. At his wish, his body was examined by autopsy and his brain was donated to the Institute of Anatomy.

Throughout the nineteenth century extraordinary new discoveries and ideas were shaping the European mind. Lombroso seems to have become gradually aware of these new ideas, although it is impossible to say exactly when, and it is impossible to determine whether he read some of the most significant publications of the time or learned of them indirectly. A score of earlier medical researchers had done individual specialized studies on medical features of criminals, but it is unknown how many of these earlier studies were known to Lombroso. His very intellectual daughters seem to have brought many ideas to his attention as they helped him throughout his lifetime to refine his thinking and edit his publications. In addition, he drew many excellent students into collaborative thinking. It was one of his most outstanding students, Enrico Ferri, who coined the term "born criminal" that became a key term in Lombroso's later publications. Like Darwin or Freud or other great nineteenth century thinkers, Lombroso brought together many earlier strands of thought, pushed ideas past their earlier forms, and created a new synthesis of ideas.

Lombroso seems never to have read the actual text of Charles Darwin's work on evolution. But the ideas were well known to Lombroso, as they were to every educated person and most especially to scholars and students in biological sciences. General ideas about evolution had been around for a long time before Darwin advanced and supported the theory with his empirical data. The notion of a possible reversal in evolution, an individual's regression to a more primitive stage, was part of the theory of dreams, a topic of great and continued interest to Lombroso. Hypnosis was another approach to regression. Dreams and hypnosis were popular areas of interest in psychiatry at that time, as interesting to Lombroso as they were to Freud and other students of mental phenomena.

Modern medications make epileptic seizures uncommon. But epileptic seizures were a more common sight in Lombroso's time. Epilepsy was viewed as a medical condition which caused short relapses to a primitive state of uncontrolled movements, biting and frenzy like an excited savage. It was generally accepted that epilepsy was a form of "atavism," that is, return to a primitive state. Epilepsy, dreams, and hypnosis all pointed to the idea that even a modern person might regress temporarily to a primitive state. Lombroso noted that epileptics and the most violent criminals were similar in many ways, suggesting that some violent criminality also might be a regression to a primitive condition. Lombroso was familiar with the work of the French hypnotist B.A. Morel whose *Treatise on Degeneracy* was published in 1857. According to Morel, hereditary and environmental factors caused physical and mental degeneration seen in epilepsy, insanity, crime and similar conditions.

Lombroso also was familiar with the biological law of recapitulation formulated by Haeckel ten years before the publication of *Criminal Man*. This law stated that ontogeny recapitulates phylogeny, which is a succinct way of saying that the development of any individual organism (ontogeny) is through stages which resemble the whole history of the evolution of the species (phylogeny). For example, the development of the individual human embryo from a tiny nondescript organism to a complex human shape mirrors the evolution of the whole human species from simple lower forms of life. At least one other biologist, Rudolf Virchow, in a book published in 1856 had noted that some organic features of lower animals can be found in humans and, further, that even on a moral or mental level humans occasionally may revert to a lower level of development. Lombroso was familiar with Virchow's book.

Lombroso reported many observations about distinct characteristics of people who lived in various regions or cities. The inhabitants of these places were more distinct to him than they might be to a modern reader. But that was because in Lombroso's time few people moved from one place to another. Generations had lived in the same place, mingling seldom with people from elsewhere. Moreover, in Lombroso's time the various regions of Italy had just merged into a single country. There was little feeling of common nationality and little mixing of people from different places. Hence, it was common for people to have stereotypes, which were not entirely unfounded, of people from different regions or cities. It was also more difficult under such circumstances to separate biological and cultural causes of behavior. People from a particular region with similar biological features also had similar cultural inheritances.

In studying biological correlates of criminality Lombroso examined the bodily characteristics of people, such as their size, bones, musculature and physical appearance. However, Lombroso was interested in explaining criminality, not predicting it. Like other social scientists he was looking for a basic understanding of things rather than trying to explain individual cases. Human behavior is very complex, and many factors must be taken into account to explain a particular case. In individual cases divergent forces, conditions that change outcomes, and just plain exceptions are commonplace. Lombroso knew this. But at the end of the nineteenth century many less learned and less sophisticated people took Lombroso's studies, as well as studies by others, and claimed to be able to predict the personalities and behaviors of individuals on the basis of their physical features. Phrenologists, for example, would make judgments about an individual's personality or character on the basis of the size, shape and bumps on the person's head. Lombroso did not do this sort of thing.

Lombroso benefited from the nineteenth century development of government bureaucracies, especially in France and Italy, which began to keep statistics on health, crime, economic conditions, etc. Statistics was a new science, and Lombroso saw statistics as another way to construct a science of criminology based on facts. He was always very careful in his studies to compare criminals with non-criminals. If he found that 27% of criminals came from a certain background or had a certain biological feature or a certain psychological characteristic, he made it a point to ask how many non-criminals had the same background, feature or characteristic. He realized that if a certain feature was common in a particular group it did not mean that everybody in the group would have the feature. He never made the mistake of saying that any one or two features could be used to identify a criminal or could be found only in criminals. Even in the extreme case of born criminals, Lombroso reported that only 33% had the atavistic physical and psychological characteristics most peculiar to them. Everything was a matter of more or less rather than yes or no, probability rather than certainty. In short, Lombroso was a skillful practitioner of the new science of statistics.

Lombroso is best known for his biological approach to explaining criminal behavior, which would be expected from a medical doctor. But it would be an inaccurate and incomplete view of Lombroso's work to look only at his medical studies. Lombroso himself emphasized that biology played a small part, and often no part, in the behavior of most criminals. Furthermore, like any doctor, Lombroso was very aware that a person's biology included not only hereditary features but also the effects of injuries and illnesses. Like any doctor, he was clearly aware of the effects of the physical environment on a person's physical and mental health. As a psychiatrist and an anthropologist he added the influences of personal relationships and society to the explanations for criminal behavior. However, both during his lifetime and afterwards Lombroso has been attacked constantly for the biological part of his criminology. It is the part which most challenged traditional beliefs about behavior being based on a "free will," which implied that individuals could make free choices and should be punished for crimes committed as a result of free choices. To Lombroso human nature was part of nature in general, and human behavior was to be explained by science like any other natural phenomenon. He viewed crimes like diseases. Quarantine and treatment might be appropriate in various cases, but not punishment as such. He was not optimistic about finding cures for crimes.

For the modern reader many of Lombroso's ideas remain provocative. His descriptions of different types of criminals, the causes of their criminality, and treatments is a reminder that crime can be dealt with only by looking at the criminal, not the crime. For example, his brief comments on "criminals by passion," which included the bomb throwing anarchists of his time, provides a different perspective on today's terrorists. The debates surrounding insanity pleas in criminal cases, including the question of whether the legal system should find defendants "not guilty by reason of insanity" or "guilty but insane," might be clarified by recourse to Lombroso's medical model of criminality. His observations on criminality in relation to civilization and education put white collar crime in a broader context than the usual explanations based on individual greed and defy the stereotype that crime is predominantly a lower class phenomenon. Lombroso's discussions of population density and immigration emphasize the complexity of these factors and how they interact with other factors when they lead to crime. The modern idea that habitual offenders suffer from biological conditions related to impulsivity and short attention span have implications which are clearer in a context like Lombroso's medical approach to criminality. Lombroso's medical perspective casts a different light on why so many people are in American prisons for drug related crimes. The consequences of his medical model with regard to the treatment or rehabilitation of criminals would broaden discussion of society's responses to crime to include treatments quite different from the usual penal model of retribution.

This selection consists of excerpts from Cesare Lombroso, *Crime: Its causes and remedies,* Part I, Chapters IV, V, and VIII; and Part III, Chapter I. (Original work published 1899) This translation was made especially for this book. In this translation some technical medical terms have been replaced with non-technical English or else supplemented with non-technical language in brackets. Also, the editors have added some notes in square brackets. Section titles have been edited. Footnotes have been renumbered and placed at the end of the selection.

.... For several months in 1870 I was carrying on research in the prisons and asylums of Pavia upon cadavers and living persons, in order to determine whether there were substantial differences between the insane and criminals, without succeeding very well. At last I found in the skull of a brigand a very long series of atavistic abnormalities, especially an enormous seam down the center of the skull and an enlargement of an interior part of the brain similar to the features which are found in lower-order vertebrates. At the sight of these strange abnormalities the problem of the nature and of the origin of the criminal seemed to me resolved: the characteristics of primitive men and of lower animals apparently are being reproduced in our times.... (Lombroso, speech at the Sixth Congress of Criminal Anthropology, Turin, April 1906.)

Cesare Lombroso
Crime: Its Causes and Remedies

Civilization and Barbarism

Among the numerous problems of society there is one especially whose definite and final solution concerns us greatly. It is the problem of the impact of civilization upon crime and insanity. If we judge by statistics alone, we shall conclude that the problem is already solved, for in every country of Europe, except England, we find that crime and insanity are each year increasing out of proportion to the growth of the population.[1] But in this connection Messedaglia rightly observes how easy it is to make a mistake in attempting to solve, on the basis of statistics alone, complex problems in which many factors play a role at the same time. The constant increase in crime and insanity might actually be explained by changes in civil and criminal laws, by a greater tendency to file charges against people, by easier access to asylums for the insane, and by more activity on the part of police.

One thing appears certain: barbarism and civilization each has crimes peculiar to it. Barbarism, by deadening moral sensibilities, diminishes the horror of homicide, which is frequently admired in barbaric societies as a heroic act. By making revenge a duty and confusing might with right, barbarism increases crimes of blood and encourages gangs of criminals, just as among the insane barbarism promotes religious delusions and obsessions, satanic delusions and obsessions, and imitative insanity. On the other hand, in barbaric societies family ties are stronger, while sexual excitement and insane ambition are less frequent, and consequently parricide, infanticide, and theft are less frequent.

According to Guglielmo Ferrero, the human race has hitherto produced two types of civilization: the type characterized by violence, and the type characterized by fraud. They are distinguished by the form which the struggle for existence takes. In primitive civilization the struggle is carried on purely by force. Wealth and power are achieved by arms, at the expense either of foreigners or of weaker fellow-citizens. Commercial competition between two peoples is carried on through armies and fleets, that is to say, by violent expulsion of competitors from coveted markets. Disputes are decided by duels. In the civilization characterized by fraud, on the other hand, the struggle for existence is carried on by cunning and deceit, and the waging of battle is replaced by legal chicanery. Political power is obtained no longer at the point of the sword but by money. Money is extracted from the pockets of others by tricks and mysterious manipulations, such as the operations of the stock-exchange. Commercial warfare is carried on through the perfection of the means of production, but still more through the perfection of the art of deceit, the skill of being able to give a purchaser the impression that he is getting a good bargain.[2] We find the first type of civilization, characterized by violence, in Corsica, part of Sardinia, Montenegro, the Italian cities of the Middle Ages, and in nearly all primitive civilizations. We find the second type of civilization, characterized by fraud, in all the modern civilized nations, that is to say, among those nations in which a capitalistic system has reached complete development. The distinction between the two types is not, however, so absolute in reality as it is in theory, for characteristics belonging to the two different types of civilization are often found mixed together in the same society.

Since in the realm of society as in the realm of the body, illness is linked to physiology [how the body functions], we discover in the criminal world these same two means of contest as in civilization, namely, violence and fraud. As a matter of fact, two forms of criminality manifest themselves in our day side by side. First, there is atavistic [primitive] criminality, in which certain individuals, who have a morbid [unhealthy, diseased] physical condition, in the struggle for existence return to the violent means which have been suppressed by civilization, such as, homicide, robbery, and rape. Second, there is "evolutive" criminality, which is no less evil in intent but more civilized in the means employed, for instead of violence it uses trickery and deceit.[3] Into the first type of criminality fall only a few individuals, who are unavoidably predisposed to crime; into the second type of criminality may fall any individual who does not have a character strong enough to resist the evil influences in his environment....

The Born Criminal:
Atavism, Epilepsy, and a Combination of Morbid Abnormalities with Atavism

Atavism [having physical and psychological characteristics of primitive people]

Up to 33% of born criminals show numerous specific characteristics that are almost always atavistic.... Many of the characteristics observed in savage races are very often found among born criminals. Examples of such characteristics include: [poor development of certain bone structures]; low cranial capacity; retreating forehead; highly developed sinus cavities behind the forehead; great frequency of bones with spongy texture; premature closing of the cranial sutures [seams in the normal skull allowing growth in childhood]; the thickness of the bones of the skull; enormous development of the jaw bones and cheekbones; jutting chin; slanting of the eyes; greater pigmentation of the skin; tufted and crispy hair; and large ears. To these we may add the primitive form of the appendix; anomalies of the ear; wide spacing of the teeth; great agility; relative insensibility to pain; dullness of the sense of touch; great visual acuteness; ability to recover quickly from wounds; blunted affections; precocity as to sensual pleasures[4]; greater resemblance between the sexes; greater incorrigibility of the woman[5]; laziness; absence of remorse; impulsiveness; bodily and mental excitability; and especially impulsivity, which sometimes appears as courage and other times as recklessness changing to cowardice. Besides these there is great vanity; a passion for gambling and alcoholic drinks; violent but fleeting passions; superstition; extraordinary sensitiveness with regard to one's own personality; and unusual ideas about God and morality. Unexpected similarities between born criminals and primitive people can be found even in small details, such as, the improvised rules of criminal gangs; the highly personal power of their leaders[6]; the custom of tattooing; the frequent cruelty of their games; the excessive use of gestures; onomatopoetic language with personification of inanimate things; and a special collection of stories recalling those of heroic times when crimes were celebrated and thought tended to clothe itself in rhythmic form.

This atavism explains the diffusion of certain crimes, such as pederasty and infanticide, whose occurrence in whole groups of people we could not explain if we did not recall the Romans, the Greeks, the Chinese, and the Tahitians, who not only did not regard them as crimes, but sometimes even practiced them as national customs. Garofalo has admirably summed up the psychological characteristics of the born criminal as the absence of the feelings of shame, honor, and pity, which are characteristics missing in savages also.[7] We may add to these the lack of industry and self-control.

To those who object, like Reclus and Krapotkin, that there are savage peoples who are honorable and chaste, we must reply that a certain degree of density of population and of association among men is necessary for crimes to develop. It is not possible to steal when property does not exist, or to swindle when there is no trade. But proof that these tendencies exist in germ in savages, is that when they begin to advance from the stage of savagery and take on a little civilization they always develop characteristics of criminality to an exaggerated degree. As Ferrero has pointed out to us, even when honor, chastity, and pity are found among savages, impulsiveness and laziness are never lacking. Savages have a horror of continuous work, so that for them the passage to diligent and methodical labor lies only by way of natural selection or of slavery. Thus, according to the testimony of Tacitus, the impulsiveness of the ancient Germans frequently resulted in the murder of a slave, committed in a fit of anger, an act which was not regarded as culpable. Tacitus also notes their lack of capacity for work. "They have," he says, "large bodies, effective for quick efforts, but they lack the patience necessary for regular work. When they are not at war they do nothing.... They sleep and eat. The strongest and most warlike live in idleness, leaving care of the house and the field to women, old men, and the weak, becoming themselves slothful brutes."

At times, on the other hand, impulsiveness, rather than sluggishness, seems to ally itself with a ceaseless need of movement, which asserts itself in savage peoples in a life of incessant vagabondage. Thus the Andaman Islanders, as Hovelacque tells us, have so restless a disposition that they remain not more than two or three days in the same place, and their wanderings have no other reason than the need for movement. This attitude seems to be the result of shifting back and forth between an inclination to physical and psychological inertia and an inclination to violent and unrestrained physical, mental, and emotional excitement. This shifting back and forth always accompanies inertia and impulsiveness. Hence it is that those peoples who are normally most lazy and indolent have the most unrestrained and noisy dances, which they carry on until they get into a kind of delirium and fall down utterly exhausted. "When the Spaniards," writes Robertson, "first saw the American Indians, they were astonished at their mad passion for dancing, and at the dizzy activity which this people, almost always cold and passive, displayed when they gave themselves up to this amusement." "The negroes of Africa," writes Du Chaillu, "dance madly when they hear the sound of the tom-tom, and lose all command of themselves." "It is," says Letourneau, "a real dancing madness, which makes them forget their troubles, public or private."

We may add that the atavism of a criminal, when he lacks absolutely every trace of shame and pity, may go back far beyond the savage stage, even to an animal stage. Pathological anatomy helps to prove our position by showing in the cases of criminals [several features of the anatomy, especially in the brain cells and the bones, which resemble the anatomical features of animals]....

These facts prove clearly that the most horrible crimes have their origin in animal instincts, of which childhood gives us a pale reflection. Repressed in civilized man by education, environment, and the fear of punishment, animal instincts suddenly break out in the born criminal without apparent cause or under certain circumstances, such as sickness, atmospheric influences, sexual excitement, or mob influence. We know that certain morbid conditions, such as head injuries, meningitis, and chronic intoxication, or certain physiological conditions like pregnancy and senility, produce complications in the nervous system, and consequently atavistic regressions occur. We can see how they may facilitate the tendency to crime, and when we take into account the short distance that separates the criminal from the savage, we come to understand why convicts so easily adopt savage customs, including cannibalism, as was observed in Australia and Guiana.[8] When we note how children, until they are educated, are ignorant of the difference between vice and virtue, and how they steal, strike, and lie without the least regret, we easily understand why the majority of abandoned children and orphans become criminals at an early age.[9] Further, atavism enables us to understand the uselessness of punishment for born criminals and why it is that they inevitably have periodic relapses into crimes....

Epilepsy

The same phenomena which we observe in the case of born criminals appear again in the rare cases of moral insanity.[10] These phenomena may be studied in detail in a large number of cases in epileptics, whether they are criminal or not[11].... All of the atavistic characteristics and behaviors shown by criminals are found in epileptics, although epileptics also show certain phenomena caused by disease, such as enlargement of the skull, degeneration of the arteries, delirium, and hallucinations. Likewise in born criminals we find, besides atavistic characteristics, certain other characteristics which appear to be entirely due to illness, or which at first sight seem more closely related to disease than to atavism....

We may recall here that Gowers often observed in epileptics some acts characteristic of animals, such as biting, barking, and mewing; he concluded "that these are manifestations of an instinctive animalism which we possess in the latent state."[12] If fully developed epileptic fits are often lacking in the case of a born criminal, this is because they remain latent and show themselves only later under the influence of the well known causes (anger, alcoholism) which bring them to the surface. With both criminals and epileptics we note an insufficient development of the higher centers of the brain. This manifests itself in deterioration of moral and emotional sensibilities, in sluggishness, in physical and psychological over-excitability, and especially in a lack of balance in the mental faculties, which, even when distinguished by genius and altruism, nevertheless always show gaps, contradictions, and on-and-off action.

A Combination of Morbid Abnormalities with Atavism

Very often certain common characteristics of criminals and epileptics have been classed as abnormal or morbid [due to disease] rather than atavistic because of the inadequacy of our knowledge of the development of the embryo and the inadequacy of our knowledge of the evolution of the species. Many of the characteristics seen in criminals and epileptics ... are due to atavism and disease at the same time, such as small skull size, excessive hardening of the skull, etc. Facial asymmetry would also appear to be atavistic when we consider the flat-fish (Penta), for example. Likewise an abnormally wrinkled face reminds us of the Hottentots and the apes. Hernias, too, as Fere correctly noted, recall conditions that are normal in the lower vertebrates and also in the human embryo.

Very often disease and atavism go back to a common cause, as Wagner[13] observes in a magnificent dissertation.

> "The idea," he writes, "that the atavism of criminals is associated with some specific disease of the fetus has been fully confirmed by the discoveries of Ettinghausen. For example, if we freeze the roots of an oak so as partly to kill it, the following year it will sprout leaves that are not like the leaves of a modern oak, but like those of an oak of the Tertiary Period. This fact explains the reappearance of intermediate and indistinct fossil forms. We see very clearly, then, that influences capable of producing a disease can bring about atavistic regressions in anatomy."

Epilepsy is the background upon which the clinical and anatomical picture of the moral lunatic and the born criminal can be drawn. The picture of the moral lunatic and the born criminal would otherwise be lost in vague semi-legal and semi-psychiatric hypotheses. However, the epileptic background explains the suddenness, periodicity, and paradoxical character of their symptoms, which are doubtless their most marked characteristics. Note, for example, in this regard, the coexistence of kindness and ferocity, of cowardice and insane recklessness, and of genius and total stupidity.

Other Types of Criminals:
The Criminaloid, Criminal Insane, Criminals by Passion, and Occasional Criminals

The Criminaloid [less atavistic species of criminal]

Criminaloids, although quite distinguishable from born criminals, also exhibit some connection with epilepsy and atavism. Thus there are more epileptics among criminaloids (10% among pickpockets) than among normal men, a greater proportion of criminal types [based on physical features] (17%), but also certain specific abnormalities, such as left-handedness, which is common among swindlers.[14]

In the biology of the criminaloid, as compared to the born criminal, we observe a smaller number of abnormalities in touch, sensibility to pain, measurements of the head, and especially less early baldness and grayness, and less tattooing. But, on the other hand, we meet with a larger number of disease related abnormalities, especially as a result of the abuse of alcoholic drinks, such as degeneration of the arteries, partial paralysis, and scars. Psychological abnormalities are especially less frequent with the criminaloid, who does not have the cynicism of the born criminal nor the passion for doing evil for its own sake. The criminaloid confesses his faults more easily and with more sincerity, and he repents more often. But he is more lascivious and more prone to alcoholism. Criminaloid women are more susceptible to suggestion.

The criminaloid is more precocious and relapses more often than a born criminal—at least this is the case with pickpockets and simple thieves. Criminaloids are often drawn into crime more by opportunity, although the lack of self-control which makes an epileptic commit crime without reason is sometimes found in the criminaloid also. We may recall that Casenova confessed that when he committed a fraud he never premeditated it, but "seemed to yield to a superior will." A pickpocket once said to me, "When the inspiration comes to us, we cannot resist." Dostojevsky depicts contraband dealers in the prison as carrying on their occupation almost without profits, not withstanding the grave risks they run and in spite of repeated promises not to relapse. Mendel and Benedict describe the impulsive nature of the vagabond, which keeps him moving without purpose and without rest.

Criminaloids, thus, differ from born criminals in degree, not in kind. This is so true that the majority of them, having become habitual criminals thanks to a long stay in prison, can no longer be distinguished from born criminals except by the lesser degree of their physical signs of criminality.

More like born criminals are those latent criminals, high in power, whom society venerates as its chiefs. They bear the signs of congenital criminality, but their high position usually prevents their criminal character from being recognized. Their families, of which they are the scourges, may discover it. Their depraved nature may be revealed too late at the expense of the whole country, to the head of which they may have risen by their shameful conduct, supported by the ignorance and cowardice of the majority of people. Even this strange species of criminal monomaniac [obsessed with one thing], who seems to differ from the epileptic in the motive of his crime and the manner of carrying it out[15], shows nevertheless the epileptic and atavistic origin of his criminality by his obsessions, short span of attention, lack of self-control, exaggerated importance given to certain details, exhaustion after his criminal crises, fondness for symbolism, excessive intermittent activity, and finally by hereditary physical signs.

The Criminal Insane

Even among truly insane criminals those forms of crime predominate which we may call the hypertrophy [extraordinary enlargement] of crime, the exaggeration of the born criminal, not only in bodily and functional characteristics but also in his manner of committing crime and in his behavior afterwards.[16] These serve to explain to us the extent of the impulsive, obscene, and cruel tendencies of the criminal insane, who are almost always unrecognized epileptics or born criminals upon whom depression and obsessive behaviors have grafted themselves. It is the natural tendency of different forms of psychological disorders to take root together in the corrupted soil of physical and mental deterioration. We have seen, likewise, how hysterical persons, alcoholics, dipsomaniacs, pyromaniacs, kleptomaniacs, and the temporarily insane reproduce many of the characteristics of epileptics. The person of unbalanced mind on the verge of insanity, on account of his habitual calm and the absence of signs of degeneracy and heredity, may also seem far removed from epilepsy; yet at times he displays epileptic characteristics, which we have seen to be the kernel of crime.[17]

Criminals by Passion [strong emotion, dedication]

Criminals of this type are a species apart. They are completely different from the born criminal—in the harmonious lines of the body, beauty of the soul, and great nervous and emotional sensitiveness, as well as in the motives for their crimes, which are always noble and powerful motives, such as love or political causes. Nevertheless they show some points of resemblance to epileptics, such as their tendency to excesses, impulsiveness, suddenness of their outbreaks, and frequent amnesia.[18]

[Editors' note: Lombroso's observations on this type of criminal reflected his time and place. Nineteenth century anarchists, especially in Italy, were the heirs of ancient democratic impulses. Italian city-states of the Renaissance had no hereditary rulers. Ambitious individuals used deceit and violence to seize power and usually ruled by means of great cruelty. To assassinate, or attempt to assassinate, a tyrant was an act of civic virtue and of glory, immortalized, for example, in Michelangelo's bust of Brutus. Most often attempts at assassination failed, and they nearly always spelled a gruesome death for the assassin because tyrants made it a point to be very closely guarded.]

Occasional Criminals

Occasional criminals, or more precisely, pseudo-criminals, are those who do not seek an occasion for crime but are practically drawn into it, or those who stumble into the net of the law for very insignificant reasons. These are the only criminals who escape all connection with atavism and epilepsy. However, as Garofalo observes, these ought not to be called criminals, properly speaking.

Crimes in Relation to Density of Population, Immigration and Education

Crime and Population Density

The influence of population density can be seen clearly in our country [Italy], especially if one examines in detail various crimes in relation to different degrees of population density. In Italy we find, for example:[19]

Number of Crimes per 100,000 Inhabitants

Population per square kilometer	Homicides	Thefts	Resistance to police	Rapes	Swindling
20 to 50	11.0	199.0	23.7	18.8	52.6
50 to 100	6.03	144.4	25.4	16.4	45.0
100 to 150	6.0	148.0	23.5	14.5	58.5
150 to 200	5.1	153.0	24.6	12.3	54.6
200 or more	3.5	158.0	29.5	18.7	50.4

We find that homicide decreases as the population density increases, especially in the great cities, so that Milan, Naples, Leghorn, and Genoa, although they have different climates and races (Greek, Celtic, Ligurian), have a lower number of homicides. In contrast we see that the number of homicides is greater where the population density is less, which is in the hotter parts of the country and in the islands, where society is more barbarous and criminal gangs are more common.

Theft, rape, and resistance to officers of the law also diminish with an increase in population density, but then rise again rapidly with the excessive density of the great cities (Padua, Naples, Milan, Venice). Swindling follows an irregular pattern, but nearly always is in the direction opposite to the population density—a fact which results from the strong involvement of the islands, especially Sardinia, in this crime, and also from the strong inclination in this direction of old native habits in the provinces of Forli and Bologna, where swindling is widespread. Bologna is proverbial for swindling, and Dante in his *Inferno* makes Venedico say, "I am not the only Bolognese weeping here; this whole place is full of them."[20]

Similarly, in recent French statistics we find the following:[21]

Population per square kilometer	Number of crimes to 100,000 inhabitants		
	Thefts	Homicides	Rapes
20 to 40	63	4.41	19.0
40 to 60	96	1.42	20.4
60 to 80	100	1.40	19.0
80 to 100	116	1.20	30.0
100 or more	196	1.88	34.0

We can see that theft becomes more and more frequent as the population density increases. Homicides and rapes, in contrast, show their highest rates in places where there is either a minimum or a maximum of population density. This contradiction is explained by the fact that the population is most compact in the great industrial (Seine-Inferieure, 92) and political (Paris, 18) centers, as well as in ports of immigration (Bouches-du-Rhone, 45). In the places with the greatest population densities the opportunities for conflict are more frequent. On the other hand, where there is a minimum of population density (Corcisa, 200; Lozere, 41; Hautes-Alpes, 24), there is a maximum of barbarism, and we have seen that in these places assaults and assassinations are often regarded more as necessities than as crimes....

Crime and Immigration

… It was already known that immigrants showed a high degree of criminality.

In recent statistics of the United States [22] it can be seen that states which have the greatest number of immigrants, especially Irish and Italians, have the highest rates of crimes. Thus:

State	Criminals per 1000 population	Immigrants
California	0.30	33%
Nevada	0.31	41%
Wyoming	0.35	28%
Montana	0.19	29%
Arizona	0.16	39%
New York	0.27	23%

On the other hand:

State	Criminals per 1000 population	Immigrants
New Mexico	0.03	6.7%
Pennsylvania	0.11	13.0%

This runs counter to the effect of population density on crime. Montana with 0.3 inhabitants to the square mile, Wyoming with 0.2, Nevada with 0.6, and Arizona with 0.4, despite their low density, have huge crime rates. This is due to immigration. New York with 151 inhabitants to the square mile, and Pennsylvania with 95 inhabitants to the square mile—two cities where the population density is great—have much lower crime rates. The District of Columbia, which has 2960 inhabitants to the square mile, also has relatively low crime rates.

Of 49,000 individuals arrested in New York, 32,000 were immigrants.[23]

Of 38,000 prisoners in North America, 20,000 were the children of foreigners.[24]

In France it has already been observed that in 1886:

of 100,000 settled residents	8 came before the courts
of 100,000 who had changed residence	29 came before the courts
of 100,000 foreigners	41 came before the courts

… Many come to the great cities honest but with false ideas of the new situation that has enticed them. Consequently, they are easily led astray; little by little they become criminals. A young girl, having yielded to seduction, becomes a prostitute. A laborer, lacking work, falls into idleness; surrounded by companions who coax him into crime and tempted by the allurements of a thousand pleasures that he sees others enjoying, he becomes a thief. There are repentant laborers who want to forget their crimes and redeem themselves by work, but they soon relapse, either as a result of running into temptation again or due to their inability to cover up their past crimes. Finally there are evildoers who come to the city specifically to commit crime. As Joly so well expressed it, in small towns it is necessary to search for opportunities for crime;

in Paris the opportunity comes to you and entices you. The big city's *bon vivants* are themselves a cause of crime, especially crimes against public decency. In Paris such crimes may be committed with such cleverness that they no longer appear to be criminal.[25]

Crime and Education

... All this explains a phenomenon which at first seems to be completely self-contradictory, namely, that education sometimes increases crime and sometimes decreases crime. When education is not yet widespread in a country and has not yet reached its full development, at first all crimes except homicide increase. But when education becomes widespread it reduces violent crimes, except, as we shall see, the less serious crimes, political crimes, commercial crimes, and sexual crimes. These increase naturally with increases in human encounters, business, and cerebral activity. However, education has an indisputable influence upon crime by changing its nature and making it less savage. Fayet and Lacassagne[26] show that in France: (1) among illiterates the crimes which predominate are infanticide, abortion, theft, formation of criminal gangs, robbery, and arson; (2) among those who can barely read and write, the predominant crimes are extortion, threatening letters, blackmail, robbery, injury to property, and assaults; (3) among those who have a moderate education, bribery, forgery, and threatening letters are most common; (4) among the well educated the predominant crimes are forgeries of commercial papers, misuse of office, forgery and falsification of public documents, and political crimes. A minimum of forgeries and a maximum of infanticides are found among illiterate people. Among convicts with a higher level of education the prevailing crimes are forgery of public documents, breach of trust, and swindling; infanticides and violent crimes are not found among the highly educated.

Hence, there is a type of crime for the illiterate, namely, the savage type; and another type for the educated, namely, the tamer but more cunning type. In the same way, according to the most recent studies of Socquet[27], we see that in France the number of illiterate criminals gradually diminished in the period 1876–1880 in comparison with the period 1831–1835. Homicides and murders have decreased among them by half, infanticides and abortions by a third, and sexual crimes by nearly a half. Violent crimes by educated criminals are generally diminishing, while their other crimes are nearly at a standstill. With regard to political crimes, these increase constantly among the educated. History teaches us that it has been the highly civilized states (Athens, Genoa, Florence) which have experienced the greatest number of revolutions. It is certainly not among the illiterate that nihilists and anarchists find their recruits, but among the more highly educated. Of this I have given abundant proof in my book, *Crime Politique*. In Austria the crimes which predominate among the illiterate are robbery, kidnapping, infanticide, abortion, murder, bigamy, homicide, malicious damage to property, and assault. In Italy, according to a remarkable study by Amati[28], we find:

[Percent of Crimes Committed by Individuals
with Different Education Levels]

Crimes, 1881–1883	Illiterate	Able to read and write	More highly educated
Political crimes	54%	36%	10.0%
Frauds	38%	55%	7.0%
Homicides	62%	37%	0.12%
Thefts	65%	34%	1.7%
Rapes	48%	44%	8.0%
Rebellions	49%	48%	3.1%

Among 500 individuals who had more education there were the following numbers of crimes in 1881–83 [The second number gives the rate per 1000 people in the population.]:

[Number and Rate of Crimes Committed by 500 Individuals
with More Education]

Forgeries	76; 152 [per 1000]	Assaults	13; 26
Homicides	44; 88	Parricides	2; 4
Thefts	40; 80	Political crimes	14; 28
Frauds	57; 114	Crimes against religion	1; 2
Extortions	38; 76	Destruction of property	4; 8
Highway robberies	22; 44	Arson	9; 18
Sexual crimes	34; 68	Instigation to crime	6; 12
Bankruptcies	33; 66	Abortions	1; 2
Perjuries	2; 4		

Looking at the types of crimes committed by individuals with a higher level of education, the figures are higher for forgery, fraud, sexual crime, bankruptcy, theft, extortion, and homicide; and lower for assault, highway robbery, parricide, and arson. Comparing people with different levels of education, the illiterate lead in homicide and theft, while the partly and fully educated together show a high figure for political crimes and a majority of rapes and frauds.

A fact of the greatest importance is that the same causes which reduce certain crimes increase others, making it difficult for a government official to devise a solution to the problem of crime. We have seen that education and wealth cause a decrease in certain brutal crimes, especially homicides and assassinations, but at the same time education and wealth increase other crimes, or even create new crimes, such as bankruptcy and swindling. And if, for example, too great a population density is the cause of many crimes, such as frauds and thefts, a sparse population, on the other hand, favors highway robbery and crimes of blood. Lack of sufficient food leads to poaching from private forests, forgeries, insurrections, and arson, but cheap grain multiplies rapes, homicides, and crimes against persons generally.

Alcohol, next to hot weather, is the most powerful producer of crime. When alcohol is cheap, it increases all the crimes against persons and against public order; but if it is expensive, alcohol increases all the crimes against property. Yet there is this strange contradiction, that more serious crimes are least numerous where alcohol is most abused. No doubt, this is because a high level of alcohol abuse occurs precisely in those localities where there is a higher degree of civilization; and a higher level of civilization, by fostering inhibition, decreases the more barbarous crimes. The school likewise is a cause of some crime. But where education is most widespread, it reduces the number and seriousness of crimes.

Footnotes

[Original references were not so complete as references are expected to be today, so, when possible, more details have been added to some references. Since parts of the original text have been omitted from this selection, the footnotes have been renumbered.]

1. In France from 1826 to 1837 there was one person indicted out of each one hundred in the population; in 1868 indictments had reached one to fifty-five (Dufau, "Traite de Statistique," 1840; Block, "L'Europe Politique," 1870). From 1825 to 1838 indictments (excluding political crimes and fiscal misdemeanors) rose from 57,470 to 80,920. In 1838 indictments increased from 237 (to the 100,000) to 375; in 1847 to 480; from 1854–55 to 1866 they sank to 389, to increase again to 517 in 1874, and to 552 in 1889. There was, then, an increase of about 133% in 50 years (Joly, "France Criminelle," 1890, p. 10).

In Austria there were:

In	1856, 1 conviction to	1238 inhabitants, 1 indictment to	832
	1857	1101	813
	1860	1261	933
	1861	1178	808
	1862	1082	740

(Messedaglia) [There is no more complete reference in Lombroso, but the reference is most likely to the Italian publication of Angelo Messedaglia, *Criminal Statistics in the Austrian Empire.*]

In England and Wales there was:

From	1811 to 1815	1 prisoner to each	1210 inhabitants
	1826 to 1830		508
	1826 to 1830 [sic]		477
	1846 to 1848		455

From 1805 to 1841 the population increased 40%, the crimes six times more than the population. In some counties, Monmouthshire for example, the population increased about 128%, crimes 720%. (Aberdeen, "Discorso," 1876).

In Italy there were:

From 1850 to 1859, 16,173 indictments for serious crimes, and 7,535 convictions

From 1860 to 1869, 23,854 indictments, and 10,701 convictions

From 1863 to 1869 crimes increased one-tenth, the population about one-twentieth

(Curcio, *op. cit.* [but no previous citation in the original])

2. Ferrero, "Violenti e Frodolenti in Romagna," in "Il Mondo Criminale Italiano," Milan, 1894.

3. Sighele, "Delinquenza Settaria," Milan, 1898.

4. Lombroso, "Homme Criminel," Vol. I, pp. 136–579. [References in the original are to the French edition, although the work was first published in Italian in 1876.]

5. Spencer. [No more complete reference in the original]

6. Tacitus, "Germ," VII.

7. "Criminologie," 2nd ed., 1895.

8. Bouvier, "Voyage a la Guyane," 1866.

9. "Homme Criminel," Vol. I, pp. 92–108.

10. "Homme Criminel," Vol. II, pp. 2–13.

11. "Homme Criminel," Vol. II, pp. 50–201.

12. "Epilepsy," London, 1880.

13. Wagner von Jauregg, "Antrittsvorlesung an der Psychiatrischen Klinik." Vienna, 1895.

14. "Homme Criminel," Vol II, pp. 216, 514, 518.

15. "Homme Criminel," Vol. II, pp. 94, 97, 408.

16. "Homme Criminel," Vol I, pp. 34 to 228; Vol. II, p. 213.

17. "Homme Criminel," Vol. II, p. 646.

18. "Homme Criminel," Vol. II, p. 226.

19. Bodio, "Annuario Statistico Italiano," 1894, Rome.

20. *E non pur io qui piango Bolognese: Anzi n'e questo luogo tanto pierno.* CANTO XVIII.

21. Ferri, "Omicidio," 1895.

22. "Compendium of the Tenth Census (1880) of the United States." Pt. II, p. 1659.

23. Brace, "The Dangerous Classes of New York," 1875.

24. Bertrami-Scalia, *op.cit.* [but no previous citation in the original]

25. Joly, "La France Criminelle," 1890.

26. Fayet, "Journal des Econ.," 1847; and Lacassagne, in Lombroso, "Archivio di Psichiatria ed Antropologia Criminale," *III.*
27. "Contribution a l'Etude de la Criminalite en France."
28. "Istruzione e Delinquenza in Italia," 1886.

Introduction to
Clifford R. Shaw and Henry D. McKay

In 1892 the University of Chicago became the first university in the United States to establish a department of sociology. The department's leading people had studied in France and Germany where emphasis was placed on social influences on human behavior and where there was a strong reliance on studying social problems by using official records, such as court and welfare records, as well as individual case histories. The first efforts to compile extensive criminal justice statistics in the United States took place at the University of Chicago. The University of Chicago became the leading university for the development of criminology.

Chicago especially became the center for criminologists interested in juvenile delinquents. There was a sense that most of the crime in Chicago was committed by juveniles. Beginning with the premise that delinquency had psychological causes, the Juvenile Psychopathic Institute was organized in Chicago in 1909. The director, Dr. William Healy, published *The Individual Delinquent* in 1915. It contained case histories and other data about 1,000 juvenile repeat offenders. Surprisingly, Healy found that poverty was rarely a factor in juvenile delinquency cases. A later study specifically addressed this issue and found that 73% of delinquents came from families with average or above average incomes (Healy & Bronner, 1926).

In 1917 the Illinois Department of Public Welfare, Division of Criminology, set up an Institute for Juvenile Research. The Institute grew from three employees to ninety in about a decade. It worked closely with clinics and parent training programs which treated delinquency as a psychological problem. When private contributions created a Behavior Research Fund for the Institute, the Institute hired Clifford R. Shaw to conduct research on delinquency in Chicago.

Clifford R. Shaw (1896–1957) had earned a M.A. in sociology at the University of Chicago in 1921. He continued with some doctoral studies until 1924 but did not complete the doctoral program. At the same time, from 1921 until 1923 he worked as a Parole Officer for the Illinois State Training School for Boys, and from 1924 until 1926 as a Probation Officer for the Cook County Juvenile Court. He became director of the sociology department at the Institute for Juvenile Research in 1926, where he remained until his death in 1957. He also taught at some colleges in the Chicago area, including the University of Chicago from 1941 until 1947.

Henry D. McKay (1899–1980) took his M.A. in sociology at the University of Chicago in 1924. He taught sociology at the University of Illinois in 1925–1926, then returned to the University of Chicago for doctoral studies. He continued his doctoral studies from 1926 until 1929 but did not complete the degree. He took a position in Clifford Shaw's sociology department at the Institute for Juvenile Research in 1927 and continued working there until his retirement.

That same year, 1927, Frederic Thrasher published *The Gang*, an extensive study of gangs in the city of Chicago. It was found that gang activity accounted for about 95% of all juvenile delinquency in Chicago. Studies of court records found that over 80% of delinquent boys acted with gangs. Particular delinquents' records linked them to older boys and to younger boys. The gangs were usually three, four, or five boys ages ten to seventeen. Their most common offenses were truancy and begging. They were not like the large cohesive gangs which developed later in the 1950s. Older brothers sometimes fenced stolen property for the gangs. The boys readily changed from one gang to another. The gangs were not stable or cohesive. Within gangs the relationships between the boys were usually selfish and competitive, each boy taking whatever he could get from the gang's activities and engaging in fistfights for leadership. The older boys taught the younger boys techniques for pulling off petty thefts, purse snatches, robberies, auto thefts, etc. Delinquent acts were often prompted more by daring and thrill seeking than by potential profit.

While working at the Institute for Juvenile Research both Shaw and McKay did case studies of individual delinquents. The case studies included, among others, an intensive study of one boy who robbed drunks, *The Jack-Roller* (Shaw, 1930), and a study of five delinquent brothers, *Brothers in Crime* (Shaw, McKay & McDonald, 1938). Case studies highlighted the role of gangs and the even greater impact of having a delinquent brother. The delinquents kept their parents ignorant of their criminal activities and squandered their criminal profits on small immediate treats and amusements, not parading their profits at home. Parents were usually honest people trying to raise their children properly but easily deceived. Typically, boys as young as three years old were taken along by truant older brothers for door to door begging excursions to better neighborhoods. They often chanced upon opportunities for thefts or burglaries.

Brothers in Crime explained criminality largely in terms of the theories of Gabriel Tarde. Tarde was a French criminologist who had died in 1904. He had rejected Lombroso's heavy biological emphasis. A biological emphasis was linked to the scientific assumption of determinism; it suggested that an individual's behavior was determined by laws of nature and inevitable social influences rather than any sort of free will. Tarde believed that crime was more a product of free choices and chance occasions than determinism. Tarde's theory focused on how criminal behavior might be learned by imitation of others. Tarde's theory of imitation was itself turned into a rather deterministic theory of crime by the American criminologists of the 1930s. American criminologists described the processes of imitation in terms of social forces, such as peer pressures, rather than free choices and chance happenings.

Shaw and McKay's *Juvenile Delinquency in Urban Areas* (1942) was a shift from case studies of delinquency to an environmental approach. Shaw and McKay were familiar with the theory of Chicago criminologists Robert E. Park and Ernest W. Burgess (1925) that social problems were due to environmental conditions. Park and Burgess' approach became known as the "ecological" approach to urban problems. Ecology was originally a concept in the field of biology. Ecology referred to the relationship between a plant or animal and its physical environment. It especially looked at how the physical environment fostered or hindered the development of an organism. Transposing this idea from biology to sociology involved thinking of society as an organism and expanding the concept of environment to include the social environment as well as the physical environment. This approach led to studies of many social problems in relation to urban areas. Besides studies of crime in relation to urban zones, there were studies of health, employment, schooling, welfare agencies, and numerous other social factors.

Shaw and McKay based the interpretation of their data about delinquents partly on the theory of Park and Burgess that there were certain natural processes which characterized the development of American cities. Cities began small and expanded outward from the center. As they grew, they incorporated surrounding towns and villages, in practice if not in legal boundaries. The city center was the downtown industrial, commercial and cultural center. A series of concentric circles surrounded the center. Next to the downtown circle was a circle of deteriorating housing, which would eventually be demolished and taken over by the expanding downtown. The third circle was predominantly residences for lower middle class workers, which was expanding outward into the fourth circle, which was mostly residences for the more prosperous middle class. Finally, the fifth circle, which was also moving outward, was home to the upper middle class, professionals and the wealthy. Industrial areas tended to be near the center; but some were in other areas, as prompted by the locations of rivers, railroads or main roads. Industrial areas had their own deteriorating boundary areas into which they were growing. The poorest people, often the latest immigrants, lived in the low income, deteriorating fringes of the downtown and industrial areas. As these people moved up the economic ladder, they moved outwards in the city, and the next newcomers replaced them in the fringe areas.

Shaw and McKay were aware of the limitations of this theory of the natural processes of urban development, especially with regard to Chicago. Chicago is not circular. It began as a settlement on the west shore of Lake Michigan where the Chicago River flows from the lakefront then forks, one branch going northwest and the other branch going southwest. The city spread more north and south along the lakefront and less to the west, so that its overall shape is a tall rectangle rather than a circle. The railroads coming to Chicago from the western plains brought live cattle and pigs to the malodorous stockyards and slaughterhouses of Chicago. The stockyards were originally at the edge of the city below the southwest fork of the river, but ended up nearer the center as the city grew outwards past them. A large industrial area grew up in the southern part of the city far from the center. Blacks occupied deteriorated enclaves in several parts of the city. A small wealthy residential enclave, the "gold coast," survived in the center of the city. Shaw and McKay were aware that the downtown area itself was starting to deteriorate and that new commercial centers were springing up far from the center. Still, Shaw and McKay believed that Park and Burgess' theory of urban growth was generally valid for Chicago and for all major American cities.

Shaw and McKay's *Juvenile Delinquency and Urban Areas* included studies done by other researchers in twenty urban areas other than Chicago. All studies found the same basic pattern as in Chicago. However, a few contained different details. Studies of four cities with Oriental neighborhoods (Seattle and Takoma, Washington; Portland, Oregon; and Vancouver, Canada) found very low delinquency rates in such neighborhoods regardless of other conditions. In Takoma police records were examined as well as court records; it was found that in a neighborhood of central European immigrants with a high rate of police records of delinquency, each boy tended to be involved in only one incident, which was attributed to strong family reactions to the incident. Takoma also had an unexpectedly low delinquency rate in one deteriorated central area, but police were said to ignore delinquency in that area. Some of the studies of other urban areas included mapping adult offenders; areas high in juvenile delinquency were also high in adult offenders. All of the studies consisted of mapping offenders' residences based on court or arrest records. None of the studies included case studies, surveys, or interviews with offenders or neighborhood residents, which might have provided direct information about people's attitudes, values or lifestyles.

Shaw and McKay used U.S. census data and some other surveys to interpret their own data. They focused on years immediately before and after a census, so that their census data would be most accurate. The census data fit neatly with Park and Burgess' theory of the processes of urban growth. People in the most deteriorated areas had the lowest incomes and included the most recent European immigrant groups and migrants from the rural south. These areas had the highest percentages of people receiving public assistance. Census data also showed that the population density in deteriorating areas of Chicago declined rapidly while it increased in the more prosperous areas, at least until 1930 when the growth of Chicago slowed notably. Population decline in fringe areas may have reflected high rates of abandoned property and the encroachment of commercial properties. Various other records and previous surveys showed that the areas where Shaw and McKay found high rates of juvenile delinquents also had high rates of truancy, adult crime, infant mortality, tuberculosis and mental illnesses. The same areas had high rates of recidivism among juvenile offenders.

Not all data fit a simple environmental, ecological view. High delinquency areas in Chicago had no shortage of schools, parks, playgrounds, boys clubs, settlement houses (centers for neighborhood activities), and other civic amenities. Some explanation was needed. Shaw and McKay believed these amenities were ineffective because they were controlled by people from outside the neighborhood instead of being run by neighborhood people. Shaw and McKay were strong advocates of neighborhood organization and control, although there was nothing in their data to provide direct support for this view.

Shaw and McKay were generally familiar with the City of Chicago and quite familiar with various studies of crime and health problems in Chicago. However, in their own study of delinquency in relation to neighborhoods, they themselves did not go into the neighborhoods, nor did they have any face to face contact with the delinquents or their families. They used existing data files. From these data they were able to determine facts about when and where delinquents lived in various parts of Chicago, but the facts contained only a few clues about the more important question of why delinquents were far more numerous in some neighborhoods than in others.

At the time of Shaw and McKay, Chicago criminologists favored the theory that delinquency was the result of a cultural conflict. The cultures in conflict were not national or ethnic cultures. They were the "conventional culture" of law abiding citizens versus the "criminal culture" of delinquent gangs. The idea of a criminal culture implied that criminals were not disorganized, maladjusted or acting in violation of their values. Shaw and McKay, and other Chicago criminologists, believed that delinquents were organized socially, well adjusted to their own social environment, and acting in accord with their own values. Their values included the conventional values of wanting prestige and financial success but also included criminal values related to how one might achieve these goals. The idea of a criminal culture implied that delinquents did not see themselves as doing wrong but only as doing what others did in the same environment (Everybody does it.) and what was the normal way to succeed in their own environment. Ironically, case studies found that delinquent boys in Chicago were quite knowledgeable about the widespread corruption of the Chicago police and other public employees.

Shaw and McKay's ecological studies of delinquents did not include any systematic research into attitudes, values or personal relationships. But they wanted to interpret their data in a way that fit with theories of social influence and cultural conflict. To do this, they relied on selected ideas from their earlier case studies when interpreting the ecological studies. However, the case studies themselves included so many factors that items from the case studies could be selected to support or contradict almost any theory.

Shaw and McKay's study of delinquents in Chicago provides a platform for reexamining many American theories about the causes of crime. Shaw and McKay's research illustrated the inadequacy of simple theories which highlight poverty, ethnicity or population density as explanations for crime. Although it is common to attribute crime to poverty or crowded living conditions, Shaw and McKay found such explanations to be inadequate. However, Shaw and McKay's own explanations seemed to have few connections to their research data, calling into question how much evidence there was to support their theories of crime and how much support other sociological theories, such as Sutherland's theory of differential association or Merton's theory of anomie, can find in the actual research evidence of the Chicago criminologists. Many recent studies in the field of criminal justice are based exclusively on large computerized data files, such as those available through The National Institute of Justice. Shaw and McKay's study raises the issue of how and how well researchers can explain their findings when they have no direct contact with the people or conditions being studied. This type of study also prompts one to consider the assumptions researchers may make regarding the accuracy and completeness of official records. The tactic of mapping data has become very popular in policing, which now utilizes computerized crime mapping. Shaw and McKay believed that mapping could pinpoint locations but could not provide explanations. From the perspective of Shaw and McKay, one could appraise the value and limits of mapping criminal justice data.

References

Healy, W., & Bronner, A.F. (1926). *Delinquents and criminals.* New York: Macmillan.

Healy, W. (1915). *The individual delinquent.* Boston: Little, Brown.

Park, R.E., & Burgess, E.W. (1925). *The city.* Chicago: University of Chicago Press.

Shaw, C.R. (1930). *The Jack-Roller: A delinquent boy's own story.* Chicago: University of Chicago Press.

Shaw, C.R., McKay, H.D., & McDonald, J.F. (1938). *Brothers in crime.* Chicago: University of Chicago Press.

Thrasher, F.M. (1927). *The gang.* Chicago: University of Chicago Press.

Clifford R. Shaw and Henry D. McKay. (1942). *Juvenile Delinquency and Urban Areas: A Study of Rates of Delinquents in Relation to Differential Characteristics of Local Communities in American Cities.* Chicago, Illinois: The University of Chicago Press. Copyright by The University of Chicago Press. Reproduced with permission.
In the following selection, Shaw and McKay summarized earlier research done by others in the "Introduction." Likewise, the "Summary and Interpretation" at the end relied heavily on earlier case studies and the work of others. Shaw and McKay's own research was presented in the middle section on "Male Juvenile Delinquents in Chicago." The editors of this selection have added any text which is within square brackets. Footnotes have been moved to the end of the selection.

Clifford R. Shaw and Henry D. McKay

Juvenile Delinquency and Urban Areas: A Study of Rates of Delinquents in Relation to Differential Characteristics of Local Communities in American Cities

Introduction

The effects of social institutions upon the personality—those ways in which the cultural pattern in one or another way affects the working out of the individual's problem—are of only academic importance unless we can in one way or another alter the environment to meet the needs that appear.[1]

Regional and Community Variations in Rates of Delinquency and Crime

As previously indicated, many studies of variation in the incidence of delinquency and crime in relation to different social and cultural backgrounds have been published during the past century. In the earliest of these studies, attention was focused primarily upon differences in rates of delinquency and crime among cities or large districts within a given country. These were followed by studies showing that such differences obtained also among local areas, communities, or neighborhoods within the corporate limits of large cities.

Among the very early ecological studies of crime were those made by Guerry in France and reported in his *Essai sur la statistique morale de la France* in 1833. In this study Guerry [2] computed crime rates for the 86 departments [government districts] of France. These rates were based upon the number of persons accused of crime during the period 1825–30, inclusive. The variations in rates were marked. The number of persons accused of crime against the person varied from 1 out of 2,199 inhabitants in Corse [Corsica], to 1 out of 37,014 in Creuse, with an average for all 86 departments of 1 out of 17,085 inhabitants. The number of persons accused of crimes against property varied from 1 out of 1,368 inhabitants in Seine, to 1 out of 20,235 inhabitants in Creuse, with an average of 1 out of 6,031 for all departments.[3]

During the early part of the past century [19th century] numerous statistical and government reports were published which indicated that the number of known criminals in relation to the population varied widely among the counties of England and Wales. As early as 1839 Rawson reported that the relative number of criminals was five times greater in certain counties than in others.[4] Twenty-three years later Mayhew published a rather exhaustive study of delinquency and crime in England.[5] Among other things, this study included a series of maps showing the incidence of criminality and various types of crime by counties. In certain counties the incidence of criminality was almost four times as great as in other counties. The number of crimes per 10,000 inhabitants in the total population ranged from 26.1 to 7.1 in the 41 counties of England and Wales....

Lombroso and Niceforo, to mention only two of the early Italian students, found that both the number of criminals per unit of population and the incidence of certain types of crimes varied widely from one city to another and from one province to another. Niceforo, in a study of criminality in the island of Sardinia, found that the ratio between the number of cases of robbery and extortion and the total population ranged widely among the districts of the island.[6] With reference to the incidence of criminality in various parts of Italy, Lombroso stated:

> In every part of Italy, almost in every province, there exists some village renowned for having furnished an unbroken series of special delinquents [offenders, not necessarily juveniles]. Thus, in Liguria, Lerice is proverbial for swindlers, Campofreddo and Masson for homicides, Pozzolo for highway robberies. In the province of Lucca, Capannori is noted for its assassinations, and Carde in Piedmont for its field thefts. In southern Italy, Soro, Melfi, and St. Fele have always had their bandits since 1860, and the same is true of Partinico and Monreale in Sicily.... But the most famous of all is the village of Artena in the province of Rome.... It is to be noted that in Sicily brigandage is almost exclusively confined to that famous valley of the Conca d'Oro.[7]...

Systematic studies of the relative incidence of delinquency in local districts within cities are, for the most part, of more recent development than the more general studies referred to in the previous pages, although the close association between conditions prevailing in particular districts within the city and the incidence of delinquency was emphasized in the very earliest investigations of the problem of delinquency. Throughout the early official reports and investigations of crime in London frequent reference is made to the so-called "low neighborhoods" in which delinquents and criminals were found in disproportionately large numbers....

After the turn of the century many students became interested in the ecological study of delinquency in American cities. In 1912 Breckinridge and Abbott published a study showing the geographic distribution of cases of juvenile delinquency in the city of Chicago. They utilized for this purpose the cases of boys and girls brought before the Juvenile Court of Cook County on petitions alleging delinquency during the years 1899–1909. Among other things they prepared a map showing the location of the homes of these children. This map indicated that a disproportionately large number of the cases were concentrated in certain districts of the city. In this connection they state:

> A study of this map makes possible several conclusions with regard to "delinquent neighborhoods." It becomes clear, in the first place, that the region from which the children of the court chiefly come is the densely populated West Side, and that the most conspicuous centers of delinquency in this section have been the congested wards [city districts] which lie along the river and the canals....
>
> ... The West Side furnished the largest quota of delinquency across the river. These are chiefly the Italian quarter of the Twenty-Second Ward on the North Side; the First and Second Wards, which together include the district of segregated vice and a portion of the so-called "black belt" of the South Side; and such distinct industrial communities as the districts near the steel mills of South Chicago and near the stockyards.[8]

It should be noted that this study did not relate the number of delinquents to the population in the various districts of the city. While the distribution map served to localize the problem of delinquency and to show the absolute number of cases in the various districts, rates by geographic units were not computed. Hence, it was not possible to conclude from this study that the observed concentration of cases was due to anything other than a greater density of population in these areas. Since the publication of the findings of Breckinridge and Abbott, studies have been carried on in which the rate of delinquents (ratio between the number of delinquents and the appropriate population group [such as, 8 delinquents per 100 residents]) has been used as a basis for comparisons among unit areas within the city....

In this attempt to analyze the variations in rates of delinquents by geographic areas in American cities a variety of statistical data are utilized for the purpose of determining the extent to which differences in the economic and social characteristics of local areas parallel variations in rates of delinquents. The methods employed include spot maps, statistical tables showing the rates of delinquents and economic and social variables computed for large zones and classes of areas.... While these maps and statistical data are useful in locating different types of areas, in differentiating the areas where the rates of delinquency are high from areas where the rates are low, and in predicting or forecasting expected rates, they do not furnish an explanation of delinquent conduct. This explanation, it is assumed, must be sought, in the first place, in the field of the more subtle human relationships and social values which comprise the social world of the child in the family and community. These more distinctively human situations, which seem to be directly related to delinquent conduct, are, in turn, products of larger economic and social processes characterizing the history and growth of the city and of the local communities which comprise it....

Male Juvenile Delinquents in Chicago

The Distribution of Alleged Delinquents Brought before the Juvenile Court of Cook County

1. The 1927–33 Juvenile Court Series

Series Studied.—These 8,411 different alleged male delinquents were brought before the Juvenile Court of Cook County from Chicago on petitions alleging delinquency during the 7-year period between January 1, 1927, and December 31, 1933. They are all separate individuals, as duplications from year to year, as well as within the separate years, have been eliminated from the series.

Distribution of Delinquents.—Map 7 shows the distribution by place of residence of the 8,411 different male delinquents. Each dot represents the home address of one delinquent boy; only one dot was used for each individual, regardless of the number of times he appeared in court from any area.[9]

Upon inspection, Map 7 reveals some very interesting characteristics. It will be observed immediately that there are areas of marked concentration of delinquents, as compared with other areas where the dots are widely dispersed. These concentrations are most obvious immediately north and northwest of the Loop [the downtown business district of Chicago] along the

Map 7
(partial reproduction, enlarged)
Outline Map of Chicago
Places of Residence of 8411 Male Juvenile Delinquents
Brought before the Juvenile Court of Cook County
during the Years 1927–1933

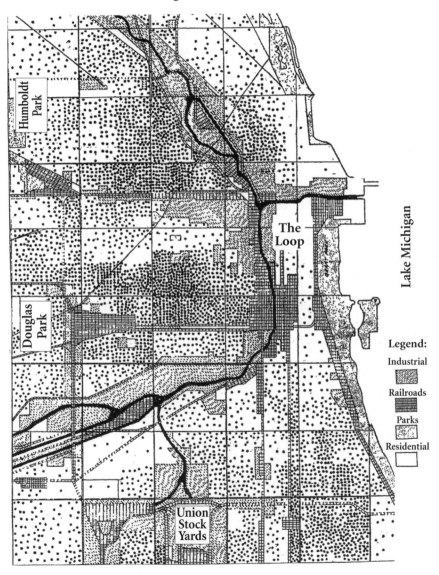

North Branch of the Chicago River, in the areas some distance south of the Loop along State Street, and in the areas immediately outside and extending westward from the northern part of the Loop. In addition to these major concentrations, lesser clusters of dots will be noted in several outlying areas, in the Back of the [Stock] Yards and the South Chicago steel-mill districts [off the bottom of the map].

This distribution of delinquents is closely related to the location of industrial and commercial areas and to the composition of the population. In the first place, as has already been noted, the areas of heaviest concentration are, in general, not far from the central business district, within or near the areas zoned for light industry or commerce. As one moves outward, away from these areas into the residential communities, the cases are more and more scattered until, near the periphery of the city, they are, in general, widely dispersed.

The concentrations of delinquents not adjacent to the central business district are, for the most part, near outlying heavy industrial areas, especially along the two branches of the Chicago River and in the Stock Yards and South Chicago districts. Comparison of the distribution map [Map 7] in turn with Maps 3, 4, and 5 [Maps 3, 4, and 5 are not reproduced here.] reveals further that the alleged delinquents are concentrated mainly in areas characterized by decreasing population and low rentals, with high percentages of families on relief [based on the 1930 U.S. census data]. Here, too, industrial workers predominate. The population in these neighborhoods was, during 1927–33, largely foreign born, with high proportions of recent arrivals, aliens, and migrants from the rural South.

As to national heritage, the area of concentration of delinquents on the Near North Side was, during the period covered, predominantly Italian; the lower Northwest Side, mainly Polish; the Near West Side, Italian and American Negro; and the Lower West Side, chiefly Czechoslovakian. Among the more outlying areas, the Humboldt Park population included Poles, Swedes, Italians, and Russian Jews; the Back of the Yards district was Polish and Lithuanian; while the predominant nationalities in South Chicago were Polish, Italian, Hungarian, Mexican, and Yugoslavian.

This scattering of delinquents among many national groups is characteristic of each of the three periods studied, though the proportions in each nationality vary. The groups producing the most alleged delinquents are, in every instance, those most recently segregated into the areas of lower economic status, as a result of the ongoing processes of American city life [i.e., the central business district and industrial districts keep expanding, their retreating fringe areas have the oldest and worst housing, new arrivals occupy the cheap housing in these fringe areas, and the better new residential areas push outward towards the edges of the city].

In order to compare the number of delinquents by areas and to relate this number in each instance to the population of the same age and sex, the city was divided into 140 areas.[10] Most of these are square miles, bounded on all four sides by the section lines of the government survey [the 1930 U.S. census]. In some instances, where much of the territory was occupied by industry or where, for other reasons, the population was sparse, it was necessary to combine several contiguous square-mile areas. In our discussion, however, these units, regardless of size, will be referred to as "square-mile areas."

When the distribution of the 8,411 delinquents is analyzed in terms of these 140 square-mile areas, wide differences are evident. In each of 3 areas there are more than 300 delinquents, while 8 have more than 150 each. At the other extreme, there is 1 area from which only 3 delinquents were taken to court, 15 with fewer than 10, and 25 with fewer than 15 delinquents. Moreover, the actual difference in concentration is greater than these comparisons suggest, since many areas with large numbers of delinquents have less residential space and population than those with fewer. *The theoretical significance of these facts is at least twofold. First, they reveal the wide variation in distribution; second, they indicate, quite apart from density of population, the differential probability of a boy's having contact with other delinquent boys in the same area or of observing their activities* [emphasis added].

Rates of Delinquents. — Map 8 shows the rates of delinquents in each of the 140 square-mile areas. [Map 8 is not reproduced here.] These rates represent the number of alleged delinquents taken to the Juvenile Court from each area during 1927–33, per hundred of the aged 10–16 male population in that area as of 1930. It should be borne in mind that the 7-year rate here presented is less than the sum of 7 yearly rates, since all duplications have been eliminated.

The range in this series is from 0.5 [less than 1 delinquent per 100 boys ages 10–16 in the area] to 18.9. The median [midpoint of the list of 140 areas] is 2.5 and the [average] rate for the city as a whole, 4.2. Three of the 140 areas have rates above 17.0, and 14 below 1.0. Similarly, there are 12 areas where the rates are more than 10.0, and 50 where they are less than 2.5. *This comparison brings out two fundamental facts, namely, that there are wide differences among areas and that the number of areas with low rates far exceeds the number where they are high* [emphasis added]. The areas with the highest rates are located directly south of the central business district, and the areas with the next highest rates north and west of the Loop. At the other extreme, low rates of delinquents will be noted in many of the outlying areas.

Most of the areas characterized by high rates of delinquents, as well as by a concentration of individual delinquents, are either in or adjacent to areas zoned for industry and commerce. This is true not only for areas close to the central business district but also for outlying areas, such as those near the Stock Yards, the South Chicago steel mills, and other industrial sections. On the other hand, the areas with low rates are, for the most part, those zoned for residential purposes.

Between the center of the city and the periphery the rates, on the whole, show a regular decrease. There are, of course, deviations from this general tendency. In some outlying sections there are areas of high rates, especially in the Stock Yards and Southwest manufacturing districts and adjacent to the South Chicago steel mills. On the other hand, not all areas close to the central business district have high rates. Area 60, for example, located just north of the Loop and including the "Gold Coast" [a wealthy area], has a rate of 2.7; and Areas 37 and 45, not far to the north, have comparatively low rates. It may be noted, however, that the physical and social characteristics of these areas differ from those of the surrounding areas.

One apparent exception to the general tendency of the rates to decrease from the center of the city outward may be noted south of the central business district, between Areas 74 and 115. Here the highest rates are in the second, third, and fourth areas (81, 87, and 93). When rates were calculated separately for the Negro and white delinquents in these areas, however, it was found that both decreased uniformly, in contrast to the combined rate. The rates for white boys, calculated necessarily on small samples [for these segregated neighborhoods], followed with some irregularities the common radial pattern, ranging from 13.4 in Area 74, the highest rate, to 2.5 in Area 115. The corresponding range for Negro delinquents was from 21.2 in the first area south of the Loop to 6.0 in the seventh area. This drop is significant because it shows that *the rates of delinquents for Negro boys, although somewhat higher than those for the whites, exhibit similarly wide variations among different communities* [emphasis added]....

2. The 1917–23 Juvenile Court Series

In the foregoing section the distribution of delinquents and the variation in rates for Chicago were studied by analyzing a series of cases brought into the Juvenile Court of Cook County during the years 1927–33 in relation to the 1930 census data. In the present section a similar series covering a period centered about the 1920 census will be presented. This series includes the

8,141 alleged male delinquents brought before the Juvenile Court of Cook County from Chicago on delinquency petitions in the 7-year period 1917–23.

Series Studied and Types of Offenses.—The 1917–23 juvenile court series was secured in the same manner and from the same sources as the 1927–33 series. With the exception of the changes in the number of areas for which rates of delinquents were calculated, the data will be analyzed in the same way. Since no important change has taken place in the basic procedure of taking boys to the Juvenile Court, these boys also represent those charged by police probation officers with relatively serious offenses.

The nature of the offenses committed by these 8,141 individuals is indicated by the classification of the 12,029 petitions filed against them in the Juvenile Court. This classification shows that 29.4 per cent of the alleged offenses were burglary, 12.2 per cent larceny of automobiles, and 20.4 per cent petty stealing. These offenses, together with a total of 7.5 per cent for other stealing offenses, such as holdup, shoplifting, and purse-snatching, give a total of 69.5 per cent classified as "all stealing." The remaining 30.5 per cent included incorrigibility, 17.1 per cent; disorderly conduct, 4.4 per cent; and all sex offenses, 2.1 per cent. There can be little doubt that these boys were, on the whole, involved in serious delinquency.

In this series, 16.7 per cent of the boys were under 13 years of age, 12.7 per cent were 13, and 18.3 per cent were 14. The highest frequencies are in the 15- and 16-year age groups, these two comprising 51.9 per cent of the total.

Distribution of Delinquents.—Map 10 shows the distribution by place of residence of the 8,141 boys in this series. This map indicates that the distribution is very similar to that previously presented and that the areas of concentration coincide quite closely with similar areas on the 1927–33 map. The one distinctive difference is that the concentrations in the areas later occupied by Negroes are much less evident in the 1917–23 series. Otherwise, the areas of heavy concentration, as in the previous series, are adjacent to the central business and industrial districts and to certain outlying industrial centers, while the areas in which the dots are widely dispersed fall in the outlying sections of the city.

The distribution indicates that this series also presents very great geographical variations in the number of delinquents. One of the 113 square-mile areas contains 6 delinquents, while another contains 312. Four areas contain fewer than 10 delinquents each, while 5 contain more than 250 each. When the distribution is analyzed further, it is found that 11 areas contain fewer than 15 delinquents, and 18 fewer than 20 delinquents each. At the other extreme, a total of 7 areas contain more than 200 delinquents each, and 14 contain more than 150.

Map 10
(partial reproduction, enlarged)
Places of Residence of 8141 Male Juvenile Delinquents
Brought before the Juvenile Court of Cook County
during the Years 1917–1923, 10–17 Years of Age

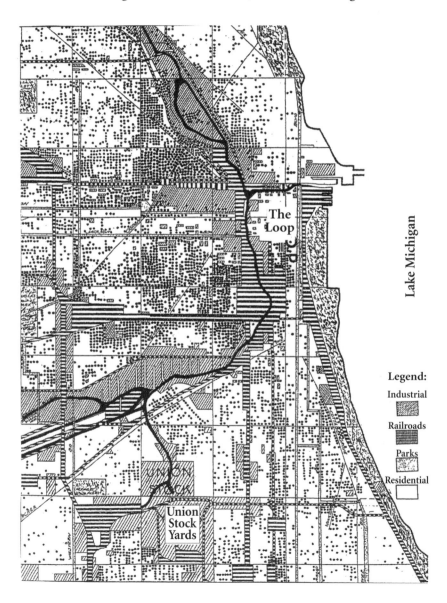

Rates of Delinquents.—The area rates for the present series are given on Map 11. [Map 11 is not reproduced here.] These represent the number of boys brought to the Juvenile Court from each of the 113 square-mile areas during the 7-year period, per 100 of the aged 10–16 male population in each of these areas as of 1920. The range of rates is from 0.8 to 19.4; the median for the series is 4.3 and the rate for the city, 5.4. Three areas have rates of less than 1.0, and a total of 19 areas less than 2.0. At the other extreme, 4 areas have rates of 15.0 or over, and 8 areas of 12.0 or over. In other words, 8 areas have rates of delinquents that are more than twelve times as great as those in 3 other areas, and more than six times as great as the rates in 19 other areas.

Map 11 reveals variations in the rates of delinquents quite similar to those of the previous series. [Map 11 is not reproduced here.] The range between high- and low-rate areas is not so great, however; and the areas with high rates of delinquents extend only about 4 miles south from the Loop in the present series, as compared with 6 or 7 miles in 1927–33.

3. The 1900–1906 Juvenile Court Series

Series Studied and Types of Offenses.—Third in this sequence is the series of 8,056 male delinquents brought into the Juvenile Court of Cook County from Chicago during 1900–1906 (the first 7 years of the Juvenile Court's existence). By comparing this series with that for 1927–33 it will be possible to determine the extent to which variations in the rates correspond and the extent to which changes in rates can be related to changes in the physical or social characteristics of the local areas.

The age distribution of the boys in the 1900–1906 series indicates that, on the whole, they were a little younger than those in the more recent series. At that time the upper age limit in the Juvenile Court was 15 instead of 16, and a somewhat larger number of boys were under 10 years of age (6.1 per cent). The highest frequencies were in ages 13, 14, and 15. With regard to offenses, it seems probable that some boys were taken to court in these earlier years on charges for which no petitions would be filed by the police probation officers at the present time. This is indicated both by the fact that the number of cases in court was greater in proportion to the population than at present and by the fact that the classification of offenses indicated a somewhat higher proportion of less serious charges.

Distribution of Delinquents.—Map 12 shows the distribution by home address of the 8,056 boys brought to court in the 7-year period 1900–1906. In this series, as in those previously discussed, it will be noted that a preponderance of the delinquent boys lived either in areas adjacent to the central busi-

Map 12
(partial reproduction, enlarged)
Home Addresses of the 8055 Male Juvenile Delinquents
Brought before the Juvenile Court of Cook County
during the Years 1900–1906, 10–17 Years of Age

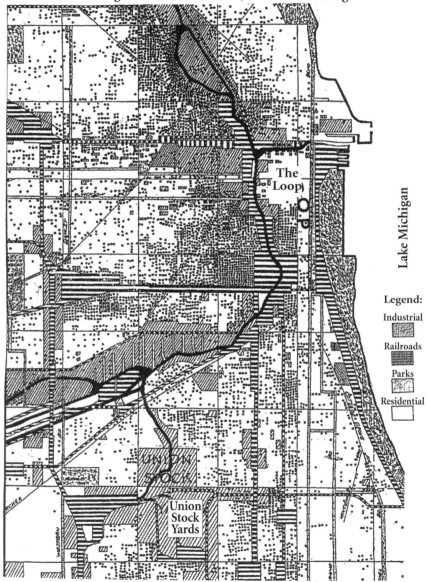

ness and industrial district or along the two forks of the Chicago River, Back of the Yards, or in South Chicago, with relatively few in other outlying areas.

While this series exhibits the same general configuration found in the others, there are two noticeable variations. First, the concentrations are somewhat more restricted and closer to the central business district and to the industrial centers than in the later series. This is to be expected, since many of the areas used for residential purposes in this early period have since been depopulated by expanding industry and commerce. Second, on this map there are relatively few delinquents in the areas east of State Street, south from the Loop. These areas, it will be remembered, contained many delinquents in the 1917–23 map and were also areas of heavy concentration in 1927–33.

Rates of Delinquents. — Map 13 shows the rates of delinquents in the 106 square-mile areas used for this 1900–1906 series. [Map 13 is not reproduced here.] The population upon which these rates were calculated was secured by combining into 106 comparable areas the 1,200 enumeration districts [used in the census] of 1900 and the 431 census tracts [used in the census] of 1910 and computing the yearly increase or decrease of population in each. The population for the midyear of this series was then estimated from the aged 10–15 male population in 1910. The areas for which rates are presented are practically the same as those used in the 1917–23 juvenile court series, except that in 7 instances it was necessary to construct combinations of the 113 areas in order to secure a larger population in districts which were sparsely settled at that time.

The rates in this series range from 0.6 to 29.8 [delinquents per 100 boys ages 10–15]. The median is 4.9 and the rate for the city as a whole 8.4. Four areas have rates of 20.0 and over; 7 have rates of 15.0 or over; and 12 have rates of 12.0 or over. At the other extreme, 3 areas have rates of less than 1.0, and 12 of less than 2.0.

Map 13 indicates that the variation in rates of delinquents is quite similar to the variations presented previously. The 4 areas with highest rates are all immediately adjacent to the Loop, and other high-rate areas are in the Stock Yards district and in South Chicago. The areas with low rates, on the other hand, are located, for the most part, near the city's periphery. As compared to rate maps for subsequent series, it can be seen that the areas with very high rates are somewhat more closely concentrated around the central business district. This is especially noticeable south from the Loop and east of State Street, where, after the first 2 miles, the rates of delinquents are below the average for the city as a whole.

4. Comparisons among Juvenile Court Series (1927–33, 1917–23, and 1900–1906)

Three methods will be employed to determine the extent to which the variations in rates of delinquents in the several time series correspond: (1) comparisons by zones, (2) area comparisons and correlations, and (3) extent of concentration.

Rates by Zones.—Rates of delinquents were calculated for each of 5 zones drawn at 2-mile intervals, with a focal point in the heart of the central business district. [The zones were a series of concentric circles drawn on the map of Chicago with the central business district as the center of the circles. See Figure 1.] These rates [for each zone] were computed on the basis of the number of delinquents and the total aged 10–16 male population in each zone.[11]

It should be borne in mind that zone rates of delinquents are presented chiefly because of their theoretical value. They show the variations in rates more conceptually and idealistically than do the rates for smaller units. The number of zones used for this purpose is not important, as it is not assumed that there are actual zones in the city or sharp dividing lines between those presented. It is assumed, rather, that a more or less continuous variation exists between the rates of delinquents in the areas close to the center of the city and those outlying, and that any arbitrary number of zones will exhibit this difference satisfactorily.

Inspection of the rate maps indicates that there are wide differentials among the rates of delinquents for the square miles within each zone, just as there are among rates for census tracts within each square-mile area. These fluctuations do not greatly affect the general trend, however; in fact, it is because the zone rates eliminate the fluctuations evident for smaller areas and present the general tendencies that they are interesting and important.

Maps A, B, and C, Figure 1, show rates of delinquents by 5 complete zones, and also by the north and south halves of the city separately, for the three juvenile court series that have been presented.... [Only the Map B part of Figure 1 is reproduced here.]

Area Comparisons and Correlations.—Of the 24 areas with the highest rates of delinquents in the 1927–33 series, 20 are among the 24 highest also in 1917–23. On the other hand, a few areas where significant changes took place in community characteristics show also marked changes in rates of delinquents.... [Despite the fact that there were great changes in 6 of the 113 areas, areas with high rates of delinquents in 1917–1923 generally had high rates in 1927–33 also, and areas with low rates in 1917–23 generally had low rates in 1927–33.]

Figure 1.
(partial reproduction, enlarged and enhanced)
**Outline Map of Chicago with Zone Rates of
Male Juvenile Delinquents, 1917–1923 Series**

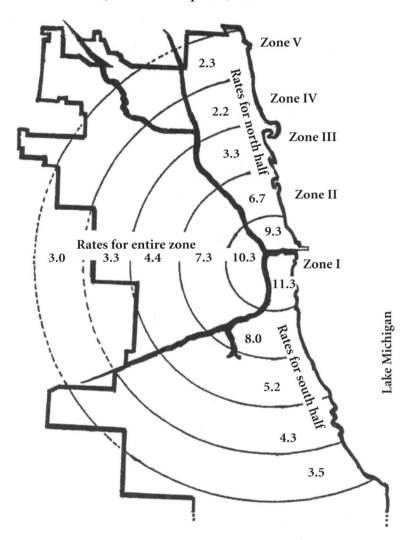

Most of the areas of high rates in the 1900–1906 series also correspond with those ranking highest in the two later series. Of the 12 highest in 1900–1906, 9 were among the 12 highest in 1927–33. Three of the 5 highest-rate areas in the latter series, but not in the former, are the same 3 found among the high-rate areas as of 1917–23. Although some new areas appear among those with high rates in the more recent series, it is significant to note that all 12 of the areas of highest rates in the 1900–1906 series are among the areas of high rates in 1927–33. Because of these areas, the correspondence between the series is even more clearly seen when comparisons involving a larger number of areas are made. Of the 25 areas with the highest rates of delinquents in the 1900–1906 series, 19 are included among the 25 highest in the 1917–23 series, and 18 among the 25 highest in 1927–33, even though these series are separated by approximately 2 and 3 decades, respectively. *This is especially significant in view of the fact that the nationality composition of the population has changed completely in some of these neighborhoods* [emphasis added]....

Summary and Interpretation
[of the Chicago Study by Shaw and McKay
and Similar Studies of 20 Other Urban Areas]

... From the data available it appears that local variations in the conduct of children, as revealed in differential rates of delinquents, reflect the differences in social values, norms, and attitudes to which the children are exposed. In some parts of the city attitudes which support and sanction delinquency are, it seems, sufficiently extensive and dynamic to become the controlling forces in the development of delinquent careers among a relatively large number of boys and young men. These are the low-income areas, where *delinquency has developed in the form of a social tradition* [emphasis added], inseparable from the life of the local community.

This tradition is manifested in many different ways. It becomes meaningful to the child through the conduct, speech, gestures, and attitudes of persons with whom he has contact. Of particular importance is the child's intimate association with predatory gangs or other forms of delinquent and criminal organization. Through his contacts with these groups and by virtue of his participation in their activities he learns the techniques of stealing, becomes involved in binding relationships with his companions in delinquency, and acquires the attitudes appropriate to his position as a member of such groups. To use the words of Frank Tannenbaum: "It is the group that sets the pattern, provides the stimulus, gives the rewards in glory and companionship, offers the protection and loyalty, and, most of all, gives the criminal life its ethical content without which it cannot persist."[12]

In these communities many children encounter competing systems of values. Their community, which provides most of the social forms in terms of which their life will be organized, presents conflicting possibilities. A career in delinquency and crime is one alternative, which often becomes real and enticing to the boy because it offers the promise of economic gain, prestige, and companionship and because he becomes acquainted with it through relationships with persons whose esteem and approbation are vital to his security and to the achievement of satisfactory status. In this situation the delinquent group may become both the incentive and the mechanism for initiating the boy into a career of delinquency and crime and for sustaining him in such a career, once he has embarked upon it.

In cases of group delinquency it may be said, therefore, that from the point of view of the delinquent's immediate social world, he is not necessarily disorganized, maladjusted, or antisocial. Within the limits of his social world and in terms of its norms and expectations, he may be a highly organized and well-adjusted person.

The residential communities of higher economic status, where the proportion of persons dealt with as delinquents and criminals is relatively low, stand in sharp contrast to the situation described above. Here the norms and values of the child's social world are more or less uniformly and consistently conventional [law abiding]. Generally speaking, the boy who grows up in this situation is not faced with the problem of making a choice between conflicting systems of moral values. Throughout the range of his contacts in the community he encounters similar altitudes of approval or disapproval. Cases of delinquency are relatively few and sporadic. The system of conventional values in the community is sufficiently pervasive and powerful to control and organize effectively, with few exceptions, the lives of most children and young people.

In both these types of communities the dominant system of values is conventional. In the first, however, a powerful competing system of delinquency values exists; whereas in the second, such a system, if it exists at all, is not sufficiently extensive and powerful to exercise a strong influence in the lives of many children. Most of the communities of the city fall between these two extremes and represent gradations in the extent to which delinquency has become an established way of life....

It should be observed that, while the tradition of delinquency and crime is thus a powerful force in certain communities, it is only a part of the community's system of values. As was pointed out previously, *the dominant tradition in every community is conventional, even in those having the highest rates of delinquents* [emphasis added].

Footnotes

1. James S. Plant, M.D., *Personality and the Cultural Pattern* (New York: Commonwealth Fund, 1937), p. 234.

2. Andre Michel Guerry, *Essai sur la statistiaue morale de la France* (Paris, 1833).

3. The maps and tables prepared by Guerry were reproduced and discussed by Henry Lytton Bulwer in his work on *France, Social, Literary, and Political* (3d ed.; London: Richard Bentley, 1836), I, 169–210. Other pertinent studies made in France include H. Joly, *La France criminelle* (Paris, 1891), and Gabriel Tarde, *Penal Philosophy*, trans. Rapelje Howell (Boston, 1912).

4. W. Rawson, "An Inquiry into the Statistics of Crime in England and Wales," *Journal of the Statistical Society of London,* II (1839), 334–44.

5. Henry Mayhew, *London Labor and the London Poor* (London, 1862), IV, 455. For similar studies reported during this early period see S. Redgrave, "Abstract of Criminal Tables for England and Wales," *Journal of the Statistical Society of London,* I (1838), 231–45; F.G.P. Neison, "Statistics of Crime in England and Wales for the Years 1834–1844," *ibid.*, XI (1848), 140–65; Joseph Fletcher, "Moral and Educational Statistics of England and Wales," *ibid.*, pp. 344–66, and *ibid.*, XII (1849), 189–336; W.M. Tartt, "Report on Criminal Returns," *ibid.*, XX (1857), 365–77; Mary Carpenter, "Importance of Statistics to the Reformatory Movement, with Returns from Female Reformatories," *ibid.*, pp. 33–40; J. Thackray Bunce, "On the Statistics of Crime in Birmingham, as Compared with Other Large Towns," *ibid.*, XXVIII (1865), 518–26; James T. Hammick, "On the Judicial Statistics of England and Wales, with Special Reference to the Recent Returns Relating to Crime," *ibid.*, XXX (1867), 375–426; and Leone Levi, "A Survey of Indictable and Summary Jurisdiction Offenses in England and Wales, 1857–1876," esp. IX, "Locality of Crime," *ibid.*, LXIII (1880), 423–56.

6. Alfredo Niceforo, *La Delinquenza in Sardegna* (Palermo, 1897).

7. Cesare Lombroso, *Crime: Its Causes and Remedies* (New York: Little, Brown & Co., 1911), pp. 23–24.

8. Sophonisba P. Breckinridge and Edith Abbott, *The Delinquent Child and the Home* (New York: Russell Sage Foundation, 1912), pp. 150–153.

9. These home addresses were plotted by street and number on a large base map of the city of Chicago, on which all streets are shown, and then copied on the outline map reproduced.

10. Rates were computed also for 60 local communities and 120 subcommunities. They reveal approximately the same variations as the rates for square-mile areas.

11. When a square-mile area was divided by one of the concentric circles, the aged 10–16 population and the number of delinquents allocated to each zone corresponded to the proportion of the area which fell in each.

12. *Crime and the Community* (New York: Ginn & Co., 1938), p. 475.

ᏕᎧ Part 2 ᏣᏮ
Legal Studies Masterworks

Introduction to Legal Studies Masterworks

The laws of European nations and, to a somewhat lesser extent, the laws of England and the United States, were greatly influenced by ancient Roman law codes and commentaries. In ancient times the chief Roman magistrate would publish a code of laws at the beginning of his term in office, which was a term of only one year. In practice, the code was just an updated edition of the code of the last chief magistrate. Besides the code, there were authoritative commentaries on the law. These Roman commentaries on the law were sometimes written by legal scholars and sometimes by their students who attended consultations between the scholars and clients. These Roman legal scholars were not judges, nor did they directly participate in trials as lawyers in most cases. But it was common for people to consult them before going to trial. The legal scholar consultants provided an understanding of the relevant legal principles. They did not limit their comments to the details of a particular case, nor did they concern themselves with what any judge decided in a particular case. Indeed, judges were expected to base their decisions on the principles expounded by the legal scholars. A judge in a particular case could easily be wrong, especially in the Roman system where judges were not scholarly themselves and served brief terms. In short, the Roman legal commentators were concerned about legal principles, not particular cases or precedents. The practice of the Roman commentators is the historical basis for modern European law which is based on legal principles, in contrast to Anglo-American law which is based on precedents. Thus, in European law schools one studies mostly legal principles, while in Anglo-American law schools one studies mostly cases and precedents to determine the meaning of laws.

The Roman Empire imposed a layer of Roman law on Europe, North Africa and the Middle East. However the Roman law did not survive the fall of the Roman Empire much more than the Roman roads, aqueducts, or other public works. Remnants could be found here and there, and some new developments were built on top of the old. But the laws of European nations returned mostly to their earlier local codes and customs. The English law was mostly an oral legal tradition handed down by sheriffs and judges with minimal paperwork. Records of cases were generally the private papers of sheriffs rather than records of the courts, with precious few surviving.

However, some English kings (Alfred, Edgar, Edward the Confessor) did compile collections of laws based on customs and legal maxims in order to standardize laws throughout the kingdom. Other compilations of laws were done not by royal initiative but by learned men who wanted a handbook of law as it stood during the reign of a particular king, such as the book of laws of King Henry. A book of laws might start with the ten commandments, followed by some other biblical passages; then laws about the rights and duties of the king, nobles, clergy, common people, and serfs; laws about property, contracts and inheritances; a collection of customary legal maxims, such as, No one shall be punished who has not been found guilty by a court; some rules on how legal procedures were to be conducted; and a list of punishments for various offenses. Whether oral or written, this body of law based on custom, to which were added records of court decisions in later times, became the "common law" of England and later the United States. The common law was not common in the sense that it served the needs of the common people, for it served mostly the needs of the upper classes. The term "common law" probably referred to the idea that these laws were to be the standardized law common to the whole kingdom, as distinct from the many local ordinances which continued to exist alongside as local laws.

The Norman conquest of England in 1066 had its legal side. The Normans were a typical European feudal society, unlike England before the conquest. European nobles had their own domains and acted as judges within them. Court fees and fines were paid to them, so that law was a profitable business. Overlapping the European nobility were the Roman Catholic clergy, the most educated people of the times, whose bishops and abbots administered provinces and had their own large estates. Soon after the Norman conquest the discovery of an ancient manuscript in Amalfi, Italy with the Code of the Emperor Justinian led to a revival of Roman law throughout Europe. Catholic clergy especially studied this law, and it also became a subject of study at the University of Bologna.

The newly discovered Justinian Code soon served as a model code for the reform of legal systems throughout Europe. The Norman conquerors tried to impose this Roman legal system on England. The Norman abbot Theobald became Bishop of Canterbury; he brought over a group of clerics trained in the new law and also had the new law placed in the curriculum of the University at Oxford. The English, however, resisted. There was resentment against Roman influence, against the early Norman kings of England who did not even bother to learn to speak English, and against the foreign clergy who tried to take control of the local courts. The English held their own. For a time the study of the Roman law was prohibited in England. Still, the Roman code was better suited to handle many problems of property and commerce, so it came to dominate the civil law. In addition, one of the great English commentators who complied a code of laws, Henry de Bracton, slipped a great deal of Roman law into his work and presented it as if it were English common law, thus arranging a secret wedding of Roman law and English common law. But for the most part the English clung to their traditional common law in criminal matters and their own sheriffs and justices of the peace rather than clergy in the administration of local courts.

The new government did insist on better record keeping by the courts, so reports of trials eventually added immensely to the body of the common law. With the advent of detailed written records of court decisions came the practice of making new court decisions based as closely as possible on older decisions. Court decisions based on legal precedents became a distinguishing feature of the Anglo-American legal systems. The practice of the law required so much knowledge of precedents and common law traditions that the law became more and more the franchise of lawyers and more and more mysterious to ordinary people.

The Norman conquest had a dramatic impact on the organization of government and the process of making law. Like ancient Roman emperors, European kings had a royal court of personal advisors and ministers. They made laws by issuing decrees. They established royal courts with their own loyal subordinates, mostly clergy, as judges. The *Magna Carta*, England's first bill of rights, was the product of a rebellion by English nobles who demanded guarantees that the king would not take away their traditional rights. The English resisted the lawmaking impulses of the royal councils. For lawmaking the English developed a two-part legislative body, the Parliament, with a House of Lords representing nobles and a House of Commons. The House of Commons did not represent the lower class. Its members were second tier aristocrats, newly made aristocrats and men quite successful in commerce or law. The House of Commons, until modern times, was not generally engaged in making criminal law. Its role was to levy taxes; deal with the administration of government; and, when requested, to give approval to acts of the king. Parliament had a recognized right to make law by statutes, at least in theory, since the time of King Edward I in the late thirteenth century, but it seldom did.

Although often opposed to one another, the Lords and the Commons united against the king's councils. By the early fourteenth century it was established that the king's councils were restricted to lawmaking in emergency situations. Even the Parliament, however, played a limited role in lawmaking, dealing mostly with problems resulting from new situations not handled adequately by the common law, conflicts between different common law courts or judgments, or legal absurdities when some item of the ancient common law no longer seemed just or reasonable. Most lawmaking was done by judges applying the common law to new cases, but guided increasingly by detailed precedents recorded in the growing body of written court reports.

The Age of Enlightenment brought a new philosophy to English law, expressed most clearly in the legal commentaries of William Blackstone, whose first volume was published in 1765, and which became the standard textbook for the study of law in England and America. As Blackstone explained, there was first the law of God, then the laws of nature implanted by God, and then the laws of society following the laws in nature, all of which are to be known by the diligent exercise of reason.

> These are the eternal, immutable laws of good and evil, to which the creator himself in all his dispensations conforms; and which he has enabled human reason to discover, so far as they are necessary for the conduct of human actions. Such among others are these principles: that we should live honestly, should hurt nobody, and should render to every one it's due; to which three general precepts Justinian has reduced the whole doctrine of the law.... [The creator] has graciously reduced the rule of obedience to this one paternal precept, "that man should pursue his own happiness." This is the foundation of what we call ethics, or natural law.... This law of nature, being co-eval [synonymous] with mankind and dictated by God himself, is of course superior in obligation to any other. It is binding all over the globe, in all countries, and at all times: no human laws are of any validity, if contrary to this; and such of them as are valid derive all their force, and all their authority, mediately [indirectly] or immediately, from this original. (Blackstone, Vol. 1, pp. 40–41)

The creator did more than give man a code of laws. The creator implanted the law in human nature. All law codes were seen simply as elaborations of the laws of nature. The legal commentaries of the ancient Roman lawyers and even the law codes developed by them were seen only as clarifications and more precise specifications of the laws of human nature. When emperors and kings made laws, they also claimed not to be making any new laws but only to be making clearer and more precise statements of the natural law or applying the natural law to new situations. It was only in the Middle Ages that kings began to assert a right to make new laws instead of just elaborating the existing laws, which were based on human nature.

If kings, and later legislatures, could not make new laws except as developments of old laws based on human nature, then they also could not repeal laws. Since the laws were based on human nature, one could no more repeal a section of the law code than one could repeal the law of gravity. Instead of being repealed, old laws which were no longer useful were simply ignored or courts decided that they did not apply to present circumstances. But the laws themselves were not subject to repeal under ordinary conditions. The only way to repeal a law was to declare that it had been a mistake to begin with because it was contrary to human nature. This was rarely done. However, such a case arose when King Edward VI made a law that all idle vagabonds should be made slaves, fed on bread and water, made to wear irons, and compelled to work. English law already included common law principles opposed to slavery, and so "the spirit of the nation could not brook this condition, even in the most abandoned rogues; and therefore this statute was repealed in two years afterwards" (Blackstone, 1765, Vol. 1, p. 412).

Statutes, the written laws decreed by kings or passed by legislative bodies and then signed into law by sovereigns, had to compete with common law in the Anglo-American legal tradition. In the Age of Enlightenment it was generally held that statutes were subject to the judgment of common law courts. In England and in the early history of the United States it was considered appropriate for courts to declare laws invalid if they were unjust, unreasonable, or contrary to human nature. Statutes were also considered invalid if they were contrary to common law, which was considered an elaboration of natural law. Before the middle of the nineteenth century legislative bodies dealt mostly with the finances, organization and administration of government, and foreign affairs, ordinarily leaving law in the hands of judges. Judges were idealized as high-minded, learned men who would not allow their self-interests to influence their legal decisions.

However, in the course of the nineteenth and early twentieth centuries, lawmaking shifted largely to legislative bodies, statutes gained dominance over common law, and courts lost most of their authority to make laws. This was the result of certain democratic ideologies and power politics. A new theory of democracy suggested that laws should be made by elected representatives of the people. However, legislators more and more represented powerful elites and business interests. Power politics named as judges those individuals who would support the agendas of the legislative and executive branches of government. Courts came to see themselves as mere interpreters of the legislature. Ironically, however, in the United States the courts acquired new power over the executive and legislative branches of government by assuming the right to decide if the actions of the executive or legislature were in violation of the Constitution, the "social contract" of the American legal system. In practice this happened most often when an angry lower class pressured a legislature to pass a law unfavorable to the upper classes. Courts often nullified such laws (see, for example, "Labor and Law" in Friedman, 1985, pp. 553–563).

The three law selections that follow examine foundations of the Anglo-American legal tradition. The first selection is a study of the relationship between law and society. William Chambliss' study of the origin and development of vagrancy laws in England and the United States raised questions about the origins and purposes of laws. Chambliss' article focused on the economic, social, and political realities which gave birth to laws. It could be seen as an illustration of Beccaria's comment that "laws, which surely are, or ought to be, compacts of free men, have been, for the most part, a mere tool of the ambitions of some or have arisen from an accidental and temporary need."

As a study of a particular set of laws, Chambliss' study is a concrete introduction to the more abstract ideas of Oliver Wendell Holmes, Jr.'s work, *The Common Law*. *The Common Law* is generally regarded as the greatest work on law written by an American. It was written when the common law was still the dominating force in American courts but about to self-destruct. It raised questions about the nature of law at a time when most lawyers viewed law as a rational science for regulating society. Holmes agreed that the purpose of law was to regulate society; but in his view reason itself had to be twisted and bent in order to twist and bend the law to meet the felt needs of society, whether rational or not. In short, Holmes suggested that the law had constructed an illusion of rationality.

Felix Frankfurter's essay on *The Reading of Statutes* acknowledged the twentieth century shift from common law to law based on statutes. It defined the problem of the modern judge as the problem of how to interpret laws made by legislatures. Frankfurter's advice to judges was not to judge the law itself but only to judge how to apply the law in particular cases. Frankfurter's emphasis on the separation of legislative and judicial powers harkened back to Beccaria's ironclad separation of the role of the legislator from the role of the judge but without the clarity and simplicity of the law itself that Beccaria demanded. Frankfurter's judge administers the law as it is, perhaps making it more urgent to reconsider Chambliss' and Holmes' questions about what the law really is.

References and Recommended Reading

Blackstone, W. (1979). *Commentaries on the laws of England: A facsimile of the first edition of 1765–1769*. Volume 1, *Of the rights of persons* (1765). Chicago: The University of Chicago Press.

Friedman, L.M. (1985). *A history of American law,* 2nd ed. New York: Simon & Schuster.

Rembar, C. (1980). *The law of the land: The evolution of our legal system.* New York: Simon & Schuster.

Introduction to
William J. Chambliss

Chambliss' "A sociological analysis of the law of vagrancy" (1964) is a classic example of a study in the field of the sociology of law. The sociology of law views the law as a product of social forces. The processes of making laws, interpretation and administration of laws are examined from the perspective of how society is organized and what forces are at work in society. There are many different theories about how societies develop and what social forces are important, and so the sociology of law includes several different sociological perspectives.

The sociological approach to law stands in marked contrast to the way law is viewed in American law schools. At the end of the nineteenth century American laws school adopted the philosophy that law is a rational science. Law was seen as mostly a product of logic created by rational lawmakers as a way to protect the morals and customs of a nation. Logical laws, based on morals and customs, would make it possible for people to live in society with due regard for each other's rights. Society itself was held together by the "social contract," which was the agreement that each member of society would respect the rights of others and would give up some freedom (e.g., give up the right to get personal revenge when wronged) in exchange for protection by lawful government and vindication when wronged. What held society together was basically a legal contract which embodied generally accepted morals and customs. The law was expected to codify and apply this contract in a logical way.

The proponents of the logical approach to law believed that laws reflected the logical requirements for a society to function efficiently. A particular law was logical insofar as it was logically necessary to maintain order in society. It was also believed that new laws needed to be logically connected to older laws. If society developed, law would develop too. But it had to be a matter of orderly development from one stage to another, not a sort of revolution which would sweep away the old and replace it with something entirely different. Law would not be a reliable guide for people's behavior if it was subject to sudden, radical changes. In the area of law, it was important to respect the history of laws and follow legal precedents when applying law to new circumstances.

A fundamental principle of legal reasoning was to judge actions from the point of view of "the reasonable man." According to this legal principle, when determining guilt the key issue was not what personal or social factors cause an individual to commit an act but instead what the reasonable man would have done in the given situation. The legal question was not, Why did this particular person do this act? Rather, the legal question was, Would the reasonable man have done this act? If the reasonable man would not have done it, then the individual who did it should be punished. "The reasonable man" did not have a life history or any individual characteristics. This somewhat fuzzy legal ideal of the reasonable man made it unnecessary to deal with the peculiarities of individuals. The law became divorced from the realities of specific people, times and places.

However, at the beginning of the twentieth century Roscoe Pound, the Dean of Harvard Law School, started a movement which eventually turned into "legal realism" in the period from 1920 to 1940 and later prompted "critical legal studies" in the 1970s. Legal realism was a belief that law should be based less on a type of logic and more on events in the real world. The real world approach shifted some of the emphasis from logic to the social policy implications of laws, from precedents to the present case, and from following the logic of the law to providing justice in fact, not merely justice in form or procedure. This shift to the real world view of law had more effect on the work of legal historians and sociologists than on the work of law schools, lawyers, and judges. Historians and sociologists began doing studies of how specific laws developed and how they affected society. One of the earliest critical studies was Chambliss' work on vagrancy laws.

Nineteenth century Europeans had already pioneered studies of law in relation to the organization of society and social forces. In 1861 Sir Henry Sumner Maine published *Ancient Law*, a study of how law changed with the development of western society. Maine found that a slow but radical change in society had produced a radical change in law. Ancient law was based on a person's social status; modern law was based on contracts.

In ancient societies people were born into a particular place in society, whether as rulers or nobles or craftsmen or peasants. People were expected to live out their lives in the roles to which they had been born. The function of the law was to specify the rights and obligations of people in their different roles. For example, when English knights surrounded King John and demanded that he sign the *Magna Carta*, it was to ensure that the nobles would be treated by the law as nobles and brought to trial by juries of their peers, other nobles. Laws were made and enforced to maintain the order in society, including keeping each person in the appropriate social status. As long as society was characterized by people living their entire lives in fixed roles, law based on the status of people seemed to be appropriate.

When society developed to the point where social mobility became possible, law also changed its basis. According to Maine, the basis of law changed from status to contracts. Instead of a person's obligations being based on a fixed place in society, a person's obligations were now based on agreements made with others. A man no longer tilled fields for the local lord because the man was a serf or a peasant; he now did it because he had a contract, even if the contract was not in writing. The theory of the "social contract" was already a familiar theory by Maine's time, so that even penal law could be viewed as a sort of contract which people entered into to provide mutual security. Thus, the function of law in relation to society was to define an individual's contractual obligations in order to assure that people would know and adhere to their mutual obligations.

Max Weber (1864–1920) was trained in law and taught legal history at the University of Berlin, but he considered himself primarily a sociologist. He considered law, politics, and economics to be interrelated. Weber concluded that the development of law in Europe was related to the development of commerce and government. As the amount of commercial trade increased in Europe and trade for money became more common than bartering goods for other goods, it became more important to develop a system of law which could regulate matters between strangers and provide all with some assurance that the agreements between them would be enforced by government when necessary. Again law was essentially based on contracts.

Weber pointed out that over time governments became more organized into bureaucratic agencies and needed more standardized ways of dealing with larger numbers of people. A kind of law which stripped people of their individuality and treated all in the same manner made it easier for governments to be efficient. This idea that all persons are "equal before the law" was a way to make all persons the same in the eyes of the law. This made it easier to administer the laws.

In his analysis of the laws of vagrancy Chambliss took a Marxist approach to law based on Karl Marx's theories that society is undergoing a class struggle based on economics. According to Marx, people who had wealth and who wanted to make profits through investments were capitalists. The capitalists were in a struggle with people who lacked wealth and who just wanted to trade whatever goods they could produce in exchange for the other goods they needed to live a decent life. In a highly industrial society, the class struggle described by Marx was epitomized in conflicts between the owners and the workers in large factories. In the nineteenth century factories were usually owned by individuals, not stock holders, and run by their individual owners, not by hired executives. The capitalist owners tried to maximize profits by paying low wages; the workers tried to increase their wages so that the fruits of their labors would be theirs. As far as Marx could see, the contracts between capitalists and workers were not proper contracts because workers were forced by their poverty to accept whatever wages capitalists would give. The laws were created and administered mostly by the capitalists to keep the workers down. Chambliss' study of the laws of vagrancy traced the origins of the vagrancy laws to an older struggle between wealthy landowners and peasants.

Chambliss' article on the vagrancy laws was written while he was working on his Ph.D. in sociology at Indiana University and taking courses in the law school. It was written for a course on labor law. It was written and published during a particularly intense anti-communist period in the United States in the course of the "cold war" between the United States and the Soviet Union. The law professor was very conservative politically and did not like the paper much. Chambliss took account of some criticisms in a later revised version of the article, but his ideas were presented most clearly in the original published version, which is the version reproduced here. Chambliss' overt Marxist approach also made the article unpopular with politically conservative readers after it was published. In the ensuing decades Chambliss continued to research, write, and teach original and thought provoking approaches to a wide variety of issues in the field of criminal justice. He wrote and edited more than twenty books and lectured all over the world. He was President of the Society for the Study of Social Problems and of The American Society of Criminology. He was awarded the highest honors of the American Sociological Association and the Academy of Criminal Justice Sciences. In addition to being a professor in the Department of Sociology at The George Washington University, he held numerous other scholarly positions, such as research director of the National Crime Control Commission from 1993 to 1995.

Chambliss' article is an invitation to think critically about the role of law in society and the law making process. Outside of law schools, very few people now think of law as primarily a rational science. Many laws are quick reactions, sometimes overreactions, to highly publicized events when people expect legislators to do something. Most people are aware that legislators often use lawmaking to impress the public and garner votes even when the lawmakers themselves realize that they are passing a law which will eventually be stricken down by the courts as unconstitutional. Most people are at least vaguely aware of the role of special interests and lobbyists in the lawmaking process. Political scientists generally view American society as an "interest group" society in which various groups of people compete against other groups to further their own interests with the expectation that the best attainable society will result from this competition and conflict among interest groups. Chambliss' article raises questions about how much powerful interest groups can control the law making process to maintain their own interests against the interests of less powerful groups or disorganized individuals. These conflicts become most visible in the cases of particular laws which reflect basic societal conflicts, such as laws regarding abortion, drug use, voting procedures, franchises, labor laws, health and welfare legislation, gun control, estate taxes, etc. Beyond all the particular legal controversies is the more fundamental unanswered question of what the role of law is, or ought to be, in a democratic society.

William J. Chambliss. (1964). A sociological analysis of the law of vagrancy, *Social Problems, 12*, 67–77. Any text which is in square brackets has been added by the editors of this book, except for "[the constables]" in one of the extended quotations, which was in the original.

William J. Chambliss
A Sociological Analysis of the Law of Vagrancy

With the outstanding exception of Jerome Hall's analysis of theft[1] "there has been a severe shortage of sociologically relevant analyses of the relationship between particular laws and the social setting in which these laws emerge, are interpreted, and take form. The paucity of such studies is somewhat surprising in view of widespread agreement that such studies are not only desirable but absolutely essential to the development of a mature sociology of law."[2] A fruitful method of establishing the direction and pattern of this mutual influence is to systematically analyze particular legal categories, to observe the changes which take place in the categories and to explain how these changes are themselves related ... [to other] changes in the society. This paper is an attempt to provide such an analysis of the law of vagrancy in Anglo-American Law.

Legal Innovation:
The Emergence of the Law of Vagrancy in England

There is general agreement among legal scholars that the first full fledged vagrancy statute was passed in England in 1349. As is generally the case with legislative innovations, however, this statute was preceded by earlier laws which established a climate favorable to such change. The most significant forerunner to the 1349 vagrancy statute was in 1274 when it was provided:

> Because that abbies and houses of religion have been overcharged and sore grieved, by the resort of great men and other, so that their goods have not been sufficient for themselves, whereby they have been greatly hindered and impoverished, that they cannot maintain themselves, nor such charity as they have been accustomed to do; it is provided, that none shall come to eat or lodge in any house of religion, or any other's foundation than of his own, at the costs of the house, unless he be required by the governor of the house before his coming hither.[3]

Unlike the vagrancy statutes this statute does not intend to curtail the movement of persons from one place to another, but is solely designed to provide the religious houses with some financial relief from the burden of providing food and shelter to travelers.

The philosophy that the religious houses were to give alms to the poor and to the sick and feeble was, however, to undergo drastic change in the next fifty years. The result of this changed attitude was the establishment of the first vagrancy statute in 1349 which made it a crime to give alms to any who were unemployed while being of sound mind and body. To wit:

> Because that many valiant beggars, as long as they may live of begging, do refuse to labor, giving themselves to idleness and vice, and sometimes to theft and other abominations; it is ordained, that none, upon pain of imprisonment shall, under the colour of pity or alms, give anything to such which may labour, or presume to favour them towards their desires, so that thereby they may be compelled to labour for their necessary living.[4]

It was further provided by this statute that:

> ... every man and woman, of what condition he be, free or bond, able in body, and within the age of threescore years, not living in merchandize nor exercising any craft, nor having of his own whereon to live, nor proper land whereon to occupy himself, and not serving any other, if he in convenient service (his estate considered) be required to serve, shall be bounded to serve him which shall him require.... And if any refuse, he shall on conviction by two true men, ... be committed to gaol [jail] till he find surety to serve. And if any workman or servant, of what estate or condition he be, retained in any man's service, do depart from the said service without reasonable cause or license, before the term agreed on, he shall have pain of imprisonment.[5]

There was also in this statute the stipulation that the workers should receive a standard wage. In 1351 this statute was strengthened by the stipulation:

> And none shall go out of the town where he dwelled in winter, to serve the summer, if he may serve in the same town.[6]

By 34 Ed 3 [law of the 34th year of the reign of King Edward III] (1360) the punishment for these acts became imprisonment for fifteen days and if they "do not justify themselves by the end of that time, to be sent to gaol till they do."

A change in official policy so drastic as this did not, of course, occur simply as a matter of whim. The vagrancy statutes emerged as a result of changes in other parts of the social structure. The prime mover for this legislative innovation was the Black Death which struck England about 1348. Among the many disastrous consequences this had upon the social structure was the fact that it decimated the labor force. It is estimated that by the time the pestilence had run its course at least fifty per cent of the population of England had died from the plague. This decimation of the labor force would necessitate rather drastic innovations in any society but its impact was heightened in England where, at this time, the economy was highly dependent upon a ready supply of cheap labor.

Even before the pestilence, however, the availability of an adequate supply of cheap labor was becoming a problem for the landowners. The crusades and various wars had made money necessary to the lords and, as a result, the lord frequently agreed to sell the serfs their freedom in order to obtain the needed funds. The serfs, for their part, were desirous of obtaining their freedom (by "fair means" or "foul") because the larger towns which were becoming more industrialized during this period could offer the serf greater personal freedom as well as a higher standard of living. This process is nicely summarized by Bradshaw:

> By the middle of the 14th century the outward uniformity of the manorial system [vast estates with serfs and tenant farmers] had become in practice considerably varied ... for the peasant had begun to drift to the towns and it was unlikely that the old village life in its unpleasant aspects should not be resented. Moreover the constant wars against France and Scotland were fought mainly with mercenaries after Henry III's time and most villages contributed to the new armies. The bolder serfs either joined the armies or fled to the towns, and even in the villages the free men who held by villein tenure [unbreakable labor contracts] were as eager to commute their services as the serfs were to escape. Only the amount of 'free' labor available enabled the lord to work his demesne [estate] in many places.[7]

And he says regarding the effect of the Black Death:

> ... in 1348 the Black Death reached England and the vast mortality that ensued destroyed that reserve of labour which alone had made the manorial system even nominally possible.[8]

The immediate result of these events was of course no surprise: Wages for the "free" man rose considerably and this increased, on the one hand, the landowners problems and, on the other hand, the plight of the unfree tenant [farmer]. For although wages increased for the personally free laborers, it of course did not necessarily add to the standard of living of the serf;

if anything it made his position worse because the landowner would be hard pressed to pay for the personally free labor which he needed and would thus find it more and more difficult to maintain the standard of living for the serf which he had heretofore supplied. Thus the serf had no alternative but flight if he chose to better his position. Furthermore, flight generally meant both freedom and better conditions since the possibility of work in the new weaving industry was great and the chance of being caught small.[9]

It was under these conditions that we find the first vagrancy statutes emerging. There is little question but that these statutes were designed for one express purpose: to force laborers (whether personally free or unfree) to accept employment at a low wage in order to insure the landowner an adequate supply of labor at a price he could afford to pay. Caleb Foote concurs with this interpretation when he notes:

> The anti-migratory policy behind vagrancy legislation began as an essential complement of the wage stabilization legislation which accompanied the breakup of feudalism and the depopulation caused by the Black Death. By the Statutes of Labourers in 1349–1351, every able bodied person without other means of support was required to work for wages fixed at the level preceding the Black Death; it was unlawful to accept more, or to refuse an offer to work, or to flee from one county to another to avoid offers of work or to seek higher wages, or to give alms to able-bodied beggars who refused to work.[10]

In short, as Foote says in another place, this was an "attempt to make the vagrancy statutes a substitute for serfdom."[11] This same conclusion is equally apparent from the wording of the statute where it is stated:

> Because great part of the people and especially of workmen and servants, late died in pestilence; many seeing the necessity of masters, and great scarcity of servants, will not serve without excessive wages, and some rather willing to beg in idleness than by labour to get their living: it is ordained, that every man and woman, of what condition he be, free or bond, able in body and within the age of threescore years, not living in merchandize, (etc.) be required to serve....

The innovation in the law, then, was a direct result of the aforementioned changes which had occurred in the social setting. In this case these changes were located for the most part in the economic institution of the society. The vagrancy laws were designed to alleviate a condition defined by the lawmakers as undesirable. The solution was to attempt to force a reversal, as it were, of a social process which was well underway; that is, to curtail mobility of laborers in such a way that labor would not become a commodity for which the landowners would have to compete.

Statutory Dormancy: A Legal Vestige

In time, of course, the curtailment of the geographical mobility of laborers was no longer requisite. One might well expect that when the function served by the statute was no longer an important one for the society, the statutes would be eliminated from the law. In fact, this has not occurred. The vagrancy statutes have remained in effect since 1349. Furthermore, as we shall see in some detail later, they were taken over by the colonies and have remained in effect in the United States as well.

The substance of the vagrancy statutes changed very little for some time after the first ones in 1349–1351 although there was a tendency to make punishments more harsh than originally. For example, in 1360 it was provided that violators of the statute should be imprisoned for fifteen days[12] and in 1388 the punishment was to put the offender in the stocks and to keep him there until "he find surety to return to his service."[13] That there was still, at this time the intention of providing the landowner with labor is apparent from the fact that this statute provides:

> and he or she which used to labour at the plough and cart, or other labour and service of husbandry, till they be of the age of 12 years, from thenceforth shall abide at the same labour without being put to any mistery [skilled craft or trade] or handicraft: and any covenant of apprenticeship to the contrary shall be void.[14]

The next alteration in the statutes occurs in 1495 and is restricted to an increase in punishment. Here it is provided that vagrants shall be "set in stocks, there to remain by the space of three days and three nights, and there to have none other sustenance but bread and water; and after the said three days and nights, to be let out and set at large, and then to be commanded to avoid the town."[15]

The tendency to increase the severity of punishment during this period seems to be the result of a general tendency to make finer distinctions in the criminal law. During this period the vagrancy statutes appear to have been fairly inconsequential in either their effect as a control mechanism or as a generally enforced statute.[16] The processes of social change in the culture generally and the trend away from serfdom and into a "free" economy obviated the utility of these statutes. The result was not unexpected. The judiciary did not apply the law and the legislators did not take it upon themselves to change the law. In short, we have here a period of dormancy in which the statute is neither applied nor altered significantly.

A Shift in Focal Concern

Following the squelching of the Peasant's Revolt in 1381, the services of the serfs to the lord "tended to become less and less exacted, although in certain forms they lingered on till the seventeenth century.... By the sixteenth century few knew that there were any bondmen in England ... and in 1575 Queen Elizabeth listened to the prayers of almost the last serfs in England ... and granted them manumission [freedom]."[17]

In view of this change we would expect corresponding changes in the vagrancy laws. Beginning with the lessening of punishment in the statute of 1503 we find these changes. However, instead of remaining dormant (or becoming more so) or being negated altogether, the vagrancy statutes experienced a shift in focal concern. With this shift the statutes served a new and equally important function for the social order of England. The first statute which indicates this change was in 1530. In this statute (22 H. 8. c.12 1530) it was stated:

> If any person, being whole and mighty in body, and able to labour, be taken in begging, or be vagrant and can give no reckoning how he lawfully gets his living; ... and all other idle persons going about, some of them using divers and subtil crafty and unlawful games and plays, and some of them feigning themselves to have knowledge of ... crafty sciences ... shall be punished as provided.

What is most significant about this statute is the shift from an earlier concern with laborers to a concern with criminal activities. To be sure, the stipulation of persons "being whole and mighty in body, and able to labour, be taken in begging, or be vagrant" sounds very much like the concerns of the earlier statutes. Some important differences are apparent however when the rest of the statute includes those who "can give no reckoning how he lawfully gets his living"; "some of them using divers subtil and unlawful games and plays." This is the first statute which specifically focuses upon these kinds of criteria for adjudging someone a vagrant.

It is significant that in this statute the severity of punishment is increased so as to be greater not only than provided by the 1503 statute but the punishment is more severe than that which had been provided by any of the pre-

1503 statutes as well. For someone who is merely idle and gives no reckoning of how he makes his living the offender shall be:

> had to the next market town, or other place where they [the constables] shall think most convenient, and there to be tied to the end of a cart naked, and to be beaten with whips throughout the same market town or other place, till his body be bloody by reason of such whipping.[18]

But, for those who use "divers and subtil crafty and unlawful games and plays," etc., the punishment is "whipping at two days together in manner aforesaid."[19] For the second offense, such persons are:

> scourged "two days, and the third day to be put upon the pillory from nine of the clock till eleven before noon of the same day and to have one of his ears cut off.[20]

And if he offend the third time "to have like punishment with whipping, standing on the pillory and to have his other ear cut off."

This statute (1) makes a distinction between types of offenders and applies the more severe punishment to those who are clearly engaged in "criminal" activities, (2) mentions a specific concern with categories of "unlawful behavior," and (3) applies a type of punishment (cutting off the ear) which is generally reserved for offenders who are defined as likely to be a fairly serious criminal.

Only five years later we find for the first time that the punishment of death is applied to the crime of vagrancy. We also note a change in terminology in the statute:

> … and if any ruffians … after having been once apprehended … shall wander, loiter, or idle use themselves and play the vagabonds … [he] shall be eftsoons [immediately] not only whipped again, but shall have the gristle of his right ear clean cut off. And if he shall again offend, he shall be committed to gaol till the next sessions [of the court]; and being there convicted upon indictment, he shall have judgment to suffer pains and execution of death, as a felon, as an enemy of the commonwealth.[21]

It is significant that the statute now makes persons who repeat the crime of vagrancy a felon. During this period then, the focal concern of the vagrancy statutes becomes a concern for the control of felons and is no longer primarily concerned with the movement of laborers.

These statutory changes were a direct response to changes taking place in England's social structure during this period. We have already pointed out that feudalism was decaying rapidly. Concomitant with the breakup of feudalism was an increased emphasis upon commerce and industry. The commercial emphasis in England at the turn of the sixteenth century is of particular importance in the development of vagrancy laws. With commercialism came considerable traffic bearing valuable items. Where there were 169 important merchants in the middle of the fourteenth century there were 3,000 merchants engaged in foreign trade alone at the beginning of the sixteenth century.[22] England became highly dependent upon commerce for its economic support. Italians conducted a great deal of the commerce of England during this early period and were held in low repute by the populace. As a result, they were subject to attacks by citizens and, more important, were frequently robbed of their goods while transporting them. "The general insecurity of the times made any transportation hazardous. The special risks to which the alien merchant was subjected gave rise to the royal practice of issuing formally executed covenants of safe conduct through the realm."[23]

Such a situation not only called for the enforcement of existing laws but also called for the creation of new laws which would facilitate the control of persons preying upon merchants transporting goods. The vagrancy statutes were revived in order to fulfill just such a purpose. Persons who had committed no serious felony but who were suspected of being capable of doing so could be apprehended and incapacitated through the application of vagrancy laws once these laws were refocused so as to include "any ruffians ... [who] shall wander, loiter, or idle use themselves and play the vagabonds."[24]

The new focal concern is continued in 1 Ed 6. c. 3 (1547) and in fact is made more general so as to include:

> Whoever man or woman, being not lame, impotent, or so aged or diseased that he or she cannot work, not having whereon to live, shall be lurking in any house, or loitering or idle wandering by the highway side, or in streets, cities, towns, or villages, not applying themselves to some honest labour, and so continuing for three days; or running away from their work; every such person shall be taken for a vagabond. And ... upon conviction of two witnesses ... the same loiterer (shall) be marked with a hot iron in the breast with the letter V, and adjudged him to the person bringing him, to be his slave for two years.

Should the vagabond run away, upon conviction, he was to be branded by a hot iron with the letter S on the forehead and to be thenceforth declared a slave forever. And in 1571 there is modification of the punishment to be inflicted, whereby the offender is to be "branded on the chest with the letter V" (for vagabond). And, if he is convicted the second time, the brand is to be made on the forehead. It is worth noting here that this method of punishment, which first appeared in 1530 and is repeated here with somewhat more force, is also an indication of a change in the type of person to whom the law is intended to apply. For it is likely that nothing so permanent as branding would be applied to someone who was wandering but looking for work, or at worst merely idle and not particularly dangerous per se. On the other hand, it could well be applied to someone who was likely to be engaged in other criminal activities in connection with being "vagrant."

By 1571 in the statute of 14 E. 1. c. 5 the shift in focal concern is fully developed:

> All rogues, vagabonds, and sturdy beggars shall ... be committed to the common gaol ... [He] shall be grievously whipped, and burnt thro' the gristle of the right ear with a hot iron of the compass of an inch about.... And for the second offense, he shall be adjudged a felon, unless some person will take him for two years into his service. And for the third offense, he shall be adjudged guilty of felony without benefit of clergy.

And there is included a long list of persons who fall within the statute: "proctors, procurators, idle persons going about using subtil, crafty and unlawful games or plays and some of them feigning themselves to have knowledge of ... absurd sciences ... and all fencers, bearwards [owners of performing bears], common players in interludes, and minstrels, ... all juglers, pedlars, tinkers, petty chapmen [hawkers], ... and all counterfeiters of licenses, passports and users of the same." The major significance of this statute is that it includes all the previously defined offenders and adds some more. Significantly, those added are more clearly criminal types, counterfeiters, for example. It is also significant that there is the following qualification of this statute: "Provided also, that this act shall not extend to cookers, or harvest folks, that travel for harvest work, corn or hay."

That the changes in this statute were seen as significant is indicated by the following statement which appears in the statute:

> And whereas by reason of this act, the common gaols of every shire are like to be greatly pestered with more number of prisoners than

heretofore hath been, for that the said vagabonds and other lewd persons before recited shall upon their apprehension be committed to the said gaols; it is enacted.[25]

And a provision is made for giving more money for maintaining the gaols. This seems to add credence to the notion that this statute was seen as being significantly more general than those previously.

It is also of importance to note that this is the first time the term rogue has been used to refer to persons included in the vagrancy statutes. It seems, a priori, that a "rogue" is a different social type than is a "vagrant" or a "vagabond"; the latter terms implying something more equivalent to the idea of a "tramp" whereas the former (rogue) seems to imply a more disorderly and potentially dangerous person.

The emphasis upon the criminalistic aspect of vagrants continues in Chapter 17 of the same statute:

> Whereas divers *licentious persons* wander up and down in all parts of the realm, to countenance their *wicked behavior*; and do continually assemble themselves armed in the highways, and elsewhere in troops, *to the great terror* of her majesty's true subjects, *the impeachment of her laws*, and the disturbance of the peace and tranquility of the realm; and whereas many outrages are daily committed by these dissolute persons, and more are likely to ensue if speedy remedy be not provided. (Italics added)

With minor variations (e.g., offering a reward for the capture of a vagrant) the statutes remain essentially of this nature until 1743. In 1743 there was once more an expansion of the types of persons included such that "all persons going about as patent gatherers, or gatherers of alms, under pretense of loss by fire or other casualty; or going about as collectors for prisons, gaols, or hospitals; all persons playing of betting at any unlawful games; and all persons who run away and leave their wives or children; ... all persons wandering abroad, and lodging in alehouses, barns, outhouses, or in the open air, not giving good account of themselves," were types of offenders added to those already included.

By 1743 the vagrancy statutes had apparently been sufficiently reconstructed by the shifts of concern so as to be once more a useful instrument in the creation of social solidarity. This function has apparently continued down to the present day in England and the changes from 1743 to the present have been all in the direction of clarifying or expanding the categories covered but little has been introduced to change either the meaning or the impact of this branch of the law.

We can summarize this shift in focal concern by quoting from Halsbury. He has noted that in the vagrancy statutes:

> elaborate provision is made for the relief and incidental control of destitute wayfarers. These latter, however, form but a small portion of the offenders aimed at by what are known as the Vagrancy Laws, ... many offenders who are in no ordinary sense of the word vagrants, have been brought under the laws relating to vagrancy, and the great number of the offenses coming within the operation of these laws have little or no relation to the subject of poor relief, but are more properly directed towards the prevention of crime, the preservation of good order, and the promotion of social economy.[26]

Before leaving this section it is perhaps pertinent to make a qualifying remark. We have emphasized throughout this section how the vagrancy statutes underwent a shift in focal concern as the social setting changed. The shift in focal concern is not meant to imply that the later focus of the statutes represents a completely new law. It will be recalled that even in the first vagrancy statute there was reference to those who "do refuse labor, giving themselves to idleness and vice and sometimes to theft and other abominations." Thus the possibility of criminal activities resulting from persons who refuse to labor was recognized even in the earliest statute. The fact remains, however, that the major emphasis in this statute and in the statutes which followed the first one was always upon the "refusal to labor" or "begging." The "criminalistic" aspect of such persons was relatively unimportant. Later, as we have shown, the criminalistic potential becomes of paramount importance. The thread runs back to the earliest statute but the reason for the statutes' existence as well as the focal concern of the statutes is quite different in 1743 than it was in 1349.

Vagrancy Laws in the United States

In general, the vagrancy laws of England, as they stood in the middle eighteenth century, were simply adopted by the states. There were some exceptions to this general trend. For example, Maryland restricted the application of vagrancy laws to "free" Negroes. In addition, for all states the vagrancy laws were even more explicitly concerned with the control of criminals and undesirables than had been the case in England. New York, for example, explicitly defines prostitutes as being a category of vagrants during this period. These exceptions do not, however, change the general picture significantly and it is quite appropriate to consider the U.S. vagrancy laws as following from England's of the middle eighteenth century with relatively minor changes. The control of criminals and undesirables was the *raison d'e-*

tre of the vagrancy laws in the U. S. This is as true today as it was in 1750. As Caleb Foote's analysis of the application of vagrancy statutes in the Philadelphia court shows, these laws are presently applied indiscriminately to persons considered a "nuisance." Foote suggests that " ... the chief significance of this branch of the criminal law lies in its quantitative impact and administrative usefulness."[27] Thus it appears that in America the trend begun in England in the sixteenth, seventeenth and eighteenth centuries has been carried to its logical extreme and the laws are now used principally as a mechanism for "clearing the streets" of the derelicts who inhabit the "skid rows" and "Bowerys" of our large urban areas.

Since the 1800s there has been an abundant source of prospects to which the vagrancy laws have been applied. These have been primarily those persons deemed by the police and the courts to be either actively involved in criminal activities or at least peripherally involved. In this context, then, the statutes have changed very little. The functions served by the statutes in England of the late eighteenth century are still being served today in both England and the United States. The locale has changed somewhat and it appears that the present day application of vagrancy statutes is focused upon the arrest and confinement of the "down and outers" who inhabit certain sections of our larger cities but the impact has remained constant. The lack of change in the vagrancy statutes, then, can be seen as a reflection of the society's perception of a continuing need to control some of its "suspicious" or "undesirable" members.[28]

A word of caution is in order lest we leave the impression that this administrative purpose is the sole function of vagrancy laws in the U. S. today. Although it is our contention that this is generally true it is worth remembering that during certain periods of our recent history, and to some extent today, these laws have also been used to control the movement of workers. This was particularly the case during the depression years and California is of course infamous for its use of vagrancy laws to restrict the admission of migrants from other states.[29] The vagrancy statutes, because of their history, still contain germs within them which make such effects possible. Their main purpose, however, is clearly no longer the control of laborers but rather the control of the undesirable, the criminal and the "nuisance."

Discussion

The foregoing analysis of the vagrancy laws has demonstrated that these laws were a legislative innovation which reflected the socially perceived necessity of providing an abundance of cheap labor to landowners during a period when serfdom was breaking down and when the pool of available labor was depleted. With the eventual breakup of feudalism the need for such laws eventually disappeared and the increased dependence of the economy upon industry and commerce rendered the former use of the vagrancy statutes unnecessary. As a result, for a substantial period the vagrancy statutes were dormant, undergoing only minor changes and, presumably, being applied infrequently. Finally, the vagrancy laws were subjected to considerable alteration through a shift in the focal concern of the statutes. Whereas in their inception the laws focused upon the "idle" and "those refusing to labor," after the turn of the sixteenth century an emphasis came to be upon "rogues," "vagabonds," and others who were suspected of being engaged in criminal activities. During this period the focus was particularly upon "roadmen" who preyed upon citizens who transported goods from one place to another. The increased importance of commerce to England during this period made it necessary that some protection be given persons engaged in this enterprise and the vagrancy statutes provided one source for such protection by refocusing the acts to be included under these statutes.

Comparing the results of this analysis with the findings of Hall's study of theft we see a good deal of correspondence. Of major importance is the fact that both analyses demonstrate the truth of Hall's assertion that "The functioning of courts is significantly related to concomitant cultural needs, and this applies to the law of procedure as well as to substantive law."[30]

Our analysis of the vagrancy laws also indicates that when changed social conditions create a perceived need for legal changes that these alterations will be effected through the revision and refocusing of existing statutes. This process was demonstrated in Hall's analysis of theft as well as in our analysis of vagrancy. In the case of vagrancy, the laws were dormant when the focal concern of the laws was shifted so as to provide control over potential criminals. In the case of theft the laws were reinterpreted (interestingly, by the courts and not by the legislature) so as to include persons who were transporting goods for a merchant but who absconded with the contents of the packages transported.

It also seems probable that when the social conditions change and previously useful laws are no longer useful there will be long periods when these laws will remain dormant. It is less likely that they will be officially negated. During this period of dormancy it is the judiciary which has principal responsibility for not applying the statutes. It is possible that one finds statutes being negated only when the judiciary stubbornly applies laws which do not have substantial public support. An example of such laws in contemporary times would be the "Blue Laws." Most states still have laws prohibiting the sale of retail goods on Sunday yet these laws are rarely applied. The laws are very likely to remain but to be dormant unless a recalcitrant judge or a vocal minority of the population insist that the laws be applied. When this happens we can anticipate that the statutes will be negated.[31] Should there arise a perceived need to curtail retail selling under some special circumstances, then it is likely that these laws will undergo a shift in focal concern much like the shift which characterized the vagrancy laws. Lacking such application the laws will simply remain dormant except for rare instances where they will be negated.

This analysis of the vagrancy statutes (and Hall's analysis of theft as well) has demonstrated the importance of "vested interest" groups in the emergence and/or alteration of laws. The vagrancy laws emerged in order to provide the powerful landowners with a ready supply of cheap labor. When this was no longer seen as necessary and particularly when the landowners were no longer dependent upon cheap labor nor were they a powerful interest group in the society the laws became dormant. Finally a new interest group [traveling merchants] emerged and was seen as being of great importance to the society and the laws were then altered so as to afford some protection to this group. These findings are thus in agreement with Weber's contention that "status groups" determine the content of the law.[32] The findings are inconsistent, on the other hand, with the perception of the law as simply a reflection of "public opinion" as is sometimes found in the literature.[33] We should be cautious in concluding, however, that either of these positions is necessarily correct. The careful analysis of other laws, and especially of laws which do not focus so specifically upon the "criminal," are necessary before this question can be finally answered.

In conclusion, it is hoped that future analyses of changes within the legal structure will be able to benefit from this study by virtue of (1) the data provided and (2) the utilization of a set of concepts (innovation, dormancy, concern and negation) which have proved useful in the analysis of the vagrancy law. Such analyses should provide us with more substantial grounds for rejecting or accepting as generally valid the description of some of the processes which appear to characterize changes in the legal system.

Footnotes

[Citations of English statutes should be read thus: "3 Ed. 1. c. 1." means the laws of the third year of King Edward the First, chapter one.]

l. Hall, J., *Theft, Law and Society*, Bobbs-Merrill, 1939. See also, Alfred R. Lindesmith, "Federal Law and Drug Addiction," *Social Problems* Vol. 7, No. 1. 1959, p. 48.

2. See for example, Rose, A., "Some Suggestions for Research in the Sociology of Law," *Social Problems* Vol. 9, No. 3. 1962, pp. 281–283 and Geis, G., "Sociology, Criminology, and Criminal Law," *Social Problems* Vol. 7, No. 1, 1959, pp 40–47.

3. 35 Ed. 1. c. 1.

4. 35 Ed. 1. c. 1.

5. 23 Ed. 3.

6. 25 Ed. 3 (1351).

7. Bradshaw, F. *A Social History of England*, p. 54.

8. *Ibid.* [the same as above]

9. *Ibid.*, p. 57.

10. Foote, C., "Vagrancy Type Law and Its Administration," *Univ. of Pennsylvania Law Review* (104), 1956, p. 615.

11. *Ibid.*

12. 34 Ed. 3 (1360).

13. 12 R. 2 (1388).

14. *Ibid.*

15. 11 H. & C. 2 (1495).

16. As evidence for this note the expectation that " ... the common gaols of every shire are likely to be greatly pestered with more numbers of prisoners than heretofore ..." when the statutes were changed by the statute of 14 Ed. c. 5 (1571).

17. Bradshaw, *op. cit.*, p. 61.

18. 22 H. 8. c. 12 (1530).

19. *Ibid.*

20. *Ibid.*

21. 27 H. 8. c. 25 (1535).

22. Hall, op. cit., p. 21.

23. *Ibid.*, p. 23.

24. 27 H. 8. c. 5 (1535).

25. 14 E 1. c. 5. (1571).

26. Earl of Halsbury, *The Laws of England*, Butterworth & Co., Bell Yard, Temple Bar, 1912, pp. 606–607.

27. Foote, *op. cit.*, p. 613. Also see in this connection, Irwin Deutscher, "The Petty Offender," *Federal Probation*, XIX, June, 1955.

28. It is on this point that the vagrancy statutes have been subject to criticism. See for example, Lacey, Forrest W., "Vagrancy and Other Crimes of Personal Condition," *Harvard Law Review (66)*, p. 1203.

29. Edwards vs California. 314 S: 160 (1941).

30. Hall, *op. cit.*, p. XII.

31. Negation, in this instance, is most likely to come about by the repeal of the statute. More generally, however, negation may occur in several ways including the declaration of a statute as unconstitutional. This later mechanism has been used even for laws which have been "on the books" for long periods of time. Repeal is probably the most common, although not the only, procedure by which a law is negated.

32. M. Rheinstein, *Max Weber on Law in Economy and Society*, Harvard University Press, 1954.

33. Friedman, N., *Law in a Changing Society*, Berkeley and Los Angeles: University of California Press, 1959.

[End note: A revised version of this article was published in William J. Chambliss, Ed., *Criminal law in action* (New York: John Wiley & Sons, 1984). The revision was a shorter version but it had additional material in the section on Vagrancy Laws in the United States. It discussed the use of a vague vagrancy statute of Jacksonville, Florida which permitted police to arrest individuals on vague grounds even when police had no reasonable suspicion that any particular crime might be committed by the individual. The Supreme Court, in Papachristou v. City of Jacksonville, 405 U.S. 156 (1972), stated, "Future criminality, however, is the common justification for the presence of vagrancy statutes.... The Jacksonville ordinance cannot be squared with our constitutional standards."

Introduction to
Oliver Wendell Holmes, Jr.

Oliver Wendell Holmes, Jr. was born in Boston on March 8, 1841. He was the first of three children of the celebrated poet, writer, and professor of medicine at Harvard, Oliver Wendell Holmes and Amelia Lee Jackson. His father was a descendant of the Puritan poetess Anne Bradstreet, and his mother's father was a chief justice of the Supreme Court of Massachusetts. Holmes, Jr. attended private school for education in the Greek and Latin classics and then Harvard College. Holmes was always proud and outspoken about his heritage. Honor, duty, and chivalry were his creed.

At the outbreak of the war between the states, Holmes dropped out of Harvard for a few months to enlist and drill as a private in the 4th Battalion Infantry, but the battalion was not called up. After graduation the next year, at the age of twenty, Holmes was commissioned a first lieutenant in the 20th Massachusetts Volunteers. His letters and diaries vividly described his experiences in the war. Although he saw the war as "an organized bore," and later said, " … I was not born to it and did nothing remarkable in any way," he was wounded seriously at the battle of Ball's Bluff, again at Antietam, and yet again at Fredericksburg. In poor physical condition, he left the army after three years, having attained the rank of lieutenant colonel. Several of Holmes' friends also served in the war. They disagreed among themselves about whether the war was just, and whether the northern states were right to impose their will on the southern states by force of arms. But all did their duty with distinction despite personal qualms. The war left Holmes with the conviction that sometimes it could be difficult to determine what is just, but one must do one's duty regardless. The war made a realist of the young Boston patrician but did not dampen his idealism.

In the autumn of 1864 Holmes entered Harvard Law School without a sense of vocation. His father, who had studied law for a year before turning to the study of medicine at Cambridge, Paris, and back at Harvard, asked, "What's the use of that, Wendell? A lawyer can't be a great man." There was no deep connection between the short, candid, outgoing father and the tall, quiet, shy son. Holmes found the law curriculum uninspired. He later said that the science, philosophy and history of law were slighted for what he called "the small change of legal thought." Holmes himself was to become more distinguished for his knowledge of the law than for his practice as a lawyer. Finishing law school in 1866, he made the then standard aristocratic tour of Europe visiting England, France and Switzerland where he met many distinguished individuals. For the rest of his life he corresponded with the English legal historians Sir Frederick Pollack and Harold J. Laski.

Holmes was admitted to the bar in 1867 and for fifteen years practiced law as an undistinguished member of some Boston law firms. In the great nineteenth century seaport of Boston some of Holmes' law practice involved admiralty law, the law of the sea. But his leanings were scholarly. From 1870 to 1873 he edited the *American Law Review*. In 1873 he edited the twelfth edition of Chancellor James Kent's (1763–1847) classic survey of early American law, *Commentaries on American Law*.

Throughout his youth and early career as a practicing lawyer Holmes maintained a long courtship with Fanny Bowditch Dixwell, the daughter of his old prep school master. They married in 1872. Though a long and happy marriage, the couple was childless. When Fanny Holmes died on April 30, 1932, Holmes wrote to his friend Sir Frederick Pollack, "For sixty years she made life poetry for me."

In 1881 Holmes was invited to lecture on law at the Lowell Institute in Boston. In those days it was very common for educated people to spend evenings at lectures sponsored by intellectual societies. The upper class was educated mostly in the classics and history but open to knowledge in all areas. Lectures usually were written out, read verbatim, and later published. Holmes' lectures became his book *The Common Law*.

Holmes' career took flight. In 1882 Holmes was made Weld Professor of Law, a chair created for him at Harvard. However, Holmes' ambition had always been to be a judge, not a professor, because judges were the people who cultivated the growth of the law. After less than a year as professor, Holmes accepted an appointment to the Supreme Judicial Court of the State of Massachusetts, where his grandfather had served. He remained there for twenty years, becoming its Chief Justice in 1899. In 1901 President Theodore Roosevelt appointed him an Associate Justice of the United States Supreme Court, where he served more than three decades before retiring on January 2, 1932, at the age of almost 91. He died a few days before his ninety-fourth birthday on March 6, 1935.

Holmes himself played a major role in the extraordinary changes in the nature of the law which took place during his time on the bench. But he was too far ahead of his time. Holmes began his career when the law consisted mostly of the common law, which was the scholarly legal tradition based on commentaries and cases going back all the way to ancient Roman law. The study of law and the decisions of courts were based on general principles and specific cases which established binding precedents. The cases and the principles were enshrined in written commentaries on the law. Law was regarded as a somewhat exotic species of logic which untrained persons would have trouble understanding. Every effort was made to explain current law and base current decisions on the legal traditions which had developed through two thousand years of legal practice. In fact, most laws were made by judges in the process of deciding cases, not by legislatures. Sometimes it took a very arcane kind of reasoning to see the connections between principles and cases as stated in the venerable common law tradition and the modern application of the law.

Holmes' great work *The Common Law* followed in the path of earlier scholars who turned to history for an understanding of law. In 1861 Henry Sumner Maine, an English scholar, published *Ancient Law*, which traced the history of law from primitive to modern times. Holmes studied Maine's book assiduously. Maine thought that the idea of a contract, which had evolved over thousands of years, was the best idea for governing a society. He was skeptical about a legal system and system of government based on human nature because the very idea of human nature was so vague and open to various interpretations. Maine preferred the American system which was based on a written Constitution, in effect a social contract.

Maine thought that early societies were patriarchal groups with all rights belonging to the father. From this evolved the rights of kings. The development of law was essentially a splintering of the patriarch's power; others besides the patriarch gradually acquired independence and rights of their own. With the development of law came "legal fictions," which were untrue statements or assumptions which were accepted in the law as if they were true. The most striking and important legal fiction was adoption, which enabled a patriarch or king to say that a certain person was his son although everybody knew it was not true. The legal fiction of adoption enabled the patriarch or king to pass on his power to a person of his choice, even if he had no son at all.

In a broader sense, Maine regarded the entire Anglo-American legal system as a legal fiction. The fiction was that all current law is logically derived from ancient common law principles. To Maine the ancient Roman law was equally a fiction insofar as it claimed to be just an elaboration of some universal natural law inherent in human nature. Both English case law and Roman law were assumed to be logical developments of a few very basic, immutable principles based on human nature. "The *fact* is in both cases that the law has been wholly changed; the *fiction* is that it remains what it always was" (Maine, 1861, p. 16). Maine explained that change is necessary but people resent change and want to believe that the law is something more permanent. As Beccaria put it, people do not want a law system based on the good or bad digestion of a judge. Hence, those who practice and cultivate the law make the needed changes but create artful explanations to make it look like no real changes have occurred.

During Holmes' lifetime more and more of the law was being created by legislatures, and less and less of the law was being created by judges deciding cases. Law broke loose from natural law and was seen more as a product of the government trying to codify the will of the people. The idea that the legislature should create the laws and the judiciary should simply apply the laws to particular cases had not been accepted much in practice before the twentieth century. The laws passed by the American Congress in its first century were mostly laws related to the budget and operations of the federal government in the areas of foreign affairs and interstate matters. Most civil and criminal law was common law together with some statutes from state laws. However, unlike most other judges of the nineteenth century, Holmes favored the idea that laws should be made mostly by legislatures and applied to cases as literally as possible by the courts. Holmes believed that making laws is the business of legislative bodies, not courts, and within the general framework of constitutional bounds, the people have a right to whatever laws they choose to make—good, bad or indifferent—through their representatives. The duty of a judge was not to make or correct laws but only to apply existing laws to cases.

However, Holmes was somewhat out of step with the basic principle of the Enlightenment that all rights begin as the rights of individuals and individuals should yield their rights to the state only to the minimum degree necessary to maintain the social contract for mutual protection. Born to the ruling class, Holmes was more inclined to the view that a benevolent government should be considered the origin of rights, although government should not intrude upon individuals more than necessary for the common good. Beccaria's idea that the purpose of law was to procure the greatest happiness for the greatest number had been taken up by the English philosopher Jeremy Bentham and magnified into the principle that the happiness of the majority should determine the content of the law. It was only a shift in emphasis, but a shift in emphasis favoring the common good rather than the individual right. Indeed, Holmes was part of a fringe movement in the law in Europe and America to create a whole new kind of legal system based not on rights but rather on the duties a person should have towards others. It was what one might expect from an upper-class person with a strong sense of *noblesse oblige*, i.e., a noble person is obligated to act towards common people in a noble manner.

During the thirty years Holmes served on the Supreme Court he became known as The Great Dissenter. He had a habit of ending up on the losing side when the Justices voted on Supreme Court decisions and he often wrote the dissenting opinions for the losing side. Sometimes his opinions were to uphold the rights of individuals, especially free speech, or the rights of corporations. But often his opinions were in favor of upholding actions of the federal government, which was constantly trying to extend its reach into the growing areas of interstate commerce, federal regulations, and social programs well beyond what the writers of the U.S. Constitution had imagined. Homes took a flexible approach to the Constitution.

Other judges of the time might view the enactments of legislators as clumsy amateur lawmaking inconsistent with the legal traditions of the common law and too much of a stretch for the Constitution, especially when it came to laws expanding the powers of the federal government beyond the expectations of the founding fathers. But Holmes fully subscribed to the radical ideas that, one, lawmaking should be done by elected legislators and, two, that laws should meet the current needs of government policy, whether logically consistent with older laws or not. Learned Hand, who was a judge of the U.S. Court of Appeals in New York, where most of the important business cases of the twentieth century were decided, told this anecdote about Holmes:

> Remember what Justice Holmes said about "justice." I don't know what you think about him, but on the whole he was to me the master craftsman certainly of our time; and he said: "I hate justice," which he didn't quite mean. What he did mean was this. I remember once I was with him; it was a Saturday when the Court was to confer. It was before we had a motor car, and we jogged along in an old [horse drawn] coupe. When we got down to the Capitol, I wanted to provoke a response, so as he walked off, I said to him: "Well, sir, goodbye. Do justice!" He turned quite sharply and he said: "Come here. Come here." I answered: "Oh, I know, I know." He replied: "That is not my job. My job is to play the game according to the rules." (Hand, 1958, pp. 306–307.)

Holmes is generally regarded as the father of "legal realism." His was a realistic or pragmatic approach to law based on society's present needs. In fact, he was a member of a small group in Boston which called themselves "The Metaphysical Society." The group included William James, chief proponent of the American philosophy of pragmatism. Pragmatism began with the premise that there are no absolute values, only market values. Things are worth whatever value they have to people at a particular time and in a particular place. Law should be whatever happens to be the will of the people at the time. In making legal decisions, as in all matters, one should be guided by results. The judge should be asking, "If I make such and such a decision, what will the results be?"

The year that Holmes retired, 1932, was the year that Franklin D. Roosevelt became President. The Roosevelt administration, reacting to the Great Depression and then World War II, wanted to expand greatly the lawmaking powers of the federal government to control the economy and bring about changes in society. It was after Holmes' retirement that his philosophy overtook the Supreme Court through the appointment of new Justices who subscribed to his view and backed the legislative programs of the Roosevelt administration. This sparked a period of rapid expansion of federal powers in areas previously left unregulated or left to state governments, including the economy, labor practices, unemployment and retirement programs, education, health care, crime, housing, transportation, and so on. Thus Holmes provided the legal foundation for so many government policies and programs which are taken for granted today.

Holmes' *Common Law* provokes fundamental questions about the systems of laws governing society. One question concerns the extent to which law is a product of social or political goals rather than logic. Holmes pointed out that law is not logical unless one accepts certain illogical assumptions, such as the assumption in admiralty law that a ship is a person. Modern corporation law is based on the idea that a corporation is a person. How does this legal fiction serve modern policy needs? Turning to Holmes' idea that the original purpose of liability law was revenge, not compensation, does modern law still focus on revenge? Consider lawsuits for "punitive damages" in addition to actual damages and the movement to give victims a right to have a voice in determining sentences. Would it be possible for law to abandon the pretense of being a logical body of doctrines and to adopt the principle that legal decisions should be guided by what would be in the best interests of society? If that were done, what would be the legal arguments in a trial? Would legal arguments based on present needs of society be more appropriate than legal arguments based on decisions made in earlier cases (precedents)? Would this change the definition of "justice"? The British and American legal systems, unlike other legal systems, are based on precedents; as a result, they preserve old law more than do other modern legal systems. Will the British and American legal systems become incomprehensible except to lawyers, and will they become so overburdened with old law that they will eventually collapse like the common law and have to be replaced with a simpler legal system?

References

Hand, L. (1958). A personal confession. In *The spirit of liberty: Papers and addresses of Learned Hand.* Chicago: University of Chicago Press.

Maine, H.S. (1861). *Ancient law.* London: Dent. [Reprinted 1965 by J.M. Dent & Sons, London.]

Oliver Wendell Holmes, Jr. (1881). *The Common Law.* Boston: Little, Brown and Co. Holmes' numerous references have been omitted; they referred mostly to ancient sources and sometimes included quotations in Latin. The editors of this selection have added section headings. Also the editors have added a glossary of names and terms at the end of this reading. If there is an asterisk at the end of a word in the text, that word is included in the glossary. In addition, throughout the text words within square brackets have been added by the editors.

Oliver Wendell Holmes, Jr.

The Common Law

Lecture I: Early Forms of Liability

The Life of the Law Has Not Been Logic

The object of this book is to present a general view of the Common Law. To accomplish the task, other tools are needed besides logic. It is something to show that the consistency of a system requires a particular result, but it is not all. The life of the law has not been logic: it has been experience. The felt necessities of the time, the prevalent moral and political theories, intuitions of public policy, avowed or unconscious, even the prejudices which judges share with their fellow-men, have had a good deal more to do than the syllogism* in determining the rules by which men should be governed. The law embodies the story of a nation's development through many centuries, and it cannot be dealt with as if it contained only the axioms and corollaries of a book of mathematics. In order to know what it is, we must know what it has been, and what it tends to become. We must alternately consult history and existing theories of legislation. But the most difficult labor will be to understand the combination of the two into new products at every stage. The substance of the law at any given time pretty nearly corresponds, so far as it goes, with what is then understood to be convenient; but its form and machinery, and the degree to which it is able to work out desired results, depend very much upon its past

In Massachusetts today, while, on the one hand, there are a great many rules which are quite sufficiently accounted for by their manifest good sense, on the other, there are some which can only be understood by reference to the infancy of procedure among the German tribes, or to the social condition of Rome under the Decemvirs*.

I shall use the history of our law so far as it is necessary to explain a conception or to interpret a rule, but no further. In doing so there are two errors equally to be avoided both by writer and reader. One is that of supposing, because an idea seems very familiar and natural to us, that it has always been so. Many things which we take for granted have had to be laboriously fought out or thought out in past times. The other mistake is the opposite one of asking too much of history. We start with man full grown. It may be assumed that the earliest barbarian whose practices are to be considered, had a good many of the same feelings and passions as ourselves.

The first subject to be discussed is the general theory of liability civil and criminal. The Common Law has changed a good deal since the beginning of our series of reports*, and the search after a theory which may now be said to prevail is very much a study of tendencies. I believe that it will be instructive to go back to the early forms of liability, and to start from them.

Law Based on Vengeance for Intentional Wrongs

It is commonly known that the early forms of legal procedure were grounded in vengeance. Modern writers have thought that the Roman law started from the blood* feud, and all the authorities agree that the German law began in that way....

Vengeance imports a feeling of blame, and an opinion, however distorted by passion, that a wrong has been done. It can hardly go very far beyond the case of a harm intentionally inflicted: even a dog distinguishes between being stumbled over and being kicked.

Whether for this cause or another, the early English appeals* for personal violence seem to have been confined to intentional wrongs. Glanvill* mentions melees, blows, and wounds,—all forms of intentional violence. In the fuller description of such appeals given by Bracton* it is made quite clear that they were based on intentional assaults....

It was only at a later day, and after argument, that trespass* was extended so as to embrace harms which were foreseen but which were not the intended consequence of the defendant's act. Thence again it extended to unforeseen injuries....

I do not know any very satisfactory evidence that a man was generally held liable either in Rome or England for the accidental consequences even of his own act. But whatever may have been the early law, the foregoing account shows the starting point of the system with which we have to deal. Our system of private liability for the consequences of a man's own acts, that is, for his trespasses, started from the notion of actual intent and actual personal culpability.

New Reasons for Old Rules

A very common phenomenon, and one very familiar to the student of history, is this. The customs, beliefs, or needs of a primitive time establish a rule or a formula. In the course of centuries, the custom, belief, or necessity disappears, but the rule remains. The reason which gave rise to the rule has been forgotten, and ingenious minds set themselves to inquire how it is to be accounted for. Some ground of policy is thought of, which seems to explain it and to reconcile it with the present state of things; and then the rule adapts itself to the new reasons which have been found for it, and enters on a new career. The old form receives a new content, and in time even the form modifies itself to fit the meaning which it has received. The subject under consideration illustrates this course of events very clearly.

I will begin by taking a medley of examples embodying as many distinct rules, each with its plausible and seemingly sufficient ground of policy to explain it. [The remainder of this chapter will trace the historical development of the legal principles embodied in the following four examples.]

[1] A man has an animal of known ferocious habits, which escapes and does his neighbor damage. He can prove that the animal escaped through no negligence of his, but still he is held liable. Why? It is, says the analytical jurist, because, although he was not negligent at the moment of escape, he was guilty of remote heedlessness, or negligence, or fault, in having such a creature at all. And one by whose fault damage is done ought to pay for it.

[2] A baker's* man, while driving his master's cart to deliver hot rolls of a morning, runs another man down. The master [baker] has to pay for it. And when he has asked why he should have to pay for the wrongful act of an independent and responsible being [the driver], he has been answered from the time of Ulpian* to that of Austin*, that it is because he was to blame for employing an improper person. If he answers that he used the greatest possible care in choosing his driver, he is told that that is no excuse; and then perhaps the reason is shifted, and it is said that there ought to be a remedy against some one who can pay the damages, or that such wrongful acts as by ordinary human laws are likely to happen in the course of the service are imputable to the service.

[3] Next, take a case where a limit has been set to liability that had previously been unlimited. In 1851, Congress passed a law, which is still in force, and by which the owners of ships in all the more common cases of maritime loss can surrender the vessel and her freight [transport charges] then pending to the losers; and it is provided that, thereupon, further proceedings against the owners

shall cease. The legislators to whom we owe this act argued that, if a merchant embark a portion of his property upon a hazardous venture, it is reasonable that his stake should be confined to what he puts at risk—a principle similar to that on which corporations* have been so largely created in America during the last fifty years.

[4] It has been a rule of criminal pleading in England down into the present century, that an indictment for homicide must set forth the value of the instrument causing the death, in order that the king or his grantee might claim forfeiture of the deodand*, "as an accursed thing," in the language of Blackstone*.

I might go on multiplying examples; but these are enough to show the remoteness of the points to be brought together. As a first step towards a generalization, it will be necessary to consider what is to be found in ancient and independent systems of law.

Liability of Animals, Things, Children and Slaves in Ancient Laws

[1] There is a well-known passage in Exodus, which we shall have to remember later: "If an ox gore a man or a woman, that they die: then the ox shall be surely stoned, and his flesh shall not be eaten; but the owner of the ox shall be quit*." When we turn from the Jews to the Greeks, we find the principle of the passage just quoted erected into a system. Plutarch*, in his Solon*, tells us that a dog that had bitten a man was to be delivered up bound to a log four cubits [about six feet] long. Plato* made elaborate provisions in his Laws for many such cases. If a slave killed a man, he was to be given up to the relatives of the deceased. If he wounded a man, he was to be given up to the injured party to use him as he pleased. So if he did damage to which the injured party did not contribute as a joint cause. In either case, if the owner failed to surrender the slave, he was bound to make good the loss. If a beast killed a man, it was to be slain and cast beyond the borders. If an inanimate thing caused death, it was to be cast beyond the borders in like manner, and expiation was to be made. Nor was all this an ideal creation of merely imagined law, for it was said in one of the speeches of Aeschines*, that "we banish beyond our borders sticks and stones and steel, voiceless and mindless things, if they chance to kill a man; and if a man commits suicide, bury the hand that struck the blow afar from its body." This is mentioned quite as an everyday matter, evidently without thinking it at all extraordinary, only to point an antithesis to the honors heaped upon Demosthenes* [who committed suicide]. As late as the second century after Christ the traveler Pausanias* observed with some surprise that they still sat in judgment on

inanimate things in the Prytaneum*. Plutarch attributes the institution to Draco*.

In the Roman law we find the similar principles of the *noxae* deditio* [obligation to hand over the guilty thing for punishment] gradually leading to further results. The Twelve* Tables (451 B.C.) provided that, if an animal had done damage, either the animal was to be surrendered or the damage paid for. We learn from Gaius* that the same rule was applied to the actions of children or slaves, and there is some trace of it with regard to inanimate things. The Roman lawyers, not looking beyond their own system or their own time, drew on their wits for an explanation which would show that the law as they found it was reasonable. Gaius said that it was unjust that the fault of children or slaves should be a source of loss to their parents or owners beyond their own bodies, and Ulpian reasoned that *a fortiori* [even more strongly] this was true of things devoid of life, and therefore incapable of fault.

An Innocent Owner Could Pay
Instead of Surrendering Property

This way of approaching the question seems to deal with the right of surrender as if it were a limitation of a liability incurred by a parent or owner, which would naturally and in the first instance be unlimited. But if that is what was meant, it puts the cart before the horse. The right of surrender was not introduced as a limitation of liability, but, in Rome and Greece alike, payment was introduced as the alternative of a failure to surrender.

The action was not based, as it would be nowadays, on the fault of the parent or owner. If it had been, it would always have been brought against *the person who had control of the slave or animal at the time it did the harm complained of*, and who, if any one, was to blame for not preventing the injury. So far from this being the course, *the person to be sued was the owner at the time of suing*. The action followed the guilty thing into whosesoever hands it came. And in curious contrast with the principle as inverted to meet still more modern views of public policy, if the animal was of a wild nature, that is, in the very case of the most ferocious animals, the owner ceased to be liable the moment it escaped, because at that moment he ceased to be owner. There seems to have been no other or more extensive liability by the old law, even where a slave was guilty with his master's knowledge, unless perhaps he was a mere tool in his master's hands. Gaius and Ulpian showed an inclination to cut the *noxae deditio* down to a privilege of the owner in case of misdeeds committed without his knowledge; but Ulpian is obliged to admit, that by the ancient law, according to Celsus*, the action was noxal [compensation could be paid instead of surrendering the guilty party] where a slave was guilty even with the privity [knowledge] of his master.

All this shows very clearly that the liability of the owner was merely a way of getting at the slave or animal which was the immediate cause of offence. In other words, vengeance on the immediate offender was the object of the Greek and early Roman process, not indemnity from the master or owner. The liability of the owner was simply a liability of the offending thing. In the primitive customs of Greece it was enforced by a judicial process expressly directed against the object, animate or inanimate. The Roman Twelve Tables made the owner, instead of the thing itself, the defendant, but did not in any way change the ground of liability, or affect its limit. The change was simply a device to allow the owner to protect his interest.

Things Were Held Liable for Injuries
Expiation, Not Compensation

But it may be asked how inanimate objects came to be pursued in this way, if the object of the procedure was to gratify the passion of revenge. Learned men have been ready to find a reason in the personification of inanimate nature common to savages and children, and there is much to confirm this view. Without such a personification, anger towards lifeless things would have been transitory, at most. It is noticeable that the commonest example in the most primitive customs and laws is that of a tree which falls upon a man, or from which he falls and is killed. We can conceive with comparative ease how a tree might have been put on the same footing with animals. It certainly was treated like them, and was delivered to the relatives, or chopped to pieces for the gratification of a real or simulated passion.

In the Athenian process there is also, no doubt, to be traced a different thought. Expiation is one of the ends most insisted on by Plato, and appears to have been the purpose of the procedure mentioned by Aeschines. Some passages in the Roman historians which will be mentioned again seem to point in the same direction.

Another peculiarity to be noticed is that the liability seems to have been regarded as attached to the body doing the damage, in an almost physical sense. An untrained intelligence only imperfectly performs the analysis by which jurists carry responsibility back to the beginning of a chain of causation. The hatred for anything giving us pain, which wreaks itself on the manifest cause, and which leads even civilized man to kick a door when it pinches his finger, is embodied in the *noxae deditio* and other kindred doctrines of early Roman law. There is a defective passage [damaged, unclear section in the ancient manuscript] in Gaius, which seems to say that liability may sometimes be escaped by giving up even the dead body of the offender. So Livy* relates that Brutulus Papius having caused a breach of truce with the Romans, the Samnites* determined to surrender him, and that, upon his avoiding disgrace and punishment by suicide, they sent his lifeless body. It is noticeable that the surrender seems to be regarded as the natural expiation for the breach of treaty, and that it is equally a matter of course to send the body when the wrong-doer has perished....

Later Laws Spread Liability to Owners

[2] It will readily be imagined that such a system as has been described could not last when civilization had advanced to any considerable height. What had been the privilege of buying off vengeance by agreement, of paying the damage instead of surrendering the body of the offender, no doubt became a general custom. The Aquilian* law, passed about a couple of centuries later than the date of the Twelve Tables, enlarged the sphere of compensation for bodily injuries. Interpretation enlarged the Aquilian law. Masters became personally liable for certain wrongs committed by their slaves with their knowledge, where previously they were only bound to surrender the slave. If a pack-mule threw off his burden upon a passerby because he had been improperly overloaded, or a dog which might have been restrained escaped from his master and bit anyone, the old noxal action, as it was called, gave way to an action under the new law to enforce a general personal liability.

Still later, ship-owners and innkeepers were made liable as if they were wrong-doers for wrongs committed by those in their employ on board ship or in the tavern, although of course committed without their knowledge. The true reason for this exceptional responsibility was the exceptional confidence which was necessarily reposed in carriers and innkeepers. But some of the jurists, who regarded the surrender of children and slaves as a privilege intended to limit liability, explained this new liability on the ground that the innkeeper or ship-owner was to a certain degree guilty of negligence in having employed the services of bad men. This was the first instance of a master being made unconditionally liable for the wrongs of his servant. The reason given for it was of general application, and the principle expanded to the scope of the reason.

The law as to ship-owners and innkeepers introduced another and more startling innovation. It made them responsible when those whom they employed were free, as well as when they were slaves. For the first time one man was made answerable for the wrongs of another who was also answerable himself, and who had a standing before the law. This was a great change from the bare permission to ransom one's slave as a privilege. But here we have the history of the whole modem doctrine of master and servant, and principal and agent. All servants are now as free and as liable to a suit as their masters. Yet the principle introduced on special grounds in a special case, when servants were slaves, is now the general law of this country and England, and under it men daily have to pay large sums for other people's acts, in which they had no part and for which they are in no sense to blame. And to this day the reason offered by the Roman jurists for an exceptional rule is made to justify this universal and unlimited responsibility.

Limited Liability and Personification of Inanimate Things, Especially Ships

[3] We will now follow the history of that branch of the primitive notion which was least likely to survive—the liability of inanimate things.

It will be remembered that King Alfred* ordained the surrender of a tree, but that the later Scotch law refused it because a dead thing could not have guilt. It will be remembered, also, that the animals which the Scotch law forfeited* were escheat* [handed over] to the king. The same thing has remained true in England until well into this century, with regard even to inanimate objects. As long ago as Bracton, in case a man was slain, the coroner was to value the object causing the death, and that was to be forfeited as deodand* "*pro rege*." It was to be given to God, that is to say to the Church, for the king, to be expended for the good of his soul. A man's death had ceased to be the private affair of his friends as in the time of the barbarian folk laws. The king, who furnished the court, now sued for the penalty. He supplanted the family in the claim on the guilty thing, and the Church supplanted him.

In Edward* the First's time some of the cases remind us of the barbarian laws at their rudest stage. If a man fell from a tree, the tree was deodand. If he drowned in a well, the well was to be filled up. It did not matter that the forfeited instrument belonged to an innocent person. "Where a man killeth another with the sword of John at Stile, the sword shall be forfeit as deodand, and yet no default is in the owner." That is from a book written in the reign of Henry VII, about 1530. And it has been repeated from Queen Elizabeth's time to within one hundred years, that if my horse strikes a man, and afterwards I sell my horse, and after that the man dies, the horse shall be forfeited. Hence it is, that, in all indictments for homicide, until very lately it has been necessary to state the instrument causing the death and its value, as that the stroke was given by a certain penknife, value sixpence, so as to secure the forfeiture. It is said that a steam engine has been forfeited in this way.

I now come to what I regard as the most remarkable transformation of this principle, and one which is a most important factor in our law as it is today. I must for the moment leave the common law and take up the doctrines of the Admiralty*. In the early books which have just been referred to, and long afterwards, the fact of motion is adverted to as of much importance. A maxim of Henry Spigurnel, a judge in the time of Edward I, is reported, that "where a man is killed by a cart, or by the fall of a house, or in other like manner, and the thing in motion is the cause of the death, it shall be deodand." So it was said in the next reign that "omne illud quod movet cum eo quod occidit homines deodandum domino Regi erit, vel feodo clerici." ["Anything which moves and kills a man shall be handed over to God by the king, through the safekeeping of the clergy."] The reader sees how motion gives life to the object forfeited.

The most striking example of this sort is a ship. And accordingly the old books say that, if a man falls from a ship and is drowned, the motion of the ship must be taken to cause the death, and the ship is forfeited—provided, however, that this happens in fresh water. For if the death took place on the high seas, that was outside the ordinary jurisdiction. This proviso has been supposed to mean that ships at sea were not forfeited; but there is a long series of petitions to the king in Parliament that such forfeitures may be done away with, which tell a different story. The truth seems to be that the forfeiture took place, but in a different court. A manuscript of the reign of Henry VI, only recently printed, discloses the fact that, if a man was killed or drowned at sea by the motion of the ship, the vessel was forfeited to the admiral upon a proceeding in the admiral's court, and subject to release by favor of the admiral or the king.

A ship is the most living of inanimate things. Servants sometimes say "she" of a clock, but every one gives a gender to vessels. And we need not be surprised, therefore, to find a mode of dealing which has shown such extraordinary vitality in the criminal law applied with even more striking thoroughness in the Admiralty. It is only by supposing the ship to have been treated as if endowed with personality, that the arbitrary seeming peculiarities of the maritime law can be made intelligible, and on that supposition they at once become consistent and logical.

New Uses for Old Legal Doctrines

[4] By way of seeing what those peculiarities are, take first a case of collision at sea. A collision takes place between two vessels, the Ticonderoga and the Melampus, through the fault of the Ticonderoga alone. That ship is under a lease at the time, the lessee has his own master in charge, and the owner of the vessel has no manner of control over it. The owner, therefore, is

not to blame, and he cannot even be charged on the ground that the damage was done by his servants. He is free from personal liability on elementary principles. Yet it is perfectly settled that there is a lien on his vessel for the amount of the damage done, and this means that that vessel may be arrested and sold to pay the loss in any admiralty court whose process will reach her. [But common law is different.] If a livery stable keeper lets a horse and wagon to a customer, who runs a man down by careless driving, no one would think of claiming a right to seize the horse and wagon. It would be seen that the only property which could be sold to pay for a wrong was the property of the wrong-doer.

But, again, suppose that the vessel, instead of being under lease, is in charge of a pilot whose employment is made compulsory by the laws of the port which she is just entering. The Supreme Court of the United States holds the ship liable in this instance also. The English courts would probably have decided otherwise, and the matter is settled in England by legislation. But there the court of appeal, the Privy Council, has been largely composed of common-law lawyers, and it has shown a marked tendency to assimilate common-law doctrine. At common law one who could not impose a personal liability on the owner could not bind a particular chattel [personal property] to answer for a wrong of which it had been the instrument. But our Supreme Court has long recognized that a person may bind a ship, when he could not bind the owners personally, because he was not their agent.

It may be admitted that, if this doctrine were not supported by an appearance of good sense, it would not have survived. The ship is the only security available in dealing with foreigners, and rather than send one's own citizens to search for a remedy abroad in strange courts, it is easy to seize the vessel and satisfy the claim at home, leaving the foreign owners to get their indemnity as they may be able. I dare say some such thought has helped to keep the practice alive, but I believe the true historic foundation is elsewhere. The ship no doubt, like a sword, would have been forfeited for causing death, in whosesoever hands it might have been. So, if the master and mariners of a ship, furnished with letters of reprisal*, committed piracy against a friend of the king, the owner lost his ship by the admiralty law, although the crime was committed without his knowledge or assent. It seems most likely that the principle by which the ship was forfeited to the king for causing death, or for piracy, was the same as that by which it was bound to private sufferers for other damage, in whose hands soever it might have been when it did the harm.

If we should say to an uneducated man today, "She did it and she ought to pay for it," it may be doubted whether he would see the fallacy, or be ready to explain that the ship was only property, and that to say, "The ship has to pay for it," was simply a dramatic way of saying that somebody's property was to be sold, and the proceeds applied to pay for a wrong committed by somebody else.

It would seem that a similar form of words has been enough to satisfy the minds of great lawyers. The following is a passage from a judgment by Chief Justice Marshall,* which is quoted with approval by Judge Storey* in giving the opinion of the Supreme Court of the United States: "This is not a proceeding against the owner; it is a proceeding against the vessel for an offence committed by the vessel; which is not the less an offence, and does not the less subject her to forfeiture, because it was committed without the authority and against the will of the owner. It is true that inanimate matter can commit no offence. But this body is animated and put in action by the crew, who are guided by the master. The vessel acts and speaks by the master. She reports herself by the master. It is, therefore, not unreasonable that the vessel should be affected by this report." And again Judge Storey quotes from another case: "The thing is here primarily considered as the offender, or rather the offence is primarily attached to the thing."

In other words, those great judges, although of course aware that a ship is no more alive than a mill-wheel, thought that not only the law did in fact deal with it as if it were alive, but that it was reasonable that the law should do so. The reader will observe that they do not say simply that it is reasonable on grounds of policy to sacrifice justice to the owner to security for somebody else, but that it is reasonable to deal with the vessel as an offending thing. Whatever the hidden ground of policy may be, their thought still clothes itself in personifying language.

Let us now go on to follow the peculiarities of the maritime law in other directions. For the cases which have been stated are only parts of a larger whole.

By the maritime law of the Middle Ages the ship was not only the source, but the limit, of liability. The rule already prevailed, which has been borrowed and adopted by the English statutes and by our own act of Congress of 1851, according to which the owner is discharged from responsibility for wrongful acts of a master appointed by himself upon surrendering his interest in the vessel and the freight [payment for shipping] which she had earned. By the doctrines of agency he would be personally liable for the whole damage. If the origin of the system of limited* liability which is believed to be so essential to modern commerce is to be attributed to those considerations of public policy on which it would now be sustained, that system has nothing to do with the law of collision. But if the limit of liability here stands on the same ground as the noxae deditio, it confirms the explanation already given of the liability of the ship for wrongs done by it while out of the owner's hands, and conversely the existence of that liability confirms the argument here....

Adapting Laws to Support Sensible Policies

The foregoing history, apart from the purposes for which it has been given, well illustrates the paradox of form [outward appearance] and substance [inner reality] in the development of law. In form its growth is logical. The official theory is that each new decision follows syllogistically from existing precedents. But just as the clavicle in the cat only tells of the existence of some earlier creature to which a collarbone was useful, precedents survive in the law long after the use they once served is at an end and the reason for them has been forgotten. The result of following them must often be failure and confusion from the merely logical point of view.

On the other hand, in substance the growth of the law is legislative. And this in a deeper sense than that what the courts declare to have always been the law is in fact new. It is legislative in its grounds. The very considerations which judges most rarely mention, and always with an apology, are the secret root from which the law draws all the juices of life. I mean, of course, considerations of what is expedient for the community concerned. Every important principle which is developed by litigation is in fact and at bottom the result of more or less definitely understood views of public policy, most generally, to be sure, under our practice and traditions, the unconscious result of instinctive preferences and inarticulate convictions, but none the less traceable to views of public policy in the last analysis. And as the law is administered by able and experienced men, who know too much to sacrifice good sense to a syllogism, it will be found that, when ancient rules maintain themselves in the way that has been and will be shown in this book, new reasons more fitted to the time have been found for them, and that they gradually receive a new content, and at last a new form, from the grounds to which they have been transplanted.

But hitherto this process has been largely unconscious. It is important, on that account, to bring to mind what the actual course of events has been. If it were only to insist on a more conscious recognition of the legislative function of the courts, as just explained, it would be useful, as we shall see more clearly further on.

What has been said will explain the failure of all theories which consider the law only from its formal side, whether they attempt to deduce the *corpus** from *a priori* postulates, or fall into the humbler error of supposing the science of the law to reside in the *elegantia* juris*, or logical cohesion of part with part. The truth is, that the law is always approaching, and never reaching, consistency. It is forever adopting new principles from life at one end, and it always retains old ones from history at the other which have not yet been absorbed or sloughed off. It will become entirely consistent only when it ceases to grow.

Glossary of Names and Terms

Glossary items are in alphabetical order.

Admiralty: the branch of English government in charge of maritime matters. The "Admiral" is the official in charge of the Admiralty. The Admiralty has its own courts which conduct trials related to incidents or lawsuits concerning ships. "The doctrines of the Admiralty" are, in effect, the law of the sea. Holmes' own Boston law practice included cases involving ships and related matters of the law of the sea.

Aeschines: 389–314 B.C. Athenian orator and politician who favored policies which helped Philip of Macedonia's conquest of Greece. He was charged with treason by Demosthenes but acquitted.

Alfred ("King Alfred ordained the surrender of a tree"): under the laws of King Alfred (ninth century English king), a tree which was involved in the death of a man had to be surrendered to the man's relatives. Trees were valuable property.

Appeals for personal violence: cases brought to court in which the charge was assault.

Aquilian law: Aquilia was an important city in Italy in the Roman Empire.

Austin: John Austin (1790–1859), English jurist who wrote commentaries on the English law.

Baker's man: employee of a baker who used horse and wagon to deliver bread house to house in the early morning hours.

Blackstone: Sir William Blackstone (1723–1780), English jurist, whose commentaries on the English law were the basic text for training lawyers in England and America well into the nineteenth century.

Blood feud: If A sheds the blood of B, then someone from B's family must shed the blood of A or one of A's relatives.

Bracton: Henry de Bracton, 13th century writer of commentaries on the English laws. Bracton made considerable use of Roman law in his commentaries, creating the illusion that English law had deeper roots in Roman law.

Celsus: Aulus Cornelius Celsus, first century A.D., author of an encyclopedia covering agriculture, military science, medicine, rhetoric, philosophy, and law.

Corporations: Modern law regards a corporation as a person. A corporation, not the owners or share holders, is held liable for its actions.

Corpus ("the *corpus*"): Latin for "body." In this case, the body of laws, the legal code as a whole.

Decemvirs: Ten men commissioned to codify the laws of Rome in 451 B.C.

Demosthenes: 384–322 B.C. Athenian orator and statesman, opposed to Philip of Macedonia's conquest of Greece. Demosthenes advocated an independent Athens. He was a bitter opponent of Aeschines. At the end of a tempestuous career, implicated in rebellion, Demosthenes committed suicide by poison.

Deodand: An object involved in a crime, such as a knife, was forfeited to the king, who in turn gave it to God by giving it to a church or monastery. "Deodand pro rege" (Latin) means "handed over to God" (deodand) "on behalf of the king" (pro rege).

Draco: Seventh century B.C. Draco wrote the first Athenian law code.

Edward the First: Edward I became King of England in 1272.

Elegantia juris (Latin): The "elegance" or logical consistency of the laws.

Escheit: The modern spelling is "escheat." Ownership of property goes to the king or to the state, particularly when someone dies without heirs.

Forfeited ("animals which the Scotch law forfeited"): Animals which did harm had to be surrendered according to old Scottish law.

Gaius: 110–180 A.D. (dates ?) Roman jurist, commentator on the Roman laws.

Glanville: 12th century writer of commentaries on the English laws.

Limited liability ("The system of limited liability which is believed to be so essential to modern commerce"): limiting the liability of a corporation to the corporate assets. The modern corporation is considered to be a "person" in matters of law. Thus corporations, not their owners, are liable for the actions of corporations. For example, a lawsuit against a corporation is against the assets of the corporation, not a suit against individual owners or stockholders. "Limited liability partnerships" are somewhat similar.

Livy: Titus Livius, 59 B.C.-A.D. 19, Roman historian.

Marshall: John Marshall, born 1755, Chief Justice of the U.S. Supreme Court from 1801 until his death in 1835. Marshall established the Supreme Court's right to rule on the constitutionality of actions by the President (Marbury v. Madison) and the Congress.

Noxae deditio: Latin legal term denoting that a thing, animal, slave or child which has done some harm must be handed over for punishment. This later developed into the legal doctrine that an owner or employer is to be held liable for some harm or damages.

Pausanius: c. 150 A.D. Greek traveler, geographer and historian, who wrote a history of the Olympic games and a ten volume travelogue entitled *Descriptions of Greece*.

Plato: 427–347 B.C. Greek philosopher, whose writings included *The Republic*, a description of a model government and an extended discussion of what is justice.

Plutarch: 46–120 A.D. (?) Greek who wrote biographies of famous Greeks and Romans as inspirational works, commonly known as *Plutarch's Lives*.

Prytaneum: A building in Athens (and other ancient Greek cities) like a town hall with a hearth kept burning at all times and a public meeting hall. In some places it also served as a publicly supported dining hall for certain people, such as past winners of Olympic games.

Quit ("The owner of the ox shall be quit."): free from any further liability (The owner shall be free from any further liability).

Reports: Written records of trials.

Reprisal (letters of reprisal): Authorization from a government to attack merchant ships of an enemy country. Letters of reprisal used to be given to private ships in wartime. The private ships with letters of reprisal acted as mercenaries. It was a legal form of piracy in wartime.

Samnites: Ancient people who inhabited the central part of the Italian peninsula.

Solon: 638–559 B.C. Lawmaker of Athens, whose biography was included in Plutarch's work.

Storey: Joseph Storey, born in 1779, Massachusetts lawyer, author of legal commentaries, appointed Associate Justice of the Supreme Court in 1811 and served until his death in 1845.

Syllogism: A three-step form of logic, as in this example: (1) Major premise: All figures with three sides are triangles. (2) Minor premise: This particular figure has three sides. (3) Conclusion: This particular figure is a triangle.

Trespass: One person's offense against another, any offense.

Twelve Tables: The twelve tables (stone tablets set up in the marketplace) to proclaim the laws of Rome, the ancient Roman law code which every Roman boy had to memorize.

Ulpian: Domitius Ulpianus, died 228 A.D. (?). Roman jurist and commentator on the law.

Introduction to
Felix Frankfurter

Oliver Wendell Holmes, Jr. was the father figure of a group of judges and lawyers who changed American government. The group included Louis Brandeis, Benjamin Cardozo and Felix Frankfurter. After Harvard Law School, Louis Brandeis had been a very successful Boston lawyer. Brandeis was appointed a Supreme Court Justice in 1916. On the court Brandeis was a strong legal ally of Holmes. Together they stood for legal realism and "judicial restraint," the doctrine that judges should be very reluctant to overturn acts of a legislature. Brandeis was famous for writing legal opinions replete with social and economic arguments, legal cross-references and footnotes. Among lawyers the term "a Brandeis opinion" became a way of describing any very exhaustive legal opinion which sorted out details and traced precedents painstakingly before arriving at a decision.

Benjamin Cardozo was educated at Columbia University and admitted to the bar in 1891. Cardozo was an elected New York Supreme Court judge before he replaced Holmes on the U.S. Supreme Court when Holmes retired in 1932. Quite different from the meticulous Brandeis in legal style when formulating opinions, Cardozo cherished the broad general principles of the law as it had developed through history and the inherent flexibility of the U.S. Constitution. Whereas Brandeis wrote for lawyers, Cardozo wrote for the general public. Cardozo was highly regarded for his literary style. His best known writing was an essay entitled, ("The Law as Literature.") Cardozo believed that the major function of the law was to be a teacher and guide to life. Hence, he believed that judges' decisions should be written in a beautiful style that would inspire people to follow the law.

Felix Frankfurter was born in Vienna, Austria on November 15, 1882. His family emigrated to the United States in 1894. Frankfurter graduated from the City College of New York in 1902 and from Harvard University Law School in 1906. At the Law School he became a student and disciple of Louis Brandeis. Upon admission to the bar, Frankfurter became an Assistant United States Attorney in New York under Henry L. Stimson. When Stimson became Secretary of War in 1911, before the beginning of the First World War, Frankfurter followed him to Washington. In 1914 Frankfurter accepted an appointment as a professor of law at Harvard, a post he retained until 1939. However, he took a leave from Harvard in 1917 during World War I to serve in Washington as counsel to the Industrial Mediation Board and then served for the next two years as chairman of the War Labor Policies Board. While still on leave from

Harvard, Frankfurter persuaded President Woodrow Wilson to send him to the Paris Peace Conference at the end of the war. Frankfurter maneuvered to obtain a diplomatic assignment and negotiated a Zionist-Arab agreement with T.E. Lawrence, known as Lawrence of Arabia, who represented the Bedouin King Faisal.

Frankfurter returned to Harvard in 1919. He became one of the founders of The American Civil Liberties Union in 1920. Later he served as an advisor to the National Consumers League and the National Association for the Advancement of Colored People. At Harvard, Frankfurter was a prolific writer for scholarly legal journals and a constant contributor to *The New Republic*, a journal of political opinion. As a civil libertarian Frankfurter protested the unfairness of the legal proceedings in the highly publicized Boston trial of alleged anarchists Sacco and Vanzetti in a March 1927 article in *The Atlantic Monthly*, which later appeared as a book. Frankfurter wrote annual summaries of Supreme Court cases, a definitive text on labor law, and coauthored a book about the Supreme Court.

Although many Americans today think of the Constitution as a liberal document which protects individual rights, for its first 150 years the Constitution was mainly the tool of southern plantation owners and northern industrialists intent on holding down the urban and rural poor, blacks, women and child laborers. The Constitutional clauses protecting the sovereignty of states, contracts of all kinds, and virtually unlimited property rights kept blacks in servitude for many generations after the Civil War ended, blocked women from voting, kept farmers agonizing under the yokes of rapacious banks and railroad shippers, and left children toiling in sweatshops for decades. The Constitution was the scourge of the underclass.

When Franklin D. Roosevelt became President in 1932, the United States was caught in a worldwide depression. Roosevelt believed that the government should take a very active role in leading the country out of the depression, instead of leaving the economy in the hands of private capitalists. Traditional law emphasized that government should not interfere with the freely negotiated contracts between industry and workers. Radical new ideas, based mostly on European models, like legally mandated minimum wages, legally mandated contributions to government managed unemployment and disability insurance, and a social security system were generally considered unconstitutional. To protect his new programs from Constitutional challenges in the courts, Roosevelt proposed legislation to force Supreme Court justices to retire at age seventy or else be supplemented by additional justices. He would appoint new justices who favored his programs. Congress eventually rejected this attempt to enlarge the Supreme Court, but popular sentiment was so much for it that "the nine old men" of the Court feared for their future and quickly changed their constitutional opinions, prompting the remark, "A switch in time saves nine."

Within the next few years Roosevelt was able to appoint a number of new justices to the Supreme Court, creating a more liberal Supreme Court and, hence, a more liberal reinvention of the Constitution. Brandeis and Frankfurter were among the judges and lawyers who agreed with Roosevelt's political philosophy that the federal government should take the leading role in the economy. Frankfurter maintained frequent contact and correspondence with Roosevelt. Brandeis, Frankfurter and their students provided legal arguments and legal counsel to further Roosevelt's "New Deal" policies. In 1939 Frankfurter gave up his post at Harvard when Roosevelt appointed him an Associate Justice of the Supreme Court.

Long before arriving at the Supreme Court Frankfurter had expressed his opinion that the courts should be very reluctant to declare laws unconstitutional. Most of the time when the Supreme Court had declared laws unconstitutional the laws which were invalidated were those which attempted to curb the powers of the commercial and industrial upper classes, such as laws against child labor. (The Constitution prohibited interfering with private contracts.) Although the north had won the Civil War militarily, the south joined hands with the "robber barons" of the north to control the country for the next hundred years. (The Congress, especially the Senate, blocked nearly all laws giving rights or benefits to the underclasses, black or white.) On the rare occasions when liberal legislation could not be blocked, the courts could be counted on to nullify the law. Working class Americans had a very low opinion of Congress and the courts. Black veterans of World War I and World War II were not the only ones who felt that the democracy which America claimed to fight for abroad was seriously deficient at home. The Constitution had become the protective mantel of individual states and industrial magnates who wanted no interference by the federal government in their affairs.

Frankfurter sided with the growing view expressed in the 1890s by James Bradley Thayer, later expressed albeit in dissent by Oliver Wendell Holmes, Jr. and still later by Louis Brandeis and Chief Justice Harlan F. Stone, that where there was a reasonable basis for the enactment of a law the courts had no right to overrule it. Frankfurter stuck to this view even when a law seemed to infringe on some constitutional rights. He often reminded the Court that Congress and the state legislatures were also responsible for the preservation of liberty. However, in cases involving criminal confessions, police searches and seizures Frankfurter insisted on strict observance of constitutional limits. He was also stalwart in defense of political and academic freedom. Frankfurter's civil liberties record was somewhat bewildering, for sometimes he sided with the liberal Justices and sometimes with the conservative Justices when voting on civil liberties cases. (This may have been a consequence of a philosophy of law based more on social policies and legislative acts than on legal principles.) Illness compelled Frankfurter to retire from the Court in 1962. He died in Washington on February 22, 1965.

Frankfurter's legacy was tarnished in 1982 when Bruce A. Murphy published an investigative study, *The Brandeis/Frankfurter Connection: The Secret Political Activities of Two Supreme Court Justices.* Prior to that publication Frankfurter had been seen as a paragon of judicial virtues. Indeed, Frankfurter had presented himself in his letters to friends as a person whose role as judge required him to remain above politics. Then as now, a judge was expected to avoid political entanglements. In fact, however, Frankfurter could not restrain his political zeal to work with Brandeis behind the scenes to control the course of government activities through his direct connection with President Roosevelt and through the former students who were placed in federal agencies as legal counsel.

While Frankfurter was still a professor at Harvard, Justice Brandeis had enlisted him as his associate in a campaign to redefine the role of government. Brandeis wanted the federal government to take an active role in what is now called "nation building" in the western part of the United States. To Brandeis the west had the noble characteristics of freedom and individualism and liberty but not the financial resources necessary to build a great society. Much of the west was as undeveloped as many countries of South America or Asia. For example, there were minimal roads, no electricity, no great irrigation systems to support farming. It seemed to Brandeis that only the federal government had the resources to develop the west, but that would require the federal government to step far beyond the role of government envisioned by the Constitution. It took Supreme Court decisions to clear the path for the federal government to engage in businesses related to nation building, such as building dams on the great rivers of America to generate electricity and control irrigation for farming.

Frankfurter shared Brandeis' enthusiasm for developing the west. It was the idea that government could legitimately engage in nation building which also transformed Frankfurter from a rather low key Jewish believer to an ardent advocate of Zionism and supporter of the state of Israel, as Brandeis was. To them these were opportunities to create new utopian societies. With this shared passion for nation building, Brandeis and Frankfurter worked together for over twenty-five years to place their protégés in positions of influence so that they could shape government policy in these matters. Some became law clerks to Supreme Court Justices, and many became clerks with other federal judges. Many became legal counsel to government agencies. After Frankfurter himself became a Justice of the Supreme Court he continued to use his personal influence to place promising young lawyers with compatible convictions in the legal departments of federal agencies, thus guiding the agencies to enlarge their activities, increasing and strengthening the role of the federal government in American society.

Some Reflections on the Reading of Statutes was first delivered as a lecture in honor of Benjamin Cardozo. It was intended to guide judges and lawyers in the murky area of how to interpret written laws. (Interpreting laws is also called "constructing statutes.") To construct a statute is to interpret it. Blackstone's (1765) commentaries had guided most judges through the eighteenth century with five simple rules explained in less than three pages: (1) Words are to be understood as they are usually used among ordinary people. (2) If doubts persist, the context may clarify the meaning of a word. (3) The particular subject matter of a law may help determine the meaning of any technical word. (4) If the consequences of taking any words literally are absurd, one must deviate a little from the literal meaning. (5) When still in doubt about the meaning of a law, one should consider the reason and spirit of it and the causes which moved the legislator to enact it. Blackstone noted that when Roman judges were in doubt about the meaning or application of a law, (the judge had to put the case in writing and ask for the emperor's opinion on it.) The emperor's responses were called "rescripts" and then had the force of law. But Blackstone was against such a practice: "To interrogate the legislature to decide particular disputes, is not only endless, but affords great room for partiality and oppression" (Vol. 1, p. 58).

For the interpretation of the common law and for the interpretation of statutes, over the centuries judges established hundreds of rules, called "canons." Some canons were very simple, such as, "A statute which changes the common law must be interpreted narrowly." Other canons might refer to a specialized area of law or introduce subtle distinctions, such as, "A penal statute may not be so broadened by judicial construction as to make it cover and permit the punishment of an act which is not denounced by the fair import of its terms.(From these examples one may appreciate that canons do not make the interpretation of law simple or automatic. They merely provide some guidelines for a judge.)

By the end of the eighteenth century the common law of England and America had lost its usefulness. To understand the common law required extraordinary knowledge, and to apply the common law to new cases required great skill in the contorted reasoning of common law judges and lawyers. The common law had begotten too many subtle distinctions, tortuous procedures and legal fictions in the effort to hold onto ancient legal baggage. The Age of Enlightenment called for laws which could be understood by ordinary people. Vigorous efforts to replace the English common law with plainly written statutes had been the goal of reformers such as the Puritans in seventeenth century England. At the start of the nineteenth century Napoleon simplified French law and organized it into a comprehensive legal code. Envy and admiration of the *code Napoleon* prompted many American lawyers and legislators to push the movement from common law to law in the form of a code of statutes. Over the course of the nineteenth century the common law was almost entirely replaced by statutory law in the United States.

The problem of how to interpret laws remained even after the transition from common law made largely by judges to statutes enacted by elected legislatures. Common law decisions strove to be consistent with earlier law, whereas statutes may introduce abrupt changes. In creating statutes legislators find it difficult to imagine all the different situations in which a law might be applied, yet they must settle on some specific wording. Legislators are also prodded to make laws by lobbyists and political campaign contributors who have special interests in having certain laws made. In addition, elected legislators must cater to voters who may favor certain laws. In election years it is fairly common for legislators to pass laws which are tough on crime in order to gather votes. Sometimes, as in the federal Omnibus Crime Control Act of 1968, laws are passed by legislators although the legislators themselves know that the laws are unconstitutional and will be struck down by the courts as soon as anyone tries to apply them. Such a political strategy enhances the public reputation of the legislators but makes the courts look soft on crime in the eyes of the public.

In addition, Frankfurter complained that legislators sometimes passed laws which the legislators themselves did not understand, leaving it to the courts to figure out what the laws mean and how to apply them. The problem of biased and bad legislation creates special problems in the interpretation of statutes. One hundred years ago many thought that the transition from common law to statutory law would make the law simpler and easier to interpret. But statutory law may be guided less by reason and consistency than the common law, making it at least as difficult to interpret and apply to particular cases.

To Frankfurter the interpretation of statutes seems to have been more an art than a science. He pointed out that the proper way to study art is to look at the works of the great masters. Similarly, he suggested, one may learn best how to interpret statutes by looking at how the great masters of the law have done it. In particular, Frankfurter suggested that one should look at how laws were interpreted by three great masters: Holmes, Cardozo and Brandeis. According to Frankfurter, there were differences in style between these three judges, but they agreed on basic principles which should govern the interpretation of statutes. Frankfurter's approach in "The Reading of Statutes" was to state principles and then illustrate them mainly from cases decided by Holmes, Cardozo and Brandeis.

Although Frankfurter rejected the notion that the real lawmaker is the judge who interprets a law, the reader may wonder to what extent laws have definite meanings and to what extent laws may be interpreted to fit preconceived ideas of a judge. Frankfurter raised the question of whether there can be hard and fast rules, or canons, to govern the interpretation of statutes, and whether hard and fast rules would be desirable. Debates about mandatory sentencing are part of this dilemma. The reader must also consider the implications of Frankfurter's principles about the duties of judges versus the duties of lawmakers, especially in a diverse society where there might be a tyranny of the majority over minorities or a tyranny of the upper classes over the lower classes. From time to time politicians may complain about "activist" judges who seem to be making laws instead of simply interpreting statutes, particularly if judges' decisions are contrary to the politicians' positions. Should judges view themselves as servants of the legislature, as suggested by Frankfurter, rather than independent ministers of justice? In the British and U.S. legal systems, where precedents determine the decisions in future cases, is the role of judges inevitably more legislative than in legal systems which do not honor precedents? Are these systems of government more or less democratic than the U.S. system? In a somewhat complicated discussion of what is meant by the "intention" of a law, Frankfurter skirted the perennial issue of how much a judge should follow the intention or "spirit" of a law versus the "letter" of a law. Frankfurter ended his lecture on the interpretation of statutes by saying that society's ultimate protection against abuses in judicial interpretation is to entrust this task "only to those who are equal to the demands." Was that a despairing conclusion that there can be no firm guidelines for interpreting laws? Is it a legal fiction that law is objective rather than subjective interpretations by various judges? Should steps be taken to end the practice of "judge shopping" by both prosecutors and lawyers, in which they try to get cases heard by a particular judge whose positions on various issues are well known to them? Should judges be elected?

Reference

Murphy, B.A. (1982). *The Brandeis/Frankfurter connection: The secret political activities of two Supreme Court Justices.* New York: Oxford University Press.

Felix Frankfurter. (1947). The reading of statutes. *Record of the Association of the Bar of the City of New York, 2,* 213–239. Reprinted with permission from The Record of The Association of the Bar of the City of New York (c) 1947, 2 The Record 6. Section titles have been added. Italics have been added to provide emphasis in some places. Any text in square brackets has been added by the editors.

Felix Frankfurter

The Reading of Statutes

The Change from Common Law to Statutory Law

A single volume of 320 octavo pages contains all the laws passed by Congress during its first five years, when measures were devised for getting the new government under way; 26 acts were passed in the 1789 session, 66 in 1790, 94 in 1791, 38 in 1792, 63 in 1793. For the single session of the 70th Congress [1928], to take a pre-Depression period, there are 993 enactments in a monstrous volume of 1,014 pages—quarto [four pages per printer's sheet] not octavo [eight pages per printer's sheet]—with a comparable range of subject matter. Do you wonder that one for whom the statutes at large constitute his staple reading should have sympathy, at least in his moments of baying at the moon, with the touching Congressman who not so long ago proposed a "Commission on Centralization" to report whether "the Government has departed from the concept of the founding fathers" and what steps should be taken "to restore the Government to its original purposes and sphere of activity"?

Inevitably the work of the Supreme Court reflects the great shift in the center of gravity of law-making. Broadly speaking, the number of cases disposed of by opinions has not changed from term to term. But even as late as 1875 more than 40 per cent of the controversies before the Court were common-law litigation [legal cases based on common law], fifty years later only 5 per cent, while today cases not resting on statutes are reduced almost to zero. (It is therefore accurate to say that courts have ceased to be the primary makers of law in the sense in which they "legislated" the common law) It is certainly true of the Supreme Court that almost every case has a statute [a law enacted by a legislature] at its heart or close to it.

Language and Other Difficulties of Interpreting Statutes

This does not mean that every case before the Court involves questions of statutory construction [interpretation of laws enacted by a legislature]. If only literary perversity or jaundiced partisanship can sponsor a particular rendering of a statute there is no problem. When we talk of statutory construction we have in mind cases in which there is a fair contest between two readings, neither of which comes without respectable title deeds. A problem in statutory construction can seriously bother courts only when there is a contest between probabilities of meaning.

Though it has its own preoccupations and its own mysteries, and above all its own jargon, judicial construction ought not to be torn from its wider, nonlegal context. Anything that is written may present a problem of meaning, and that is the essence of the business of judges in construing legislation. The problem derives from the very nature of words. They are symbols of meaning. But unlike mathematical symbols, the phrasing of a document, especially a complicated enactment, seldom attains more than approximate precision....

The difficulties are inherent not only in the nature of words, of composition, and of legislation generally. They are often intensified by the subject matter of an enactment. The imagination which can draw an income tax statute to cover the myriad transactions of a society like ours, capable of producing the necessary revenue without producing a flood of litigation, has not yet revealed itself.[2] Moreover, government sometimes solves problems by shelving them temporarily. The legislative process reflects that attitude. Statutes as well as constitutional provisions at times embody purposeful ambiguity or are expressed with a generality for future unfolding....

The intrinsic difficulties of language and the emergence after enactment of situations not anticipated by the most gifted legislative imagination reveal doubts and ambiguities in statutes that compel judicial construction [interpretation]. The process of construction, therefore, is not an exercise in logic or dialectic: the aids of formal reasoning are not irrelevant; they may simply be inadequate. (The purpose of construction being the ascertainment of meaning, every consideration brought to bear for the solution of that problem must be devoted to that end alone)

To speak of it as a practical problem is not to indulge a fashion in words. It must be that, not something else; not, for instance, an opportunity for a judge to use words as "empty vessels into which he can pour anything he will"—his caprices, fixed notions, even statesmanlike beliefs in a particular policy. Nor, on the other hand, is the process a ritual to be observed by unimaginative adherence to well-born professional phrases. To be sure, it is inescapably a problem in the keeping of the legal profession and subject to all the limitations of our adversary system of adjudication. When the judge, selected by society to give meaning to what the legislature has done, examines the statute, he does so not in a laboratory or in a classroom. Damage has been done or exactions made, interests are divided, passions have been aroused, sides have been taken. But the judge, if he is worth his salt, must be above the battle....

Lessons from the Masters:
How Holmes, Brandeis, and Cardozo Constructed Statutes

When one wants to understand or at least get the feeling of great painting, one does not go to books on the art of painting. One goes to the great masters. And so I have gone to great masters to get a sense of their practice of the art of interpretation....

And so I have examined the opinions of Holmes, Brandeis, and Cardozo and sought to derive from their treatment of legislation what conclusions I could fairly draw, freed as much as I could be from impressions I had formed in the course of the years.

Holmes came to the Supreme Court before the great flood of recent legislation, while the other two, especially Cardozo, appeared at its full tide. The shift in the nature of the Court's business led to changes in its jurisdiction, resulting in a concentration of cases involving the legislative process. Proportionately to their length of service and the number of opinions, Brandeis and Cardozo had many more statutes to construe. And the statutes presented for their interpretation became increasingly complex, bringing in their train a quantitatively new role for administrative regulations. Nevertheless, the earliest opinions of Holmes on statutory construction, insofar as he reveals himself, cannot be distinguished from Cardozo's last opinion, though the latter's process is more explicit....

If it be suggested that Mr. Justice Holmes is often swift, if not cavalier, in his treatment of statutes, there are those who level the same criticism against his opinions generally. It is merited in the sense that he wrote, as he said, for those learned in the art. I need hardly add that for him "learned" was not a formal term comprehending the whole legal fraternity. When dealing with problems of statutory construction also he illumined whole areas of doubt and darkness with insights enduringly expressed, however briefly. To say "We agree to all the generalities about not supplying criminal laws with what they omit, but there is no canon against using common sense in construing laws as saying what they obviously mean"[8] is worth more than most of the dreary writing on how to construe penal legislation. Again when he said that "the meaning of a sentence is to be felt rather than to be proved,"[9] he expressed the wholesome truth that the final rendering of the meaning of a statute is an act of judgment. He would shudder at the thought that by such a statement he was giving comfort to the school of visceral jurisprudence.

Judgment is not drawn out of the void but is based on the correlation of imponderables, all of which need not, because they cannot, be made explicit. He was expressing the humility of the intellectual that he was, whose standards of exactitude distrusted pretensions of certainty, believing that legal controversies that are not frivolous almost always involve matters of degree, and often degree of the nicest sort. Statutory construction implied the exercise of choice, but precluded the notion of capricious choice as much as choice based on private notions of policy. One gets the impression that in interpreting statutes *Mr. Justice Holmes reached meaning easily, as was true of most of his results, with emphasis on the language in the totality of the enactment and the felt reasonableness of the chosen construction.* He had a lively awareness that a statute was expressive of purpose and policy, but in his reading of it he tended to hug the shores of the statute itself, without much re-enforcement from without.

Mr. Justice Brandeis, on the other hand, in dealing with these problems as with others, would elucidate the judgment he was exercising by proof or detailed argument. In such instances, especially when in dissent, his opinions would draw on the whole arsenal of aids to construction.(More often than either Holmes or Cardozo, Brandeis would invoke the additional weight of some "rule" of construction.)But he never lost sight of the limited scope and function of such "rules." Occasionally, however, perhaps because of the nature of a particular statute, the minor importance of its incidence, the pressure of judicial business, or even the temperament of his law clerk, whom he always treated as a co-worker, Brandeis disposed of a statute even more dogmatically, with less explicit elucidation, than did Holmes.

For Cardozo, statutory construction was an acquired taste. He preferred common-law subtleties, having great skill in bending them to modern uses. But he came to realize that problems of statutory construction had their own exciting subtleties and gave ample employment to philosophic and literary talents. Cardozo's elucidation of how meaning is drawn out of a statute gives proof of the wisdom and balance which, combined with his learning, made him a great judge. While the austere style of Brandeis seldom mitigated the dry aspect of so many problems of statutory construction, Cardozo managed to endow even these with the glow and softness of his writing. The differences in the tone and color of their style as well as in the moral intensity of Brandeis and Cardozo became apparent when they wrote full-dress opinions on problems of statutory construction. Brandeis almost compels by demonstration; Cardozo woos by persuasion.

The Judicial Function in a Democracy: Freedom and Restraint

From the hundreds of cases in which our three Justices construed statutes one thing clearly emerges. The area of free judicial movement is considerable. These three remembered that laws are not abstract propositions. They are expressions of policy arising out of specific situations and addressed to the attainment of particular ends. The difficulty is that the legislative ideas which laws embody are both explicit and immanent. And so the bottom problem is: What is below the surface of the words and yet fairly a part of them? Words in statutes are not unlike words in a foreign language in that they too have "associations, echoes, and overtones."[10] Judges must retain the associations, hear the echoes, and capture the overtones. In one of his very last opinions, dealing with legislation taxing the husband on the basis of the combined income of husband and wife, Holmes wrote: "The statutes are the outcome of a thousand years of history.... They form a system with echoes of different moments, none of which is entitled to prevail over the other."[11]

What exactions such a duty of construction places upon judges, and with what freedom it entrusts them! John Chipman Gray was fond of quoting from a sermon by Bishop Hoadley that "Whoever hath an absolute authority to interpret any written or spoken laws, it is he who is truly the lawgiver to all intents and purposes, and not the person who first wrote or spoke them."[12] By admitting that there is some substance to the good Bishop's statement, one does *not* subscribe to the notion that they are lawgivers in any but a very qualified sense.

Even within their area of choice the courts are not at large. They are confined by the nature and scope of the judicial function in its particular exercise in the field of interpretation. They are under the constraints imposed by the judicial function in our democratic society. As a matter of verbal recognition certainly, no one will gainsay that *the function in construing a statute is to ascertain the meaning of words used by the legislature. To go beyond it is to usurp a power which our democracy has lodged in its elected legislature.* The great judges have constantly admonished their brethren of the need for discipline in observing the limitations. A judge must not rewrite a statute, neither to enlarge nor to contract it. (Whatever temptations the statesmanship of policy-making might wisely suggest, construction must eschew interpolation and evisceration.) He must not read in by way of creation. He must not read out except to avoid patent nonsense or internal contradiction. "If there is no meaning in it," said Alice's King [in *Alice in Wonderland*], "that saves a world of trouble, you know, as we needn't try to find any." Legislative words presumably have meaning and so we must try to find it.

This duty of restraint, this humility of function as merely the translator of another's command is a constant theme of our Justices. It is on the lips of all judges, but seldom, I venture to believe, has the restraint which it expresses, or the duty which it enjoins, been observed with so consistent a realization that its observance depends on self-conscious discipline. Cardozo put it this way: "We do not pause to consider whether a statute differently conceived and framed would yield results more consonant with fairness and reason. We take this statute as we find it."[13] It was expressed more fully by Mr. Justice Brandeis when the temptation to give what might be called a more liberal interpretation could not have been wanting. "The particularization and detail with which the scope of each provision, the amount of the tax thereby imposed, and the incidence of the tax, were specified, preclude an extension of any provision by implication to any other subject…. What the Government asks is not a construction of a statute, but, in effect, an enlargement of it by the court, so that what was omitted, presumably by inadvertence, may be included within its scope."[14] (An omission at the time of enactment, whether careless or calculated, cannot be judicially supplied however much later wisdom may recommend the inclusion.)

Interpreting Law and Making Law

The vital difference between initiating policy, often involving a decided break with the past, and merely carrying out a formulated policy, indicates the relatively narrow limits within which choice is fairly open to courts and the extent to which interpreting law is inescapably making law. To say that, because of this restricted field of interpretive declaration, courts make law just as do legislatures is to deny essential features in the history of our democracy. It denies that legislation and adjudication have had different lines of growth, serve vitally different purposes, function under different conditions, and bear different responsibilities. The judicial process of dealing with words is not at all Alice in Wonderland's way of dealing with them. Even in matters legal some words and phrases, though very few, approach mathematical symbols and mean substantially the same to all who have occasion to use them. (Other law terms like "police power" are not symbols at all but labels for the results of the whole process of adjudication.) In between lies a gamut of words with different denotations as well as connotations.

There are not wanting those who deem naive the notion that judges are expected to refrain from legislating in construing statutes. They may point to cases where even our three Justices apparently supplied an omission or engrafted a limitation. Such an accusation cannot be rebutted or judged in the abstract. In some ways, as Holmes once remarked, every statute is unique.

Whether a judge does violence to language in its total context is not always free from doubt. Statutes come out of the past and aim at the future. They may carry implicit residues or mere hints of purpose. Perhaps the most delicate aspect of statutory construction is not to find more residues than are implicit nor purposes beyond the bound of hints. Even for a judge most sensitive to the traditional limitation of his function, this is a matter for judgment not always easy of answer. But a line does exist between omission and what Holmes called "misprision or abbreviation that does not conceal the purpose."[15] Judges may differ as to the point at which the line should be drawn, but the only sure safeguard against crossing the line between adjudication and legislation is an alert recognition of the necessity not to cross it and instinctive, as well as trained, reluctance to do so.

In those realms where judges directly formulate law because the chosen lawmakers have not acted, judges have the duty of adaptation and adjustment of old principles to new conditions. But where policy is expressed by the primary lawmaking agency in a democracy, that is by the legislature, judges must respect such expressions by adding to or subtracting from the explicit terms which the lawmakers use no more than is called for by the shorthand nature of language....

Interpreting the Words of Congress: The Text

Let me descend to some particulars.

The text: Though we may not end with the words in construing a disputed statute, one certainly begins there. You have a right to think that a hoary platitude, but it is a platitude not acted upon in many arguments. In any event, it may not take you to the end of the road. The Court no doubt must listen to the voice of Congress. But often Congress cannot be heard clearly because its speech is muffled. Even when it has spoken, it is as true of Congress as of others that what is said is what the listener hears. Like others, judges too listen with what psychologists used to call the apperception mass, which, I take it, means in plain English that one listens with what is already in one's head. One more caution is relevant when one is admonished to listen attentively to what a statute says. One must also listen attentively to what it does not say.

We must, no doubt, accord the words the sense in which Congress used them. That is only another way of stating the central problem of decoding the symbols. It will help to determine for whom they were meant. Statutes are not archaeological documents to be studied in a library. They are written to guide the actions of men. As Mr. Justice Holmes remarked upon some Indian legislation, "The word was addressed to the Indian mind."[16] If a statute is written for ordinary folk, it would be arbitrary not to assume that Congress intended its words to be read with the minds of ordinary men. If they are addressed to specialists, they must be read by judges with the minds of the specialists.

(And so we assume that Congress uses common words in their popular meaning, as used in the common speech of men) The cases speak of the "meaning of common understanding," "the normal and spontaneous meaning of language," "the common and appropriate use," "the natural, straightforward and literal sense," and similar variants. In *McBoyle v. United States*,[17] Mr. Justice Holmes had to decide whether an airplane is a "motor vehicle" within the meaning of the Motor Vehicle Theft Act. He thus disposed of it: "No doubt etymologically it is possible to use the word to signify a conveyance working on land, water or air, and sometimes legislation extends the use in that direction…. But in everyday speech 'vehicles' calls up a picture of a thing moving on land."

Sometimes Congress supplies its own dictionary. It did so in 1871 in a statute defining a limited number of words for use as to all future enactments. It may do so, as in recent legislation, by a section within the statute containing detailed definitions. Or there may be indications from the statute that words in it are the considered language of legislation. "If Congress has been accustomed to use a certain phrase with a more limited meaning than might be attributed to it by common practice, it would be arbitrary to refuse to consider that fact when we come to interpret a statute. But, as we have said, the usage of Congress simply shows that it has spoken with careful precision, that its words mark the exact spot at which it stops."[18] Or words may acquire scope and function from the history of events which they summarize or from the purpose which they serve.

However colloquial and uncertain the words had been in the beginning, they had won for themselves finally an acceptance and a definiteness that made them fit to play a part in the legislative process. They came into the statute … freighted with the meaning imparted to them by the mischief to be remedied and by contemporaneous discussion. In such conditions history is a teacher that is not to be ignored.[19]

Words of art bring their art with them. They bear the meaning of their habitat whether it be a phrase of technical significance in the scientific or business world, or whether it be loaded with the recondite connotations of feudalism. Holmes made short shrift of a contention by remarking that statutes used "familiar legal expressions in their familiar legal sense."[20] The

154

peculiar idiom of business or of administrativ⸱
meaning that ordinary speech assigns to language.
transplanted from another legal source, whether th
legislation, it brings the old soil with it.

Interpreting the Words of Congress: The Co⸱.

The context: Legislation is a form of literary composition. ⸱
tion is not an abstract process equally valid for every compositio⸱
for every composition whose meaning must be judicially ascertai⸱
nature of the composition demands awareness of certain presuppo⸱
For instance, the words in a constitution may carry different meanings ⸱
the same words in a statute precisely because "it is a *constitution* we are e⸱
pounding." The reach of this consideration was indicated by Mr. Justice
Holmes in language that remains fresh no matter how often repeated:

> When we are dealing with words that also are a constituent act, like
> the Constitution of the United States, we must realize that they have
> called into life a being the development of which could not have been
> foreseen completely by the most gifted of its begetters. It was enough
> for them to realize or to hope that they had created an organism; it
> has taken a century and has cost their successors much sweat and
> blood to prove that they created a nation. The case before us must be
> considered in the light of our whole experience and not merely in that
> of what was said a hundred years ago.[21]

And so, the significance of an enactment, its antecedents as well as its later
history, its relation to other enactments, all may be relevant to the construction of words for one purpose and in one setting but not for another. Some
words are confined to their history; some are starting points for history.
Words are intellectual and moral currency. They come from the legislative
mint with some intrinsic meaning. Sometimes it remains unchanged. Like
currency, words sometimes appreciate or depreciate in value.

(Frequently the sense of a word cannot be got except by fashioning a mosaic of significance out of the innuendoes of disjointed bits of statute.) Cardozo phrased this familiar phenomenon by stating that "the meaning of a
statute is to be looked for, not in any single section, but in all the parts together and in their relation to the end in view."[22] And to quote Cardozo once
more on this phase of our problem: "There is need to keep in view also the
structure of the statute, and the relation, physical and logical, between its
several parts."[23]

Considering the Purpose of a Statute:
The Lawmaker's "Intentions"

The generating consideration is that legislation is more than composition. As an active instrument of government which, for purposes of interpretation, means that laws have ends to be achieved. It is in this connection that Holmes said, "words are flexible."[24] Again it was Holmes, the last judge to give quarter to loose thinking or vague yearning, who said that "the general purpose is a more important aid to the meaning than any rule which grammar or formal logic may lay down."[25] And it was Holmes who chided courts for being "apt to err by sticking too closely to the words of a law where those words import a policy that goes beyond them."[26] Note, however, that he found the policy in "those words"!

You may have observed that I have not yet used the word "intention." All these years I have avoided speaking of the "legislative intent" and I shall continue to be on my guard against using it. The objection to "intention" was indicated in a letter by Mr. Justice Holmes which the recipient kindly put at my disposal:

> Only a day or two ago—when counsel talked of the intention of a legislature, I was indiscreet enough to say I don't care what their intention was. I only want to know what the words mean. Of course the phrase often is used to express a conviction not exactly thought out—that you construe a particular clause or expression by considering the whole instrument and any dominant purposes that it may express. In fact intention is a residuary clause intended to gather up whatever other aids there may be to interpretation beside the particular words and the dictionary.

If that is what the term means, it is better to use a less beclouding characterization.... We are not concerned with anything subjective. We do not delve into the mind of legislators or their draftsmen, or committee members. Against what he believed to be such an attempt Cardozo once protested:

> The judgment of the court, if I interpret the reasoning aright, does not rest upon a ruling that Congress would have gone beyond its power if the purpose that it professed was the purpose truly cherished. (The judgment of the court rests upon the ruling that another purpose, not professed, may be read beneath the surface, and by the purpose so imputed the statute is destroyed.) Thus the process of psychoanalysis has spread to unaccustomed fields. There is a wise and ancient doctrine that a court will not inquire into the motives of a legislative body...."[27]

English Courts Ignore Legislative History

... How then does the purpose which a statute expresses reveal itself, particularly when the path of purpose is not straight and narrow? The English courts say: Look at the statute and look at nothing else. Lord Reading so advised the House of Lords when a bill was before it as to which the attorney general had given an interpretive explanation during its passage in the House of Commons:

> Neither the words of the Attorney General nor the words of an ex-Lord Chancellor, spoken in this House, as to the meaning intended to be given to language used in a Bill, have the slightest effect or relevance when the matter comes to be considered by a Court of Law. The one thing which stands out beyond all question is that in a Court of Law you are not allowed to introduce observations made either by the Government or by anybody else, but the Court will only give consideration to the Statute itself. That is elementary, but I think it is necessary to bring it home to your Lordships because I think too much importance can be attached to language which fell from the Attorney General.[30]

How narrowly the English courts confine their search for understanding an English enactment is vividly illustrated by the pronouncements of Lord Haldane, surely one of the most broad-minded of all modern judges. He said in *Viscountess Rhonddas Claim*[31] [a case famous in the English feminist movement; in 1922 Lady Rhonddas petitioned, unsuccessfully, to be allowed to take a seat in the House of Lords]:

> My Lords, the only other point made on the construction of the Act was that this Committee might be entitled to look at what passed while the Bill was still a Bill and in the Committee stage in the House. It was said that there amendments were moved and discussions took place which indicated that the general words of s. I [section one] were not regarded by your Lordships' House as covering the title to a seat in it. But even assuming that to be certain, I do not think, sitting as we do with the obligation to administer the principles of the law, that we have the least right to look at what happened while the Bill was being discussed in Committee and before the Act was passed. Decisions of the highest authority show that the interpretation of an Act of Parliament must be collected from the words in which the Sovereign has made into law the words agreed upon by both Houses. The history or previous changes made or discussed cannot be taken to have been known or to have been in view when the Royal assent was given. The contrary was suggested at the Bar, though I do not think

the point was pressed, and I hope that it will not be thought that in its decision this Committee has given any countenance to it. To have done so would, I venture to say, have been to introduce confusion into well-seeded Law. In *Millar v. Taylor* the principle of construction was laid down in words, which have never, so far as I know, been seriously challenged, by Willes J. as long ago as in 1769: "The sense and meaning of an Act of Parliament must be collected from what it says when passed into a law; and not from the history of changes it underwent in the house where it took its rise. That history is not known to the other house or to the sovereign."

These current English rules of construction are simple. They are too simple. If the purpose of construction is the ascertainment of meaning, nothing that is logically relevant should be excluded. The rigidity of English courts in interpreting language merely by reading it disregards the fact that enactments are, as it were, organisms which exist in their environment. One wonders whether English judges are as confined psychologically as they purport to be legally. The judges deem themselves limited to reading the words of a statute. But can they really escape placing the words in the context of their minds, which after all are not automata applying legal logic but repositories of all sorts of assumptions and impressions? Such a modest if not mechanical view of the task of construction disregards legal history.... To be sure, early English legislation helped ascertainment of purpose by explicit recitals [statements of the reasons for making a law]; at least to the extent of defining the mischief against which the enactment was directed. To take a random instance, an act in the reign of Edward VI reads: "'Forasmuch as intolerable Hurts and Troubles to the Commonwealth of this Realm doth daily grow and increase through such Abuses and Disorders as are had and used in common Alehouses and other Houses called Tipling houses: (2) it is therefore enacted by the King our Sovereign Lord, etc."[33] Judicial construction certainly became more artificial after the practice of elucidating recitals ceased. It is to be noted that Macaulay, a great legislative draftsman, did not think much of preambles. He believed that too often they are jejune because legislators may agree on what ought to be done, while disagreeing about the reasons for doing it. At the same time he deemed it most important that in some manner governments should give reasons for their legislative course.[34] When not so long ago the parliamentary mechanism was under scrutiny of the Lord Chancellor's Committee, dissatisfaction was expressed with the prevailing practice of English courts not to go outside the statutes. It was urged that the old practice of preambles be restored or that a memorandum of explanation go with proposed legislation.[35]

U.S. Courts Have Changed:
They Now Consider Legislative History and Administrative Practices

At the beginning, the Supreme Court reflected the early English attitude. With characteristic hardheadedness Chief Justice Marshall struck at the core of the matter with the observation: "Where the mind labours to discover the design of the legislature, it seizes everything from which aid can be derived."[36] This commonsensical way of dealing with statutes fell into disuse, and more or less catchpenny canons of construction did service instead. To no small degree a more wooden treatment of legislation was due, I suspect, to the fact that the need for keeping vividly in mind the occasions for drawing on all aids in the process of distilling meaning from legislation was comparatively limited.

As the area of regulation steadily widened, the impact of the legislative process upon the judicial brought into being, and compelled consideration of, all that convincingly illumines an enactment, instead of merely that which is called, with delusive simplicity, "the end result." Legislatures themselves provided illumination by general definitions, special definitions, explicit recitals of policy, and even directions of attitudes appropriate for judicial construction. Legislative reports were increasingly drawn upon, statements by those in charge of legislation, reports of investigating committees, recommendations of agencies entrusted with the enforcement of laws, *et cetera*. When Mr. Justice Holmes came to the Court, the U.S. reports were practically barren of references to legislative materials. These swarm in current volumes.

The change I have summarized was gradual. Undue limitations were applied even after courts broke out of the mere language of a law. We find Mr. Justice Holmes saying, "It is a delicate business to base speculations about the purposes or construction of a statute upon the vicissitudes of its passage."[37] And as late as 1925 he referred to earlier bills relating to a statute under review, with the reservation "If it be legitimate to look at them."[38]

Such hesitations and restraints are in limbo. Courts examine the forms rejected in favor of the words chosen. They look at later statutes "considered to throw a cross light" upon an earlier enactment.[39] The consistent construction by an administrative agency charged with effectuating the policy of an enactment carries very considerable weight. While assertion of authority does not demonstrate its existence, long-continued, uncontested assertion is at least evidence that the legislature conveyed the authority. Similarly, while authority conferred does not atrophy by disuse, failure over an extended period to exercise it is some proof that it was not given. And since "a page of history is worth a volume of logic,"[40] courts have looked into the background of statutes, the mischief to be checked and the good that was designed, looking sometimes far afield and taking notice also as judges of what is generally known by men.

Limitations of Rules for Interpreting Statutes

Unhappily, there is no table of logarithms for statutory construction. No item of evidence has a fixed or even averse weight. One or another may be decisive in one set of circumstances while of little value elsewhere. A painstaking detailed report by a Senate Committee bearing directly on the immediate question may settle the matter. A loose statement even by a chairman of a committee, made impromptu in the heat of debate, less informing in cold type than when heard on the floor, will hardly be accorded the weight of an encyclical.

Spurious use of legislative history must not swallow the legislation so as to give point to the quip that only when legislative history is doubtful do you go to the statute. While courts are no longer confined to the language, they are still confined by it. Violence must not be done to the words chosen by the legislature, unless, indeed, no doubt can be left that the legislature has in fact used a private code, so that what appears to be violence to language is merely respect to special usage. In the end, language and external aids, each accorded the authority deserved in the circumstances, must be weighed in the balance of judicial judgment.

Only if its premises are emptied of their human variables, can the process of statutory construction have the precision of a syllogism. We cannot avoid what Mr. Justice Cardozo deemed inherent in the problem of construction, making "a choice between uncertainties, we must be content to choose the lesser."[41] But to the careful and disinterested eye, the scales will hardly escape appearing to tip slightly on the side of a more probable meaning.

Nor can canons of construction save us from the anguish of judgment. Such canons give an air of abstract intellectual compulsion to what is in fact a delicate judgment, concluding a complicated process of balancing subtle and elusive elements. All our three Justices have at one time or another leaned on the crutch of a canon. But they have done so only rarely, and with a recognition that these rules of construction are not in any true sense rules of law. So far as valid, they are what Mr. Justice Holmes called them, axioms of experience.[42]

In many instances, these canons originated as observations in specific cases from which they were abstracted, taken out of the context of actuality, and, as it were, codified in treatises. We owe the first known systematic discussion of statutory interpretation in England to the scholarship of Professor Samuel E. Thorne, Yale's law librarian. According to Professor Thorne, it was written probably prior to 1567. The latest American treatise on the subject was published in 1943. It is not unfair to say that in the four intervening centuries not much new wisdom has been garnered. But there has been an enormous quantitative difference in expounding the wisdom. "A Discourse upon the Exposicion & Understandinge of Statutes" is a charming essay of not more than thirty pages. Not even the freest use of words would describe as charming the latest edition of Sutherland's *Statutory Construction*, with its three volumes of more than 1,500 pages....

Legislative Ambiguity and Judicial Construction of Statutes

The quality of legislative organization and procedure is inevitably reflected in the quality of legislative draftsmanship. Representative Monroney told the House last July that "ninety-five percent of all the legislation that becomes law passes the Congress in the shape that it came from our committees. Therefore if our committee work is sloppy, if it is bad, if it is inadequate, our legislation in ninety-five percent of the cases will be bad and inadequate as well."[43] And Representative Lane added that "in the second session of the 78th Congress 953 bills and resolutions were passed, of which only 86 were subject to any real discussion."[44]

But what courts do with legislation may in turn deeply affect what Congress will do in the future. Emerson says somewhere that mankind is as lazy as it dares to be. Loose judicial reading makes for loose legislative writing. It encourages the practice illustrated in a recent cartoon in which a senator tells his colleagues: "I admit this new bill is too complicated to understand. We'll just have to pass it to find out what it means." A modern Pascal might be tempted at times to say of legislation what Pascal said of students of theology when he charged them with "a looseness of thought and language that would pass nowhere else in making what are professedly very fine distinctions." And it is conceivable that he might go on and speak, as did Pascal, of the "insincerity with which terms are carefully chosen to cover opposite meanings."[45]

But there are more fundamental objections to loose judicial reading. In a democracy the legislative impulse and its expression should come from those popularly chosen to legislate, and equipped to devise policy, as courts are not. The pressure on legislatures to discharge their responsibility with care, understanding, and imagination should be stiffened, not relaxed. Above all, they must not be encouraged in irresponsible or undisciplined use of language. In the keeping of legislatures perhaps more than any other group is the well-being of their fellow men. Their responsibility is discharged ultimately by words. They are under a special duty therefore to observe that "exactness in the use of words is the basis of all serious thinking. You will get nowhere without it. Words are clumsy tools, and it is very easy to cut one's fingers with them and they need the closest attention in handling; but they are the only tools we have, and imagination itself cannot work without them. You must master the use of them, or you will wander, forever guessing, at the mercy of mere impulse and unrecognized assumptions and arbitrary associations, carried away with every wind of doctrine."[46]

Perfection of draftsmanship is as unattainable as demonstrable correctness of judicial reading of legislation. Fit legislation and fair adjudication are attainable. The ultimate reliance of society for the proper fulfillment of both these august functions is to entrust them only to those who are equal to their demands.

Footnotes

[Some of the footnotes in the original text were in sections which have been omitted in this selection, namely, footnotes 1, 3–7, 28–29, and 32. The footnotes below are numbered as in the original text. Many of the references are to legal cases, e.g., *Roschen* v. *Ward*, 279 U.S. 337, 339 (1929). This is the citation for the case of Roschen versus Ward, in Volume 279 of the U.S. Reports, starting on page 337 but the reference is specifically to something on page 339, for the year 1929.]

2. I Report of Income Tax Codification Committee, Cmd. 5131, pp. 16–19 (England 1936).
8. *Roschen* v. *Ward*, 279 U.S. 337, 339 (1929).
9. *United States* v. *Johnson*, 221 U.S. 488, 496 (1911).
10. Barker, *The Politics of Aristotle* lxiii (1946).
11. *Hoeper v. Tax Comm'n*, 284 U.S. 206, 219 (1931).
12. Gray, *Nature and Sources of the Law* 102, 125, 172 (2d ed., 1921).
13. *Anderson* v. *Wilson*, 289 U.S. 20, 27 (1933).
14. *Iselin* v. *United States*, 270 U.S. 245, 250, 251 (1926).
15. *St. Louis-San Francisco Ry.* v. *Middlekamp*, 256 U.S. 226, 232 (1921).
16. *Fleming* v. *McCurtain*, 215 U.S. 56, 60 (1909).
17. 283 U.S. 25, 26 (1931).
18. *Boston Sand & Gravel Co.* v. *United States*, 278 U.S. 41, 48 (1928).
19. Mr. Justice Cardozo in *Duparquet Co.* v. *Evans*, 297 U.S. 216, 220, 221 (1936).
20. *Henry* v. *United States*, 251 U.S. 393, 395 (1920).
21. *Missouri* v. *Holland*, 252 U.S. 416, 433 (1920).
22. *Panama Refining Co.* v. *Ryan*, 293 U.S. 388, 433, 439 (1935) (dissenting).
23. *Duparquet Co.* v. *Evans*, 297 U.S. 216, 218 (1936).
24. *International Stevedoring Co.* v. *Haverty*, 272 U.S. 50, 52 (1926).
25. *United States* v. *Whitridge*, 197 U.S. 135, 143 (1905).
26. *Olmstead* v. *United States*, 277 U.S. 438, 469 (1928) (dissenting).
27. *United States* v. *Constantine*, 296 U.S. 287, 298, 299 (1936) (dissenting).
30. 94 H.L. Deb. 232 (5th ser. 1934). [House of Lords debate]

31. (1922) 2 A.C. 339, 383.

33. 6 Edw. VI, c. 25 (1552).

34. *Lord Macaulay's Legislative Minutes*, 145 *et seq.* (Dharker ed., 1946).

35. Laski, Note to the *Report of the Committee on Minister's Powers*, Cmd. 4060, Annex V, 135 (1932).

36. *United States* v. *Fisher*, 2 Cranch 358, 386 (U.S. 1805).

37. *Pine Hill Coal Co.* v. *United States*, 259 U.S. 191, 196 (1922).

38. *Davis* v. *Pringle*, 268 U.S. 315, 318 (1925).

39. *United States* v. *Aluminum Co. of Amer.*, 148 F. 2d 416, 429 (C.C.A. 2d 1945).

40. *New York Trust Co.* v. *Eisner*, 256 U.S. 345, 349 (1921).

41. *Burnet* v. *Guggenheim*, 288 U.S. 280, 288 (1933).

42. *Boston Sand & Gravel Co.* v. *United States*, 278 U.S. 41, 48 (1928).

43. 92 Cong. Rec. 10040 (1946). [Congressional Record]

44. 92 Cong. Rec. 10054 (1946).

45. Pater, Essay on Pascal in *Miscellaneous Studies*, 48, 51 (1895).

46. Allen, Essay on Jeremy Bentham in *The Social and Political Ideas of the Revolutionary Era*, 181, 199 (Hearnshaw ed., 1931).

ᛒᚩ Part 3 ᚳᛉ
Police Studies Masterworks

Introduction to Police Studies Masterworks

In the late 1800s there was some hope of developing a new social and technological science of policing. The new discipline was called "police science." The principal architects of police science were well educated German, British, and American police administrators. They were attracted to new technologies which could be used in police work, such as photography, fingerprinting, laboratory analyses of physical evidence from crime scenes or crime victims, telephone systems, and later one-way radios and then two-way radios, motorcycles and automobiles for rapid response to crime scenes, and the development of scientific management in the private sector with its counterpart public administration in government agencies. These new technologies and management sciences were expected to turn police work into a bona fide profession with its own hybrid science, provided that police agencies could hire educated people and provide them with training as well as the resources for a police science. However, over the course of the next century the natural science and technological aspects of police work faded into the background largely due to lack of funding for science and technology, and social science studies of police dominated the end of the twentieth century. "Police science" became better known as "police studies."

In the United States in the period 1830–1880 systematic study of police work, police departments, and police officers consisted of studies by politicians considering the idea of establishing more formal police departments. This was the time when large cities were changing from a police system based on magistrates and watchmen, with help from nearby citizens when needed, to paramilitary police departments based on a model developed in France and subsequently implemented in London in 1829. New York City politicians, for example, journeyed to London to look at the new police model before implementing something like it in New York.

The impetus for this new kind of police in London had been large scale urban "disorders" by lower-class people seeking political reform, especially rights to vote, and by the restive factory workers of the new industrial age. Factory owners, including Sir Robert Peel who established the London police, needed something like an army to control riots and protect their property. In American cities also, such as Philadelphia and New York, it was major riots which moved politicians to opt for the new style of paramilitary police. The American riots were often directed against blacks, but the riots also sprang from the social upheaval of the new age of industry.

Prior to setting up the London police, Sir Robert Peel had established the Irish constabulary on a military model to control English occupied Ireland.

Paramilitary police forces already existed in Europe, and Peel copied particularly from the Paris police. The Irish Constabulary was viewed by Peel as an experiment in preparation for a London police force. The new paramilitary police for large urban areas even in the homeland were designed along the lines of a military occupation force with emphasis on patrol, surveillance, and no citizen involvement. Many politicians and citizens had misgivings about paramilitary police forces, but they seemed to be useful for maintaining order in riot prone cities.

After the political inquiries into the organization of paramilitary police forces, the next wave of police studies consisted of investigations of police departments by various committees probing brutality and corruption. Although the old system of magistrates and watchmen was often corrupt, their corruption was limited by the very limited number of officials involved in police work and by their dependence on cooperation from citizens when maintaining order or making an arrest. The large new paramilitary police departments enabled brutality to develop and corruption to increase to an extent unimaginable in earlier times. Police officers were often corrupt individually as well as in an organized manner. The new police system gave police virtually unlimited powers in practice, posted them in every neighborhood, and unified them as a group. In the United States they were under the control of local politicians and acted pretty much as the strong arm of neighborhood politicians. Their roles expanded rapidly, so that they soon took on the tasks of providing such social services as shelters for the homeless and soup kitchens as well as enforcing local ordinances related to health, housing, employment, and business practices. They were in charge of running elections, often making sure that their political bosses stayed in office. The opportunities for graft were abundant, and police work became a very lucrative occupation. Hence, it was not surprising that the landmark studies of police in the last half of the nineteenth century were investigations of police corruption.

Notable but not exceptional among the investigations of police in the late nineteenth century was an investigation of the New York City police by the Lexow Committee of the State Senate in 1894. The Committee found the Police Department to be thoroughly permeated by brutality and graft, beginning with bribes paid by people to get police jobs and bribes paid by police officers to get promotions. But investigatory commissions brought little change to policing. Decades later in 1933 the federal Wickersham Commission looked at many police departments as well as courts nationwide and found comparable brutality and graft. Throughout the twentieth century federal and local investigatory commissions kept unearthing brutality and graft in American police departments, although it was somewhat reduced towards the end of the century. But even in 2001 a judge allowed a Los Angeles police precinct to be indicted under federal law as an organized crime syndicate. The reports of investigatory commissions constitute the principal documents for the study of police up to about 1960 and the reports of later commissions are some of the key documents for the study of police in the later decades.

To the studies done by investigatory commissions in the period 1880–1960 must be added the journalistic exposes of police and journalistic accounts of police incidents and trials. Many journalistic accounts looked beyond stories of police brutality and corruption to include accounts of heroism, peace keeping, and crime solving ingenuity. Some reported how ordinary policemen went about their routine work. Until late in the twentieth century big-city policemen were often assigned a beat soon after being hired and worked the same beat twenty to thirty years until their retirement. H.L. Mencken's "Recollections of Notable Cops" (in *The Vintage Mencken*, New York: Vintage Books, 1990) was a journalist's story of how one policeman presided over a neighborhood with considerable talent for peace keeping although little concern for the law. Journalistic accounts were the predecessors of more formal social science studies of police work.

The earliest social science studies of police tended to be studies of police management. The classics were Raymond Fosdick's *European Police Systems* (1915) and *American Police Systems* (1920). Later came Bruce Smith's *Police Systems in the United States* (1940). August Vollmer, the police chief of Berkeley, California from 1905–1932, developed a strong relationship with the local campus of the University of California and set up a School of Criminology there. Vollmer was an advocate of police science, embracing both its technological and management components. One of his disciples, Orlando W. Wilson, reformed the Wichita, Kansas police department and then returned to Berkeley as the Dean of the School of Criminology. Wilson wrote the classic text *Police Administration*, laying the foundation for that aspect of police studies. He took over the management of the Chicago Police Department from 1960–1967.

The first social science study of how ordinary police officers do their work was conducted by William A. Westley about 1950. It was a doctoral dissertation study for a degree in sociology from the University of Chicago, which had been the hothouse for earlier studies in delinquency and criminology. Although Westley's study was of no interest to publishers for two decades, it became well known among sociologists interested in police. Other pioneering studies of how ordinary policemen (when there were no police women) did their work were Michael Banton's *The Policeman in the Community* (New York: Basic Books, 1964), Jerome Skolnick's *Justice Without Trial* (New York: John Wiley and Sons, 1966), and Egon Bittner's "Police on Skid Row: A Study of Peacekeeping" (*American Sociological Review*, 1967, *32*, 699–715). At a time when police denied that they used discretion rather than enforcing the law equally all the time, the American Bar Foundation conducted a nationwide study (1974) of the use of discretion by police officers in routine law enforcement. These early studies documented that police officers were generally unsupervised by their superiors and handled their beats in whatever ways they saw fit. The early studies by social scientists embarrassed police departments and made it more difficult for other researchers to gain cooperation from police agencies. But they forced police departments to face themselves and eventually to become more accountable to the public.

Social science studies of police accelerated rapidly in the 1960s and 1970s when federal government commissions and academic researchers began looking at police both as organizations and as individuals. The President's Commission on Law Enforcement and the Administration of Justice (especially the *Task Force Report on the Police*) and the National Advisory Commission on Civil Disorders were among the many federal commissions on various matters which employed social scientists as researchers. Both individually and as organizations, police had played a major role in opposing the civil rights movement, in opposing anti-Vietnam war demonstrators, and in triggering the hundreds of urban riots which mauled American cities in the 1960s. Questions were raised about "the police personality," "the police culture," relationships between police and the community, and control of police by elected officials, courts, and the media. Police were highly resistant to most of these studies.

However, studies supported by the federal government or by think tanks with ties to police departments (e.g., The Rand Institute, The Police Foundation, The Police Executive Research Forum, The National Institute of Justice) have had the backing and cooperation of reform minded police administrators. They have examined the effectiveness of various police administrative, patrol, and investigative practices. The landmark study of this type was the Kansas City study of random preventive patrol, which found that routine police patrol did not deter crime. Other studies have questioned the value of foot patrol, the value of rapid police response time, the effectiveness of detective work, the reliability of crime lab reports, the effectiveness of sting operations, the effectiveness of police strategies for many kinds of situations, such as domestic disputes, use of deadly force, situations involving mentally ill people, public intoxication, high speed pursuits, and so on. More and more, the results of these studies found their way into training programs for police officers. By the end of the twentieth century some police administrators began looking at social science studies for guidance in developing policy for dealing with many of these problems.

The masterworks chosen for this anthology are classic studies of policing at three different levels. Westley's study looked at policemen operating at the street level. Fogelson's study focused mainly on the management level in policing, which has tended to be somewhat cut off from street level policing. Goldstein's study examined policing at the political level where a police department encounters the currents of local government. Together they provide an opportunity to explore key ideas about how police operate as individuals and as organizations and what their place is in a democratic society.

Suggested Reading

Vila, B., and Morris, C. (1999). *The role of police in American society: A documentary history*. Westport, CT: Greenwood Press.

Introduction to
William A. Westley

William A. Westley was the first social scientist to study police. There was a rich journalistic literature on police extending back more than a hundred years which gave vivid accounts of what police officers did and how they did it. There were also numerous reports of legislative committees or commissions which had investigated police. The journalistic literature emphasized sensational events and extraordinary personalities in police work. The investigative reports focused on corruption and brutality in particular places at particular times; they almost always were reactions to situations which had become so notorious and flagrant that legislators had to do something to restore public confidence in police.

Westley was the first person to attempt a study of how ordinary police officers see themselves and do their work. Although Westley's study was published in book form in 1970, the study itself was done some twenty years earlier and was already well known. At the time of the study Westley was a doctoral student in sociology at the University of Chicago, and his study of the police was his doctoral dissertation. Westely wanted to do his research in a city where he was doing some teaching as an adjunct professor at a small college. The city was Gary, Indiana. Gary was a steel town whose huge mills provided steady wages for a blue collar population. His dissertation mentor, Professor Joseph D. Lohman, made the necessary arrangements. No claim was made that Gary had either a typical police department or an exceptional one. Gary seems to have been rather similar to other industrial cities of the time.

The police of Gary were not happy to have someone doing research in their department. But Professor Lohman had considerable political clout in Illinois and Indiana; some people considered him a possible candidate for President of the United States. Lohman compelled the chief in Gary to go along with Westley's research and warned that the chief would be held responsible if any harm came to Westley. Subsequently the chief tried to undermine Westley's research, but Westley confronted the chief and had him sign the stencil of a letter to all officers urging cooperation. Westley then mailed the letter, signed by the chief, to all officers.

Westley was a threat to the police because of what he might learn about unlawful practices. Westley knew that his life was in danger, shielded only by Professor Lohman. Even Lohman had warned him, "You will know so much after three weeks they will kill you." He had to proceed carefully. He was aware of some corruption in the Gary police department but considered that too dangerous a subject to pursue. Instead he focused on police use of physical force and the police code of silence.

At the time of Westley's study the study of various occupational subcultures, such as teachers and lawyers, was an established field of inquiry, but no one had studied police in a social science manner. As a sociologist Westley was guided by the idea of *functionalism*, which was a widely accepted perspective among sociologists. *Functionalism* was the belief that every component of a society or culture has a function, that is, serves a purpose. Hence, if police use physical force, force must serve some purpose for them. If police have a code of silence, it also must have some function in the police society. The challenge for Westley was to discover the scope and depth of violence and secrecy in the police culture and to determine what purposes they served. Whatever purposes violence and secrecy served, they had to fit into these police officers' view of themselves and their world. As Westley noted in the Preface to his book, the major analytical problem of his study was how to resolve the paradox "about the incompatibility between the lives of these men as decent, humble, urban men, usually with wives, children, and small homes, and their lives as policemen in an antagonistic relationship with the community."

Westley viewed police violence and secrecy as a matter of morality. Morality is not something entirely objective or determined by others. It consists of norms of behavior not merely adopted but adapted by an individual with more or less influence from others in the individual's social circles or society at large. Among police, violence and secrecy could be understood within the framework of a special morality, the morality of police. There are several occupations which have developed their own morality, and sometimes even their own explicit code of ethics, because people in those occupations do some things which are questionable in terms of standard morality. Lawyers do their best to get an acquittal for a criminal who is guilty, doctors give or withhold treatments which are morally unacceptable to some people (such as abortions), military people deliberately kill people, and so on. Occupations which involve violations of conventional morality develop their own norms of right and wrong so that they can carry out their customary activities and still see themselves as morally good people, despite the contrary moral views of some other people. Westley coined the term "legitimation" to describe the mental process by which individuals find a justification for acting a certain way. "Legitimations" could be based on truths, half-truths, falsehoods, or some combination of these. Westley's analysis of violence and secrecy among police viewed these actions in the context of a police morality based on legitimations commonly accepted among police officers.

Police in the 1950s had a well established role as peacekeepers. It was also well established that they did their work in whatever ways they saw fit or found necessary. The police officers themselves were recruited from the lower middle class of laborers and civil servants. They seldom had more than high school education, often less. They were given virtually no training as police officers before being assigned to patrol beats. They learned police work from older colleagues and followed the customary practices of their departments. They were expected to be tough enough and willing enough to take on neighborhood thugs. It was a time when most people did not have automobiles. Police, like most people, both lived and worked in the same neighborhood, often for a lifetime, except for those police officers assigned to a city's desperate neighborhoods. Their job was to keep the neighborhood under control. They knew who the troublemakers were and where the trouble spots were. They did not allow their authority to be questioned. Not yet equipped with hand held radios, most police officers worked on foot and had only minimal contact with their police stations once they set out on a tour of duty. As isolated practitioners they worked with little supervision. They had a reputation for using their batons freely to enforce their will. Judges backed them up routinely.

Until the middle of the twentieth century police had only a vague relationship with law. The peacekeeping role did not require thinking about the law most of the time. If a situation could be handled informally with a reprimand, an order to do something or stop doing something, or a lesson taught with a few swings of the baton, there was no need to make the matter complicated by invoking the law. Police had no training in law. Except for extraordinary cases, most people who had been arrested by police were tried in various types of "police courts" where even the judges or magistrates had no training in law but rather were political appointees. The charges against a person were not specified in legal terms but in colloquial terms, such as "being drunk" or "fighting." A defense lawyer was a rare sight and would be less useful than a good word from a local politician or from a respectable citizen.

As a result of the movement to professionalize the police, and also as a result of the civil rights disorders of the 1950s, police work began to be redefined as law enforcement. The civil rights movement faulted police for upholding segregation laws. It was in response to complaints that some of the things done by police were unreasonable or unjust, especially enforcing segregation laws, that police chiefs took the position that police had no choice but to enforce the laws. They said that it was not the role of police to question a law but only to enforce it. If there was a problem with a law, it was up to legislators to change it. In short, police administrators took the position that police have no discretion. It was in this narrow sense that police began to call themselves "law enforcement officers."

The idea that police were law enforcement officers was new when Westley did his study. It was an idea that progressive chiefs were trying to impose on police officers who had operated with a different understanding of their job for the preceding hundred years. One problem Westley encountered was that the police officers in his study thought of him as someone on the side of the chief trying to change the way they did their job. But even if there had not been a struggle in progress between old and new definitions of the police job, Westley would have encountered problems in doing his study. Previous studies of police had been investigations of corruption and brutality. Such studies had never been good for the self images of police or the reputations of police departments. Westley's study had the potential for doing damage to the police department and to individual officers but little likelihood of doing them any good.

Completing this study was so stressful and threatening to Westley that when it was completed he went on to other areas of interest in sociology. He became a professor of sociology at McGill University in Montreal, Canada. He was involved in a ten year study of mental health. He also studied adolescent behavior and, in more recent years, the sociology of organizations. He has done consulting work on organizational efficiency. However, Westley did one later study of police. For the Canadian government he did a study of police control of crowds in five cities (*The Formation, Nature, and Control of Crowds*, Defence Research Board, Department of National Defence, Canada, 1956). This study was also hampered by the resistance of police to an outsider doing research.

After Westley other sociologists as well as psychologists began to study police organizations, culture, and "the police personality." Their research confirmed that there is a somewhat standard police subculture characterized by distinctive norms, attitudes, and practices which can be found in most police departments. There seemed to be less corruption in police departments at the beginning of the twenty-first century. However, efforts to change the police subculture by raising educational standards for police, refining police hiring practices, increased training for police, and more diligent investigations of police brutality or corruption have not notably changed the police subculture. The police subculture seems to have endured without very much change since Westley's study, making his research as relevant today as it was decades ago. Police administrators, who may have been more influenced by reforms than police officers, still bemoan the "blue curtain" of silence and solidarity. Police officers still take their cues more from fellow officers than from superiors, and relationships between police and area residents, especially in minority areas, are still often abrasive. An advantage of Westley's study was that, more than most other studies, Westley's analysis went beyond merely describing the actions of police; he got into the minds of the officers and provided insight into how police view themselves and their actions. When reading Westley's study one may ask to what extent the police behaviors, attitudes, and rationalizations described by him are still characteristic of police.

William A. Westley. (1970). *Violence and the Police: A Sociological Study of Law, Custom and Morality.* Cambridge, MA: The Colonial Press. This selection is reproduced with permission of the copyright holder, The MIT Press. Some section titles have been altered, and two content footnotes from the original have been incorporated into the text where they have been placed in square brackets.

William A. Westley

Violence and the Police: A Sociological Study of Law, Custom, and Morality

Preface: The Research Methods and Issues

This book looks back some twenty years to a different time, a different police department, and certainly to a different sociologist. What can I now add to what these have wrought? That the author was a young man hanging on the edge of his first real sociological venture, full of hope, strung tight with the experience but passionately devoted to communicating an understanding of the police and of how their world operated. He was afraid of the police after forcing himself to listen to the tune of violence in their lives, but full of the need to comprehend their humanity within this violence, to understand how the forces of work and community gave this shape to their humanity. He found it hard to so share their point of view that he had rapport with their actions, and yet ask them to bare details of self-incriminating conduct. There was a terrible tension in the flow of this semi participant research, for to understand, he had to sympathize; but in attempting to sympathize he wanted to be liked. To be liked, he had to play by their rules and not ask too many questions. Thus, the work went in waves of carefully building up confidence and inevitably becoming involved in their regard, then asking questions, sharp probing questions, that soon caused rejection. This proved to be both personally painful, in the sense that thereafter he had to push himself on men who he felt disliked and were afraid of him, and practically disastrous, since if the men refused to talk to him the research would stop.

On one occasion, after asking a series of men probing questions in a very sensitive area, everyone stopped talking to him and failed to meet their interview appointments. Days went by when he would sit in the squad room, and the men would not even pass the time of the day with him. The ice broke only when he observed one day that the hard-bitten patrol sergeant came in, evidently delighted with himself, and explained that he had just helped a lady put some packages in her car. This was so incongruous that the interviewer checked his field notes and found a series of small incidents in which different policemen had expressed what he felt to be excessive pleasure in helping someone. He reasoned that this must be because they felt so rejected by the public that they were hungry for approval. He then tested this hypothesis by going to the sergeant and explaining that he was in trouble, that his career depended on getting the research done and asking the sergeant to help him. The response was overwhelming. The sergeant immediately expressed sympathy, called all the men together the next morning and gave them hell for not helping the interviewer, and then personally vouched for him. Thereafter, all the men talked very freely and were exceptionally cooperative. This was a real gain in insight into the police, achieved, however, at considerable emotional cost to the sociologist.

There were other occasions when, for different reasons, the department became uncooperative and it was difficult to continue the research. The solution was to stay around for such long and continuous periods that it was not humanly possible for the men to keep up the pretense of being the kind of men they wanted the interviewer to believe they were. Sooner or later a major slip was bound to occur, witnessed by the interviewer. After that the men would relapse into their daily routines. Observation of the detective bureau was a case in point. Just as soon as he began talking to the detectives, he was aware that they were maintaining a front. He then determined to wait them out and literally just sat in the detective bureau for days on end. Finally, after ten days of sitting, something broke. They had brought in a small Negro man, and when the detective sergeant, who was a huge muscular man, asked him what he had been doing that afternoon and the man said something that was obviously considered false, the sergeant slapped him across the side of the head with such force that the man was knocked off his feet. Immediately the sergeant glanced over at the interviewer, then raced over and picked up the man. He did him no more violence, but thereafter all the detectives began to discuss their cases and their tactics quite openly, and the interviewer was invited to go along on raids. This was an alarming incident, since the interviewer found himself in a moral quandary. Observing the violence was upsetting in itself. If they could do that kind of thing to the other man, what might they do to the interviewer should they decide that he was dangerous (because he already possessed a lot of incriminating information)? [Footnote: Evidently there were some grounds for his fears, since his sponsor, Joseph D. Lohman, had warned him to be careful or he might just be found in an alley with his head smashed. Lohman had, in fact, implied to the Chief that he (the Chief) was responsible for the safety of the interviewer. It sounds melodramatic, but for the interviewer it was just plain frightening.] But if they had continued to hit the Negro man, what should he have done? He felt he would have had to do something. What if the Negro had asked the interviewer to be his witness? Furthermore, how could he possibly sympathize with men who acted in this way? These were very painful conflicts.

These were some of the big issues. Sandwiched between them were a host of less formidable but still significant events. One was the evening when the interviewer was alone in the home of a policeman with a reputation for brutality; the policeman described in detail how he used violence to control sexual offenders. Then, when he was asked what he would do to a man who had killed a policeman, he leaped to his feet, towering above the thoroughly cowed interviewer and shouted down at him: "I'd beat him to death with a two-by-four." Two weeks later this man wandered into an office in which the interviewer was talking to a sergeant; the sergeant very quickly shoved him out the door, but not before the interviewer noticed that the man's clothes were wet and sticky with what appeared to be blood. A subsequent contact with an informant revealed that the man had that day practically beaten someone to death.

Yet there were very few men on the force like this. A surprising number so abhorred violence that they took dull desk jobs to avoid it. Most confessed to the interviewer that brutality brought a bad name to the department. But not one of them was willing to protest openly such violence, and certainly not to report the men who were violent. They all believed that policemen had to use violence at times to protect themselves and that if they exposed this brutality, it harmed the department. The use of violence had deep emotional significance to those policemen, and talking to them about it was always a very delicate matter.

Especially delicate was the problem of letting the men know that one really knew what was going on, so they would feel that they didn't have to protect secrets, while at the same time making them understand that this information would not be used against them. It was widely reputed that in certain sections of the force the men were accepting graft. Because of this, every man on the force was either involved in this graft or he had heard stories about others who were. Naturally, they were very secretive about this and were suspicious of anyone asking questions around the department. In fact, they were often so sensitive about this that they were afraid that if they talked with the interviewer the others might think that they were informers. Thus, the problem was to convince them that they had nothing to hide and that the purpose of the interviews was not to find out about graft. In the beginning, when the interviewer really knew nothing about what was going on, there was no way in which he could indicate that he was knowledgeable. But later, when quite gradually he came to know both what was going on and who was involved, he was able to manifest a sophistication about these matters which was reassuring to the policemen because it made them feel that the interviewer already knew the story and that therefore they had nothing to hide. In fact, some were so re-assured that they proceeded to provide facts and figures about graft accepted by their colleagues—much to the horror of the interviewer, who felt that they might later develop guilt feelings about this, or that others would think that gathering such information was the purpose of the research. Again it was often touch and go, but with time and increasing skill the interviewer found it easier and easier to get information.

It is difficult to describe the sense of paradox that he had about the in-compatibility between the lives of these men as decent, humble, urban men, usually with wives, children, and small homes, and their lives as po-licemen in an antagonistic relationship with the community. The resolu-tion of this paradox proved to be the major analytical problem of the study. He felt that he personally had to be able to understand how these men could be both these things, how it would have been possible for him to have held these views. He imaginatively tried to live through what they were living through. He retraced their steps, first in the community, then in the recruit school, then in their early days in the squad cars and on the foot beat. As explanations came to him, he asked the men whether they had had such experiences and feelings. He asked himself what the conse-quences of having such feelings would be and then went to find out whether, indeed, other men had the same reactions as he. He talked to the rookies, to the experienced men, to their wives and children. Thus, think-ing, working, listening, taking detailed notes, and then brooding over them, he came to construct an explanation of their world that made these apparently diverse and contradictory viewpoints coherent....

The Morality of Secrecy and Violence

Policemen find that in order to endure their work they must relate to the public in ways that protect their self-esteem. Since they see the public as hostile to the police and feel that their work tends to aggravate this hostility, they sep-arate themselves from the public, develop strong in-group attitudes, and con-trol one another's conduct, making it conform to the interests of the group.

They insist that all policemen maintain strict secrecy about police affairs; act in such a way as to maintain public respect for the police; and use whatever methods are necessary for the apprehension of the felon. These form broad rules of conduct in terms of which they decide how to act in specific situations.

This chapter deals with these rules of conduct, with the way in which they are articulated in action, and with their impact on law enforcement and the policeman's self-conception, social role, and morality.

The Roots of Morality:
The Police Society Creates Its Rules

The policemen in City X are deeply concerned with the hostility they feel from the public. It is a pressure that they constantly endeavor to alleviate or repudiate. Their job requires that they be in constant interaction with the public—it is an ever-present factor in their experience—and they become extremely sensitive to these public accusations. They lean on one another for moral support; they depend on one another for practical support. Against unpleasant experience they have the bulwark of in-group, interpersonal strength. Even if the public doesn't appreciate them, their fellows do. The public must be repudiated and the group affirmed. "We are only one hundred forty against one hundred forty thousand" is a running commentary on their position, expressing their feelings of affinity against a hostile world. The feeling is a powerful lever projecting the policeman into the group.

Public hostility includes the policeman in his symbolic status. It includes an assessment of collective responsibility or guilt by association, in terms of which every member of the force is made responsible for the actions of the individual officer. The result is that the individual policeman finds that his own interests have been forcibly identified with those of the group. Any action that incriminates or smears a member of the force has the same impact on all the others before the bar of public opinion. In City X the public frame of reference represents the police so negatively that every vice is added to their character and every virtue is forgotten. This is the feeling of the police when they complain so bitterly about the unfair publicity that the city newspaper gives them. It is encompassed in the words of an officer, who said, "You have two strikes against you as soon as you put on the uniform." Almost in spite of themselves, the policemen come to protect the actions of their comrades and to see little in them that is bad. Almost any beating becomes just; even graft becomes permissible. The policeman is thus permitted to breach the law, for to apprehend him would only do the apprehender harm. The prejudice and the stereotype bind the police together and give them a common front against the community.

Through the hostility and through the stereotype, the police become a close, social group, in which collective action is organized for self-protection and an attack on the outside world. These become expressed in two major rules. The vehicle of self-protection is the rule of silence—secrecy. The vehicle of attack is the emphasis on the maintenance of respect for the police.

The Rule of Secrecy

The stool pigeon, the squealer, the one who tells, is anathema to almost any social group. He is an outcast among the police. To him is applied the most powerful sanction the group has available—the silent treatment. This is powerful because it deprives the unfortunate man of information vital to his continued success and necessary to his happiness, and because he works alone. This is the penalty for a serious abrogation of the rule of silence. It is a penalty for a threat to the secrecy of the group.

Secrecy among the police stands as a shield against the attacks of the outside world; against bad newspaper publicity, which would make the police lose respect; against public criticism, from which they feel they suffer too much; against the criminal, who is eager to know the moves of the police; against the law, which they too frequently abrogate. Secrecy is loyalty, for it represents sticking with the group, and its maintenance carries with it a profound sense of participation. Secrecy is solidarity, for it represents a common front against the outside world and consensus in at least one goal.

Secrecy and silence are among the first rules impressed on the rookie. "Keep your mouth shut, never squeal on a fellow officer, don't be a stool pigeon," is what the rookie has dinned into his ears; it is one of the first things he learns.

Secrecy does not apply to achievements—these should be publicized. It applies to mistakes, to plans, to illegal actions, to character defamation. Among the police it applies to mistakes in arrests, to the abrogation of departmental rules, to criminal suspects, to illegal actions, to personal misdemeanors. These are important insofar as they represent a breach in the protective coating that the policeman tries to present to society.

Method for Testing Strength of Secrecy. Obtaining concrete data on secrecy among the police represented one of the most difficult problems in the research. The interviewer was at all times an outsider, one from whom secrets were to be withheld. Because of this it was decided to make a frontal attack on the problem by designing a question that would leave every alternative unpleasant. Such an approach had to be limited, however, lest it seriously impede the research project (which it did). Thus, a question was designed, presented to 16 men in a series, and then dropped. Even so, it resulted in a wholesale cancellation of interviews for a period of two weeks, and much persuasion was needed before they could be resumed.

Each man was given the following problem:

I'd like to pose an imaginary situation and see how you would handle it. You and your partner pick up a drunk who is breaking up a bar. While you are patting him down you discover he has five hundred dollars on him. You take him into the station. You drive and your partner sits in the back with the drunk who is raising hell. When you get to the station and check him in with the turnkey the money doesn't show up. The drunk yells for his dough. Your partner says he never saw the money. You realize that your partner has clipped him. What would you do?

When they had replied, a further situation was posed:

The drunk prefers charges against you. In court your partner testifies that as far as he knew the drunk didn't have a cent on him. There are no other witnesses, and there is no further evidence. How would you testify?

These questions "put the men on the hook" because a refusal to answer *looked* incriminating, a failure to report the partner or to perjure oneself *was* incriminating, and reporting and/or testifying against the partner was making oneself a stool pigeon. All the questions were pressed, and most of the men responded. Seventy-seven percent of the men stated that they would perjure themselves. The results are summarized in Tables 1 and 2.

Table 1. Proportion of Policemen Willing to Report Other Policemen for Stealing

Response	Frequency	Percentage
Would report	4	27
Would not report	11	73
Total	15	100

Table 2. Proportion of Policemen Willing to Testify Against Other Policemen

Response	Frequency	Percentage
Would not testify	10	77
Would testify	3	23
Total	13*	100

* Two men refused to answer the question.

One man stated that he would both report and testify against his partner. He was a rookie. The last man to be interviewed completely evaded the question by stating:

... Now about this business of a policeman rolling a drunk. That doesn't happen very often. Your partner doesn't do anything without your knowing about it. Of course once in a while you will pick up a drunk and you don't take them all to jail. Might be a nice fellow. Your partner might say, "Let's take him home, he's a nice guy." You will take him home, put him to bed and then you will be driving away. You will leave the guy and be driving away and your partner will reach over and say here's yours, and hand you a twenty dollar bill. Well when that happens very often you begin not to trust that partner because you know it may be that if he is giving you twenty dollars he probably took a hundred because a guy that will steal from a drunk will steal from you.

The full significance of the responses becomes apparent only if it is realized (1) that the support and enforcement of the law is the basic legal function of the police, and they are quite conscious of the fact; (2) that the policemen themselves maintain that biased testimony only leads to trouble in the long run; and (3) that the detection of perjury by the authorities would result in the suspension of the man from the force, causing him to lose both his job and his pension time, would seriously hinder him in any future profession, and would make him liable to imprisonment.

From the responses it is clear that in spite of these dangers the illegal action is preferable to breaking the secrecy of the group, to being categorized as a stool pigeon. Undoubtedly, the verbal responses cannot be correlated with the actual actions. If they were faced with a perjury charge, many would probably change their mind. However, this does not diminish the significance of the responses, which represent a choice among alternatives. We would suggest, therefore; that the data are indicative of the strength of two characteristics of the police force: (1) secrecy constitutes one of the most important definitions and is represented in the rule of silence, and (2) law enforcement is subordinate to the ends of the group....

Legitimate and Illegitimate Uses of Police Powers

For the police, action in large measure is confined to action toward the people of the community. It involves, on the one hand, the nature of police powers, and on the other, their decisions about using these powers.

Police power has two aspects: the positive which involves coercion in power to arrest and to use violence in making arrests; and the negative, which involves the power of withdrawal of protection. Policemen's legal privileges entitle them to the first source of power and forbid them the second.

Both are used. Although the police are legally entitled to certain powers, these powers are utilized for their personal ends as well as in the line of duty

As a group they tend to use the power that they possess to gain their ends as a group, ends that we have indicated are basically embodied in the maintenance of secrecy, the maintenance of respect for the police, and the apprehension of the felon. In addition to the extension of their legal sources of power, they also tend to draw on certain illegal sources of power which are at their disposal. Principal among these is their power to withdraw their protection. In this sense they come to regard protection as a personal commodity, the extension of which is a reward for compliance and the withdrawal of which is a punishment for noncompliance. This source of power is almost completely reserved for expediting the ends of the police, whatever they may be, and is seldom used to back up their legal function. [Footnote: Thus, when graft becomes an important end of the police, this source of power is frequently used to force the cooperation of the unwilling gambler, bartender, and the like.]

The Range of Police Action Choices

Police action can be seen as a continuum ranging from letting it pass, or giving a warning, to the arrest and/or a beating. Actions in this range can be legally supported or rationalized. The decision on the part of the individual policeman as to what kind of action to take in a specific situation involves the interrelation of three variables: the enforcement of the law, the maintenance of respect for the police, and the apprehension of the felon, or the making of a "good pinch."

The enforcement of the law, *ceteris paribus*, will be confined to actions utilizing the legal sources of power and will seldom extend beyond the arrest. Persons involved in misdemeanors, who constitute the largest number of offenders, will generally be treated with respect, and will be warned more frequently than arrested. The speeder, the drunk, the public nuisance, and so forth are seldom taken seriously by the police. It is only as one or both of the other variables come into play that the enforcement of the law involves more stringent types of action. Thus, when a drunk curses or reviles a policeman, especially in front of an audience, and when the policeman interprets this as demeaning the police, as influencing the public respect for the police, as threatening his dignity, the drunk will be susceptible to the more stringent types of police action—the arrest, and very possibly rough treatment. How far the policeman will go will depend (1) on how threatened he feels, (2) on the current attitude toward the police in the city and (3) on that portion of the public into which he categorizes the drunk. If the policeman feels seriously threatened, if the public attitude toward the police has been quiet, and if the policeman sees the drunk as a professional criminal, or a Negro, some type of rough treatment will probably be the result.

This does not imply that there are not legitimate bases on which the policeman resorts to violence; there are many situations in which he may have to choose this course of action, such as when the prisoner refuses to accept arrest, when the policeman is attacked, when the policeman has to prevent someone from injuring another person or from committing a serious crime. However, even in these situations, frequently he can refrain from injuring the offender by overpowering him. Police usually work in pairs, and the situation, therefore, is frequently one in which they are two against one.

In addition, there are individual differences in the frequency with which the policeman resorts to force based largely on propensity and strength. Some men seem to work out their fears and aggressions on the job. Some men are so powerful that they seldom experience resistance on the part of the public, and when they do they can easily overpower the offender. Other men, who are smaller, seem to pose a challenge to the offender because of their very size, and they will frequently experience resistance and have to use the club to overcome this resistance. Nevertheless, the amount of force used by the police and the situations in which it is applied cannot be accounted for fully under the categories of necessity in the line of duly and personal propensities and strength; they appear to be a matter of prescription in terms of ends not thus accounted for.

This, then, affords an opportunity to test our hypothesis that the maintenance of respect for the police and the apprehension of the felon represent major occupational norms of the police.

Legitimations for Police Actions
Reveal Norms of Police Morality

Although the prevalence of similar attitudes among a large proportion of the men, and their logical integration with the problem of the occupation, would suggest that these attitudes reflect group norms, it does not demonstrate the point. Similar experiences may generate similar attitudes which have no collective basis. However, the legitimation of action offers an index which does have such a basis. This becomes clear if one considers the subjective meaning of norms for the men involved.

Here one can assume (1) that a norm regulates action not only because of the sanctions it involves, but also because it represents to the actor the morally correct choice; (2) that any important norm should function as a source of moral authority to the actor so that he will justify his actions in terms of it; (3) that the more extreme the action, the more likely it will be applied toward ends (normatively defined) that are of importance; and (4) that the more subject to criticism the action is, the more likely the man will feel called upon to justify it.

On the basis of these assumptions it was possible to identify the major norms of the police by asking them to justify certain forms of extreme action. The use of force or violence is such an action, since it is both extreme and subject to heavy criticism by the people of the community. Therefore, the ways in which the police justify the use of force would indicate their major norms.

Legitimations for Violence

Seventy-four policemen in Department X were asked, "When do you think a policeman is justified in roughing a man up?" Their responses were essentially prescriptive in that they tried to indicate to the interviewer the type of situation in which they would prescribe the use of force. The situations for which force was prescribed represented those in which the policemen felt its use would be justified; therefore, these situations could be considered as sources for its legitimation.

Their answers frequently had elements in common, and thus it was possible to group them into rough categories which are indicative of the norms they represent (see Table 3). Since many of the respondents gave more than one basis for the use of force, their responses are first classified in terms of the major orientation, summarized in the column "primary responses." Each response in this column indicates a separate case. Their remaining rationalizations are summarized in the column "secondary response." Each item in this column represents an additional rationalization advanced by a respondent listed in the primary response column.

Table 3. Bases for the Use of Force

Basis	Primary Response Num.	Primary Response %*	Secondary Response Number	Total Num.	Total %*
1. Disrespect for the police	27	37	2	29	39
2. Only when impossible to avoid	17	23	0	17	23
3. To obtain information	14	19	3	17	23
4. To make an arrest	6	8	3	9	12
5. For the hardened criminal	5	7	3	8	11
6. When you know the man is guilty	2	3	1	3	4
7. For sex criminals	2	3	4	6	8
8. For self-protection	0	0	4	4	5
9. When pressure is on you	0	0	1	1	1
Total	74	100	20	94	

* Percentages computed only to the nearest 1%

Interpretation:

1. The evidence of 39% [Total % column] of the men giving disrespectful behavior as a basis for the use of force supports the thesis that the maintenance of respect for the police is a major orientation of the police.

2. That 23% of the men legitimate the use of force to obtain information that would lead to the solution of a crime or the conviction of the criminal would support the thesis that the apprehension of the felon is also a major orientation of the police.

3. That 66% of the men gave as their *primary* rationalization an illegal basis for the use of force (categories 1, 3, 5, and 6) while only 8% gave a legal basis (category 4) would indicate that the group-engendered values are relatively more important to the men than their legal function.

4. The fact that 23% of the men stated that force should be avoided if possible is indicative of the social situation in which the interview took place rather than the feelings of the men. At the time the interviews were being made the chief of police was carrying on a program to reduce the amount of force being used and was applying penalties to deviants; the interviewer was suspected of being connected with the chief. Under these conditions the safest response was to condemn the use of force. Thus although some of the men undoubtedly indicated their true feelings, the proportion of 23% probably exaggerates the number. On the other hand, these same conditions would indicate that the proportion of the men endorsing the use of force is biased conservatively.

5. The apparent guilt of the man and his identification as a hardened criminal as bases for the use of force in 15% of the cases does not indicate

that these are motivational factors but rather that they represent conditions under which the use of force can take place. They represent the feeling on the part of the men that force must be used with caution because of the possibility of a lawsuit against them.

In support of each of these interpretations, the actual statements of the respondents are more convincing than the number of times they occur. Therefore, we cite at length several typical responses in each category.

Legitimations for Violence in the Maintenance of Respect

That 39% of the respondents gave disrespectful behavior as a reason for using force is indicative of the profound meaning that the maintenance of respect has for the police. The responses conveyed this meaning in three general ways: by implication—"You gotta be tough with these fellows"; on a personal basis—"If anybody kicks me you can bet he is going to get it back"; and in terms of the group's needs—"If you don't use force when you have to you can't do your job because it spreads like wild fire" and "as a matter of fact there are a lot of people who know a policeman won't use a gun and they take advantage of the fact and try to push him around." The symbol of disrespect for the police is the "wise guy," the fellow who thinks he knows more than they do, the fellow who talks back, the fellow who insults the policemen. The "wise guy" epitomizes what the police hate in the public. If they think they can get away with it, they will deal with him harshly. He appears in the following response:

> Well there are cases. For example when you stop a fellow for routine questioning. Say a wise guy, and he starts talking back to you and telling you you are no good and that sort of thing. You know you can take a man in on a disorderly conduct charge but you can practically never make it stick. So what you do in a case like that is to egg the guy on until he makes a remark where you can justifiably slap him and then if he fights back you can call it resisting arrest.

This policeman points up the need that he feels to punish the "wise guy," to bring him into line. He formulates possible lines of action. He points out that legally he can't do a thing to the man. He figures out a way to punish the man, to beat him up and not get in trouble, and to hit him on legal grounds.

Many of the responses indicated that the men felt sensitive about public opinion concerning the use of force. They recognized that the use of force was in many instances illegal, that it could get them in trouble. In particular, they recognized that the Negro was no longer so politically impotent and could cause trouble if they beat him up....

The presence of an audience seems to be the ultimate incentive to the use of force in one sense. The policeman who is insulted in front of an audience feels that his prestige is really dropping. Two men illustrated how they reacted in situations of this type.

> I am not afraid to bust a guy. Some of the fellows may be but I am not. Like the other day. We came down there. It was a corner in one of the taverns. It was a bunch of these white chippies. Well, they were raising a lot of hell and all of a sudden this blonde whore comes running out. She really had her machine going. She was plenty excited and she had plenty of drinks in her. We told her she couldn't be coming up like that and she started to get a little sassy, and all those other whores were standing around the comer, watching. So what do I do? I throw her into the car and clear out.

This man was extremely conscious of "all those other whores ... standing around the corner, watching." He felt this was a good reason to get tough with the offender. He suggests but does not state that he did a lot more than throw her into the car. However, this in itself constitutes rough treatment, for he meant it literally....

Legitimations for Violence
in the Apprehension of the Felon

Twenty-three percent of the men interviewed listed obtaining information as a basis for the use of force. The figures are deceptive, however, since the "third degree" has in recent years received a lot of adverse publicity, and the men were afraid to admit the existence of such a practice. This publicity has reduced the use of the third degree, in the police station, to a considerable extent, but it has not been eliminated even there. Out of the station, however, the use of force to make a suspect talk is still prevalent and sanctioned.

The use of force in this area is the product of two general factors. The first of these is that the "good pinch," the apprehension of the felon, or the breaking of a big case is a major source of prestige in the department. A man who makes a lot of good pinches and breaks several big cases has a reputation among the other men for being a good policeman. In addition, the police define the criminal as having abrogated many of his rights as a citizen, and they are therefore willing to use measures they would feel reluctant to use otherwise. The result is that the men, eager to obtain the prestige and having no compunctions about the criminal, feel that the end justifies the means. The group sanctions and the men use, therefore, almost anything they think they can get away with to obtain a confession or to get the offender to lead them to the evidence.

The second factor is the competition between the patrol and the detective divisions. This is mostly one-sided, the patrolman feeling that he doesn't get an even break in the solution of cases and the consequent publicity and prestige. Thus, when the patrolman apprehends a suspect, he is eager to close the case before he has to hand it over to the detectives. He has to act fast to do this and to him force seems a legitimate way to make the man talk. Besides, he can usually get away with it by saying that the man resisted arrest.

The use of force against the suspect is justified by the men on the basis that they are acting in the best interests of the community. They feel that they are only using the methods of the suspect, and that in doing so they frequently apprehend men who are a danger to the people in the community. One can not overlook this as a form of self-justification for the men involved: Feeling as they evidently did that such an explanation made their actions reasonable in terms of the values held by the interviewer, it is very likely that it likewise served as an answer to those values as they internalized them. Therefore, it is likely that the individual men faced with specific situations, make their decisions in terms of a complex of factors that are not easily disentangled but among which their desire for prestige, their feeling that they are performing a community service, and their definition of the criminal as having abrogated his rights as a citizen form a substantial basis for the use of force....

The protection of the people in the community as legitimation for the use of force is evident in the following case:

> The third-degree methods are justified in certain cases. For example, four potential killers pull a job. One is caught. The freedom of the other three is a menace to the community. In that case third-degree methods are essential in getting the other three men.

Legitimations for Violence
Based on the Law

The policeman is legally entitled to the use of force in the performance of his duty. He has to and does use force in this connection. In making an arrest, in defending himself, in maintaining the peace of the community, the policeman frequently finds himself in situations that require that he use force to perform his duty and to go about his job. This legal entitlement is the basic refuge that the policeman has whenever he uses force for whatever reasons. He can always say that it was in self-defense, or that the offender was resisting arrest.

Seventeen percent of the men mentioned their duty as a basis for the use of force. This came up in two forms: to make an arrest [12%] and for self-protection [5%]. Only 7% of the men felt that force should be limited to cases involving these characteristics. The following are representative cases:

1. On this force business you have to use it. Like this case where we caught a fellow. He was a drug addict. He was fighting us all the way. I put him in the car. He lashed out with his feet and caught me in the face. We had to work him over and we opened his scalp a little bit. You have to work men over like that. They may be dangerous. You often have to do it to get things done.
2. When he resists arrest any time. That lets you use force enough to complete an arrest but the amount is up to you.
3. Force is legitimate only when necessary to make an arrest.
4. The average man has to use force only once or twice a year. Of course, there are individuals who never have to use force because they never bother about arresting anybody.

Guilt as a Precondition to Violence

The policemen, aware of the community's condemnation of brutality and of the legal dangers in the misuse of force, tend to utilize the apparent guilt of the offender as a basis for escaping both. They feel that if the man is guilty, they are doing the people of the community a favor by forcing him to confess, since this protects the community against his further depredations. The more serious the crimes attributed to the offender, the more likely they are to feel this way. In addition, they feel that the necessity for using force to apprehend the felon who is found guilty is more believable and at the same time more excusable. This is the structure of their rationalization. We do not question its validity, in terms of effective police work; however, its illegality and misuse are obvious.

The rationalization does not, however, incorporate or reveal two other factors that underlie and are important in police actions of this type. Both of these involve the prestige of the policeman. As we have previously indicated, the solution of a crime, the making of a "good pinch" is one of the most important sources of prestige for the policeman on the police force and in the community. Second, the relationship between the policeman and the criminal is one of conflict. The policeman pits his will and resources against those of the criminal. The failure to obtain a confession or a conviction, therefore, represents a kind of defeat in which the policeman's own competence is threatened. The lower the status of the offender, the greater the threat....

For the policeman the ultimate guilt arises out of an attack and injury to a policeman. To be suspected of this crime is to endanger one's life as this case clearly indicates:

> ... If he killed a cop I'd beat him with a two by four. I'd break every bone in his body. Put him in the hospital for six months....

Police Action and the Law

Law enforcement is the legal job of the police. Theoretically, this, with the protection of the community and a host of other services, constitutes the function of the police. Yet there are strong grounds for believing that for the police themselves, law enforcement is only an incidental function and is frequently utilized not for the community but to further the ends of the police.

The contacts that the police have with the courts soon teach them that the law is not inviolable. They see it used to further political ends; they see it available for purchase; they frequently find themselves punished for its enforcement by undue time spent in attempts at prosecution. They tend to lose respect for the law.

In his contacts with the public, the policeman finds that law enforcement is not popular. He sees great numbers of people operating their businesses and conducting their lives in disregard of the law. He finds reflected in the eyes of the community a lack of respect for the law. When he does enforce the law, he receives only insults from the public that takes the trouble to let him know what they think—the offenders.

It is not surprising, therefore, that the police, who are referred to as the pillars of the law, should see its enforcement as an end of dubious value. They recognize that it sets limits to their actions; they recognize that a too-obvious flaunting of negligence would result in the loss of their jobs; they recognize that it is fundamentally what gives meaning to their job; they recognize these things, and the recognition exerts sufficient pressure on their behavior so that their function is far from a mockery. Law is thus in a very real sense, an end of the police. Yet, when contrasted to other ends it plays a subordinate role....

Although the police are not oblivious to their responsibilities with respect to law enforcement and of their role as agents of the state, the law is for them a secondary end to be enforced when it is convenient. Thus, when the enforcement of the law conflicts with the ends of the police, the law is not enforced; when it supports the ends of the police, they are fully behind it; and when it bears no relationship to the ends of the police, they enforce it as a matter of routine.

Introduction to
Robert M. Fogelson

Robert M. Fogelson has written several books on urban history and urban affairs. His book, *Downtown: Its Rise and Fall, 1880–1950* (2001), provided a history of the transformation of American cities from cities with one main urban center to metropolitan areas with multiple urban and suburban centers. In 2005 he published a complementary book, *Bourgeois Nightmares: Suburbia, 1870–1930*. Fogelson received a B.A. from Columbia University in 1958 and a Ph.D. from Harvard in 1964. In 1968 he accepted a joint appointment in History and Urban Studies at the Massachusetts Institute of Technology.

The 1960s and '70s were turbulent times in American cities with civil rights and anti-Vietnam war protests and scores of riots erupting in major cities all across the country. Police were in the center of the controversies. They played their role as peace keepers in a rather one-sided and heavy handed manner, making themselves the focal points of these crises in American society. Academics, government commissions and private research foundations turned their spotlights on police. The National Advisory Commission on Civil Disorders, commonly known as The Riot Commission, found that some minor police action had been the trigger of nearly every riot. The deeper causes of riots were social and economic conditions, such as widespread poverty, hunger, inadequate housing and lack of medical care for the poor, but the triggers which set off riots were relatively insignificant police actions which escalated out of control. People who lived in the run down parts of major cities viewed police as hostile outsiders who were like a foreign army occupying the territory and using repressive tactics against the local community. The government responded with new programs to combat poverty, hunger, housing and medical care shortages as well as new programs to improve police. It was in this historical context that Fogelson undertook his research on the problems of big cities and police.

In 1967 Fogelson published *The Fragmented Metropolis: Los Angeles, 1850–1930* with support from The Joint Center for Urban Studies. The following year, his study with R.B. Hill, "Who Riots? A Study of Participation in the 1967 Riots" appeared in the supplemental studies of The Riot Commission. In 1969 Fogelson published *The Los Angeles Riots*, in which he reviewed the reports of commissions which had examined riots which had wrought massive destruction in parts of that city. In 1971 Fogelson published *Violence as Protest: A Study of Riots and Ghettos*. Seven years later Fogelson completed *Big-City Police*, an historical study of police departments done for The Urban Institute, of which Fogelson was a fellow from 1970–1975.

Big city policing is quite different from small town policing. Big city policing is mostly anonymous policing in which the police and the people in a particular neighborhood are strangers who distrust one another. Big cities often are divided into competing interest groups, especially class and ethnic groups, rather than homogeneous communities. In a big city different groups can segregate into different parts of the city, exacerbating their differences. In a big city setting it has been common for just one ethnic group, or two, to gain control of the police department, with the result that the police department reflects and intensifies community conflicts. Thus, the differences between small town policing and big city policing are not only a matter of size. Fogelson's *Big-City Police* highlighted the class and ethnic factors which have shaped big city police.

The history of policing in the United States is a history of half-hearted reform efforts. In the period 1830–1860 big city governments transformed their day and night watchmen organizations into more structured police departments. They generally followed the model of the London police, which was essentially a military organization to patrol and control an urban area, based on the Paris police and the Irish Constabulary. However, the personnel of the new police organizations were the same watchmen as before, and their reputation was unflattering. The effort to transform an undisciplined, lazy and corrupt gang of police into a respectable arm of the law advanced in fits and starts over the next century. The model of a military organization was the first blueprint for reforming police. But police do not resemble a military organization because most police officers work alone in whatever way they see fit; superiors barely know what goes on and are very seldom present to provide leadership or direction. At the end of the nineteenth century big city police were still corrupt and inefficient but they had gained considerable power over a wide range of urban affairs. Police ran elections, were in charge of building and sanitary law enforcement, issued licenses for a variety of businesses, and ran soup kitchens and homeless shelters, as well as maintaining order on the streets. All these enterprises were opportunities for graft. The Lexow Committee investigation of the New York City Police Department in 1894 found that people paid large bribes to neighborhood politicians with party connections to get hired as police officers and enormous bribes for promotions within the police department because it was such a profitable job.

At the beginning of the twentieth century there was an alternative model for the police. An alternative to the military model was the professional model. At that time many jobs were being transformed into professions. Prior to professionalization, jobs were learned by informal, on-the-job training and apprenticeships. The transformation into a profession required that, before beginning work, the job holders had to be trained in a specific body of knowledge appropriate to the work, that they had to pass job knowledge tests to get licensed, and that their work performance be guided by clear performance and ethical standards. Following this route, teachers, nurses, civil engineers, lawyers, dentists, and hundreds of other worker groups transformed themselves from apprentice type jobs to professions. With professionalization came higher status in society and sometimes more money.

Some police were attracted by the professional model. Police salaries were never low compared to other jobs available to people with their qualifications. Apart from the money available through graft, police salaries generally surpassed the salaries of low level professionals such as teachers or civil engineers, were on a par with run of the mill lawyers, but were less than the income of upper level professionals like doctors or corporate lawyers. Although police may have had an eye on the income levels of doctors and corporate lawyers, what they probably wanted most of all was the respect that would come from being a profession. However, police were not willing to professionalize all the way. They wanted to mix the military model with the professional model, to keep the apprenticeship form of training rather than require prior professional knowledge, to avoid job knowledge testing, licensing and objective standards of performance. Police were particularly keen on mimicking the professions by being accountable only to themselves, although the police version of accountability required that police officers be judged only by other officers from the same police department whereas professional review boards are composed of members of the same profession who do not all work in the same organization. Thus it was a diluted version of professionalization which the police sought.

In *Big-City Police* Fogelson detected two major reform movements among big city police. The first was in the late nineteenth and early twentieth centuries. It was part of a larger movement to reform all aspects of government. This was the "progressive" movement. The progressives wanted more businesslike government, although they realized that the main problem in American government was its control by big business. The political leaders of the progressives, most notably President Theodore Roosevelt and later President Woodrow Wilson, felt that most federal politicians as well as state politicians had become the servants of wealthy bankers and industrialists. Together with politicians, the Supreme Court protected "robber barons" of all types by narrow interpretations of the Constitution's clauses on contracts and property rights. The progressives called for a peaceful revolution. Among other things, they succeeded in getting the U.S. Senate more into the hands of the people by a Constitutional Amendment mandating direct election of senators instead of the original Constitutional provision of election of senators by state legislatures, which were controlled by the wealthy. They attempted municipal reforms by inventing new forms of local government, such as governing commissions and city managers.

The progressive movement wanted to run cities the way a successful business would be run. The emphases were on honesty and efficiency. This demanded that the person at the top of the organization be well informed about everything going on in the organization, that the person at the top make the decisions and control the resources of the organization, and that the organization operate by fixed and well known procedures. It also required that workers be well trained in their particular jobs, that complex jobs should be broken down into specialized parts, and that some workers should be trained as specialists to handle these more specialized tasks. The people who led the progressive movement at state and local levels were mostly religious leaders from the upper class Protestant churches, together with upper middleclass business people and people from notable old families. Although they claimed that they wanted to separate police from politics, in reality they wanted to wrest police from the diverse hands of local ethnic politicians in big city neighborhoods and put police in the hands of city-wide politicians who were more beholden to these upper-middle-class reformers. The progressives felt that they and their ideas would have more impact on mayors or citywide councilmen than on the various neighborhood politicians.

The second great reform movement was led by police administrators. It was a more focused movement towards turning police into some kind of profession. In many ways the founder of the movement was August Vollmer. Like so many police reformers, he was chief in a college town, Berkeley, California. He took up the idea that there could be a science of policing as a basis for professionalization. The university in town was a good place to start compiling and teaching this body of knowledge. Starting in 1906, for nearly three decades Vollmer led a movement to select and train police officers more carefully and to introduce modern technology into police work, such as the use of automobiles and the polygraph. One of his protégés, Orlando W. Wilson, eventually took charge of the Chicago police department from 1960–1967, where he continued the reform movement with efforts to use modern management approaches to manpower utilization and such technology upgrades as increased use of radios and computers. Most notable among other police chief reformers was William H. Parker, who brought the reform movement to the Los Angeles police department, where he was chief from 1950–1968. However, these reformers were most concerned about the inner workings of police departments, the problems of administration and technology. They were not particularly in touch with what typical police officers were doing in the routine performance of their jobs. The second great reform movement aimed at police professionalism but overlooked everyday police work at the street level. A gap developed between the police administrators and the police officers, with the police officers mostly continuing their traditional ways of doing the job. The visions of the reformers and the realities of the streets clashed and buckled in the conflicts of the 1960s and '70s.

In the final chapter of *Big-City Police* Fogelson concluded that police reform had come to a standstill. The reader may ask whether the conditions described by Fogelson a quarter century ago still provide a fairly accurate description of American police forces and whether reform of police is still at a standstill. If reform is considered from the point of view of the professional model, then one may ask whether there has been any notable advancement in police education and training requirements, accountability, technical proficiency, and so on. On the other hand, one may ask whether the professional model itself has been abandoned. One might ask whether police administrators ever really wanted a professional type of police or whether they wanted only selected aspects of professionalism. In Fogelson's account of the reform efforts based on professionalism there were discussions of residency requirements for police, more hiring of minorities, civilian review boards, neighborhood anti-crime organizations, and other possible indications of a different model of reform. This might be loosely described as a sort of new "community model" of policing starting to emerge but not yet recognized in the 1970s. However, one must consider whether these reforms in turn have made any substantial progress. One may also ask whether police themselves actually want "community policing."

Robert M. Fogelson. (1977). *Big-City Police*. Cambridge, MA: Harvard University Press. This selection is reproduced with permission of Robert M. Fogelson. It includes a short segment from Chapter 6, "The Professional Model," and most of Chapter 11, "Reform at a Standstill," which was the concluding chapter of *Big-City Police*. Section titles have been added. Footnotes have been renumbered. A glossary of police organizations and investigatory commissions has been appended. Any text in square brackets has been added by the editors of this selection.

Robert M. Fogelson

Big-City Police

A Second Generation of Reformers

On October 19, 1933, Dr. William Jay Schieffelin, Judge Samuel Seabury, and several hundred other notable New Yorkers assembled in Town Hall to pay tribute to the Reverend Charles H. Parkhurst, who had died several weeks before at the age of ninety-one. The meeting was a memorable occasion. It started out as a service for Dr. Parkhurst, the fiery pastor who had led the campaign against the New York City Police Department in the 1890s. But it turned into a rally for Fiorello H. La Guardia, the colorful ex-congressman who had been picked by the reformers to run for mayor on the fusion or anti-Tammany ticket in the first municipal election after the Seabury Committee investigation.[1] The meeting thus marked the passing of the first generation of reformers—which included, in addition to Dr. Parkhurst, Clarence Lexow, Gustav Schwab, John Goff, Theodore Roosevelt, and William Strong—and the arrival of the second generation. It was the second generation that carried on the reform campaign from the early 1930s through the late 1960s....

Hence Dr. Parkhurst's death marked not only the departure of one generation of reformers and the arrival of another but also the end of the first wave of police reform, which was inspired by the Progressive movement, and the beginning of the second, which was dominated by the law enforcement community. [The Progressive movement consisted of upper class people who formed various civic groups and campaigned for government to be run efficiently like a business, for more accountability to the public, and against corruption in all parts of government. The second wave of police reform focused only on police and was led by police administrators.] This is a vital, if not a rigid, distinction. August Vollmer of Berkeley, Richard Sylvester of Washington, James L. Beavers of Atlanta, William P. Rutledge of Detroit, and other high-level police officials had supported the reform effort before 1930. But the chambers of commerce, ministerial alliances, municipal leagues, and other nonpartisan organizations had led the first wave of reform. Far from abandoning the reform campaign, these groups rendered invaluable and in some cases indispensable financial, political, and moral assistance after 1930. But outside of Chicago and a few other cities where most policemen and politicians felt little or no sympathy for the reform effort, the voluntary associations had a deep-seated reluctance to take a commanding role in the second wave of reform. This transition, in which the leadership of the reform crusade shifted from the Progressive elites to the law enforcement groups, was far from over by the 1930s; but it was well underway and, with hindsight, just about irreversible.

The second generation of reformers was troubled by much the same things as the first, though not necessarily to the same degree or for the same reasons. Although its members were broadminded about some infractions of the blue laws, they were offended by gambling, prostitution, pornography, and other forms of commercial vice and were appalled by the use and sale of marijuana, heroin, and other so-called dangerous drugs.

They were disturbed by the insidious influence of partisan politics, which in their opinion undermined the integrity of the police forces and other parts of the criminal justice system.[2] They were irritated by the incompetence of the welfare bureaus, school boards, and other institutions, which in their judgment increased the responsibility of the police departments and decreased the legitimacy of the public authorities. They were dismayed by the sharp rise of serious crime, particularly of racketeering and extortion in the 1930s and 1940s, of organized crime and juvenile delinquency in the 1940s and 1950s, and of muggings, attacks, and drug abuse in the 1950s and 1960s. Unlike their predecessors, however, these reformers were driven not so much by their distaste for deviant behavior, machine politics, administrative inefficiency, and criminal activity as by their concern about the low status of the big-city police....

The Professional Model

[The second generation of reformers wanted to make police more like a profession.] Applying the professional model to the big-city police, the reformers arrived at three distinct yet closely related recommendations, which incorporated and extended the Progressive prescription for police reform.[3] The first recommendation was that the departments had to overcome the obstacles that had stymied their attempts to gain the same degree of autonomy as medicine, law, and the other professions. Hence the reformers called on the authorities to increase the chiefs' power, enhance their tenure, insulate them from partisan pressures, and otherwise strengthen their position vis-àvis ward and even city-wide politicians. Close down as many additional precincts as possible, they proposed, and transfer as many additional activities as possible from ordinary patrolmen attached to the precincts to special squads assigned to headquarters. In line with contemporary organizational theory, the reformers urged the departments to set up planning and research units, reorganize the force along functional instead of territorial lines, and clarify the division of responsibility among the precincts, squads, and other units. Form special inspectional units to keep a close watch over day-to-day operations, they suggested, and untangle the chain of command by reducing the number of officials who reported directly to the chiefs....

The second recommendation was that the departments had to surmount the hurdles which had thwarted their plans to bring the rank-and-file up to the same level as architects, professors, and other professionals. Thus the reformers pressed the authorities not only to accept only high school or college graduates, subject them to a thorough psychiatric screening, and otherwise tighten the physical, mental, and moral requirements, but also to raise salaries, increase pensions, improve working conditions, abolish residency requirements, and permit lateral entry. The reformers further encouraged the departments to expand existing training programs for recruits and develop in-service training facilities for veterans; to forbid the rank-and-file to solicit rewards, take part-time jobs, join labor unions, and engage in other activities that were inconsistent with professional status; and to devise promotional procedures that inhibited political interference, emphasized on-the-job performance, increased the chief's discretion, and reduced the number of years an officer had to serve at one rank to be eligible for advancement to another. Lastly, the reformers implored the authorities to shift the disciplinary proceedings from the city councils, police commissions, and civil service boards to the police chiefs, departmental trial boards, or other internal bodies....

The third recommendation was that the departments had to deal with the constraints which had handicapped their efforts to develop the same degree of proficiency as engineering, accounting, and the other professions. Hence the reformers suggested that the authorities should relieve the police of the responsibility to run ambulances, operate lockups, take censuses, provide special details for private concerns and public agencies, and carry out other tasks remotely if at all related to crime prevention. The departments should not only employ civilians in all sorts of clerical, secretarial, technical, and other positions currently filled by policemen but also curtail foot patrols, replace two-man with one-man squad cars, and deploy the uniformed force according to scientific formulas. Possibly in conjunction with sociologists, psychologists, criminologists, and other experts on deviance and delinquency, the profession should work out a theory of crime prevention that rested on something more substantial than dubious assumptions and antiquated prejudices. The departments should also compile and report criminal statistics in a more careful and less capricious style so that police administrators and ordinary citizens could compare criminal activity from one precinct to another, one city to the next, and one year to another....

Reform at a Standstill:
The Doubts of the Reformers

On October 24, 1968, Gordon E. Misner appeared before the National Commission on the Causes and Prevention of Violence. A prominent criminologist, Misner had impeccable reform credentials. As a product, in his words, of "California policing" he had preached the gospel according to August Vollmer, earned his Ph. D. at Berkeley's School of Criminology and worked with Joseph D. Lohman, who had succeeded O.W. Wilson as dean of the school. Yet in his testimony Misner expressed grave reservations about the conventional wisdom of the reform movement.[4] He observed that the Philadelphia police which "nobody ever accused of being a professional [force]," did a pretty good job without imposing stiff entrance requirements and maintaining high professional standards. He remarked that several other departments, which had carried out most of the reform recommendations, had run into all sorts of problems that Vollmer, Wilson, and other reformers had failed to anticipate. Misner's testimony, given two years after Wilson had retired and only one year after William H. Parker had died, revealed that by the late 1960s a few reformers were having second thoughts about some of the cardinal tenets of the reform movement.

A few of their second thoughts were predictable. Some reformers were worried about the growth of the special squads, a concern that had been voiced by Public Safety Director Smedley D. Butler of Philadelphia as early as the mid-1920s. Some of these units were essential, the reformers conceded; but if allowed to proliferate, they subverted the command structure, blurred the responsibility between patrolmen and plainclothesmen and provided the uniformed force with an excuse for inaction. The Knapp Commission revealed that, unless closely supervised, they also turned into the principal sources of graft and corruption in most departments. As Jerry V. Wilson, chief of the Washington, D.C., police, remarked, these squads posed still other problems that were less obvious but even more serious. They developed a strong esprit de corps, a conviction that they were superior to the uniformed force, which severely undermined the morale of the rest of the department. They also siphoned off from the uniformed force many of its most competent and committed members, who regarded a transfer to a plainclothes unit as the next best thing to a promotion.[5] Since the patrolmen and not the plainclothesmen dealt with ordinary citizens on a day-to-day basis, this practice did little to enhance the public image of the big-city police.

Some reformers were troubled as well by the operation of the civil service, an anxiety that had been articulated by Commissioner Arthur Woods of New York City as early as the late 1910s. Some regulations were necessary, they acknowledged, to insulate personnel practices from partisan politics. But the promotional procedures, which relied heavily on written tests, seniority, oral interviews, and field evaluations, were not reliable indicators of potential leadership, Commissioner Robert J. diGrazia of Boston charged. Instead of moving up promising commanders, the civil service rewarded run-of-the-mill patrolmen who were anxious to increase their pay and raise their status and had a knack for taking tests and avoiding trouble. In a striking departure from the conventional wisdom, a few reformers even criticized the appointments process. According to James M. Murray, personnel director of the Washington, D.C. police in the late 1960s, there was little correlation between IQ levels, test scores, or other recruitment criteria and ordinary performance measures. According to the Rand Corporation, which did a survey of minority recruitment in New York City in the early 1970s, the civil service was so slow that many qualified candidates dropped out of the running.[6]

Some reformers were also critical of the efforts to enforce the vice laws, a position that had been spelled out by Chief August Vollmer as early as the mid-1920s. Gambling, prostitution, and drunkenness were deplorable, they admitted. But in the face of the pervasive indifference, not to mention the out-and-out opposition, of many Americans, there was nothing much the police could do about these activities. As James F. Ahern, chief of the New Haven police in the late 1960s, wrote, the police also paid a high price for trying.[7] Well aware that gamblers, bookies, prostitutes, and numbers runners often operated with virtual impunity, many citizens drew the conclusion that the police were either corrupt or incompetent. And according to the Seabury, Knapp, and other official commissions that looked into the activities of the vice squads, this conclusion was not wide of the mark. To many reformers, this price seemed exorbitant in the early 1970s. They did not see how the police could justify spending so much time and money on gambling and other morals offenses at a time when murder, rape, robbery, and burglary were on the rise. Nor did these reformers see how the police could justify assigning so many officers to vice squads at a time when many departments were being forced to put a freeze on appointments and even to lay off veteran officers.

But some of the second thoughts about the cardinal tenets of the reform movement were unexpected. A few reformers were skeptical about the validity of the professional model, a notion that had been sacrosanct down through the late 1950s. This skepticism took several different forms. To Misner, professionalism had gone too far; the gap between politics and policing had grown too wide. "I don't want City Hall to be out of the police department," he told the Violence Commission. "I don't want the day-to-day interference with operating routine.... But I do want the participation of ... the political leadership in the long-range planning and policy development." To Ahern, however, professionalism had not gone far enough; it had reached the chiefs, but it had not been extended to the patrolmen. Most departments paid lip service to the professional model, he pointed out; in practice, they continued to treat the rank-and-file like "military operatives." And to Jerry Wilson, professionalism was simply inappropriate, a reflection of an elitist attitude toward ordinary work. Rather than following undertakers, salesmen, janitors, and other groups in the ludicrous quest for professional status, Wilson wrote, police officers should model themselves on carpenters, bricklayers, plumbers, and the other so-called "master craftsmen."[8]

A few reformers also doubted the wisdom of requiring a college degree of all recruits, a requirement that had been endorsed by the President's Crime Commission in the late 1960s. Jerry Wilson based his objections on several grounds other than the difficulty of persuading college graduates to go into policing. First, the police should be "reasonably representative" of the community, which was full of citizens who did not start, much less finish, college. Second, the police should serve as "a ladder" to the middle class for blacks and other newcomers who would be hard pressed to meet this requirement. And third, the police do a good deal of tedious work which would probably bore many college graduates, a point also stressed by Misner. Wilson did not object to higher education for police officers; on the contrary, he encouraged the rank-and-file to attend college classes and supported plans to give them extra pay for college credits. But he strongly objected to the proposal to make the college degree an entrance requirement, a proposal that in his view reflected the law enforcement community's drive for professional status and its infatuation with formal credentials. Attacking the conventional wisdom of the reform movement, Wilson insisted that anyone with a solid education through the tenth grade should have no trouble assimilating police training and understanding departmental regulations.[9]

A few reformers were critical too of the rhetoric of the "war on crime," a rhetoric that had been employed by the Johnson Administration in the mid-1960s. As Misner pointed out, the police spend most of their time, probably as much as 90 percent, directing traffic, helping people, and doing all sorts of other things which by no stretch of the imagination are related to crime prevention. The police do not use the remaining 10 percent of their time very well, Ahern added. They still do not know what causes crime, and notwithstanding the widespread acceptance of the Uniform Crime Reports, they still cannot measure criminal activity with much precision. A few reformers also insisted that the public tended to expect too much of the police. Addressing a Police Foundation conference, Patrick Murphy spoke out against this tendency, which he attributed to the tradition of the frontier marshal, a susceptibility to easy solutions, and the rhetoric of law and order. "Somehow," he told his audience, "we must let the American public know that neither the police nor other elements in the criminal justice system have anything approaching a complete answer to the problems of crime." [10]

Misner, Murphy, Ahern, and Jerry Wilson did not repudiate the campaign for police reform. They had no wish to return to the days when public service was a means of social mobility, local control was a source of political legitimacy, ethnic life-styles were an expression of American culture, and the police department was an adjunct of the political machine. Nor did they speak for the majority of their fellow reformers. Most of them were more concerned about political interference than bureaucratic isolation, more troubled by undereducated officers than overeducated officers, and more inclined to stress the progress of policing than to emphasize its limitations. But Misner and the other skeptics expressed reservations about the reform campaign which cannot be lightly dismissed. These reservations not only raised questions that threatened the ideological consensus on which the reform movement was based—questions about the relationship between policing and politics, credentials and qualifications, crime and society. These reservations also reflected a growing concern about the course of police reform among millions of Americans, many of whom had supported the reform campaign down through World War II and even into the 1960s.

The Doubts of Citizens about the Course of Police Reform

Many Americans were concerned about the course of police reform for traditional reasons. These Americans, who were represented by the crime commissions, chambers of commerce, taxpayers outfits, and other agents of the financial and commercial elites, placed a high priority on public order, managerial expertise, and governmental efficiency. Direct descendants of the Progressives, they had long accepted the reformers' assumptions about the nature of public service, political legitimacy, and American culture as well as their convictions about the relationship between politics and policing. They had also shared the reformers' confidence that if the local authorities changed the structure, personnel, and function of the police departments in line with the reform prescription, they would solve the police problem and in time the crime problem as well. But lately these Americans had begun to think that their confidence was misplaced. For despite the special squads and precinct consolidations, the civil service and service pensions, and the Uniform Crime Reports and preventive patrol, the big-city police still left much to be desired—not so much as in the 1890s, when the Lexow Committee [see the glossary] held its hearings, or in the 1930s, when the Wickersham Commission issued its report, but enough to raise serious doubts about the long-run efficacy of the reform movement.

Two things in particular troubled these Americans. The first was that the reformers had not put an end to the corruption, incompetence, and lawlessness of the big-city police. In 1974, a decade and a half after Commissioner Thomas J. Gibbons left the Philadelphia police, the Pennsylvania Crime Commission uncovered evidence "of systematic, widespread corruption at all levels of the Department." Similar revelations rocked New York, Seattle, Indianapolis, and several other cities in which the reformers had gained control of the police force after World War II. In 1972, a decade and a half after Commissioner Stephen P. Kennedy quit the New York City police, the New York Times reported that many officers were working at what one senior commander estimated at no more than 50 percent efficiency. Although the New York City Police Department had an unenviable reputation, there was no reason to believe that it was much less efficient than other big-city forces. In 1973, less than a decade after Superintendent O.W. Wilson retired from the Chicago police, a blue-ribbon panel charged that many officers employed excessive force in the black and Puerto Rican communities. Shortly thereafter the Chicago Tribune published an eight-part series that not only confirmed the panel's charges but also concluded that police brutality was common in the white neighborhoods as well.[11]

The second source of concern was that the big-city police had not put an end to crime in the streets. Notwithstanding the saturation squads, field interrogations, crime labs, Uniform Crime Reports, and other innovations, the police were hard put to do much about what Newsweek magazine referred to in 1965 as a condition of epidemic criminality. Whether crime was worse in the 1960s than in the 1920s, when the second wave of police reform got underway, is impossible to say because the available statistics are not reliable enough to permit generalizations from one decade to another. But crime was probably on the rise in the 1960s, and in any case most citizens thought it was. Of five hundred persons who were asked in the mid-1960s whether violent crime had increased in the District of Columbia over the last five years, 60 percent said very much, 22 percent a little, 10 percent not much, and 3 percent not at all. Only one percent said it had decreased.[12] Conditions were much the same in most other big cities. Out of respect for the FBI and a reverence for hard data most Americans took at face value the results of the Uniform Crime Reports, which as a rule revealed a steady and often sharp rise in criminal activity in urban America. And they accepted as gospel the jeremiads of Hoover, Parker, and other well-known law enforcement officials who were not averse to exploiting the fear of crime to justify their requests for additional manpower and increased resources.

The critics were no doubt too hard on the reformers. The big-city police were less corrupt, incompetent, and lawless in the late 1960s than in the early 1930s and the middle 1890s, a mark of progress for which the reformers deserved much of the credit. And if the police had not made much headway against crime, neither had the prosecutors, courts, and correctional institutions. But the reformers had only themselves to blame for the growing skepticism about the reform movement. For two decades they had claimed that the big-city police would be free of corruption, incompetence, and lawlessness once their structure, personnel, and function were revised according to the reform prescription. They had also contended that once the police were reorganized along the lines of the military analogy or the professional model, they would greatly cut down, if not completely wipe out, crime in urban America. The reformers had been persuasive. Over the years they had prevailed on most Americans not only to adopt their goals and support their efforts but also to accept their standards. Hence their fellow citizens evaluated the reform movement not from an historical viewpoint, which might have given a proper perspective, but by the reformers' own criteria. By these criteria the results were somewhat less than satisfactory.

Perhaps for lack of a viable alternative, some Americans remained loyal to the reform campaign. Along with the Knapp Commission and the Pennsylvania Crime Commission, they held that the big-city police were still prone to corruption, incompetence, and lawlessness not because the reform proposals were ill-advised but because they had not been put into practice. Despite the valiant efforts of Wilson, Murphy, and the other reformers, the police still bowed to pressure from the local politicians, still appointed too many unqualified applicants, and still spent too much energy on chores other than crime prevention. Now was the time to rally behind the reformers, these Americans concluded, not to abandon them. This viewpoint was not limited, to conservatives. Testifying before the Violence Commission, Ramsey Clark, attorney general in the Johnson Administration and a Democrat with outstanding liberal credentials, insisted that the solution to the police problem was, in a word, professionalization. Two years later Clark recommended that the big-city police require college degrees of all recruits, appoint specialists with graduate degrees in medicine, law, criminology, and related disciplines, and focus their efforts exclusively on crime prevention.[13] Although characterized by Tom Wicker of the New York Times as "the most revolutionary public voice in America," Clark said little that ran counter to the conventional wisdom of the reform movement.

Signs of Dwindling Confidence in Police

But many Americans lost faith in the reform campaign. Stunned by the revelations of the Knapp Commission and other investigative agencies, they no longer believed that the big-city police could stamp out corruption and incompetence, much less wipe out violent crime. The great popularity of *Serpico* and *Dirty Harry* was one sign of the dwindling confidence in the big-city police. *Serpico*, a movie about the New York City police, described how Officer Frank Serpico discovers that with one or two exceptions everyone is "on the take" and no one, not the commissioner and not even the mayor, does anything about it. A dedicated officer, who to the delight of the middle- and upper-middle-class audiences combines an Italian-American background with a Greenwich Village life style, Serpico is shot in the head for his attempts to expose the system. *Dirty Harry*, a film about the San Francisco police, depicted the plight of Detective Harry Calahan, another dedicated and courageous officer, who is stymied by self-serving politicians, woolly headed judges, and nitpicking commanders. Calahan finally gets his man, but only by defying his superiors and taking the law into his own hands. In *Magnum Force*, the sequel to *Dirty Harry*, Calahan has no choice but to throw away his badge.[14]

Another sign of the dwindling confidence in the big-city police was the deep-seated reluctance to report criminal activity. According to the nationwide victimization survey sponsored by the LEAA [see the glossary] in the early 1970s, roughly one of every three crimes went unreported in Newark and St. Louis, one of every two in New York, Baltimore, and Atlanta, three of every five in Cleveland, Dallas, and Portland, two of every three in Chicago, Denver, and Los Angeles, and a whopping four of every five in Philadelphia.

There were many reasons that the victims failed to call the police. According to another nationwide victimization study, published by the President's Crime Commission in the late 1960s, some Americans felt the crime was a private matter; others were afraid of reprisals; some could not spare the time; a few were worried about the offenders; and others were too confused or upset by the incident. But according to this and other surveys, the victims did not report crimes partly because they lacked confidence in the police forces. Of several hundred victims who were asked to account for their reluctance to call the police, 28 percent replied that the officers would not want to be bothered, 58 percent said that the police could not do anything about it anyway, and 31 percent answered that even if they tried, the police would not necessarily arrest the right person.[15]

Still another sign of the dwindling confidence in the big-city police was the widespread enthusiasm for community policing, self-defense, and even vigilante activity. The North Ward Citizens Committee patrolled the Italian neighborhoods of Newark and the Maccabees Safety Patrol policed the Jewish communities of Brooklyn. The Crime Prevention Institute set up an escort service in New York's Harlem; and with the support of LEAA the Sav-Mor Association organized a house-watch program in Boston's Roxbury. As the President's Crime Commission reported, many persons stayed home after dark, put iron bars on their windows, left the lights on at night, and kept a dog on the premises. Many others attended judo and karate classes, bought mace cans and tear-gas pens, carried knives or handguns, and took other drastic steps to protect themselves. Few Americans were ready to tangle with dangerous criminals. But many were quick to applaud Paul Kersey, the hero of the movie *Death Wish*, a well-to-do architect who seeks out muggers and summarily executes them after his wife and daughter are brutally assaulted. A one-man vigilante squad, Kersey reflects the growing sentiment that the lone gunman was, in the words of Penelope Gilliatt, one of the *New Yorker's* film critics, "a big city's only hope of law and order."[16]

The Rising Costs of Policing

To make matters worse for the reformers, the price of policing and other public services was, as the Washington *Post* put it, "sky-rocketing." The rise was steep in New York. Between 1963 and 1973, a decade in which the size of the force increased from 26,700 to 31,500, or roughly 18 percent, the cost of operations went up from $299 million to $587 million or roughly 96 percent. But the rise was just as steep, if not steeper, in most other big cities. By the early 1970s Chicago spent more than $200 million on policing, Los Angeles,

Detroit, and Philadelphia more than $100 million, Baltimore and Boston more that $50 million, and Cleveland and Houston more than $25 million. Assured by the reformers that the departments had to raise salaries, benefits, and pensions in order to attract and retain qualified officers, most citizens were willing to go along with the increases through the 1960s. But dismayed by the inflation of the early 1970s and the recession that followed, they now began to wonder not only whether the cities were getting their money's worth but also whether they could afford the mounting costs of the reform movement. Summing up this sentiment, Vice-President Nelson A. Rockefeller, chairman of the National Commission on Productivity and Work Quality, told a conference, "Our citizens' right to have safe streets can no longer be sought at any cost." [17]

The costs of policing were skyrocketing for two principal reasons other than the steady increase in the number of officers. One reason was that under pressure from the police unions and to a lesser degree the reform groups most big cities gave the rank-and-file substantial raises in the late 1960s and early 1970s. New York was extremely generous. Between 1966 and 1974 a patrolman's base pay after five years experience went up from $8,500 to $15,300, an increase of close to 80 percent, and his direct earnings, which included longevity increments, paid holidays, and night-shift differentials, rose from $8,800 to $16,800, an increase of over 90 percent. By virtue of a pegging system the superior officers—who as a result of a trend that went back to the turn of the century and reached a peak in the early 1970s now made up one-third of the sworn personnel and one-fourth of the entire force in most cities—received comparable raises. But many other cities were just as generous. By 1974 a patrolman started at more than $14,000 in San Francisco, more than $11,000 in Seattle, Los Angeles, Chicago, Cleveland, and Detroit, more than $10,000 in Boston and Houston, and, more than $9,000 in Pittsburgh, Denver, and Phoenix. A patrolman with five to nine years experience earned that year at least $15,000 in San Francisco, Los Angeles, and Detroit, at least $14,000 in Chicago, Boston, and San Diego, and al least $13,000 in New Orleans, Milwaukee, and Philadelphia. [18] The superior officers received 33 to 100 percent more in most of these cities....

Concerns about Police Autonomy, Citizens' Rights, and Civil Rights

Many Americans were concerned about the course of police reform for different reasons. These Americans, who were represented by the civil liberties unions and civil rights groups, put a high priority on personal liberty, racial equality, and bureaucratic accountability. What troubled them was not so much the corruption and incompetence of the police or the high cost of policing as the much-heralded autonomy of the police. To put it another way, these Americans were distressed not because the reform movement had done too little or because it had gotten too expensive but because it had done too much. From their perspective, which was shared by Misner and a few other reformers, the movement had not only separated policing from politics, which was admirable, but also removed it from popular control, which was deplorable. In addition to denying the local politicians their sources of influence, the movement had deprived the ordinary citizens of their avenues of redress; if scrupulous officers could operate with impunity, so could the unscrupulous. The reform movement had improved the quality of policing in a number of ways, these Americans conceded; but in the process it had fostered a degree of bureaucratic irresponsibility that was out of place in a democratic society.

This concern surfaced in the late 1950s and early 1960s when the United States Commission on Civil Rights revealed that many blacks felt powerless to do anything about police malpractice. Some of the commission's advisory committees later confirmed these revelations; so did the University of California School of Criminology and the Atlanta, Boston, and New York City chapters of the ACLU. According to the President's Crime Commission, the blacks had reason to feel this way. Drawing on a nation-wide survey of police-community relations by Michigan State University, the commission reported that police officers were rarely convicted and punished on the basis of a complaint by citizens. These revelations had a strong impact on many Americans, whites as well as blacks. For one thing, they came in the wake of a number of studies by the NAACP and ACLU which showed that a generation after the Wickersham Commission report on lawless law enforcement the big-city police still arrested citizens without a warrant, detained them without cause, and otherwise violated their civil liberties. For another thing, they came in the heyday of the civil rights crusade, a time when the intense emotions aroused by the Montgomery bus boycott, the Birmingham sit-ins, the March on Washington, and the other efforts to undermine the racial status quo had reached their peak.[19]

As some Americans realized, this problem was largely an out-growth of the reform movement, which had persuaded the authorities that the responsibility for handling complaints against the police should be entrusted to the police, and to them alone. Out of a deep concern for the reputation of their departments the internal affairs units and other special squads that assumed this responsibility employed a host of reprehensible tactics to discourage citizens from filing complaints against officers. They threatened complainants with criminal libel in New York City, demanded that they take a lie detector test in

Cleveland, and charged them with disorderly conduct, resisting arrest, and other offenses in Philadelphia; Washington, D.C.; and Los Angeles. If the citizens filed a complaint anyway, many departments intimidated them and their witnesses. If the citizens requested a hearing, which in light of the expensive, complicated, and protracted proceedings involved was highly unlikely, many departments refused to provide them with counsel or allow them access to the files. In other words, the police behaved as if the complainants, not the officers, were on trial.[20] As a result most departments upheld so small a fraction of the complaints that many citizens concluded that self-policing, one of the principal corollaries of the professional model, was a sham.

Led by the ACLU and NAACP, these citizens called on the authorities to shift the responsibility for handling complaints from the police departments to outside review boards, or as they were commonly referred to, civilian review boards. These boards would serve several purposes, their sponsors claimed. They would restrain the many officers who in the absence of an effective disciplinary system engaged in brutality, harassment, and other improper and even illegal practices. By ensuring a thorough and impartial investigation of all complaints, they would protect the other officers against malicious, misguided, and otherwise unfounded accusations. They would provide the blacks and other ethnic minorities an avenue of redress, which would help restore their dwindling confidence in the police departments and other municipal agencies. They would explain police procedures to the citizens, review enforcement requirements with the police, and start a genuine dialogue in place of mutual recrimination. By curbing police malpractice and improving police-community relations, the review boards would greatly enhance the quality of law enforcement in urban America.[21] The boards would have "no disciplinary powers whatever," their backers assured the police; they would only make recommendations to the departments, which would deal with the officers as they saw fit.

The proposed boards incensed most police officers, who regarded them as a severe threat to their professional aspirations and especially to their determination to set their standards and discipline their colleagues without outside interference. Led by the IACP, ICPA, and FOP [see the glossary], the police lashed out against the proposal. The amount of malpractice is greatly exaggerated, they insisted; the cries of brutality and harassment are usually nothing but attempts to subvert law enforcement. The police departments, the courts, and the Justice Department all provide adequate avenues of redress on the rare occasion when a citizen is mistreated by an officer. The review boards would be inequitable, impractical, and undesirable—inequitable because they would draw invidious distinctions between the police departments and other municipal agencies, impractical because they would ask people with no expertise or experience to sit in judgment on police officers, and undesirable because they would inject politics into policing and set the reform movement back several decades. If put into practice, these boards would demoralize the police, weaken their authority, impair their efficiency, and thus exacerbate the crime problem. Rather than press ahead with this hare-brained scheme, the police spokesmen concluded, the civil liberties and civil rights groups should lend their support to the ongoing efforts to professionalize the big-city police.[22]...

The controversy was not particularly inspiring. The ACLU and NAACP overstated the case for the review boards almost, though not quite, as much as the ICPA and FOP exaggerated the case against them. If the experience of the Philadelphia advisory board is indicative, the review boards would not have greatly curbed police malpractice or improved police-community relations, but neither would they have severely hamstrung the police forces or exacerbated the crime problem. The controversy was illuminating, however. It not only revealed that the rank-and-file groups were now a force to be reckoned with in most cities and that they would use their formidable power to conserve many of the reform legacies of which their members were the principal beneficiaries. More than any other issue of the decade, it also showed that many citizens who had hitherto supported the reform campaign were no longer willing to go along with the notion of self-policing and the assumptions about politics, policing, and professionalism underlying it. The controversy indicated too that out of a genuine concern for the plight of the blacks and other minorities some of these citizens were prepared to tolerate a degree of political interference and to sacrifice a degree of professional autonomy in order to enhance the accountability of the big-city police.

Minority Access

The civil liberties and civil rights groups would probably not have pushed so hard for the civilian review boards if the big-city police had been representative of the communities they served. But as the President's Riot Commission pointed out, most departments were overwhelmingly white. Nowhere did nonwhites hold a fair share of the jobs. They were underrepresented by a factor of two in Philadelphia and San Francisco, three in New York and Kansas City, four in Atlanta and Newark, five in Boston and Cincinnati, six in Baltimore and Buffalo, and eight or more in Oakland, Detroit, and New Orleans.[23] To many citizens it seemed that in an effort to upgrade the force the big-city police had excluded not only the illiterate, incapacitated, and unsavory but also the blacks, Mexicans, and Puerto Ricans. No doubt some of the minority candidates were unqualified, but what, these citizens asked, about the rest of them? In the absence of a satisfactory answer some Americans who had previously supported the reform campaign concluded that exclusion of these racial and ethnic minorities was indefensible.

This issue emerged in the South in the late 1940s and early 1950s when the Southern Regional Council reported that with one or two exceptions none of the region's leading cities employed more than a handful of black police officers. But the issue did not surface outside the South until the early and middle 1960s when the United States Commission on Civil Rights pointed out that blacks and other minorities fared only slightly better in the rest of the nation. And it did not come to a head until the late 1960s when the President's Crime Commission and the President's Riot Commission, whose reports reached a wide audience and generated a good deal of interest, confirmed the findings. These reports had a profound impact on many Americans, whites as well as blacks. For one thing, they came out in the midst of the civil rights movement, when the campaign to prohibit discrimination in private employment which culminated in the passage of the Civil Rights Act of 1964 had left Americans extremely sensitive to charges of discrimination in the public sector. For another thing, the reports came out at the height of the 1960s riots, when Los Angeles. Newark and Detroit, and the other major cities were so racked by violent protest that for the first time in history Americans were forced to consider whether the big-city police could maintain law and order in the black ghettos.[24]

As some Americans realized, this problem was largely an outgrowth of the reform movement, which had persuaded the authorities to adopt a number of policies that severely, if inadvertently, discriminated against blacks and other groups. Under pressure from the reformers the authorities abolished the residency requirements, which slowed down the turnover of the Irish-Americans and other second- and third-generation immigrants and also reduced the competitive edge of blacks and other first-and second-generation newcomers. They underwrote vigorous recruiting efforts, which were aimed not at central city churches, YMCAs and high schools, which were mainly black, Mexican, and Puerto Rican, but at out-of-town colleges, universities, and military bases, which were predominantly white. They put great emphasis on written tests, which winnowed out a higher percentage of blacks, Mexicans and Puerto Ricans than of whites. They tightened the character checks, which disqualified a disproportionate number of blacks and other newcomers on the grounds that they had picked up a criminal record, changed jobs too often, or received a less than honorable discharge from the armed forces.

Surely, many Americans concluded, it was time for the authorities to find other ways to raise the caliber of the big-city police....

It was also time for them to take steps to increase the number of black officers. Following this line, many Americans called on the authorities to do their recruiting in the central cities, a move, they claimed, that would encourage more blacks and other newcomers, at least some of whom would be qualified, to consider a career in policing....

Many Americans also called on the authorities to reimpose the residency requirements, a move, they argued, that would not only increase the competitive edge of the blacks and other minorities, but also improve the quality of law enforcement and alleviate the fiscal crisis of the cities. But the rank-and-file outfits strongly objected to this proposal. Stressing that it would violate the civil liberties of the officers and, by excluding qualified candidates from out of town and compelling veteran officers to choose between their jobs and their homes, lower the caliber of the police departments, they opposed it in one city after another....

Many Americans called on the authorities to change the entrance requirements too, a move, they insisted, that would increase the probability that blacks and other newcomers who applied would be appointed. But under intense pressure from the reform groups and rank-and-file outfits, which charged that this proposal would lower the quality of the big-city police, the authorities were extremely reluctant to do so. Thus the Massachusetts Law Reform Institute and other public and quasi-public law firms filed suit in Boston, Philadelphia, Oakland, and several other cities in the late 1960s and early 1970s. They charged that the written tests, character checks, and other entrance requirements discriminated against the blacks and other minorities and therefore violated the equal protection clause of the Fourteenth Amendment. In their defense the authorities insisted that these requirements were applied in a nondiscriminatory way and, citing prominent reformers, added that they were needed to maintain the caliber of the big-city police. But the denials were not persuasive. As Thomas A. Mela of the Law Reform Institute brought out in his examination of Arthur C. Cadegan, Jr., deputy superintendent of personnel and training of the Boston Police Department, the defendants could not produce any studies, surveys, or other evidence to support their contention that the entrance requirements were predictive of on-the-job performance.[25]... As a result, the plaintiffs won a series of major cases in the early 1970s....

Population Changes and Attitudes toward Police

The course of police reform aroused concern not only among many lower- and lower-middle-class blacks but also among many upper-middle- and upper-class whites, who had formed the basis of the reform coalition since the turn of the century....

The course of police reform was only one of several reasons for the breakup of the reform coalition. Of the other reasons the most important was a marked change in the make-up of the upper-middle-class Americans. Prior to 1900 these Americans were a fairly homogeneous group. The grandsons and great grandsons of northern and western Europeans, most of them had been born in the mid-nineteenth century, brought up as Protestants, and raised in the villages and small towns of rural America. They came of age in the late nineteenth century, a time when the political machines were in their heyday, the police forces were in disrepute, and municipal corruption seemed to be the most critical domestic problem. All this changed over the next sixty or seventy years as a large number of second- and third-generation immigrants managed to climb into the upper-middle class. The sons and grandsons of southern and eastern Europeans, many of these immigrants had been born after World War I, brought up as Catholics or Jews, and raised in the great cities of the Northeast, Midwest, and Pacific Coast. They came of age after World War II, by which time the political machines were on the wane, the police departments were on the mend, and racial discrimination had replaced municipal corruption as the country's most serious domestic problem....

For the first time a good many upper-middle-class Americans were skeptical about the conventional wisdom of the reform movement too. Now that the ward bosses had little or no power over the big-city police, they wondered why the authorities should attempt to consolidate or close down precincts over the strenuous objections of the local residents. Now that most officers were appointed in their early or middle twenties, they questioned whether the authorities should allow the police to retire on a handsome pension after only twenty or twenty-five years of service. Now that the local politicians had little to say about appointments, they wondered whether the authorities should impose written tests and other entrance requirements that discriminated against blacks and other minorities. And now that the rank-and-file were well organized and their unions bargained over promotional practices, disciplinary procedures, and other issues, they questioned the point of retaining the civil service. In view of the disaffection of the upper-middle-class Americans with the course of police reform it is little wonder that the reform coalition was shattered in the 1960s and 1970s.

A function of a fundamental realignment of social classes and ethnic groups, the breakup of the reform coalition brought the second wave of police reform to a standstill by the early 1970s. Not that the reformers stopped trying. On the contrary, they worked as hard as ever. Led by Murphy and other influential figures, they called on the departments to require a college degree of all recruits, shift from two-man to one-man squad cars and employ computers to allocate manpower. They urged the universities, foundations, and federal agencies to lend support to the schools of criminology and departments of police science that transmitted the gospel of professionalism to the next generation of law enforcement officials. They appealed to the IACP, whose members had applauded reform rhetoric at their annual meetings and whose staff had incorporated reform principles into their field surveys, to take a more active role in the reform campaign. They asked the LEAA and the Police Foundation, which were supposed to upgrade policing by encouraging innovation, experimentation, and evaluation, to underwrite concrete, though as a rule fairly conventional reforms in one department after another.

But the reformers ran into stiff resistance. Their efforts aroused the opposition not only of many police officers, which was bad enough, but also of many upper-middle-class Americans, which was even worse. These Americans were a formidable lot. They were well educated, well off, and sophisticated; they knew their way around the courts, the legislatures, the press, and the other institutions that molded the big-city police. They were not inclined to compromise, especially on civil rights issues; nor were they easily intimidated or bought off. They also gained strength from the demand for community control, the assault on civil service and the other attempts to dismantle the monuments of the Progressive movement. By the mid-1970s they had the reformers on the defensive. Far from moving ahead with their plans, the reformers were hard pressed to preserve the entrance requirements, disciplinary procedures, and other legacies of two generations of police reform. Whether the reformers would regain the initiative in the face of this resistance remained to be seen. But the prospects were poor, indeed so poor that it is safe to say that by the mid-1970s, or roughly eighty years after the Lexow Committee opened its hearings, the campaign for police reform had come to a standstill.

Footnotes

1. New York *Times*, Sept. 9, Oct. 20, 1933; Mitgang, *Man Who Rode the Tiger*, ch. 17; Arthur Mann, *La Guardia Comes to Power, 1933* (Philadelphia, 1965), ch. 3.
2. V.W. Peterson to Charles W. White, July 17, 1951, Chicago Crime Commission Files.

3. [The reader is referred to an earlier footnote, as follows:] In addition to *Municipal Police Administration* and *Police Administration*, I have based my interpretation of the reform diagnosis and prescription on many other documents, perhaps the most revealing of which are Vollmer, "Police Conditions in the United States"; Citizens' Police Committee, *Chicago Police Problems*; Vollmer, *Police and Modern Society*; Smith, *Police Systems in the United States*; Smith, ed., *New Goals in Police Management*; Donald C. Stone, "Recruitment of Policemen," IACP's *Bulletins on Police Problems*, no. 1, August 1938; August Vollmer, "Police Bureau Survey: City of Portland Oregon" (Portland, 1947); Finance Commission of the City of Boston, *The Boston Police Survey* (Boston, 1949); Institute of Public Administration, *The New York Police Survey* (New York, 1952); Bruce Smith, "Report of a Survey of the San Francisco, California Police Department" (1957); Institute of Public Administration, "The Atlanta Police Survey" (1957); President's Commission on Crime in the District of Columbia, *Report on the Metropolitan Police Department* (Washington, D.C., 1965); O.W. Wilson, "Police Organization and Administration," *National Municipal Review*, December 1936, 700ff. The IACP's *Police Yearbook*, the Southern Institute for Law Enforcement's *Proceedings*, and *the Journal of Criminal Law and Criminology* are also quite revealing.

4. President's Violence Commission, *Transcript of Proceedings*, Oct. 24, 1968, pp. 1,898–1,902.

5. Wilson and McLaren, *Police Administration*, pp. 79–86, 321–327; *Kanpp Commission Report*, pp. 1–3; Jerry Wilson, *Police Report* (Boston, 1975), p. 142.

6. Benjamin Shimberg and Robert J. diGrazia, "Promotion," in O. Glenn Stahl and Richard A. Staufenberger, eds., *Police Personnel Administration* (Washington, D.C., 1974), pp. 101–124; Terry Eisenberg and James M. Murray, "Selection," in ibid., pp. 76–79; Bernard Cohen, *Minority Recruiting in the New York City Police Department*, Part II. *The Retention of Candidates* (New York, 1971), pp. 50–57.

7. Ahern, *Police in Trouble*, pp. 143–150.

8. President's Violence Commission, *Transcript of Proceedings*, Oct. 24, 1968, p. 1,902; Ahern, *Police in Trouble*, pp. 192–193; Wilson, *Police Report*, p. 198.

9. Wilson, *Police Report*, pp. 174–178; Wilson's letter to Washington *Post*, Dec. 19, 1970.

10. Police Foundation, "News Release," April 29, 1974, p. 3; President's Violence Commission, *Transcript of Proceedings*, Oct. 24, 1968, p. 1,912; Ahern, *Police in Trouble*, pp. 150–155.

11. *Pennsylvania Crime Commission Report*, p. 1; *Knapp Commission Report*, pp. 1–3; Williams, *Vice Squad*, pp. 56–62; New York *Times*, Aug. 10, 1972; Mar. 4, 1974; *Christian Science Monitor*, Mar. 19, 1974; George Bliss, "Bad Apples on the Beat," *The Nation*, Feb. 9, 1974, pp. 171–174.

12. *Newsweek*, Aug. 16, 1965, p. 20; Biderman *et al.*, *Victimization and Attitudes Toward Law Enforcement*, p. 133.

13. President's Violence Commission, *Transcript of Proceedings*, Sept. 18, 1968, pp. 17, 22; Ramsey Clark, *Crime in America* (New York), p. 9, ch. 9.

14. For reviews of these movies, see the New York *Times*, Dec. 23, 1971; Nov. 25, Dec. 26, 1973.

15. New York *Times*, April 15, 1974; Ennis, *Criminal Victimization in the United States*, pp. 43–47; Biderman *et al.*, *Victimization and Attitudes Toward Law Enforcement*, pp. 153–155.

16. Dick Russell, "Police Action—Yes! Vigilantes—No!" *Parade*, June 22, 1975, pp. 8–10; Albert J. Reiss, Jr., "Public Perceptions and Recollections about Crime, Law Enforcement, and Criminal Justice," in *Studies in Crime and Law Enforcement in Major Metropolitan Areas*, I, Section II, 102–112; *The New Yorker*, Aug. 26, 1974, p. 50.

17. Washington *Post*, May 10, 1975; Raymond D. Horton, "Economic Brief for the City of New York," brief prepared for the impasse proceeding between the city and the PBA in 1975, pp.76, 85; ICMA, *The Municipal Year Book* (Washington, D.C., 1973), pp. 175–176.

18. Horton, "Economic Brief," pp. 109, 142; *The Municipal Year Book* (Washington, D.C., 1975), pp. 52–53.

19. U.S. Commission on Civil Rights, *Hearings Held in Detroit, Michigan, December 14–15, 1960* (Washington, D.C., 1961), pp. 379–388; U.S. Commission on Civil Rights, *Hearing [Held in] Newark, New Jersey, September 11–12, 1962* (Washington, D.C., 1963), pp. 473–483; American Civil Liberties Union, *Police Power and Citizens' Rights: The Case for an Independent Police Review Board*, pp. 8–19; Joseph D. Lohman and Gordon E. Misner, *The Police and the Community*, report prepared for President's Crime Commission (Washington, D.C., 1966), I, 167–175; II, 164–165; *Crime Commission Report*, p. 196; Harold Norris, "Arrest Without Warrant," *The Crisis*, October 1958, pp. 481–486; American Civil Liberties Union, Illinois Division, *Secret Detention by the Chicago Police* (Glencoe, Ill., 1959), pp. 22–29; *Congressional Report*, vol. 108, pt. 15, Sept. 26, 1962, pp. 20, 913–20,919; *Crime Commission Report*, pp. 186–188; Anthony Lewis, *Portrait of a Decade* (New York, 1965).

20. ACLU, *Police Power and Citizens' Rights*, pp. 35–38; Lohman and Misner, *The Police and the Community*, II, 213–217; David W. Abbott, Louis H. Gold, and Edward T. Rogowsky, *Police, Politics and Race: The New York Referendum on Civilian Review* (Cambridge, 1969), pp. 5–6; National Capital Area Civil Liberties Union, "A Proposed Revision of the System for Processing Civilian Complaints against Police Misconduct in the District of Columbia" (1964), Metropolitan Police Department Files.

21. Fogelson, *Violence as Protest*, p. 72.

22. Ibid., p. 73.

23. *Riot Commission Report*, p. 169. This assumes that nonwhites would have been fully represented on the police forces if the percentage of nonwhite officers had been about equal to the percentage of nonwhite residents.

24. Rudwick, *The Unequal Badge*, pp. 3–4; *Crime Commission Report*, pp. 167–168; *Riot Commission Report*, pp. 1165–169; Lewis, *Portrait of a Decade*, pp. 105–108; Fogelson, *Violence as Protest*, ch. 1.

25. *Penn v. Stumpf*, 308 F.Supp. 128 (1970), Plaintiff's Brief; *Castro v. Beecher*, 334 F.Supp. 930 (1971), 934–942; *Commonwealth of Pennsylvania v. O'Neill*, 348 F.Supp. 1084 (1972), 1,088–1,101; *Bridgeport Guardians, Inc. v. Members of Bridgeport Civil Service Commission*, 345 F.Supp. 788 (1973), 783–794; *Guardians Association of New York City Police Department, Inc. v. Civil Service Commission of City of New York*, 490 F.2d 400 (1973), Plaintiff's Brief; Herzog, "Tests on Trial"; Deposition of Arthur C. Cadegan, Jr., taken on behalf of the plaintiffs on Oct. 19 and 20, 1970, in the case of *Castro v. Beecher* (United States District Court, District of Massachusetts, Civil Action No. 70-122OW), I, 77, 95–96; II, 35–36, 49–50, Massachusetts Law Reform Institute Files, Boston.

Glossary of Organizations and Commissions

ACLU: American Civil Liberties Union.

FOP: Fraternal Order of Police, a nationwide police officer organization which acts as a police advocacy group and also fulfills some functions as a union.

IACP: International Association of Chiefs of Police.

ICPA: International Conference of Police Associations.

Knapp Commission: Commission which investigated police corruption in New York City in the 1970s.

LEAA: Law Enforcement Assistance Administration, a federal agency which provided funding for various criminal justice system projects, especially for police departments.

Lexow Committee: New York State Senate committee which investigated police corruption in New York City in 1894.

NAACP: National Association for the Advancement of Colored People.

PBA: Policemen's Benevolent Association, the union for New York City police officers.

Seabury Committee: The Seabury Committee investigated corruption in the New York City Police Department from 1930–1932, forcing Mayor Jimmy Walker to resign.

Wickersham Commission: The federal commission officially named the National Commission on Law Observance and Enforcement, appointed in 1929 and chaired by Attorney General George W. Wickersham, which made extensive investigations and reported widespread corruption in police departments, courts, and correctional agencies throughout the United States.

Introduction to
Herman Goldstein

Herman Goldstein grew up in New London, Connecticut. He graduated from the University of Connecticut in1953. Goldstein's first acquaintance with the workings of a police department was with the Philadelphia police when he was a graduate student in governmental administration at the University of Pennsylvania. Subsequently he was an assistant to the city manager of Portland, Maine. There he assisted O.W. Wilson in a study of that city's police administration. In 1956–1957 he worked as a researcher for the American Bar Foundation's Survey of the Administration of Criminal Justice. In this capacity Goldstein observed the street level operations of police in Wisconsin and Michigan. Among other things, this research documented beyond doubt, despite the denials of police administrators, that police do not simply enforce the law; police exercise great amounts of discretion in choosing which laws to enforce and whether to enforce them by powers of arrest or by less formal powers of coercion. From 1960–1964 Goldstein was executive assistant to O.W. Wilson, who was then the reform minded superintendent of the Chicago Police Department. In 1964 Goldstein became Professor of Criminal Justice Administration at the Law School of the University of Wisconsin at Madison.

Goldstein has been a consultant to numerous local and national organizations and government commissions, including, among others, the President's Commission on Law Enforcement and Administration of Justice, the National Institute of Law Enforcement and Criminal Justice, the Police Foundation, the Knapp Commission to Investigate Allegations of Corruption in the New York City Police Department, and the Police Executive Research Forum. Goldstein wrote extensively on the role of police, police discretion and policy making, control of police conduct, police relationships with minorities, and the political accountability of police. He worked on numerous specific problems and on developing innovative programs with police agencies throughout the United States and in various other countries.

Over the course of his career Herman Goldstein took the lead in redefining the role of police in American society in modern times. Perhaps more than any other person, Goldstein moved police work from a reactive philosophy of maintaining order and apprehending criminals to a proactive philosophy of supporting democratic values and enhancing public safety through a problem solving approach to crime. Notions of community policing, however that may be understood in various towns and cities, have borrowed their clearer ideas from Goldstein's philosophy of policing. In particular, it was Goldstein's concept of problem oriented policing which became the core of community policing ideas in the United States. Problem oriented policing emphasized the need for police to deal with problems which underlie recurrent crime instead of simply reacting to crimes one by one as they occurred.

Goldstein's approach to police accountability emphasized a democratic ideal of accountability to elected officials. From the earliest days of American police departments, a crucial question has been, "Who will police the police?" The professionalism movement in policing answered that the police will police themselves. But this has not been effective. In practice the answer has been that the media, the courts, and various government officials will police the police. A basic premise of American society is that a free press is the watchdog keeping an eye on all branches of the government. Especially since the middle of the twentieth century the courts have attempted to control the actions of police in various circumstances. Efforts to control police have also taken the form of control over police by elected officials or by appointed officials, sometimes individuals and sometimes committees or commissions. In various places and at various times the heads of police forces have been elected sheriffs, civil service chiefs selected through promotional exams, or appointed chiefs selected by a mayor or by a city or town council, or some combination of appointment processes.

A century ago it was fairly common to place police departments under a board of commissioners consisting of representatives of different political parties in an effort to reduce the influence of partisan politics in policing. Although political control of police generally has been considered desirable, partisan politics has been considered undesirable. Partisan politics is government based on belonging to a particular political party. For example, if a democrat won an election and replaced a republican mayor, republican police officers would be dismissed and replaced by democratic police officers. Usually bipartisan commissions operated at the local level, but occasionally local police were put under control of a state commission, often as a way of shifting power from local politicians to state politicians. Some commissions were given real power to run police departments; other commissions were just advisory bodies, which police chiefs politely ignored. Even when police departments were placed under the control of mayors, some city governments authorized "strong mayors" with considerable power over police, whereas other city governments limited the powers of a mayor by giving a share in the power to a city council of some sort. At the peak of the professionalism movement in policing, some police departments were placed under a civil service chief who ran the police department independent of all political officials. In some of these cases police chiefs who lost touch with the community or even became embattled with the community were impossible to remove.

In most nations other than the United States police are controlled largely by the central government. Police forces tend to be national police forces. Where there are both national and local police forces, as in Italy, the national police force takes the leading role in serious criminal matters while the local forces take the leading role in more routine matters such as traffic control and minor offenses. In England police forces are jointly controlled by the local government and the national government. In the United States the founding fathers never imagined a federal police force. It was by clever manipulation that President Teddy Roosevelt, who had been one of the police commissioners in New York City and loved running a police department, took a few Secret Service officers assigned for his protection and converted them into a bureau of investigation, despite objections from members of Congress that these investigators would be used for partisan political investigations. They were soon proven right. But the bureau keep increasing in size and expanding its activities until finally Congress approved the existence of a Federal Bureau of Investigation, so that it would no longer be just a president's personal investigative bureau.

Once established, federal policing grew and multiplied into various separate federal agencies. These federal agencies have consistently lobbied Congress to increase their powers and their numbers and vigorously sought to take over the roles played by local police departments. However, the historical tradition in the United States has been that police departments are operations of local government. For the past half century the federal government has been gaining ever greater control over local police departments by the power of the purse, that is, by using federal funds to influence the policies and practices of local police. Whether the continuing shift of policing from local government to federal government control is for better or for worse, the shift itself is a major historical development in policing.

The diversity and complexity of the United States is hardly noticed by Americans themselves. The existence of so many separate legal systems, so many separate police agencies, and so many separate correctional systems with different and sometimes conflicting components is bewildering only to foreigners. American government, at all levels, is itself an unfinished set of experiments with numerous ideas in play at any particular time. At the local level there are governments run by hired professional city managers, and there are governments run by elected mayors. Among the professional city managers there are some who are given a rather free hand by the town council which hired them, and there are some who are controlled quite closely by the town council. Among elected mayors some are "strong mayors" with great power to make decisions and appoint officials on their own, and some other mayors have very little power other than to carry out the decisions and endorse the appointments of a city council. Indeed, in the history of the very same town or city, one may find that the government has been redesigned from time to time, shifting powers here and there, and sometimes shifting back to earlier government arrangements. The government itself is an unfinished creation, and the search for a better form of government is carried on by each government acting in response to its own problems and political power struggles without much regard for what some other government in the next city or town may be doing. Such diversity and change in government has been the American way.

In the 1920s and 1930s many state and local governments were streamlined to add power and control to the top elected official. For example, New York State had nearly two hundred elected state officials at the beginning of this period. Since each was elected, they did not come under the control of the governor. Being governor was almost meaningless because none of these elected officials running state agencies had to pay any attention to the governor. Then the New York State constitution was revised so that there were only four elected state officials; all the rest became appointed officials who had to follow policies established by the governor and legislature. The result was that the governor could manage the state more effectively and could be held accountable for nearly all of the state's operations. However, in the 1960s the trend towards centralized power invested in a single elected official began to reverse. There was a desire for more community participation in government and more governmental adaptation to individual communities. Governments and individual agencies began to decentralize with more powers being placed in neighborhood hands.

In *Policing a Free Society* Goldstein raised the question of how a police department should be fitted into the government of a town or city. The governmental arrangements for police departments are as diverse and changing as local government itself. Besides proposals for the overall position of a police department in local government, Goldstein made recommendations for the manner in which police policies and operations should be made accountable to citizens. On a very fundamental level Goldstein rejected the basic premise of the police professionalism movement that these matters are police business and should be left to the police. Goldstein pointed out that much of what police do has little to do with crime. Police are a multi-function agency of local government which handles such diverse tasks as facilitating the movement of people and traffic, aiding lost or injured people, and providing security in public places. Furthermore, police have great latitude in deciding how to do their tasks; they are not limited to bringing legal charges against people.

Goldstein assumed that in a democratic society citizens should have a say, even a deciding role, in all matters, including those which are assigned to police as their work. Goldstein also assumed that police should be as accountable and responsive to the public as any other government agency. This was apparent in a recommendation by Goldstein that, in many cases, police departments should follow the administrative rule making practices of many federal and state agencies. Since police do exercise discretion about what laws to enforce and how to enforce them, police department policies which embody these discretionary decisions should be public knowledge. The administrative rule making procedure is a five step process which begins with (1) a study of a particular problem, (2) publishing a draft of a proposed rule or policy, (3) soliciting comments from the public, (4) revising the rule or policy as needed in light of the comments, and, at last, (5) publishing the final rule or policy. Goldstein proposed that police departments should follow this administrative rule making procedure in determining many of their policies and procedures.

In Goldstein's philosophy of policing, making police a more democratic institution will not weaken the ability of police to fulfill their roles in government. To the contrary, he believed, a more democratic police force will be a more effective police force. But this does not resolve the practical problem of how to make police a more democratic institution. Sometimes the very nature of democracy raises more problems than it solves. For example, Goldstein assumed that a city-wide official like a mayor represents all the people of a city. However, in a city characterized by racial politics a mayor might come to power, and stay in power, only because a voting majority approves a mayor's anti-minority policies.

Coming from a background in government and political science, Goldstein's characteristic way to support his arguments was with case studies. The evidence he would cite to prove that something was, or was not, a good idea was most often an account of what happened in some place where an attempt was made to implement the idea. A case study might draw on somewhat informal sources such as newspaper accounts or more formal sources such as government reports or detailed case studies done by social scientists.

The problems and proposed solutions discussed by Goldstein in this reading are an invitation to debate the many ways in which police might be made into a more accountable and democratic institution. Goldstein himself noted the limitations of many of his proposals. How police fit into the structure of local government and the arrangements by which they can be made to serve the public have varied so much from one place to another, and even varied so much in the same place at different times, that establishing a democratic form of police must still be considered an unfinished and uncertain business. Among the specific debatable issues touched on by Goldstein were residency requirements for police officers, the job security of police chiefs, the role of civilian review boards, the political influence of police organizations, the power of elected officials to direct police and hold them accountable, majority pressures for police to crack down on minorities, and adapting law enforcement policies to particular neighborhoods.

Herman Goldstein. (1977). *Policing a Free Society.* Cambridge, MA: Ballinger Publishing Co. This selection is reproduced with permission of the Board of Regents of the University of Wisconsin. Footnotes have been renumbered. A brief summary of an omitted section has been printed in square brackets.

Herman Goldstein
Policing a Free Society

Directing Police Agencies through the Political Process

To whom are the police accountable? How do we give meaning to the widespread assumptions that the police are subject to control by the citizenry and that they are fully answerable for the manner in which they use their authority?

Establishing new mechanisms for the review and control of police discretion ... contributes toward achieving greater accountability. But it cannot, by itself, provide the total government apparatus that is required to assure accountability with regard to all aspects of an agency's operations. Accountability, in its broadest sense, includes much more than responsibility for determining policies in discretionary areas. It covers every aspect of administration of an agency, including, for example, its operating efficiency, its hiring and promotion practices, and its financial management. Accountability encompasses as well responsibility for the conduct of individual employees for the use which they make of their authority and for their integrity. These two concerns are so important and raise such complicated issues that they are dealt with separately in chapters 7 and 8. This chapter examines the processes by which citizens can, in a positive way, influence and sometimes alter the policies and administration of a police agency.

The Basic System and the Problems It Presents

Compared to other nations the most distinctive characteristic of policing in the United States is the extent to which the police function is decentralized. The President's Crime Commission estimated that there are approximately 40,000 police departments in the country and that all but 250 of these are local agencies.[1] This organizational arrangement reflects the widely held belief that maintaining local control over police operations is the most effective means for avoiding abuse and assuring a popular voice in directing the police. Almost invariably, proposals for the consolidation of small agencies and for the creation or expansion of agencies at the federal, state, and regional levels have been strongly opposed. Even when the trend has been to consolidate units of government, such as school districts, to increase efficiency and reduce costs, the public has clung tenaciously to the practice of organizing police services at the lowest level of government.[2]

The traditional means by which citizens are assumed to exert positive influence on the police is through their elected officials. The influence is most direct in the case of sheriffs, who continue to be selected by popular election in most jurisdictions. At the municipal level a police chief who is by legislation required to function under the direction of an elected mayor and who is appointed by the mayor, is obviously considered responsible to the mayor for all aspects of police operations. The mayor, in turn, is considered by the electorate to have the ultimate responsibility for the police. Theoretically, then, citizens who want to influence police operations should be able to do so, in a general way, through their vote for mayor and subsequently by directing their complaints and suggestions about the police to the mayor.

But the lines of accountability to the citizenry and the formal channels for influencing police operations are rarely so open or so clearly defined. And herein lies one of the major paradoxes in policing in this country. We have insisted on maintaining the police as a responsibility of local government in order to assure accountability and an opportunity for local influence over so potentially powerful a government activity. Yet at the same time we have constructed various devices which, in attempting to protect the police from pernicious influences at the local level, effectively shield the police from the communities they serve. The net result of these conflicting aims is that considerable ambiguity exists as to who in fact is responsible for the many decisions that are made in the running of a police agency, and there is a great deal of uncertainty over how the public is supposed to control police operations.

Various Administrative Arrangements for Achieving Accountability

Much of the current ambiguity regarding the arrangements for supervising police operations is traceable to the pervasive influence that partisan politics had on police agencies in this country from the early years of their development and lasting well into this century. Not only were jobs filled by patronage. The police—and police authority—were used in various ways to enforce party loyalty and even to deliver elections. Friends were rewarded by lax law enforcement. Enemies were harassed. And honest efforts to provide equitable police service were constantly undermined. The fact that the police were beholden to a political party rather than the electorate often made a shambles out of their operations.[3]

In attempts to gain more effective control over the police so they would better serve the needs of the total community, various organizational arrangements were tried. Experiments were carried out in the second half of the nineteenth century with independent administrative boards, with elected boards, with bipartisan boards, and with state control over municipal police. By 1900 most municipalities whose police had been placed under state government won back control. But experimentation with the various forms of administrative boards continued into the first several decades of this century. These schemes not only failed to achieve the desired objectives, they were actually used to gain political control as often as they were used to insulate the police from partisan considerations.[4]

Starting early in the 1900s, as part of a general trend in city government, gradual support developed for the appointment of a single executive to head a police agency who would be protected from political influence through tenure. But this movement drew opposition because of the immunity that such an individual would have from appropriate citizen influence. Noting this resistance, the Wickersham Commission, which published the results of its investigation of police operations in 1931 and which reflected the viewpoint of the new breed of professional police administrators who were emerging at the time, observed:

> Seeking to avoid repression and to preserve democratic ideals, the people have virtually turned over their police departments to the most notorious and frequently the most dangerous persons in their communities, who do not hesitate to use them for every type of oppression and intimidation. Therefore, their attempt to protect themselves from a powerful autocratic chief of police has served to place them and the government in the hands of unscrupulous cutthroats, murderers, and bootleggers.[5]

When the commission was conducting its investigations, a strong movement was already under way to reform city government. Primarily in order to increase operating efficiency, independent administrative boards were gradually being eliminated as three forms of city government became popular—the commission, the strong-mayor, and the city-manager plans. All three called for the police chief to be more directly accountable to an elected official. Under the commission form of government the police were directed by one of the elected commissioners. Under the strong-mayor form the chief was under the direct supervision of the mayor. And under the city-manager plan the chief was accountable to the city manager who, in turn, was accountable to the city council. Interestingly, the Wickersham Commission saw these changes as steps backward unless special measures were taken to guarantee the chief's independence.

> Limiting the powers of the police executive by placing absolute control of police under the mayor, commissioners, or city manager has opened wide the door for every conceivable type of incompetency, political corruption, and organization demoralization. The theory that the mayor, representing the people, will exercise wisdom in conducting the business of the city and, being directly responsible to the electors, will do his utmost to protect the lives and property of inhabitants and preserve the peace, has been badly shattered, judging by the caliber of the police service which is to be found in the majority of the communities in this country....
>
> The chief must be surrounded with every protective civil service device imaginable. When that is done the citizens may take more interest in the appointment of their chief police executive. With security of tenure, with intelligence, with training, with honesty, and with sincerity of purpose, the criminal element can be controlled. Without these virtues and with political control as it now exists, police departments must go on unorganized, inefficient, and corrupt.[6]

Today most police agencies are headed by a single administrator. In a survey of 1,774 cities having a population in excess of 5,000, the International City Management Association reported in 1972 that the chiefs in 1,018 were appointed by the mayor, city manager, or other chief administrative officer; 252 were appointed by the mayor and city council; 195 were appointed by the council; 199 were appointed by a civil service commission; 80 by independent boards; and 30 were elected.[7]

Included among these are some vestiges of the older arrangements where the channel of accountability is unclear. Boards with varying degrees of authority can be found, for example, in Chicago, Los Angeles, San Francisco, and Milwaukee. And the police departments of such large cities as Kansas City (Missouri) and St. Louis not only have boards but, along with Baltimore, continue to operate under state control.

Even where they are directly appointed, however, most chiefs enjoy some form of protection from political influence through civil service. So, although the vast majority of chiefs are, in a formal sense, directly responsible to the municipal chief executive and, through him, to the citizenry, accountability is in fact limited in a variety of ways.

Emergence of Police Autonomy as a Virtue

The effect that partisan political pressures had on the police through much of their history was apparently so catastrophic that fear of a recurrence has given rise to a fetish of sorts that equates any form of citizen involvement in directing police agencies with the most nefarious form of political corruption. As a result, even though most police chiefs are now directly responsible to the chief executive officer of a municipality, the chief executive tends to refrain from exercising the authority granted to him. In contrast with their relationship with other departments of city government, mayors and city managers have sought to avoid involvement in police business—especially as it relates to the way in which the law is to be enforced—deferring to the autonomy of the department or to the prosecutors, judges, and legislatures from whom the police are commonly assumed to receive their instructions.

Those running for the office of mayor for the first time often promise to grant autonomy to the police. And it is not uncommon for mayors running for reelection to brag about the degree of independence they allowed their police departments. Mayors often take pains to disassociate themselves from decisions upon which controversial police actions are based.

The startling result of this aversion to putting any political pressure on the police is that the police now actually have greater autonomy than other agencies of government that exercise much less authority. Yet most people seem unconcerned over this rather curious state of affairs. Apparently holding the traditional view that police are merely automatons and that the law defines their authority and function in precise terms, citizens are likely to support the mayor who, in disclaiming responsibility for police actions, is abdicating a responsibility which is clearly his. And they are likely to join in allegations that a mayor who questions police policies or attempts to influence the manner in which the police function is guilty of "political interference."

Negative By-Products of Autonomy

The intense concern over improper pressures has affected more than the system of accountability; it has had a major influence on all efforts to improve the police and has profoundly affected the internal arrangements for running a police agency. Indeed, freedom from partisan political influence has come to be synonymous with the professional movement among police personnel. Some of the consequences of the pervasive concern with neutrality and objectivity have only recently become obvious.

Because the professional movement evolved as a reaction to politically dominated policing, it naturally followed that little heed was paid to facilitating communication between the citizenry and the police. On the contrary, every effort was made to destroy existing relationships and to frustrate continuing contacts through rules or other administrative devices. Thus, for example, police officers were prohibited in some jurisdictions from talking to citizens except "in the line of duty." In the larger departments they were prohibited from working in the neighborhoods in which they resided, lest they be improperly influenced by those with whom they were most familiar. State police agencies were held up as models because of the extent to which they achieved objectivity through their policies of assigning personnel to areas away from their homes. Personnel in all agencies were transferred frequently in order to minimize the likelihood that familiarity with the citizens in an area would give rise to corrupt relationships. As police operations were centralized in order to achieve greater efficiency, the breaking of a network of relationships between locally organized police and the community they served was seen as having positive value. Subsequent events have made it clear that the highly impersonal form of policing that these changes produced has been among the major factors contributing to the hostility demonstrated toward police in recent years.

The priority placed on autonomy has also had a negative impact, in many situations, upon the capacity of police leaders to lead. In their study of the problems in governing New York City, Wallace Sayre and Herbert Kaufman observed that police commissioners in that city have long sought freedom from supervision by the mayor, from interventions by party leaders, and from jurisdictional invasions by other government agencies. But they point out that autonomy for the department has also meant isolation for the commissioner from sources which might help him in his difficult task of securing internal control.[8] Writing fifteen years ago, Sayre and Kaufman concluded that the overall effect of isolation, in the case of New York City, was to limit seriously a commissioner's potential for achieving change. The commissioner, they claim, must "yield to the necessity of being more the spokesman and the advocate than the leader and the innovator."[9] Although the experiences of New York City police commissioners may be assumed to be unique because of the size of their operations, the description of the commissioners' position, with some modifications, aptly fits many other police administrators in the country.

Recent Developments Pointing to Inadequacies in the Present System

Until the 1960s the ambiguity of the procedures by which police agencies were subject to influence and control went largely unnoticed by the public. But the social turbulence of the sixties gave rise to numerous controversies regarding police functioning, and these in turn stirred citizen interest in the police. In their attempts to establish responsibility for past actions and to influence future police functioning, aroused citizens found, often to their surprise, that the channels for influencing police operations were poorly defined and, in some cases, totally blocked. Interest in the accountability of the police peaked in the late 1960s but it has remained high as controversial issues involving the police continue to arise in cities across the country.[10] What, specifically, are some of the developments that have brought the problem to the surface?

Frustration of Minorities

Blacks and other minority groups became increasingly frustrated at having failed to bring about changes in police practices. For years the police in many jurisdictions had provided inadequate services to minority communities; beyond this they had engaged in indiscriminate and often illegal actions in the policing of such areas. In the period from the 1950s to about 1965, criticism of police practices tended to take the form of a specific allegation of brutality or illegality. To eliminate such incidents, campaigns were mounted to improve police functioning by conducting a more thorough screening of police personnel and by providing human-relations training to police officers. There was, as well, a major effort to establish civilian boards to review allegations of police misconduct (see chapter 7). But these projects did not solve the problems. The quality of police service remained inferior in many jurisdictions, and indiscriminate street searches, harassment of persons committing petty offenses, and other police practices that offended minority communities went on unabated. From 1965 on, it became increasingly apparent to the most militant groups that the basic policies and overall attitude of some police administrators would have to be changed in order to affect the actions of the police at the operating level. But attempts to bring about such changes were frequently thwarted. Meetings with the police (often in the form of community-relations programs) were commonly used by the police to convince complainants that the prevailing police practices were in fact beneficial to the community. Police officials would deny categorically that illegal or improper practices were condoned. Mayors and city council members, when appealed to, claimed either that they were without authority to influence the police or that they thought it improper to interfere with police operations. The frustration such experiences produced contributed in no small measure to the violence that erupted in the late 1960s. It found expression, too, in the demands for neighborhood and community control of the police—a development that is discussed in more detail later.

But not all reactions were so volatile or so radical. In Evanston, Illinois, in 1969 the shooting of a black teen-ager by a police officer resulted in a lengthy investigation that produced a report in which questions were asked that, in a calm and thoughtful manner, reflect the same frustrations and illustrate the quest for clearer lines of accountability:

Who is Responsible for the Shooting?

The Police Officer? Ultimately, of course, it was his decision. But it is too simple to blame only him. He made his decision within a framework of "duty" supplied by the Evanston Police Department. He acted as he was trained to act, and the officer that takes his place will be trained in the same way.

The Chief of Police? According to his testimony, the Chief of Police makes the policy decisions for the Evanston Police Department. This includes the policy governing the use of firearms. Although he referred to no higher authority involved in shaping police policy, the Department is not entirely autonomous. If his policies run counter to expectations, he can be fired or counseled in his decisions by the City Manager.

The City Manager? He has the direct responsibility for police administration. It is his belief that the shooting occurred within a framework of duty. But even he is subject to higher authority.

The City Council? The City Council is the policy-making body for all branches of city government. It is clear that they made no policy decisions that would prevent the shooting of Bruce Williams. These decision-makers were elected by Evanston citizens and must reflect the views of their constituents to remain in office.

The Citizens of Evanston? Evanston citizens as a whole have not demonstrated dissatisfaction by demanding a review of the police policy, or participation in determining that policy. Expressions of outrage at the implications of police policy for Bruce Williams have come only from Evanston's Black citizens. Evanston's white citizens have not been similarly aroused. There is nowhere else to place responsibility—the citizens of Evanston must assume it.[11]

Attempts by Newly Emerged Groups to Affect Policy

The sharp rise in political dissent and the rapid change in values and customs in the past decade placed the police in contact with a number of new groups, most of whose members had little prior contact with the police. Among these people were those who, for example, took to the streets in demonstrations against government policies; those who experimented with narcotics and other dangerous drugs; and those whose life-style subjected them to frequent inquiry because of the conditioned tendency of the police to be alert to deviations from the community norm. Unlike blacks and other racial minorities who are only now obtaining a voice for themselves in community affairs, individuals in these groups, since they came from the majority community, had been accustomed to immediate response to their grievances. When they clashed with the police, they moved much more rapidly to attempt to influence police functioning through established channels. Finding—as minority groups did before them—that these channels were often blocked, they began to clamor for new ways in which the citizenry could have more of a say in determining the operating policies of police agencies.

Illustrative of this reaction is the statement of a Madison, Wisconsin, alderman after a police action that resulted in the arrest of eighty persons on drug-related charges.

> If we are to defuse the issues raised as a result of that raid, we must be afforded the opportunity to explore the charges, the facts, the policies and the attitudes surrounding all of the issues involved....
>
> The police administration and the mayor have been reluctant to establish any forum, to encourage any discussion, to promote any means by which the citizens of this community can review or investigate questions about police practices and policies....
>
> To remedy that basic communications gap, that essential element in reestablishing civilian control over police policies and practices, I have introduced a resolution calling for the establishment of a five-member committee of aldermen to review police policies and practices....
>
> Were the no-knock, middle of the night tactics necessary? Were a number of people picked up in those raids and later released who had nothing at all to do with those not released? Was the way in which the raids were carried out, the timing and the targets arranged so as to terrorize the youth community? Is it the practice and the policy of the police department to deal differently with student and other minority groups than with the population as a whole? ...
>
> The only change in the policies of the police administration for which I call is the willingness on the part of the police administration to discuss the issues, to present their policies freely and openly. The police have nothing to lose and we all have much to gain from such an exchange....[12]

Rebuffs of Mayors

Although most mayors have avoided controversial issues involving the police by deferring to the autonomy the police are commonly assumed to have, some have sympathized with criticism of the police and have sought to change police policies. Those who have moved aggressively in an effort to do so, however, have suffered serious setbacks. Among the most common issues that have drawn municipal chief executives into debates over police policies have been disagreements over the form of the police response to a disturbance, over the use made of deadly force, or over the manner in which a given law has been enforced. But the conflict almost invariably gets translated into a much more simplistic debate in which the conflicting parties are characterized as either overly tough or overly permissive. In such an atmosphere there is little opportunity to discuss issues rationally. And there is a tendency, especially by rank-and-file police, to claim that the chief executive's effort to influence police operations constitutes the very kind of political interference from which the police should be shielded.

Rank-and-file personnel have demonstrated in these conflicts that they can be a formidable political force in the community.[13] In New York City in 1966 the police soundly defeated the city administration's effort to establish a civilian review board by arranging to have the issue submitted to the voters in a referendum and by then carrying out an intensive campaign that resulted in the overwhelming defeat of the proposal at the polls.[14] In Cleveland, when the city turned down police requests for pay increases, the police took their case to the people through a referendum. They conducted an energetic campaign that resulted in the adoption in 1967 of a charter amendment that requires the city to pay its policemen 3 percent above police salaries being paid in any other city with a population of more than 50,000 in the state.[15] In several large cities (Minneapolis and Philadelphia, for example) the political power of the police and the support they have been able to enlist have resulted in police personnel being elected mayor.

Commenting on the demonstrated capacity of the police to exert political "muscle," former Mayor Carl B. Stokes of Cleveland is quoted as having said:

> There is simply no question of the political power of the police in any city. They can make all kinds of appeals to the people for support, and they can eventually ruin almost any politician.
>
> In most of the big cities, if there is some friction between political leaders and the police, you would probably find a great portion of the people siding with the police, and simplifying all the issues terribly. There is a great danger in this situation to the very order of society.[16]

... Many people believe it is good that mayors and other political figures cannot influence police policies. They see this as proof that the system developed over the years to shield the police from improper political influences is working effectively. Others argue that those conflicts that have been taken to the voters have been resolved in the most democratic fashion. But both of these positions fail to acknowledge the complexity of the problem. The kind of influences from which the police have been successfully shielded are often precisely those to which the police in a democracy should be subjected. And majority votes on issues and candidates are not the ultimate test of the appropriateness of police policies. On the contrary—and herein lies the heart of the problem—the real test of a police force in a democracy is the degree to which it responds to the legitimate demands of minorities, whether the minorities be racial, religious, political, geographical, or even criminal. That minorities have experienced difficulty in pressing their claims and that elected officials have been rebuffed in their efforts to represent them should be cause for grave concern. And when, to this state of affairs, is added the great political power of rank-and-file police personnel, the situation is troubling indeed....

Essential Elements for Achieving Greater Accountability

It is quite natural that those who are concerned with achieving greater accountability by the police and more citizen input into decision-making, on recognizing the weakness of recent proposals, should continue their search for an ideal plan that could be applied universally to solve all existing problems without producing any negative results. But no single model is available, nor is it likely that one will evolve in the near future. There are simply too many variables from one community to another. Moreover, our experience in attempting to elicit greater community involvement at the neighborhood level in large cities and in structuring police discretion—which are two important components of any system of accountability—is extremely limited, so there is little to build on. It appears, therefore, that the next several decades will be a period of experimentation in which the dynamics and needs of different municipalities will lead to a variety of arrangements aimed at improving the process by which citizens can influence and exert appropriate control over police operations.

Although no single model can be recommended, recent attempts to provide a clearer form of accountability suggest that some minimal elements are essential if the system is to work....

[One essential element is to include all aspects of police functioning in any program for achieving greater police accountability. Not just certain activities but all activities of police should be subject to accountability. Another essen-

tial element for achieving greater accountability is to facilitate public participation and scrutiny in police policy making. Whatever policies guide police in
their operations should be subject to public review. One way to do this is to
implement the public rule making procedure used by federal agencies, in
which an agency announces a proposed rule, gets citizen input, then finalizes
and publishes the rule.]

Decentralizing to the Maximum Degree

It is only natural that the frustrations of community groups who failed to
change police operating policies should have produced demands in the large
cities for absolute neighborhood control of the police. The movement reflects the common tendency to solve the problem of most immediate concern
without full regard for the impact that the solution will have in other areas.
In many respects the reaction is similar—in its extreme character—to the
earlier reactions to the destructive effects of partisan politics, which resulted
in insulating police agencies from legitimate influences as well.[17]

But the problems likely to be created by total decentralization of the police
function ought not to blind us to the desirability of establishing new channels
by which residents of a small area within a larger community can—when
there is no compelling reason to apply a policy uniformly throughout a city—
have a voice in determining the policies affecting service in their neighborhood. There is a far greater difference in the makeup and character of selected
neighborhoods within a large city than there is in the makeup of smaller cities
located within the same state. And yet a large-city police department is usually committed, at least formally, to providing a uniform style of police service to all neighborhoods, whereas the form of police service in smaller communities differs significantly in accord with the wishes of local residents.

That independently organized police agencies are more effective than the
larger city-wide departments in meeting the demands of citizens residing in
their communities is the major point made in a study reported by Elinor Ostrom and Gordon Whitaker.[18] They based their conclusions on measurements of such factors as the rate of victimization of residents; the amount of
assistance rendered citizens; the promptness with which police responded to
calls for help; and citizens' assessment of police-community relations and the
kind of job they thought the police were doing.[19] A major problem with such
inquiries is that measures of police responsiveness and citizen satisfaction are
not always indicative of the quality of police service. A police agency may be
very responsive to citizen demands and be rated highly by the people it
serves, but when its actions are measured against standards of legality and
propriety the quality of the service may be poor.

The residents of neighborhoods within large cities would in all probability realize a higher degree of satisfaction if police services were under their direct control, but this might be at the cost of a deterioration in the quality of the service a person traveling through the neighborhood would receive. The challenge in the larger cities is in trying to achieve some of the benefits of neighborhood-oriented policing without sacrificing the commitment that the larger jurisdiction must maintain toward providing a high level of service to citizens moving between areas—including those who enter the larger jurisdiction from the smaller communities.

This poses some fundamental questions. What decisions can be left to a neighborhood or some other subdivision of a larger municipality? It is unlikely that anyone would seriously suggest that state statutes prohibiting homicide or rape should be enforced differently in different areas of a city or even in different sections of a state. But a strong case could be made for adopting different operating policies for resolving conflict in order to acknowledge different cultural practices and preferences. How does one decide what an appropriate sub-division of a large community would be for purposes of determining these police policies and practices? By what mechanisms can a community arrive at its position? Are local elected boards desirable? Should these be institutionalized or should they be maintained on an ad hoc basis? Would they provide the degree of accountability that is required for decision-making? And what status should their decisions have? Would they be binding or simply advisory?

The suggestion that some substantive decisions concerning the form of police service be made at a level lower than that of municipal government is probably the most controversial of all the proposals for achieving greater police accountability. The idea runs contrary to the whole movement of recent years, in which emphasis was placed on achieving uniformity, objectivity, and equal enforcement of the law within a jurisdiction. But it deserves serious consideration, given our new awareness of the degree to which the quality of police service is influenced by police acknowledgment of variations in the life-styles of different neighborhoods.

Meeting the Continuing Need for Insulation

Given the history of domination of police agencies by partisan political interests, it is clearly essential that the system of political accountability be designed to minimize the likelihood that political parties will be in a position to manipulate the police to their advantage. Moreover, police administrators and police officers must be free to enforce the law without fear that the person or class of offenders against whom they take action has the power to retaliate against the enforcing officers. Obvious as this should be, it is nevertheless important to stress that much of what the police do—whether it be issuing a summons for speeding or prosecuting a case against organized criminals—places them in an adverse relationship with members of the community. Persons without police experience do not realize the magnitude of this problem and the extremes to which individuals will go to "get even" with the police. It would make for an intolerable situation if such individuals, properly and legally proceeded against and afforded an opportunity for judicial review of the charges against them, were able to use the channels for citizen direction of the police as a means of revenge.

Beyond these concerns, proper police functioning, as was previously noted, requires that the police act in a number of different circumstances without regard to the interests and demands of the community that they are serving and the citizens who may in fact be paying their salaries. They must be insulated from local pressures when fulfilling a responsibility that is theirs by virtue of legislation or other form of direction promulgated at a level higher than that of the municipal government, be it a provision of the United States Constitution or a state statute. The citizens of a given neighborhood, for example, should not be allowed to interfere with police action designed to protect the right of an individual to move into the neighborhood. The police should be free to provide adequate protection to a person speaking on behalf of an unpopular cause, however strong the objection within the community might be to the speaker. The police should be insulated from community pressures that demand they use their authority and their coercive power to proceed improperly and illegally against individuals whose actions have offended broad segments of the community. And the police should be sufficiently insulated to enable them to guarantee the constitutional rights of individuals taken into custody.

Police administrators also require independence and flexibility in order to administer an agency within the policies established by the appropriate bodies. Citizen groups should provide guidance on direction and priorities, but they ought not become involved in developing detailed instructions on how policies are to be implemented. A chief's day-to-day control over personnel, equipment, and resources cannot be reduced without seriously detracting from his ability to manage.

The results of various administrative arrangements to provide needed insulation in the past make it appear unwise to resort, once again, to the creation of independent boards and commissions to serve as buffers between the police and the community. Nor does it seem desirable, given recent experience, to give police administrators ironclad tenure. Yet some security in office is essential. Without it a chief would be too vulnerable to the numerous pressures exerted on him. Aside from being subject to outside pressures, an administrator would find it extremely difficult to maintain control over personnel. Many subordinates will not cooperate fully with a chief who does not have tenure and who appears in danger of being fired because of his actions or the positions he takes—especially if the subordinates themselves are tenured. If every administrative decision has the potential of becoming a test of the chief's capacity to stay in office, qualified candidates will not apply for the chief's job in the first place.

One method for providing needed tenure without sacrificing accountability to the public appears to have considerable merit, but has not been widely employed. It calls for appointment of the chief to a set term of office, with the provisions of his employment established by contract. The length of service could be sufficiently long to enable a chief to gain a foothold in the first years, when the pressures are likely to be greatest and when conflict-producing changes must be carried out. By contract, a community could commit itself to providing financial security in the form of salary for the full length of the term while reserving the right to terminate the service of a chief before the term expires. The financial obligation that would be incurred if the contract were terminated before the incumbent's term expired would serve as some protection against frivolous dismissals. Yet the cost involved in "buying out a contract," especially after several years had passed, would not be an unreasonable price to pay if a community concluded that its desires and the policies of its chief were irreconcilable.

Pinpointing Responsibility

Even though police actions derive from policies formulated by a range of officials and legislative bodies, the police should be accountable to a single public official and through that official to the citizenry for the manner in which these policies are carried out. The logical official is the mayor or appointed chief executive of a municipality who is responsible to either the electorate or the city council. This provides the clearest and most direct means for achieving political accountability. It is consistent with the concept, advanced in chapter 2, that the police should be viewed primarily as an agency of municipal government in which is housed a whole range of functions. And it supports prevalent feeling that, in order to bring about a more coordinated response to the complex problems of' urban areas, the authority of municipal chief executives to supervise municipal government should be strengthened. It has the additional advantage of being in line with public expectations, for although most municipal chief executives have very limited control over city government, citizens tend to look to the mayor or city manager as the official in overall charge.

Holding the municipal chief executive responsible for police functioning in this manner does not mean that he or she would make all the decisions or exercise unlimited supervision. On the contrary, a major responsibility would be to see to it that the police agency conformed with legislation and policies established at a higher level of government. Likewise, it would be the municipal chief executive's job to assure that the agency carried out its responsibilities to consult community groups in formulating policies. If increased use were made of administrative rule-making as a way of structuring discretion, the mayor or city manager would be expected to oversee this process personally and participate in the formulation of new policies.

It follows that on occasion the municipal chief executive, in accounting to the community for a specific police action or practice, will have to point out that what the police were doing was in conformity with constitutional requirements, or legislative mandate, or the wishes of the city council. It will be an improvement over current arrangements in many jurisdictions if there is a single official who, even if he cannot act on citizen requests and complaints, can, with some authority, advise citizens where they should go in order to alter policies and practices to which they object....

Footnotes

1. President's Commission on Law Enforcement and Administration of Justice, *Task Force Report: The Police* (Washington, D.C.: Government Printing Office, 1967), p. 7. Some have used a smaller figure. A survey by LEAA in 1970 found that there were 208 enforcement agencies at the state level, 4,800 at the county level, and 14,603 at the local level—but this survey did not include agencies of municipalities with a population of less than 1,000. See United States Department of Justice, Law Enforcement Assistance Administration, *Criminal Justice Agencies in the United States: Summary Report, 1970* (Washington, D.C.: Government Printing Office, 1971), pp. 11–13. Whatever differences there may be in calculating the exact total, it is clear that a large number of police agencies exist in this country, and almost all of them are organized at the local level of government.
2. For a recent review of the efforts that have been made to consolidate police agencies, see National Advisory Commission on Criminal Justice Standards and Goals, *Police* (Washington, D.C.: Government Printing Office, 1973), pp. 108–117.
3. There are many detailed accounts of the sordid conditions created by the alliance between the police and political-party organizations in this period and up to the present. See, for example, Raymond B. Fosdick, *American Police Systems* (1920; reprint ed., Montclair, N.J.: Patterson Smith, 1969); Leonhard F. Fuld, *Police Administration* (1909; reprint ed., Montclair, N.J.: Patterson Smith, 1971); National Commission on Law Observance and Enforcement, *Report on Police* (Washington, D.C.: Government Printing Office, 1931; reprint ed., Montclair, N.J.: Patterson Smith, 1968); Lincoln Steffens, *The Shame of the Cities* (New York: McClure-Phillips, 1904). For an account of a contemporary situation, see John A. Gardiner, *The Politics of Corruption* (New York: Russell Sage Foundation, 1970).

4. The most comprehensive summary of the various systems employed in an effort to achieve effective control of the police in this country—up to 1920—is contained in Fosdick, *American Police Systems*, pp. 58–187.

5. National Commission on Law Observance and Enforcement, *Report on Police*, p. 51.

6. Ibid., p. 49 and 52.

7. International City Management Association, *The Municipal Yearbook* (Washington, D.C.: International City Management Association, 1972), p. 276.

8. Wallace S. Sayre and Herbert Kaufman, *Governing New York City* (New York: Russell Sage Foundation, 1960), p. 290.

9. Ibid., p. 292.

10. Most recently there has been much greater concern with the accountability of enforcement agencies at the federal level, as debates have taken place over the practices of the FBI, and IRS, and the CIA. In a classic restatement of the problem the FBI has been attacked for being too responsive to political direction (in helping, as some allege, to cover up the Watergate incident) and too immune from citizen control (as, for example, in adopting a policy of infiltrating anti-war groups). The first complaint leads to urgings that the Bureau be more tightly insulated from the influence of politicians; the second leads to demands that it be made more susceptible to political control. So far this has resulted in suggestions for limiting the tenure of the director and creation of a congressional committee to oversee FBI operations. In what may appear to some as a contradictory development, the Director of the FBI promised that there will be no presidential interference in the functioning of the Bureau. "Kelly, With Nixon at Side, Pledges Integrity of F.B.I.," *New York Times*, 10 July 1973. To whom is the FBI responsible? As an agency of the executive branch it is formally accountable to the attorney general and, through him, to the president. But the ambiguity surrounding this arrangement mirrors the confused situation that exists at the local level of government.

11. *Community, Police, and Policy, The Report Emerging from the Bruce Williams Case by the Police Hearing Board of the Evanston Human Relations Commission* (Evanston, Illinois: Evanston Human Relations Commission, 1969), pp. 8–9.

12. "Birkley Tells Optimists: 'Drug Furor Proves Police Review Need,'" *Madison, (Wis.) Capital Times*, 31 January 1972.

13. For an interesting study of three large jurisdictions, see Leonard Ruchelman, *Police Politics: A Comparative Study of Three Cities* (Cambridge, Mass.: Ballinger Publishing Co., 1974).

14. In addition to Ruchelman, *Police Politics*, see David W. Abbott, Louis H. Gold, and Edward T. Rogowsky, *Police, Politics and Race: The New York City Referendum on Civilian Review* (New York: American Jewish Committee, 1969).

15. See Hervey A. Juris and Peter Feuille, Police Unionism (Lexington, Mass.: Lexington Books, D.C. Heath, 1973), p. 120.

16. Mayor Carl B. Stokes as quoted by D.J.R. Bruckner in "Stokes Target of Bitter Battle," *Madison (Wis.) Capital Times*, 29 October 1968.

17. For a discussion of some of the problems in implementing neighborhood control of the police, see James Q. Wilson, *Varieties of Police Behavior* (Cambridge, Mass.: Harvard University Press, 1968), pp. 284–299; and Albert J. Reiss, Jr., *The Police and the Public* (New Haven: Yale University Press, 1971), pp. 207–212.

18. Elinor Ostrom and Gordon Whitaker, "Does Local Community Control of Police Make a Difference? Some Preliminary Findings," *American Journal of Political Science* 17 (1973): 48–76. See also Elinor Ostrom et al., *Community Organization and the Provision of Police Services* (Beverly Hills, Calif.: Sage Publications, 1973).

19. Ostrom and Whitaker, "Does Local Community Control of Police Make a Difference?" pp. 61–74.

❧ Part 4 ☙

Correctional Studies
Masterworks

Introduction to
Correctional Studies Masterworks

In the history of ideas the path from the primitive idea of justice to present ideas of corrections sometimes branched off in different directions, sometimes crossed the paths of other ideas, and sometimes doubled back. From one time to another corrections changed direction to pursue punishment, or reform of individuals, or deterrence of other individuals, restitution to society or to victims, incapacitation of the offender, or protection of society, or the pursuit of several goals at once.

As Holmes pointed out in *The Common Law*, the early idea of justice was simply revenge. The ordinary form of revenge was physical punishment. In primitive societies individuals sought vengeance for crimes against themselves or their kinfolk. In ancient times there was no notion of "correcting" an individual. What had to be corrected was the balance of justice in the world. For every injustice there had to be retribution. In western civilization for the past two thousand years the most common symbol of justice has been "The Lady of Justice." She is blindfolded; she holds a scale with balance pans in one hand and a sword in the other hand. The scale represents the idea that for every offense there must be a punishment of equal weight. The sword represents the necessity of punishment.

However, the idea of retribution for crimes was challenged in the Middle Ages by the emerging idea that people's intentions were as important as their actions, and maybe even more important. Attention shifted from the crime to the criminal. The idea that right or wrong was a matter of intentions, not just deeds, was connected to the philosophical idea of "free will." The concept of free will was that people's behavior was controlled by mental choices. A person could imagine a variety of options and could choose one over another without compulsion by physical needs or habits. If this theory was correct, a person's bad behavior was a result of bad choices and could be changed by making right choices in the future. In short, people could be corrected. Reform could replace punishment as the core of justice.

The next question was how a person could be corrected. Since the earlier idea of justice was to avenge crimes through physical punishment, one easy way for the legal system to adapt to the idea of reforming people was simply to continue punishing people and to view the punishment itself as a means of correction. Hence, the law could continue to impose punishments, but punishments would now be regarded as instruments of reform instead of instruments of revenge. The idea was that punishments would induce people to make different, socially acceptable choices in the future. But different people might need different amounts of reforming, so the amount of punishment had to be adapted to the individual offender rather than being equal to the crime.

Until the eighteenth century the punishments for crimes were usually fines, physical punishments such as whipping or branding, penal servitude such as rowing on a galley, banishment to a colony which needed laborers, or death. Imprisonment itself was not a punishment. Prisons were used to hold debtors until their debts were paid, to hold captives for ransom, to hold political prisoners who were considered dangerous but not necessary to execute, and, as far as criminals were concerned, to hold people awaiting trial or waiting for their sentences to be carried out. Prisons acquired a new purpose with the emergence of the ideas that people could be reformed and that reform did not necessarily require harsh physical punishment. The new idea was that prison should be a place where people will reform.

When prisons were first used as places for reform, reform was seen as a matter of the individual choosing to reform. Hence, prison would be a place where a person could reform, not a place where the person would be reformed by others. In the deeply religious world of the eighteenth and early nineteenth centuries, drawing from the traditional practices of medieval monasteries, the model prisons in Europe first sought to reform people by providing a place of solitude and silence furnished with a bible, so that the criminal could reflect upon his evil deeds, repent, and reform himself.

However, the idea that prisons should reform people by providing a sort of monastic setting did not last long. One reason was its cost. Soon prisoners also were expected to labor in order to defray the expenses of a prison. Labor was compatible with monastic solitude and silence. But between 1830 and 1870 American prisons shifted the main emphasis from solitude and silence to labor as the chief component of the prison regimen. Prisoners provided very cheap labor. They were used for manufacturing goods in prisons under contracts to make such products as clothing, barrels, nails, farm machinery, and so on. Often they were rented out to private contractors, farms or businesses to build roads, clear land, quarry stone, and so on. By the late 1800s American prisons were able to not only cover their operating expenses but also to make very large profits through the labor of prisoners. Prisons became mostly places of penal servitude, that is, virtual slave labor.

New ideas about human nature and how to reform people accompanied the development of prison labor. Instead of behavior being viewed primarily as a matter of choices, behavior came to be seen as a matter of habits. Human beings were considered to be creatures of habit. Hence, the goal of reform could be achieved most effectively by drilling new habits into prisoners. The regimens of penal servitude were rationalized as a program of reforming offenders by instilling in them habits of industry which would enable them to be productive members of society after release. The harsh disciplinary practices of prisons characterized by whippings and solitary confinement under beastly conditions enforced the regimen of penal servitude. Prisons strove to turn out obedient workers.

A historic meeting of penal reformers from America and Europe was held in Cincinnati, Ohio in 1870. The meeting produced a Declaration of Principles which is still considered a statement of ideals in the field of penology. Putting the ideals into practice has been difficult. Many of the ideals were embodied in a new type of prison called a "reformatory." The reformatory was intended mostly for younger prisoners. Their prison labor would be more like skilled job training, based on the individual's vocational needs rather than prison industry productivity, and oriented towards providing the means of earning a good livelihood after release. Basic education was added to the program, especially for the youngest prisoners. The physical design and the regimen of prisons would more closely resemble the "free society" on the outside with open communication among prisoners, more relaxed eating arrangements, more teachers and counselors compared to custodial staff, and other attempts to create a more normal society inside the prison.

The first "reformatory" was erected in Elmira, New York in 1876. It became a model for the rest of the country. However, reformatories were mostly limited to young first offenders, were few compared to the number of old prisons remaining in operation, and themselves tended to slip back somewhat into the old prison regimens. For older offenders there was still the industrial prison. To a small extent some of the ideals of the reformatory won acceptance in these older prisons too, but it was usually a matter of applying reformatory ideals to only a few of the prisoners considered suitable.

In the mid-twentieth century the end of the industrial prison meant less prisoner regimentation and less call for harsh disciplinary practices. A booming prison population swollen with young, restless and occasionally violent offenders was confined to idleness. Moreover, the prison population would no longer accept the primitive living conditions, brutal punishments, and blind eye administration of most prisons. Old trusty systems which had put the everyday running of prisons into the hands of the most violent prisoners who maintained their own systems of discipline brought prisons to a boiling point. Starting in the 1950s a series of extremely violent prison riots attracted media attention to prison conditions. These events also forced courts and, to a lesser extent, legislators to pay attention. Meanwhile the black civil rights movement stirred up a number of other movements for rights—for women, for the handicapped, for the mentally ill, and even for prisoners.

The old-time prison guards who had generally been low level political appointees with no qualifications were replaced in most prisons by civil service employees who sought to upgrade the occupation. They rejected the title "guards" and insisted on being called "correction officers." Although they usually maintained custody of prisoners in a more humane manner, with occasional exceptions their role remained a custody role. Like the reformatories, prisons began employing more counseling and instructional staff and offering more treatment programs for some prisoners, especially general education programs and group counseling for alcohol or other drug addicts. Without the prison industries there was more space in the prison regimen for rehabilitation and recreational activities.

With the end of the prison industries, prisons changed from money makers for the state to expenses. Increased and more professional staffs added to costs. The pressure to reduce costs and renewed interest in rehabilitation rather than punishment led to renewed interest in alternatives to prisons. Probation instead of prison was a hundred-year-old alternative. Probation consisted of sentencing a person to a period of supervision outside of prison, usually with some restrictions on the person's activities. It was considered most appropriate in cases of first-time and non-violent offenders.

Following sharp increases in crime in the United States in the 1960s, probation began to be used in more cases and in more serious cases in order to ease the crowding and costs of prisons. This led to more stringent forms of probation. A type of "shock probation" was tried, consisting of a few days in jail followed by probation. "Intensive probation" was used in some cases; it provided much more frequent monitoring. Some prisoners were fitted with electronic monitoring devices so that probation officers could keep track of their whereabouts.

In addition to greater use of probation in the correctional system, some new programs were added to prison regimens. "Work release" programs were instituted; these released some prisoners to work during the day, or even for a week of workdays, requiring the prisoners to return to prison at night or on weekends. "Halfway houses" were another arrangement; they moved some prisoners into small facilities in urban areas and let these prisoners go out to work during the daytime while still serving the last part of a sentence. These programs were seen as more conducive to rehabilitation as well as being less expensive.

However, for most prisoners in the United States throughout the twentieth century there was little effort at rehabilitation. A new philosophy of prisons towards the end of the century stressed two themes. One theme was that prisons were for the purpose of protecting society by keeping offenders locked up. The American Law Institute's Model Penal Code specified that a court should not impose a prison sentence unless it is necessary to protect society. The intent of the rule was to prompt courts to make more use of other sentences, such as probation or restitution. But instead the emphasis on protecting society provided another rationale for more and longer prison sentences.

The second theme of late twentieth century American corrections was that prisoners should be kept locked up until they become too old to be able to engage in criminal activities. This was supported by studies which showed a drop in crime as offenders aged. The prison was a place for "aging out." In European countries prison terms became shorter with more investment in post-prison rehabilitation programs, but in the United States longer prison sentences became the norm in the late twentieth century.

These two themes, protecting society and aging out offenders, constituted the dominant American philosophy of prisons at the beginning of the twenty-first century. The idea of reform persisted but as an idea applicable to only a small percentage of offenders. Although Lombroso had believed that only a small percentage of criminals, the "born criminals," were incurable and had to be quarantined for the protection of society, the modern practice of corrections in America was based on the assumption that the majority of offenders could not be reformed. Criminal behavior was viewed as the result of deeply rooted habits, an incorrigible lifestyle, and a virtually unalterable criminal environment. Long prison sentences and scanty rehabilitation programs were the logical results of this view of crime and criminals.

Suggested Reading

Killinger, G.G., & Cromwell, P.F. (1973). *Penology: The evolution of corrections in America.* St. Paul: West Publishing Co.

Morris, N., & Rothman, D.J. (1995). *The Oxford history of the prison: The practice of punishment in western society.* Oxford: Oxford University Press.

Introduction to
Gustave de Beaumont and Alexis de Tocqueville

When John Howard became High Sheriff of Bedfordshire, England in 1773 he discovered that the prison under his authority was a miserable dungeon. He soon learned that other prisons throughout England were the same. Vicious criminals, minor offenders, people in prison for not paying debts, women as well as men, old and very young were crowded together, some of them chained, in the darkness of large chambers with vermin and disease, dead bodies lying on the floor sometimes, no water for cleaning or toilet, no light or provision for air, no heat in winter, wearing rags, preying upon one another and being preyed upon by the jailors. Jailors were given fixed budgets to run a prison, and the less they provided for the prisoners, the more they kept for themselves. Jailors earned extra money from fees paid by prisoners or their relatives for better treatment, e.g., for lighter chains, food, a less crowded cell, for having a visitor, and so on.

In search of something better, Howard made a journey to look at prisons on the continent of Europe. There he did find something better, particularly in Holland, Belgium and Italy. There he found a system of humane prisons with the philosophy that prisons should actually reform offenders instead of merely holding them. There were no chains or cruel punishments. Light, fresh air and cleanliness were the standard. These prisons had a strategy for reforming offenders which emphasized classifying and separating different kinds of prisoners for different handling within the prison. These prisons also emphasized maintaining an atmosphere conducive to reform by isolating prisoners to some extent and enforcing rules of silence. Such a system is easily understood when one considers that clergy and religious orders played a major role in developing these reform prisons, most especially those for women and children. Howard reported that the clergy were the most powerful influence on the reform of the prisoners. Upon returning to England, Howard wrote *The State of Prisons* (1777) in which he described the horrid conditions of English prisons and set forth a blueprint for reformed prisons based on what he had observed in Europe. Howard's book caused a sensation in England and in America.

The ideas of John Howard fit very neatly with the convictions of Pennsylvania's Quaker founders. The Quakers, also known as the Society of Friends, were a Christian religious group founded in England by George Fox about 1650. They believed that every individual has a direct relationship with god, so that there is no need for clergy, official creed or rituals. Fox admonished his followers to quake (tremble) at the word of the Lord. In church they meditated silently for long periods of time; because many of them did quake as they meditated, they came to be known as Quakers. There was no preaching and no formal ceremony, although a member might stand and testify to faith now and then. The Quakers had an optimistic view of human nature. They believed that by meditating individuals could discover the good in themselves and come to lead a good life. They also believed that any form of violence against another person was contrary to the will of god. Hence, they were opposed to any forms of physical punishment and opposed to war for any reason.

The Quakers encountered hostility from their neighbors in England. Under the leadership of William Penn they procured a charter from the king to set up a colony in the new world. Their colony was called Pennsylvania. However, the colony did not maintain closed borders, so non-Quakers also settled there. Although the Quakers were soon outnumbered by others in Pennsylvania, their traditions remained a strong influence. They also held on to economic and political control until the Revolution. The Pennsylvanians were very intent on reforming offenders rather than punishing them. Indeed, William Penn himself had instituted a very humane form of penal system in Pennsylvania in 1682, aimed at reform instead of punishment. But his system remained in effect only until his death in 1718. Pennsylvania's jails had degenerated after that to primitive conditions like the English prisons.

Blackstone's *Commentaries on the laws of England* was the textbook of every judge and lawyer in colonial America. Blackstone accepted Beccaria's idea that reform rather than punishment was the object of justice. Blackstone also had picked up and amplified Beccaria's idea that, as far as preventing crime is concerned, the certainty of punishment is more important than the severity of punishment. In England in 1785 William Paley published *The Principles of Moral and Political Philosophy*. Paley was another voice saying that prisons should reform criminals rather than punish. But Paley went further by specifying that prisoners should be housed individually in separate cells. In separate cells they would not be influenced by other prisoners. Alone, they could reform themselves by reflecting on their crimes and repenting. These ideas appealed to Pennsylvanians.

In May 1787 Benjamin Franklin and Benjamin Rush organized the Philadelphia Society for Alleviating the Miseries of Public Prisoners, which was concerned about abject conditions in Philadelphia's Walnut Street jail. This jail had been constructed in 1772. It was a compound about two hundred by four hundred feet containing several buildings. In 1789, responding to the Society's concerns about the prison, the Pennsylvania legislature declared that the Walnut Street prison would house prisoners from all parts of the state and ordered the construction of a new building in the compound to house the most serious offenders. The new building was constructed with sixteen solitary cells, six feet by eight, each with its own little walled-in exercise yard. The design of this building prevented any prisoner from seeing another or talking to another at any time. Prisoners were required to work at trades like shoemaking in order to defray the costs of the prison.

In 1790 Pennsylvania reformed its penal code as part of the overhaul of its penal system. The death penalty was abolished except for murder and treason, and all forms of physical punishment, such as branding and whipping, were replaced by prison sentences and labor. The Walnut Street prison was administered in accord with the new penal code.

The Walnut Street prison used a classification system for prisoners, which was regarded as essential for reforming them. The most serious offenders were in the solitary cells of the new building constructed for this purpose. For less serious offenders there was another building, which had two floors with a total of thirty-two rooms, each about eighteen by twenty feet and each housing several prisoners. A large stone building designed as a work house was used for holding debtors. Women were separated from male prisoners. Even the prison yard was divided among the different classifications of prisoners.

To further implement a reform strategy of solitude and silence, the Pennsylvania legislature authorized the construction of a large new prison at Cherry Hill, Philadelphia. It was the first building designed in America particularly to be a penitentiary type of prison. This prison, and its philosophy, triggered a prison reform movement in America, especially in Pennsylvania and New York. Most of the discussion of prison reform in the early 1800s, even in Europe, focused on the new penitentiary systems of Pennsylvania and New York.

Many people in France in the early 1800s were fascinated by America. Frenchmen who had participated in the American revolution had returned to France with vivid accounts of life in the new world. The French Revolution of the 1780s had sputtered to an end in the terrible period of French history known as "The Reign of Terror." Many people thought that the ideals of the revolution could be seen at work more in America than in France itself. Gustave de Beaumont and Alexis de Tocqueville were from aristocratic families. They had studied history and government and attended lectures at the University of Paris. They were in their late twenties and held low level positions in the French judicial system. The social circles of de Beaumont and de Tocqueville included acquaintances with personal ties to America who hosted visiting Americans and stirred interest in American society. Lafayette's house was a meeting place for French and Americans with compatible ideas, and de Beaumont was a frequent visitor there. He later married a granddaughter of Lafayette. He introduced de Tocqueville to the Lafayette circle.

When the French government saw a pressing need to do something about the horrific conditions in prisons in France, de Beaumont and de Tocqueville offered to make an official visit to America to look into the new American penitentiary system. They arrived in New York in May of 1831. Aided by their official mandate to look into American penitentiaries and by their numerous personal contacts, they made a whirlwind tour of the United States from New England to Louisiana over the course of a year, collecting documents and taking notes on everything they saw and interviewing prominent people. Their interests were in everything American, of which penitentiaries were just a small part. But they visited the prisons on Blackwell's Island (now Roosevelt Island), as well as in the towns of Auburn and Ossining (Sing Sing) in New York; Philadelphia and Pittsburgh in Pennsylvania; Wethersfield, Connecticut; Boston; Baltimore; and other cities. In some prisons they interviewed every prisoner privately. They also interviewed prison officials. Upon returning to France in May of 1832 de Beaumont and de Tocqueville wrote their report on the penitentiaries. Actually, de Tocqueville seems to have fallen into a depressed mood and could scarcely write anything, so that de Beaumont did nearly all the writing of this report. Later de Tocqueville recovered and went on to write his much more famous work, *Democracy in America*.

De Beaumont and de Tocqueville did not focus on the typical prison in America, which was quite dreadful, but rather on the so-called penitentiaries. The penitentiaries were places which were based on the new philosophy of what a prison should do and what it should be like. It was intended to be more humane than other prisons, but that was not all. It was further intended to reform the prisoners rather than just keep them locked away from society or punish them. The new penitentiaries incorporated a new set of ideas about precisely how to reform prisoners. That was what generated so much interest in them.

In their report de Beaumont and de Tocqueville drew certain conclusions about the penitentiaries in America and about prisons in general. Their purpose was not merely to describe the American prisons but to make recommendations for prison reforms in France. As evidence to support their recommendations, they relied on their personal observations as well as interviews with prisoners and prison officials, various reports on the prisons, historical sources and public information. As students of government, they were most inclined to base conclusions on case histories. The prisons of Pennsylvania and New York were their most important cases.

Although the word *penitentiary* is still used, today's prisons do not follow the ideas of the penitentiary as described by de Beaumont and de Tocqueville. The prisons they described are a vivid contrast to the din and idleness of modern American prisons. The most fundamental question remains whether offenders can reform themselves or be reformed, and whether a prison could be a suitable environment for reforming a typical offender. These questions encompass more detailed issues, such as types and conditions of labor and job training in prisons, living conditions, prison regimens, prisoner classification and separation systems, and the roles of prison staff. De Beaumont and de Tocqueville's emphasis on equality in the penitentiaries can prompt reflection on today's unequal prisons and the use of "prison consultants" by wealthy people to get placement in more comfortable prisons. Underlying all ideas about punishment and reform are assumptions about human nature, the extent to which people can change themselves or be changed by others, and what motivates behavior. De Beaumont and de Tocqueville provide an opportunity to reexamine the most fundamental questions about the purposes of prisons, prison conditions, and the goals of a criminal justice system.

Gustave de Beaumont and Alexis de Tocqueville. *On the Penitentiary System in the United States and Its Application in France.* (Originally published in 1832) This translation was made especially for this book. It consists of selected passages from Chapter 1 and Chapter 2. Subtitles were added. Some notes also were added; they are enclosed in square brackets in the text.

Gustave de Beaumont and Alexis de Tocqueville

On the Penitentiary System in the United States and Its Application in France

The Philosophy of the Penitentiary

Although the penitentiary system in the United States is a new institution, its origin must be traced back to times already long gone by. The first idea for reform in the American prisons came from a religious sect in Pennsylvania. The Quakers, who abhor all shedding of blood, had always protested against the barbarous laws which the colonies inherited from their mother country. In 1786 their voice succeeded in getting proper attention, and from that time punishments of death, mutilation, and the whip were abolished in almost all cases by the Legislature of Pennsylvania.

A less cruel fate awaited convicts after this time. Punishment by imprisonment was substituted for physical punishments. A law authorized the court to impose solitary confinement in a cell during the day and the night upon those guilty of capital crimes. It was then that the Walnut Street prison was established in Philadelphia. Here the convicts were classified according to the nature of their crimes. [They were classified into two groups: those who were to be kept in solitary confinement without work, and those who were housed in dormitories and required to work.] Separate cells were constructed for those whom the courts of justice had sentenced to total isolation. These cells also served to curb the rebellion of individuals unwilling to submit to the discipline of the prison. The prisoners in solitary confinement did not work. [However, most of the prisoners in the Walnut Street prison were not in solitary confinement and did work.]

This innovation was good but insufficient.

[The law of 1786 required classification of prisoners into different types, so that different kinds of prisoners could be confined under different conditions.] Since that time the impossibility of classifying criminals in a useful way has been acknowledged, and the imposition of solitary confinement without labor has been condemned by experience.

Nevertheless it is fair to say that the test of this theory [that convicts could be reformed by solitary confinement] was not adequate enough to be decisive. The authority given to judges in Pennsylvania by the law of April 5, 1790 and of March 22 to send criminals to the prison in Walnut Street, who formerly would have been sent to the various county jails, soon produced such a crowd of convicts that it became difficult to put all of them in the proper classifications because the number of solitary cells was inadequate.

Actually, a real penitentiary system did not yet exist in the United States. If asked why this name [penitentiary] was given to the system of imprisonment, we would answer that in America, then as well as now, abolition of the death penalty was confused with a penitentiary system. People said, *Instead of killing the guilty, our laws put them in prison; hence we have a penitentiary system.* This conclusion was not correct.

It is very true that imposing the death penalty for the majority of crimes is incompatible with a system based on imprisonment. But even with the death penalty abolished, a penitentiary system still does not necessarily exist. For a penitentiary system it is also essential that the criminal, whose life has been spared, be placed in a prison whose discipline makes him better. If a prison system, instead of reforming a criminal, tends to corrupt him still more, this would be not a penitentiary system but only a bad system of imprisonment.

This mistake of the Americans was disseminated in France for a long time. In 1794 the Duke de la Rochefoucauld-Liancourt published an interesting account of the prison in Philadelphia: he declared that this city had an excellent prison system, and everybody repeated what he said.

However, the Walnut Street prison could produce none of the effects which are expected from a penitentiary system. It had two principal faults: it worsened by mutual contact those who worked together, and it worsened by idleness those individuals who were plunged into solitude.

The real achievement of the founders of the penitentiary system was the abolition of the bloodthirsty old laws of Pennsylvania and, by introducing a new system of imprisonment, the direction of public attention to this important matter. Unfortunately, the aspects of this innovation which deserved praise were not immediately distinguished from the aspects which were undesirable.

Solitude imposed on a criminal in order to induce him to reform through reflection rests upon a valid philosophical concept. [It is true that, given an opportunity to reflect in solitude, a person will repent and reform.] But the authors of this theory had not yet found a way to put this theory into practice. Only then would it be considered practical and beneficial. However, their mistake was not immediately recognized. Success of the Walnut Street prison was boasted of in the United Stales even more than in Europe, and this biased public opinion in favor of this prison's faults as well as its advantages.

New York and Other States Imitated the Pennsylvania System

The first state which showed itself eager to imitate Pennsylvania was New York, which in 1797 adopted both new penal laws and a new prison system. Solitary co⸺   ⸺   ⸺   w York as in Philadelphi   cally for those who were s   who opposed the establis   efore, was not the ordinar   ;reat criminals who, befor   condemned to death. Tho   ogether in the prison with   inmates of the solitary cell   ·y punishment which their   ie order of the prison was

The Wal: Massachusetts, Maine, Nev   d the principle of solitary c   iminals in each of these stat   of prisons.

Nowher⸺   the hoped-for success. In ⸺⸺⸺⸺ ⸺⸺ ⸺⸺⸺⸺ ⸺⸺ ⸺⸺ ⸺⸺⸺⸺ ⸺⸺⸺⸺⸺⸺⸺⸺ and it never succeeded in reforming the prisoners. Every year the legislature of each state voted considerable funds towards the support of the penitentiaries. But the continuous return of the same individuals into the prisons proved how ineffective was the system to which they were subjected.

Such results might seem to prove the inadequacy of the whole system of the penitentiary. However, instead of condemning the theory itself, the way it was implemented was criticized. It was believed that the whole problem resulted from an insufficient number of cells and crowding of the prisoners. It was believed that the system would produce good results if some new buildings were added to the prisons already existing. New expenses, therefore, and new efforts were made.

More Penitentiary Experiments in New York and Pennsylvania

This was how the Auburn prison originated [in 1816]. This prison, which has become so celebrated, at first was founded upon a plan which was essentially erroneous. It limited itself to some classification of the prisoners. Each of the cells was designed to accommodate two convicts. It was of all combinations the most unfortunate. It would have been better to throw together fifty criminals in the same room than to separate them two by two. This mistake was soon realized, and in 1810 the Legislature of the State of New York ordered the erection of a new building at Auburn (the northern wing) in order to increase the number of solitary cells. (However it should be noted that no idea as yet existed of the system which has developed since then.) It was not intended to subject all the convicts to a system of solitary cells. It was only to apply the system of solitary cells to a greater number of prisoners.

At the same time the same theory [about solitude and reform] produced similar experiments in Philadelphia. The limited success of the Walnut Street prison would have convinced the inhabitants of Pennsylvania of its ineffectiveness if they, like the citizens of the State of New York, had not seen the faults in the way the system was implemented as a reason for continuing to believe that the basic theory was correct.

In 1817 the Legislature of Pennsylvania authorized the construction of a penitentiary at Pittsburgh for the western counties, and in 1821 it authorized construction of the penitentiary at Cherry Hill for the city of Philadelphia and the eastern counties. The principles to be followed in the construction of these two establishments were, however, not entirely the same as those on which the Walnut Street prison had been erected. In the Walnut Street prison, classification was the primary feature of the prison system; solitary confinement was secondary. In the new prisons classification was abandoned; a solitary cell was to be prepared for every convict. The criminal was not to leave his cell day or night, and all labor was denied to him in his solitude. Thus absolute solitary confinement, which in Walnut Street was only incidental, was now to become the foundation of the prison system adopted for Pittsburgh and Cherry Hill.

This experiment promised to be decisive. No expense was spared to construct these new establishments worthy of their goal. These edifices were built on elevated ground. They resembled palaces more than prisons.

In the meantime, even before the laws which ordered their construction were carried out, the Auburn prison had been tested in the State of New York. Lively debates followed in the legislature on this occasion. The public was impatient to know the results of the new experiments which had just been put into effect.

When the northern wing of Auburn prison had been nearly finished in 1821, eighty prisoners were placed there, and a separate cell was given to each. This experiment, from which such good results had been anticipated, turned out to be fatal to the majority of the convicts. In order to reform them, they had been subjected to complete isolation. But such absolute solitude, if nothing interrupts it, is beyond the strength of man. It destroys the criminal without letting up and without pity. It does not reform. It kills.

The unfortunate prisoners on whom this experiment was done fell into a state of depression so noticeable that their keepers were struck by it. Their lives seemed in danger if they remained longer in this situation. Five of them had already died during a single year. Their mental state was just as alarming. One of them had become insane; another, in a fit of despair, had taken the opportunity when the keeper brought him something, to throw himself down from his cell [onto the stone pavement below the tiers of cells], running the almost certain risk of a fatal fall.

The system was finally judged based on such effects. The Governor of the State of New York pardoned twenty-six of those in solitary confinement. The others to whom this clemency was not extended, were allowed to leave their cells during the day and to work in the common workshops of the prison. From this period (1828) the system of total isolation ceased completely to be practiced at Auburn. Proof was soon provided that this system of solitary cells, fatal to the health of the criminals, was also ineffective in producing their reform. Of the twenty-six convicts pardoned by the governor, fourteen returned to the prison a short time afterwards as a result of new offenses.

This experiment, so deadly to those who were selected to undergo it, might have endangered the success of the penitentiary system altogether. After the melancholy effects of isolation, it was feared that the whole principle of reform through solitude would be rejected. It would have been a natural reaction. The Americans were wiser. They did not give up the idea that solitude, which causes a criminal to reflect, exercises a beneficial influence. The problem was to find some means by which the bad effects of total solitude could be avoided without giving up the advantages of solitude. It was believed that this end could be attained by leaving the convicts in their cells during the night and by making them work during the day in the common workshops while obliging them to maintain total silence while doing so.

Messrs. Allen, Hopkins, and Tibbits, who in 1824 were directed by the Legislature of New York to inspect the Auburn prison, found this new system established in that prison. They praised it greatly in their report, and the Legislature sanctioned this new system by its approval....

Since the beginning the system of Auburn has had extraordinary success. It soon aroused public attention to the highest degree. A remarkable change took place at that time in the opinions of many people. The direction of a prison, formerly entrusted to obscure wardens, was now sought by persons of high standing. Mr. Elam Lynds, formerly a captain in the army of the United States, and Judge Powers, a magistrate of rare merit, were seen, with honor to themselves, filling the office of directors of Auburn.

However, the adoption of a system of cells for all convicts in the state of New York rendered the Auburn prison inadequate since it contained only 550 cells after all the successive additions which had been made. The need for a new prison was felt. It was then that the plan of Sing Sing [Ossining, New York] was resolved upon by the legislature (1825). The way it was carried out is something which deserves to be reported.

Mr. Elam Lynds, who had acquired his experience at Auburn where he had been the superintendent, left Auburn, took one hundred convicts accustomed to obey with him, and led them to the place where the new prison was to be erected. There, encamped on the bank of the Hudson River, without a place to house them and without walls to lock in his dangerous companions, he set them to work, making every one a stone mason or a carpenter, and having no other means to keep them in obedience than the strength of his character and the energy of his will. Over a period of several years the convicts, whose number was gradually increased, were at work building their own prison. At present the penitentiary of Sing Sing contains one thousand cells, all of which were built by their criminal inmates.

At the same time (1825) an establishment of another kind was erected in the city of New York. It occupies a place no less important among the improvements whose history we are attempting to trace. We mean the House of Refuge which was founded for juvenile offenders.

There is no other establishment whose usefulness has been warranted to a higher degree by experience. It is well known that most of the individuals on whom the criminal law inflicts punishments were unfortunate before they became guilty. Misfortune is particularly dangerous for those whom it befalls at a tender age; and it is very rare that an orphan without inheritance and without friends, or a child abandoned by its parents, avoids the snares laid for his inexperience, and does not pass within a short time from misery to crime. Concerned about the fate of juvenile delinquents, several charitable individuals of the city of New York conceived the plan of a House of Refuge. It was designed to serve as an asylum [place of shelter], and to provide the young people with an education and the means of earning a living which fortune had refused. Thirty thousand dollars was the amount of the first round of donations. Thus, solely by the power of a charitable association, an eminently useful establishment was founded. Perhaps it is even more important than the penitentiaries, because the penitentiaries punish crime whereas the House of Refuge tends to prevent it.

Further Experiments with Penitentiaries in Pennsylvania

The experiment made at Auburn in the State of New York, which showed the fatal effects of isolation without labor did not prevent Pennsylvania from continuing to test the effects of solitary confinement. In the year 1827 the penitentiary of Pittsburgh began to receive prisoners. Each one was locked up, day and night, in a cell in which no labor was permitted. This solitude, which in principle was to be absolute, was not really in fact. The construction of this penitentiary is so defective that it is very easy to hear in one cell what is going on in another. Hence, each prisoner found in the conversation with his neighbor a daily recreation, that is to say, an opportunity for inevitable bad influence. Since these criminals did not work, we could say that their sole occupation consisted of mutual bad influence. This prison, therefore, was even worse than the Walnut Street prison because, due to the communication with each other, the prisoners at Pittsburgh were as little occupied with their reform as those at Walnut Street. And while those at Walnut Street indemnified society to a degree by the products of their labor, those at Pittsburgh spent all their time in idleness, harmful to themselves and burdensome to the public treasury.

The failure of the Pittsburgh prison proved nothing against the system which had called it into existence, because defects in the construction of the prison rendered the implementation of the solitary system impossible. Nevertheless, the advocates of the theories on which it was founded began to grow cool. This discouragement became even more widespread in Pennsylvania when the gruesome effects caused by solitude without labor in the Auburn prison became known, and when people learned of the success of the new system at Auburn based on isolation by night and labor together during the day.

Warned by such striking results, Pennsylvania was fearful she had pursued a dangerous course. She felt the necessity of submitting to a new investigation the question of solitary imprisonment without labor, practiced at Pittsburgh and introduced into the penitentiary of Cherry Hill, the construction of which was already far advanced. The legislature of this state, therefore, appointed a committee to examine which was the better system of imprisonment. Messrs. Charles Shaler, Edward King and T.I. Wharton, commissioners charged with this mission, have described in a very remarkable report the different systems then in practice (December 20, 1827). They concluded the discussion by recommending the new Auburn system, which they proclaimed to be the best....

Pennsylvania was, perhaps more than any other state, interested in the controversy. The rival of New York, it was natural she should show herself jealous to retain in every respect the rank to which her advanced civilization entitles her among the most enlightened states of the Union. She adopted a system which at once agreed with the austerity of her manners and her philanthropic sensitiveness. She rejected solitude without labor, the fatal effects of which experience had proved everywhere, and she retained the absolute separation of prisoners. This is a severe punishment, but one which does not need the support of physical punishments.

The penitentiary at Cherry Hill, founded on these principles, is therefore a combination of Pittsburgh and Auburn. Isolation during night and day has been retained from the Pittsburgh system, but the labor of Auburn has been introduced into the solitary cell.

A Comparison of the Two Systems

We find in the United States two distinctly separate systems: the system of Auburn and that of Philadelphia. Sing Sing in the State of New York, Wethersfield in Connecticut, Boston in Massachusetts, and Baltimore in Maryland have followed the model of Auburn. On the other side, Pennsylvania stands all alone.

Although the two systems are opposed to each other on important points, they have a common basis without which no penitentiary system is possible. This basis is the *isolation* of the prisoners.

Whoever has studied the interior of prisons and the mental state of their inmates has become convinced that communication between these persons renders their reformation impossible. Communication between them becomes the inevitable cause of alarming bad influences. This observation, justified by the experience of every day, has become an almost commonplace truth in the United States. The writers who disagree most regarding how to put a penitentiary system into practice agree totally upon this point, that no beneficial system can possibly exist without separation of the criminals.

For a long time it was believed that, in order to avoid the bad effects caused by contacts between prisoners, it would be sufficient to set up a certain number of classifications in the prison to separate the prisoners into different kinds. But after having tried this plan, its inadequacy has been recognized. There are similar punishments and also crimes called by the same name, but there are no two human beings the same in regard to their character. Moreover, every time convicts are put together, there necessarily exists a harmful influence of some upon others. In any association among the wicked it is not the less guilty who influence the more criminal, but rather the more depraved who influence those who are less depraved.

Since it is impossible to stop bad influences by merely classifying prisoners into separate groups, we must agree to the separation of every one. This separation, which prevents the wicked from harming others, is also favorable to the wicked himself. Thrown into solitude, he reflects. Placed alone, remembering his crime, he learns to hate it. If his soul be not yet filled to the brim with crime, and thus have lost all taste for anything better, it is in solitude that remorse will come to assail him.

Solitude is a severe punishment, but such a punishment is merited by the guilty. Mr. Livingston justly remarks that a prison, destined to punish, would soon cease to be a fearful place if the convicts in it could enjoy the same social contacts in which they delighted before their entry into prison. Still, whatever may be the crime of a guilty prisoner, no one has the right to take his life from him, if society decrees merely that he is to be deprived of his liberty. That, however, would be the result of absolute solitude if no alleviation of its rigors were offered.

This is the reason why labor is introduced into prison. Far from being an increase in the punishment, it is a real benefit to the prisoner. But even if a criminal did not find in labor a relief from his sufferings, it nevertheless would be necessary to force him to it. It was idleness which led him to crime. With work to do he will learn how to live honestly. Labor by criminals is necessary from another point of view, too: their detention, expensive for society if they remain idle, becomes less burdensome to society if they labor.

The prisons of Auburn, Sing Sing, Wethersfield, Boston, and Philadelphia are based on these two united principles, solitude and labor. These principles, in order to be beneficial, ought not to be separated. The one is ineffective without the other....

The Philadelphia Model of Solitude and Labor

Completely convinced of these truths, the founders of the new penitentiary at Philadelphia considered it necessary for each prisoner to be secluded in a separate cell during the day as well as at night. They believed that only absolute separation of criminals can protect them from mutual bad influence, and they have applied the principle of separation in all its rigor. According to this system, a convict, once thrown into his cell, remains there without interruption until the end of his punishment. He is separated from the whole world. A penitentiary, full of offenders like himself, but every one of them entirely isolated, does not provide him with a society in prison. If it is true that in establishments of this nature, all evil originates from the contacts of prisoners among themselves, we have to acknowledge that nowhere is this contamination avoided with more certainty than at Philadelphia, where prisoners find themselves completely unable to communicate with each other. It is unquestionable that this complete isolation shields a prisoner from all harmful contamination.

Since solitude is more complete in Philadelphia than in any other prison, nowhere is the need for labor more urgent. However, it would be inaccurate to say that labor is imposed in the Philadelphia penitentiary. We could say more accurately that the favor of labor is granted. When we visited this penitentiary, we conversed with all its inmates one by one. There was not one among them who did not speak of labor with a kind of gratitude and who did not express the idea that without the relief that comes from being busy with work, life would be insufferable. What would become of a prisoner during the long hours of solitude without this relief, abandoned to himself, a prey to the regrets of his soul and the terrors of his imagination? Labor provides relief in a solitary cell; it fatigues the body and relieves the mind.

It is very remarkable that these men, the majority of whom were led to crime by laziness and idleness, should be led by the torments of solitude to find their only comfort in labor. By hating idleness, they accustom themselves to hate the primary cause of their misfortune; and labor, by comforting them, makes them love the only means which will enable them to gain their livelihood honestly when they are free.

The Auburn Model of Solitude and Labor

The founders of the Auburn prison also acknowledged the need to separate prisoners in order to prevent all communication among them and to subject them to the requirements of laboring. But the Auburn system follows a different path to arrive at the same end.

In this prison, as well as in others set up on the same model, prisoners are locked in their solitary cells only at night. During the day they work together in common workshops. Since they are subjected to the law of rigorous silence, although they are together in the same place, they are really isolated. Labor in common and in silence is the special feature which distinguishes the Auburn system from the Philadelphia system.

It is said that, owing to the silence to which the prisoners are condemned, commingling of the prisoners has no disadvantages but instead offers many advantages. They are together, but no mental connection exists among them. They see each other without knowing each other. They are in society without any interaction. There is neither dislike nor sympathy among them. A criminal who thinks about planning an escape or an attempt to kill his keepers does not know which of his fellow prisoners he could expect to give him assistance. The commingling of the prisoners is strictly physical, or, to put it another way, their bodies are together but their minds are separated. It is not the solitude of the body which is important, but that of the mind. At Pittsburgh the prisoners, although separated, are not alone, since there is communication among them [through the flimsy walls]. At Auburn they are really isolated, although no wall separates them.

Being together in the workshops, therefore, presents no hazards. On the contrary, it has a unique advantage, that of accustoming prisoners to obedience. What is the principal purpose of punishment in relation to the one who suffers it? It is to give him the habits of society, and the first of these is to teach him to obey. Proponents of the Auburn system say that it provides a clear advantage over the Philadelphia system on this point.

Perpetual seclusion in a cell is a condition which is beyond the control of a prisoner. It curbs a prisoner without a struggle and so completely eliminates any submission of a mental character. Locked up in a small space, he does not really have to observe any discipline. If he works, it is in order to escape the weariness which threatens to overwhelm him. In short, he obeys not so much the established discipline as the physical impossibility of acting otherwise.

At Auburn, on the contrary, labor, instead of being a comfort to the prisoners, is a painful task to them, which they would be glad to get rid of. In observing silence, they are constantly tempted to violate the rule. They have merit in obeying because their obedience is not merely a necessity. It is in this way that the Auburn discipline gives prisoners the habits of society, which they do not develop in the prison of Philadelphia.

We see, then, that silence is the principal basis of the Auburn system. It is this silence which establishes a mental separation between all prisoners, which deprives them of all dangerous communication, and which leaves them only those social contacts which are not harmful.

We have explained the general principles upon which the systems of Auburn and of Philadelphia rest. How are these principles put into action? How and by whom are the penitentiary establishments administered? What are the administrative arrangements, and what is the regimen of each day? This shall form the subject of the following section.

Administration of Penitentiary Systems

The administration of these prisons is entrusted everywhere to a superintendent, whose authority is more or less extensive. He employs a clerk, who is in charge of the financial affairs of the establishment. Above the superintendent are three inspectors responsible for the general direction and oversight of the prison, and under the superintendent is a more or less large number of subordinate jailors....

Although the inspectors are not the day to day administrators of the prison, they nevertheless direct it. They make the regulations, which the superintendent is obliged to enforce, and they constantly watch over their implementation. They have the power to modify the regulations as they see fit, according to the needs of changing circumstances. However, in no case do they take part in the daily administration of the prison. The superintendent alone runs the prison because he alone is answerable for it. The superintendents everywhere have the same legal authority, yet they do not exercise it in the same way in all the prisons which we are describing. Thus at Sing Sing the supervision by the inspectors appeared to us superficial, while at Auburn and at Wethersfield the inspectors took a much more active part in the affairs of the prison.

On the whole, we could say that the powers of the inspectors are much more extensive in law than in reality, while the superintendent, whose written authority is not very great, is really the soul of the administration. The most important position in the prison is, without a doubt, the superintendent. In the penitentiaries of the United States this position is usually entrusted to honorable men entitled by their talents to positions of this sort. The Auburn prison has had for directors men like Mr. Elam Lynds, a former captain of the army, and Mr. Gershom Powers, a Judge of the State of New York. At Wethersfield, Mr. Pillsbury; at Sing Sing, Mr. Robert Wiltze; and at Boston, Mr. Austin, a captain in the navy, are all men distinguished by their knowledge and their capabilities. To great integrity and a deep sense of their duty they add much experience and a thorough knowledge of men, which is so necessary in their position. Among the superintendents of the American penitentiaries, we have to mention especially Mr. Samuel Wood, director of the new Philadelphia prison. He is a man of superior mind who, motivated by religious convictions, has left behind his former career in order to devote himself entirely to the success of an establishment so useful to his community.

The lower-level staff, the under-wardens, are not as distinguished for their standing in society or for talent. However, in general, they are intelligent and honest men. In charge of supervising the labor in the workshops, they nearly always have special technical knowledge of the trades with which the prisoners occupy themselves....

We have seen that the superintendents, however lofty their character and position may be, are subject to the control of a superior authority, the inspectors of the penitentiary. But above both there is an authority mightier than all others, not written in the laws but all-powerful in a free country, namely, public opinion. The improvements in prisons have aroused general attention, public opinion focuses on these matters, and public opinion exercises its enormous influence without hindrance.

There are countries in which public establishments are considered by the government to be its own personal affair, so that people are allowed to enter them only as the government pleases, just as a home owner might refuse admission into his house as he pleases. In such countries the public establishments are sort of administrative sanctuaries which no unconsecrated person can enter. The public establishments in the United States, on the contrary, are considered to belong to everyone. The prisons are open to everyone who chooses to inspect them, and every visitor may see for himself the regimen which regulates them on the inside. There is no exception to this except in the penitentiary at Philadelphia. Yet, even in Philadelphia anyone who wishes may see the buildings and the interior of the establishment. The only thing not permitted is to see the prisoners, because visits by the public would be in direct contradiction to the principle of absolute solitude, which is the foundation of the Philadelphia system.

Instead of avoiding inspection by the public, the superintendents and inspectors of prisons seek the examination and attention of everyone. Each year the inspectors give an account, either to the legislature or to the governor, of the financial situation of the prison as well as of its proper operation. They point out existing abuses and also improvements which could be made. Their reports, which are printed by orders of the legislatures, are immediately distributed for publicity and debate. Newspapers, the number of which in the United States is immense, publish the reports faithfully. Hence, there is not a citizen of the United States who does not know how the prisons of his country are run, and everyone is able to contribute to their improvement either by his opinion or by his financial contribution....

The Prison Regimen

We have seen the elements of which the prison is composed. Let us now examine how it operates. When a convict arrives in prison, a physician checks the state of his health. He is washed, his hair is cut, and new clothing, in keeping with the uniform of the prison, is given to him. In Philadelphia he is conducted to his solitary cell, which he never leaves. There he works, eats, and rests; and the construction of this cell is so complete in its facilities that there is no need whatever to leave it.

At Auburn, at Wethersfield, and in other prisons of the same kind, the prisoner is first plunged into the same solitude, but only for a few days. After that the prisoner leaves solitary confinement in order to labor in the workshops. At daybreak a bell gives the signal for rising. The jailors open the cell doors. The prisoners arrange themselves in a line under the command of their respective jailors. First they go into the yard, where they wash their hands and faces. From there they go into the workshops, where they start to work immediately. Their labor is not interrupted until the hour for taking food. Not a single instant is given to recreation.

At Auburn when the hours of breakfast or of dinner have arrived, labor stops and all the convicts meet in the large dining hall. At Sing Sing and all other penitentiaries they return to their cells and take their meals separately. This latter arrangement appeared to us preferable to the arrangement at Auburn. It is not without difficulties and even danger that such a large number of criminals can be gathered together in the same room. Their being together makes it so much more difficult to maintain discipline.

In the evening, when the sun sets, labor stops and the convicts leave the workshops to return to their cells. Upon rising, going to sleep, eating, leaving the cells and going back to them, everything is done in the most profound silence. Nothing is heard in the whole prison but the footsteps of those who march, or sounds coming from the workshops. When the day is finished and the prisoners have returned to their cells, the silence within these vast walls, which hold so many prisoners, is that of death. We often walked at night along the monotonous and silent galleries where a lantern is always burning. We felt as if we were walking through catacombs. There were a thousand living beings, and yet it was a desert solitude.

The regimen of one day is the same as for every day of the year. One hour after another in the convict's life follows with overwhelming uniformity from the moment of his entry into the prison until the end of his sentence. Labor fills the whole day. The whole night is given to rest. Since the labor is hard, long hours of rest are necessary. The prisoner's rest is not disturbed between the moment of going to bed and the time of rising. Before his sleep as after it, the prisoner has time to reflect on his solitude, his crime, and his misery.

It is true that not all penitentiaries have the same regimen. Still, all the convicts of a prison are treated in the same way. Indeed, there is more equality in prison than in society.

Labor in Prison

All prisoners have the same clothing and eat the same bread. [In the nineteenth century upper-class people ate soft white bread, and lower-class people ate coarse dark bread.] All work. In this respect there is no distinction among them except the differences which result from some having a greater natural skill for one trade than for another. On no condition is labor to be interrupted. It has been found inappropriate to give a prisoner just a certain task to do, after which the prisoner is at liberty to do nothing. It is as essential for the convict as for the order of the prison that he should labor without interruption. It is essential for him because idleness is harmful to him; it is essential for the prison because, as Judge Powers observed, fifty individuals who work can be watched more easily than ten convicts doing nothing....

Labor is beneficial not only because it is the opposite of idleness, but also because the convict by working learns a trade which may support him after he leaves prison. The prisoners are taught only useful trades. Care is taken to choose the trades which are the most profitable and whose products are easiest to sell.

The Philadelphia system has been accused of making labor by the prisoners impossible. It is certainly more economical and advantageous to have a number of workmen labor together in a common workshop rather than have each of them work in a separate place. Moreover, it is true that a great many trades cannot be pursued properly by an individual workman in a small space. Yet the penitentiary of Philadelphia shows that the various occupations which can be pursued by isolated men are numerous enough to occupy them usefully. The same difficulty is not encountered in prisons in which convicts work in a group. At Auburn and at Baltimore a very great variety of trades is pursued. These two prisons have vast manufacturing facilities which encompass many useful occupations. However, at Boston and at Sing Sing the occupations of the convicts so far have been less varied. In these two prisons, the majority of the criminals are employed in cutting stones.... [Before the use of structural steel, stone was the choice material for large buildings, and stone cutting was a skilled occupation.]

Women in Prison

Such is the regimen established in the American penitentiaries. We have said that this discipline is applied to all prisoners in the state prisons. However, women have not been subjected to it yet, except in Connecticut. Generally the women are found together in the American prisons as with us [in France]; and in that country, as with us, they are exposed to all the vices growing out of contaminating contacts with other prisoners.

Some persons believe that it would be extremely difficult to apply to women a system based on silence. But the experiment done at Wethersfield [Connecticut], where women are, like the rest of the prisoners, subject to isolation in cells during the night and absolute silence during the day, proves that this difficulty can be overcome. It is not the difficulty of imposing silence on women which has prevented reform in the prisons of the United States. In the implementation of the new penitentiary system, the women have been omitted mostly because of the small number of crimes committed by women in that country. It is because women occupy only a little space in prison that they have been neglected. It is the same as with most evils of society—a remedy is ardently sought for things that are important; if they are not alarming, they are overlooked....

Introduction to
John Augustus

What is known about Augustus himself comes from fragments in the *Report*, published testimonies, and newspaper accounts which Augustus included as a sort of appendix incorporated in the *Report*. Augustus was born in Woburn, Massachusetts in 1784. He moved to Lexington in 1805 where he established a prosperous shoemaking business. By 1819 he was able to donate a large parcel of land to that city for the construction of a school, the Lexington Academy. In 1813 Augustus married a twenty-year-old woman known to us only as Sally. They had a child whom they named Harriet. The daughter died when less than a year old, and Sally died about the same time. Some years later Augustus married again, this time to Harriet Stearns. They had a daughter, whom they also named Harriet, who died at the age of ten. However, they also had two sons who survived. Augustus and his wife did raise at least one girl, his first child client. The little girl had been arrested together with an older sister for stealing. Augustus impulsively bailed the little one. Later he discovered that her mother, as well as her father, was an incorrigible drunkard, so her own family was unsuitable to raise her.

When Augustus moved to Boston in 1827, he again established himself as a shoemaker. His shop was at 5 Franklin Avenue, not far from the police court. He had five or six apprentices or employees. Augustus was already about 57 years old, older than the average life span at that time, when he began his labors on behalf of the unfortunate. Even so, he was a very determined, very independent, very fast talking bundle of kinetic energy who amazed people by how much he did in a day. He was described as "a thin, elderly man of medium height, his face somewhat wrinkled, and his features of a benevolent expression," a "warm-hearted and impulsive man," who "generally utters what is uppermost in his thoughts, without stopping to calculate the effect which it will be likely to produce" (*Report*, p. 75). When Augustus began posting bail for habitual drunkards in 1841, he took to working much of the night to keep his shop going. For the first two years he had only his own income to support his activity, but he began to get financial help from others after that. Still, his own financial resources were exhausted after four years. He had to give up his business after the fifth year and thenceforth was entirely dependent on help from others. He relied on Boston philanthropists to support his bail activities and even to post bail for himself when his enemies conspired to imprison him.

In addition to his labors on behalf of those in trouble with the law, Augustus was well known for the help he gave to abandoned children and to people who were ill and destitute. On one occasion, in 1848, he played a major role in persuading a church group to forego construction of a new church and instead use their funds to establish a home for abandoned children. Augustus' work on behalf of offenders was only part of his charitable activities.

The idea that people could be reformed was one of the dominant ideas of the nineteenth century. Among some of the seventeenth and eighteenth century enlightenment philosophers the idea of reforming people was based on the premise that human nature was good and reform was only a return to a natural state of goodness. The idea of reform rather than punishment for criminals had been given strong voice in the writings of Beccaria on crimes and punishments and Blackstone's commentaries on law. The idea of reform was also a powerful force in religious thinking, and not only among Quakers. Fundamentalist preachers in the nineteenth century, both local and traveling preachers, conducted religious revivals urging people to be "born again."

The idea of reform took a specific direction in the temperance movement of the nineteenth century. The temperance movement viewed alcohol as the most serious problem of society. Addiction to alcohol destroyed individuals' lives and families by making people unfit for work and violent towards others. The temperance movement was powerful in both northern Europe and America. Among the numerous temperance groups in America were the George Washington Temperance Society for men, the largest in the country, and the Martha Washington Temperance Society for women. The temperance movement seems to have been the source of John Augustus' conviction that people can and should be reformed rather than punished, whenever possible. The temperance movement continued to grow throughout the nineteenth century and into the twentieth when the movement triumphed with the passage of the Eighteenth Amendment to the U.S. Constitution in 1919. The Eighteenth Amendment prohibited all manufacture and sale of alcoholic beverages. Thus began the fifteen year period of Prohibition in the United States.

All those who sought to reform people shared the same assumption that reform was mostly a matter of will power. They viewed human beings as rational creatures with free wills. They believed people had the power to change their lives by reflecting and making a decision. Other people could only encourage and support such a decision. But to be effective the decision had to be formalized in some specific, public way. For Christian preachers individual reform was proclaimed through baptism at a gathering of believers. For temperance groups, the ritual of reform was "the pledge." The pledge was a promise never again to touch alcohol. But it was not simply a verbal promise. It was a written document signed by the individual then held by the temperance society or someone else. Most often the reformed individual also became an active member of the temperance society, which provided group support for the new abstainer. The temperance societies were the only reformers mentioned by John Augustus in his report on his own activities, although he did not officially work for a temperance society. On the first occasion when Augustus posted bail for a prisoner, Augustus had the man take "the pledge," which Augustus was apparently carrying in his pocket that day.

John Augustus' self-appointed legal role consisted of posting bail for offenders. He intervened in their trials at the point where they were convicted but not yet sentenced. After the case against the defendant was presented, Augustus injected himself into the proceeding by asking the judge to allow him to post bail. Posting bail was an accepted practice in English and American law. What was novel in the work of John Augustus was, first, that the person for whom he was posting bail was a stranger and, second, that he was posting bail for so many offenders.

Augustus asked the judge to recess the trial before sentencing the offender and to give the offender a period of "probation" before proceeding with the trial. "Probation" was not a technical term, nor did Augustus intend it to be a label for this process. "Probation" was an ordinary word, although it is now an old fashioned word, meaning "a period of testing." Augustus was asking the judge to allow a period of testing to see whether the offender would reform. He assumed that the judge would share his belief that reform was better than punishment. He also assumed that if the person went through this period of testing without relapsing into bad conduct, the punishment imposed by the judge would be mild because it would be seen as unnecessary. Unlike modern probation, the probation proposed by Augustus was not a sentence. Augustus' probationers were sentenced following the period of probation, but the sentence was usually minimal if the probation was successful.

In the mid-1800s most people lived on farms. Cities were the centers of trade and commerce. As the century rumbled on, some northern cities became more and more the centers for manufacturing textiles and then for the garment industry. The city of Boston was one of the world's great seaports with fast Yankee Clipper ships extending trade as far as the Orient. For able bodied men there was work, although it might not pay very well. For the sick, injured, infirm or old there was little of anything. Such financial supports as unemployment benefits, disability income and retirement pensions had not yet been invented. A person unable to work depended on family, neighbors and charities. Government services were minimal. Many schools, hospitals, soup kitchens and welfare societies began as private or religious philanthropies. Only later did government get involved in these activities. John Augustus' work with criminal offenders was another example of private philanthropy which later became a government activity.

In the nineteenth century few careers were open to women. Most women married, did the chores around the house or farm and raised their children. For the few women with the requisite skills there was teaching, as long as they remained unmarried. Married women were not allowed to teach. Unskilled women could earn a subsistence living by doing laundry or other menial work. Single young girls, such as new Irish immigrants in Boston, might find work in a middle- or upper-class household. Domestic work was the most common employment for women. Middle-class people commonly had live-in servants who did cleaning, laundry, cooking, sewing, and child care. These servants were given room and board and a very small amount of money. The lady of the house supervised them, taught them domestic skills, taught them manners and proper speech, might teach them to read and write, and supervised their behavior in order to safeguard the reputation of the household. However, in a world where there were few other work or educational opportunities for women, many young girls fell into prostitution. Eventually John Augustus began extending his activities to helping some of these girls and young women by placing them as domestic workers in middle class households.

A Report of the Labors of John Augustus for the Last Ten Years, in Aid of the Unfortunate ... is a terse account, despite the lengthy title, of what John Augustus did as an inventor of probation for criminal offenders in the United States. In his report, first published in 1852, Augustus described what he did, leaving it mostly to the reader to piece together the why and how of it. The stories of his labors tend to be bare bones, leaving the reader curious about the details and the thinking behind his actions. It is a record of extraordinary success from the day Augustus began such work in 1841 until publication of the report ten years later.

The *Report* seems to have been a fund raising project. Fund raising became particularly necessary when Augustus' opponents in the court created new rules requiring people who posted bail to have the necessary assets at hand. A promise would no longer be sufficient. Despite formidable opposition, Augustus managed to continue his labors at a reduced level at least until the year before his death at the age of seventy-five in 1859. The self-effacing Yankee friend to the unfortunate revealed very little about himself in his report. Nor did he take the trouble to explain what philosophy guided his actions, other than some general references to Christian charity; nor did he offer any organized presentation of what tactics he found most effective. As far as evidence to support the validity of his working practices and his conclusions is concerned, Augustus relied entirely on his own experience.

Augustus had no actual coworker or disciple to explain or carry on his labors, although similar work was apparently being done by one other Boston philanthropist, John M. Spear, of whom little is known. Coincidentally at the same time, apparently unknown to Augustus, in Birmingham, England Matthew D. Hill had begun the practice of bailing and supervising offenders in order to reform them. Starting in 1872, thirteen years after Augustus' death, Rev. Rufus W. Cook, chaplain of the Boston jail, carried on volunteer work similar to the work of Augustus and Spear until 1878 when the State of Massachusetts passed legislation to appoint an official probation officer for the city of Boston.

Augustus' *Report* is a historical account of how Augustus helped various types of offenders, starting with men who were habitual drunkards. These were not first offenders or easy cases; a "habitual" drunkard was legally defined as someone with at least two prior convictions. Hence, the common assertion that Augustus worked only with first offenders or with easy cases is wrong. More by chance than by plan, he went on to help other types of offenders. With each type of offender he had somewhat different criteria for selecting those he would work with and somewhat different strategies for helping them. Modern probation has been criticized for not having a coherent theory and not being particularly successful in reforming people. However, from Augustus' narrative one can deduce his theory and his successful strategies for working with different types of offenders, especially his emphases on family ties and work.

The *Report* of John Augustus remains relevant to the most urgent and modern issues in corrections. It can be a springboard for thinking about such correctional issues as classifications of offenders, alternatives to incarceration, the roles of probation officers, the effectiveness of probation, the criteria for selecting offenders for probation, the way probationers are supervised, privatization of corrections, the economic aspects of the criminal justice industry, the social causes of crime, and the possibilities and means of reforming offenders. His narrative provides an opportunity to reexamine the basic questions underlying the practice of probation both then and now, namely, what sorts of people are most suitable as candidates for probation, and what strategies should be used to help them reform. It can be most instructive to do this by considering Augustus' various types of cases one type at a time: male habitual drunkards, female drunkards, child offenders, one complicated case of a woman who had run a house of prostitution, and young prostitutes. For each of these types of offenders Augustus had different norms for selecting cases and different tactics for promoting the individual's reform. For Augustus reform did not mean merely refraining from criminal activity: reform involved commitments to work and family.

John Augustus. (1852). *A Report of the Labors of John Augustus, for the Last Ten Years, in Aid of the Unfortunate: Containing a Description of His Method of Operations, Striking Incidents, and Observations upon the Improvement of Some of Our City Institutions, with a View to the Benefit of the Prisoner and of Society.* Boston: Wright & Hasty. Subtitles have been added to this selection, and some notes have been added in square brackets. Some punctuation has been modernized.

John Augustus

A Report of the Labors of John Augustus

By request of my friends to whom I have been under the greatest obligations for the last few years, I now with diffidence yet with much self-gratification present a brief yet comprehensive report of a portion of my labors for the last ten consecutive years.

It is generally known that my time has been wholly devoted to the unfortunate, in seeking out the wretched who have become victims to their passions and subjects of punishment by law, and that my mission has been to raise the fallen, reform the criminal, and, so far as my humble abilities would allow, to transform the abode of suffering and misery to the home of happiness. A brief account of the manner in which my efforts have been put forth will I trust afford satisfaction to those of my friends who have contributed their means and their encouragement of my labors, and thus enabled me to accomplish what by the blessing of heaven I have done, yet what I could at first never even have hoped to accomplish.

I have spent the greater part of my time at the Jail, the Court House, and in the abodes of the unfortunate and those charged with all kinds of offences against the law, with a view to ameliorate their condition, and to effect their reformation; and here let me say that the amount of labor which I have performed in the courts alone, in the specified time, is infinitely greater than I at first believed it in my power to accomplish, and to my friends it will not appear like boasting or self-praise if I give a plain transcript of facts as I have recorded them. Every one who has the *will* to do, may do a vast amount of good in the cause in which I am engaged.

In the first place, I will answer the questions which are frequently asked as to how I receive compensation, and how I am able to bail so many, and how I manage to look to the cases of so many persons. I devote my time daily, and often a large portion of the night, in the performance of the various labors which fall within my province. I am no agent for any sect, society, or association whatever. I receive no salary, neither have I ever received a dollar for any service as a salary, nor do I know of any individual who ever became responsible for me, even to the amount of a dollar. I am therefore not accountable to any sect, society or individual for the manner in which my efforts have been applied.

I put my hand to the plough in 1841 in the Police Court, the scene of my earliest efforts to reform the drunkard, which acts on my part were wholly voluntary and have been so to the present time, and equally voluntary have these acted who have aided me to prosecute effectually the work I began.

Common Drunkards:
Selecting Cases and Strategies for Reform

I cannot better describe my mode of action in the Police Court than by introducing an every-day scene there. It was at this time that the great Washingtonian Temperance reform was exciting the attention of the public mind, and when a general interest pervaded the hearts of the philanthropic, to liberate the wretched inebriate from the prison of his own destructive vice, and to loose the bonds which held him captive, by removing from him the pernicious influences by which he had been surrounded, and by causing him to feel that he was still a man.

In the month of August, 1841, I was in court one morning, when the door communicating with the lock-room was opened and an officer entered, followed by a ragged and wretched looking man, who took his seat upon the bench allotted to prisoners. I imagined from the man's appearance that his offence was that of yielding to his appetite for intoxicating drinks, and in a few moments I found that my suspicions were correct, for the clerk read the complaint, in which the man was charged with being a common drunkard. [Note: "Common drunkard" was a legal term meaning convicted of drunkenness at least twice previously.] The case was clearly made out, but before sentence had been passed, I conversed with him for a few moments and found that he was not yet past all hope of reformation, although his appearance and his looks precluded a belief in the minds of others that he would ever become a *man* again. He told me that if he could be saved from the House of Correction, he never again would taste intoxicating liquors. There was such an earnestness in that tone, and a look expressive of firm resolve, that I determined to aid him. I bailed him by permission of the Court. He was ordered to appear for sentence in three weeks from that time. He signed the pledge and became a sober man; at the expiration of this period of probation, I accompanied him into the court room. His whole appearance was changed and no one, not even the scrutinizing officers, could have believed that he was the same person who less than a month before had stood trembling on the prisoner's stand. The Judge expressed himself much pleased with the account we gave of the man, and instead of the usual penalty—imprisonment in the House of Correction—he fined him one *cent* and costs, amounting in all to $3,76 [Note: Adjusted for inflation this was equivalent to about $70.00 in 2005; see westegg.com/inflation/infl.cgi], which was immediately paid. The man continued industrious and sober, and without doubt has been by this treatment saved from a drunkard's grave. [Note: A second account of this first case appeared later in the *Report*. The second account added that the man had a family and the prospect of ready employment.]

This was truly encouraging, and before January, 1842 I had bailed seventeen persons for a similar offence, and they had severally been sentenced in the same manner, which in all amounted to $60,87. Eleven of this number paid the fine, but the other six being too poor to raise the amount, I paid it for them.

It became a rule of this court that a person charged with being a common drunkard, if bailed on probation, the amount of the bail should be thirty dollars, and if at the expiration of the time assigned, the person reformed, the penalty for the offence was the payment of a fine of one cent and costs of court.

Out of the number whom I bailed that year, I now recollect the residence of but one, for a change of circumstances has in many cases called some of the number to various parts of the country, and several have doubtless paid the debt of nature, but so far as I have been able to ascertain, they have sacredly kept the pledge which they were then induced to take. The person to whom I here allude lives on Commercial Street, in this city, and sustains an excellent character, as a sober man and a good citizen. In an interview with this man about a month since, I remembered a remark which was made to me by a well known clergyman of this city [identified in a footnote by Augustus as Rev. Mr. Lathrop] about the time he was bailed; he said, "If one drunkard out of fifty could be saved from drunkenness and restored to the bosom of his family, it would more than pay for all the labor expended in attempting to restore the other forty-nine." This language which has been thus demonstrated, gave me great encouragement. Soon after this man was bailed, the clergyman to whom I have referred called at my shop, in Franklin Avenue, and informed me that there was a man in an alley near Haymarket Square, who was very drunk and unable to walk; he requested me to go and take care of him. I expressed my fears that he might be taken to jail by the officers before we could find him, but he offered to go with me and assist me. This offer I thought very extraordinary, for here was a clergyman *actually* going "out into the highway and hedges." Another gentleman who was present volunteered to accompany us. It was quite dark when we arrived at the spot, and groping our way about, we found the man lying upon the ground; we endeavored to urge him to leave his cold lodgings and to follow us, but he refused, and we led him from the place. We carried him to a Hotel, but at first they refused to allow him to remain in the house, giving as a reason that he did not get his liquor there. The next morning he was conveyed to his home in Waltham.

I have related this as an instance of *practical* preaching. This act of the Rev. gentleman was a noble one, and if the clergy of all denominations would preach in this way a little more than they do, I am confident that a much greater amount of good would be accomplished than now is. I had labored about a year when it became evident that much good had been and might be performed, by laboring in the field in which I had commenced operations, and to promote this object several kind and philanthropic individuals placed in my hands donations of various sums, which enabled me to accomplish a much greater amount of good than I could have done from my own limited means alone. In 1842 I continued to attend the court and to bail as many as I could attend to, those whom I believed might be benefited by such acts on my part. But here I found my efforts materially cramped, and in some measure limited, for my business affairs, of course, claimed a share of my attention, as I was at that time engaged in the boot-making business in Franklin Avenue near the court house. I generally went into court about half past nine in the morning, thinking to return to my shop in a short time, but very frequently found it impossible to leave the court room till twelve or one o'clock, as I waited to bail some unfortunate person. This course broke in upon my business engagements at my shop, and the delay which caused the evil arose in most cases from the opposition of the officers of the court to my mode of operation, and in some cases when I left the court room for a few moments, the unhappy object whose welfare was my aim, would be examined and sentenced before my return. I resolved not to be frustrated in this manner, and thus sacrificed much valuable time.

I continued on in this way for some time, and found that occasions rapidly multiplied where I was called upon to bail the prisoner, and to counsel and aid the wretched. It soon became generally known in the city that I was saving drunkards from the House of Correction, and daily calls upon my attention were increased. My business at my shop suffered sadly by neglect. In August, 1842, I found that I had bailed thirty persons.

Scarcely an hour in the day elapsed, but some one would call at my house or my shop and tell their tale of sorrow. One had a husband who had been arrested by the police; another a wife who had been dragged to the watch house; she had perhaps been taken out of bed at midnight and hurried away from her babe and her family. This was accompanied by a request for me to bail her or him. The unhappy person might add, "I work for Mr. B. We have four small children. My wife is a very good woman, and her only fault is that she drinks once in a while. If you will only get her off, I will pay you any thing you may ask." Scarcely perhaps had the person paused when a poor woman would enter to tell me that her husband, who drinks a little once in a while, went out last night and had not returned; she watched for him all night and had just learned that he had been arrested and taken to jail. She would close by saying, "Do, Mr. Augustus, go and get him out and let me return to my babe. Will you say yes? What shall I do? They will carry him to the House of Correction." The pair stand importuning me, and as I rise from my bench, there enters a little girl who can hardly speak for crying. After some kind words, the little one says, "Mr. Augustus, mother wants to have you come down to our house. Father is in jail. Mr. Stratton took him away last night. Mother is very sick and can't go out." I can do no less than to tell the little one to run home and assure her mother that I will come, and aid her all in my power, and having thus driven the tears back that had begun to flow, the little one trips away to give joy to her mother.

Similar cases were constantly occurring. I would carefully note their names and residences, then go to the court and watch perhaps for hours, till some one whose name I had entered, was brought in from the lock-up, and would then make an effort to save him.

Opposition by Police and Courthouse Officials: The Courthouse Syndicate

Frequently I suffered extreme inconvenience from the opposition of the police officers as well as the clerk of this court. I could not imagine the cause of this unfriendly spirit, until I learned that for every drunkard whom I bailed, the officer was actually losing seventy-five cents, to which he would have been entitled if the case had been otherwise disposed of. This in the aggregate amounted to quite a sum, as will be seen from a glance at the table of statistics. But for all that, I believed that generally a drunkard could more effectually be reformed by kindness than by imprisonment in the House of Correction.

I cannot better give the reader an idea of some of the troubles which I had to encounter, than to extract an article from the *Boston Daily Mail:*

Bridget H., a middle aged, long visaged woman, in a black hood and red shawl, with as much dirt as sorrow upon her pale face, was complained of by police officer Fuller for being a common drunkard. She listened to the reading of the complaint, and in answer to the usual question by the clerk, "Are you guilty or not guilty?":

Bridget. Not guilty; I never was a drunkard.

Mr. Fuller. I found her last night intoxicated, and have seen her so before.

Bridget. No; you never saw me drunk. You said I was so once, and threatened to take me to the watch house, and I gave you a silver half dollar to let me go. You would not have taken me this time if I had had silver to hire you to let me alone.

Justice Cushing. Mr. Fuller, how is this?

Fuller. It is not true—the woman will say what she pleases, and I cannot help it.

[Officer V., to ease his brother constable from an awkward position, came forward and stated to the court that the woman was not to be believed, having been in the House of Correction.]

Bridget. I never was in the House of Correction *but once in my life.*

His Honor here understood the woman to say, "I never was there in my life," and he replied, "That's false, I have your name here as an old offender, and your charge against the officer is not to be accredited a moment after this denial."

Mr. John Augustus, who was present and standing near the prisoner, mildly observed, "She said, your Honor, that she had been in the House of Correction *once.*"

Justice. She did not say so—I heard what the woman said, that *she never was in the House of Correction in her life.*

Police Officer. That is true, your Honor, she said so.

John Augustus—(warmly) But I say she did not say so! I heard the words she used, and I appeal to the spectators.

Considerable excitement began to manifest itself among the few spectators of this highly dignified dispute, and several voices exclaimed, "She did not say so—Augustus is right!" In fact there were not three persons present but heard Bridget distinctly admit that she had been in the House of Correction once.

Officer. Silence in the court!

Justice—(with temper) Mr. Augustus, hold your tongue, sir! Sit down, or I'll direct an officer to take you out of the room!

Augustus. I *will* say what I heard.

Justice. (rising with a *show* of dignity) You can't say any thing! Take a seat, instantly sir! (The incorrigible philanthropist seated himself, and the justice readjusted his spectacles.) Sir, you intrude upon the patience of the court;

you contradict me, and appeal to the spectators, as though I did not know what was said as well as they. (Augustus rising) Keep your seat and be silent, or I'll have you taken out of the room. What right have you to interfere in a question of veracity between a highly respectable officer, so far as I know, and this woman?

Augustus. But I wish to explain the—

Justice. Not another word, sir! (To the prisoner) Bridget, are you married?

Bridget. Yes; but I don't live with my husband.

An officer. Her husband is a steady man and works in Roxbury; but she is so bad he cannot live with her.

Justice. Ah, I see his name, *he has been up three or four times for beating his wife....* (To the clerk) Say four months.

Clerk. Bridget H—, the court sentences you to four months imprisonment in the House of Correction.

A Woman's Plea for Help: Selecting Cases and Reform Strategies

Again, in July, 1842, another instance occurred, the mention of which will suffice for this court. I went down to the lock-up (beneath the Court House) to see a man whom I intended to bail that day and when passing along the main passage leading to the cells, a woman who was imprisoned called to me and requested me to bail her. I told her I could not. Then she asked why I could not aid her as well as aid men. She said she had a husband and children, and expressed much regret for her conduct, and a desire to be allowed to return home. The officer, Mr. D—, who was then a constable of the court, was quite angry and ordered me to leave the place and go about my business; and as I had never bailed a woman, I declined doing so now and left the place, though with a feeling of regret that I had not offered her at least a word of encouragement and hope. As I was returning home revolving in my mind the scenes of the morning, I met a friend, and related the incident to him; the next time I met this man, which was but an hour afterwards, he informed me that he had related the affair to his wife, who expressed a desire to save the poor creature, and even offered to take her into her family, that she might be able to watch over and encourage her, but it was too late, the case had been disposed of, and the woman sentenced; as I parted with him I could but remark that if ladies generally possessed hearts like hers, few there would be who would suffer for sympathy, advice, or aid.

I made up my mind hereafter to recognize "Woman's Rights," and that the very next woman who applied to me to bail her—if I found her a worthy object of aid—I would do it, in spite of all the *rum-breaths* and the seventy-five cent fees of the Police Court, provided that the Judge would give his consent.

On the 27th of July, of this year, a woman who was engaged in the Washingtonian cause, called on me and requested me to go to the court and bail a woman in whom she felt an active interest. She said the family resided in Eliot Street, and her husband was in the employment of Mr. H—D. P—near Court Square. I promised to investigate the case further, and accordingly called to see her husband, who was employed at the restaurant, but a few rods [perhaps 30 or 40 feet] from my shop.—He appeared to be a very kind hearted man, and spoke in terms of the most tender regard of his erring wife, and with deepest emotion told me that he was willing to sacrifice every thing he had in the world, if the reformation of his wife could be effected. He also expressed a desire that the matter might be kept as secret as possible. I went over to court to watch the moving of the waters, which hitherto had borne all drunkards on its current down to the abyss of destruction and despair. When the woman was brought up, I attempted to whisper a few words of hope to her, but I was rudely ordered away by the officers, and the complaint was read to the woman, in which she was charged with being a common drunkard; the witnesses were called; the testimony was strongly against her and the case was fully made out. Just before sentence was pronounced, I told the Justice that I would, with his consent, bail her to appear on the 15th of August, to which he very cheerfully acceded. The woman went home after having promised that she would never again drink intoxicating liquor. This was on Friday, and the lady who had first interested herself, was present at the interview. On Sunday following, I called upon the woman whom I had bailed, and the interview was indeed a happy one; the children were neatly dressed, and were about to start for the Sabbath school, and the very atmosphere was redolent with peace and happiness; although so short a time had elapsed, the mother appeared like a very different woman; she had signed the pledge and most sacredly she kept it. She appeared in court at the specified time, and was fined one cent and costs. She afterwards became a *devoted* member of the Martha Washington Temperance Society. Some time during the next year, there was a tea party at Tremont Temple, the originators of which was the Martha Washington Society. Dr. Channing was present, and during the evening I heard him address a lady of the name of her whom I had bailed the year before, and I found it to be no other than her, and was assured that she was one of the most efficient members of that excellent society. Such an instance was to me additional evidence of the efficacy and humanity of my plan.

I have now related in an unvarnished manner the occasions on which I bailed the first man and first woman, and I need not therefore particularize cases which since have become more than a thousand. That year I bailed forty-six persons, of which number four were females, and thirty I have every reason to believe, abandoned the vice which brought them to the prisoner's bench; but a small proportion of the number were too strongly wedded to a career of guilt and were incorrigible.

During the year ending December 31, 1842, the amount of my bail bonds were $1,380, and the amount of fines paid $174,86.

Posting Bail for Various Offenders:
Expanding Labors, Saving Children, Continued Opposition

During the year 1843, I bailed a number of persons who were charged with various offences, my efforts hitherto having been exclusively for the benefit of the drunkard. In the latter part of this year, I bailed two little girls, aged eight and ten years, and one little boy aged eleven. The girls were sisters. These children had been indicted at the October term, and of course their cases were entered on the docket of the Municipal Court. The girls were charged with stealing five or six dollars [Note: equivalent to about $100 in today's money] from a grocery store on Washington Street. These girls sold apples, and entered the store daily to offer their fruit for sale, and at such times those employed in the store would often tease them by playfully seizing their apples. This familiarity, of course, caused the children to be pert and to act in a similar manner with the property of the grocer, and on one occasion one of them took a small sum of money from a drawer; they shared it equally, and were soon after arrested for larceny from a shop and confined in jail. The next day they were brought before the Police Court for examination. The father of the little ones was present and was allowed to speak for them if he desired, but he was evidently intoxicated; he spoke in a very unfeeling manner of the elder child, saying that "she was to blame, and might go to jail, it was good enough for her," but spoke in a different manner of the other. The Justice ordered them both to find surety each in the sum of $100, and for default to be committed to jail. I offered myself as surety for the little one and was accepted. I took the child to my house, and placed her in charge of my wife; the other went to jail. The next day I went in quest of her mother, and after some difficulty found her, but in a state of intoxication, and of course unable to converse about her children. It was not a fit place for these little ones, neither were those whom nature intended as their guardians, at all competent to take proper care of them. A few days after I had witnessed this melancholy sight, a humane gentleman, Mr. H., called on me, and expressed his desire to take the little girl who was then in jail, into his own family. I offered to bail her, and immediately proceeded to the Police Court, for that purpose, and was at once accepted as her surety. We proceeded directly to the jail, where we found the little one crying bitterly. The iron door swung creaking on its hinges, to allow of the egress of the little prisoner. I took her tiny hand in mine and led her from the place, while the child looked up into my face, and there beamed from her eyes an expression I can never forget. Who would know true joy, let him be a participant in a scene like this. I could fancy a language proceeding from that gaping cell which was now untenanted; it said in unmistakable language, "Take this infant under thy guardian care, for she has none to help her; be thou her father and her guide, then shall the blessings of those that are ready to perish come upon you. Say to her, remember this day in which you came from out the prison of bondage, for by strength of hand the Lord has brought thee out of this place."

My friend took the little one to the bosom of his own family, and the sequel is soon told;—they both became good girls, and were brought up aright; the elder one is now married happily, and resides in Worcester county of this State. At the expiration of this year (1843), upon looking over my records, I found that I had bailed fifty-three persons at the Police Court, and four in the Municipal Court. The amount of my bail bonds in the Municipal Court was $520, in the Police Court, $1,694. I have related the above instance to show the reason of my carrying my labors into the Municipal Court. Another reason for my operating in this court was that perhaps one person in ten whom I bailed for drunkenness, for various reasons did not appear at the assigned time, and of course the cases of such were defaulted. It has been a rule of the court that the defendant must subsequently appear within a specified time—ten days, or the default could not be taken off, and therefore the bonds were forfeited; occasionally defendants were sick, others absent, some perhaps forgot the time at which they were to appear, and occasionally some would be drunk, and of course unable to appear, and whenever such cases did occur, the papers were sent up to the County Attorney; it was necessary for him to sue me, which he did in cases of common drunkards. This course was necessary as a legal form, but the Judges always remitted the penalty, as such accidents are occasionally unavoidable; and from business of this character and being summoned, I found my way to the Municipal Court. Here I regret to say that I met with much opposition from the officers when they discovered the nature of my labors, but that unfriendly spirit if as rife, was not so frequently and so visibly manifested, as at the Police Court, for here I had the protection of the Judges and the Sheriff, whom I found were by no means unfavorable to my efforts. When I first attempted to enter this court, I occasionally observed the same officers lurking about, whom I had occasion to remember in the Police Court, and they were evidently alarmed at the progress I was making.

At this time I was constantly bailing some one in the Police Court to appear here for trial. Often when I attempted to enter the court room, I was rudely repulsed by the officers and told that I could not go in, as their orders were imperative to admit no one except members of the bar; on one occasion of this kind, having particular business in the court room, I informed the officer of the fact, (of which however he was previously aware) but he replied as before; I immediately addressed a note to the sheriff, which I transmitted by a member of the bar, and was at once, after this system of telegraphing, admitted. When I returned I was crowded back and not allowed a seat where the members of the bar sat, even though there were at the time a number of unoccupied chairs, but I contented myself with the thought that I was fast gaining ground. I subsequently took a seat, but was soon rudely expelled without the least cause. I would always obey, but generally returned to my seat, although I received a reprimand of the petty officials who "clothed with a little brief authority," took inconceivable delight in thus causing me inconvenience. I always endeavored to keep myself as cool and as calm as possible under such treatment, keeping my object constantly in view. By being driven back I was not infrequently brought in contiguity with the prisoner's dock, so that I could easily converse with the prisoners, and this was the very object I desired; but when they discovered this act on my part, the duties of their office required them to prohibit such conversation.

Here then, were two points gained,—to take my place with the members of the bar, and to occasionally whisper a word of hope to the desponding heart of some unfortunate and perhaps innocent person. This opposition was not unexpected or singular, for my conduct was new to them; no one had ever before attempted to aid or befriend the prisoner in this way in this court. I soon found ample occasion to address the judge, and at such times was always listened to with as much attention as was any member of the bar,—this was the greatest point yet attained, for I received that attention which I craved, and on no occasion was I ever treated otherwise than any one should be who was engaged in a work like mine.

Watching the Temple of Justice:
Justice for the Poor and the Ignorant

I became considerably acquainted with the prisoners, their offences, their wants and condition, and occasionally found those arraigned who had little cause to hope for justice by reason of their poverty and ignorance, in opposition to the power, experience and learning of the prosecuting attorney. Often I would find a very youthful prisoner, who was arraigned for the first time in his life, and who was never before within the walls of a court house; destitute of friends to advise, or money to procure counsel, which means, if within their power, might perhaps, establish the proof of their innocence.

A woman perhaps, is charged with stealing an article; she is innocent, and pleads 'not guilty,'—she is put upon trial, the evidence is strong against her, and it may be purely circumstantial,—she has no counsel, yet she is told by the court that she can ask the witness any questions,—but she dares not interrogate him; she is told that if she desires she can address the jury; here she appears abashed and bewildered, and *cannot* say a word in explanation of the act. The jury retire, and subsequently bring in a verdict of guilty, when, had she any legal adviser to assist, she might have established her innocence and been spared the infamy and punishment for the commission of a crime, which she would never have committed. There are many prisoners whose cases are thus disposed of, and who receive no justice.

Here then, was opportunity for me to labor, for I thought it as much a duty to have the temple of justice watched, and to inquire who are imprisoned that should go free, to investigate the merits of cases and to allow the innocent opportunity to show their innocence, as for the accuser to attempt to show their guilt.

If my observations have been correct, I have found that wrong customs prevail sometimes in courts of justice as well as in communities, and that the minds of the dispensers of justice may occasionally be biased in favor or against a prisoner, by the external circumstances by which he may be surrounded; in view of that state of things I resolved to bail some of the pitiable objects whenever prudence might dictate. At first I was inclined to shrink from so doing, as I was surety for a number in the Police Court, and was constantly taking upon myself other and like responsibilities, but I offered myself as bail, and was readily accepted by the court. This course opened the door for numerous applications to me to aid others in a similar manner, and I offered myself again and again, and always with approval. It should not be supposed that I assumed such obligations merely at the solicitation of the unfortunate, or without due investigation into the merits of their cases and a scrupulous examination into the history and character of each individual.

I continued this course for a time, when on one occasion, Mr. S.D. Parker, the county attorney, objected to my becoming surety, stating to the court as the ground of his objection, that I was not competent in regard to property [i.e., did not have enough money or property to guarantee the bail amount]; this objection was properly made, as he had an eye single to the interests of the State treasury, and in this was but performing his duty. I was aware of the force of his objection, but the case in hand was one of especial interest and importance; it was that of a woman who had been indicted for keeping a house of ill-fame, but who had given assurances that if I would become surety for her, she would abandon her course of life, and would return to her friends in the country; I stated the case to the court and requested to be allowed to assume the bonds; his Honor overruled all objection, and I was again accepted. The woman performed all that she had promised, and I have reason to believe abandoned her guilty career. My object was accomplished, and subsequently, by consent of the court, and of Mr. Parker, I was allowed to bail others, when by so doing the object of the law would be accomplished, and there appeared an intention to reform, in the party charged with the offence.

Continuing Labors in the Police Court and the Municipal Court: Reform versus Punishment

That year I had a great amount of labor to perform, and the character of my duties had become various. I was now obliged to bestow a share of my time and attention upon both courts, to bail large numbers of persons and to bear their cases in mind, to keep their numbers correctly, to watch the calling of the court docket, to see if the assigned cases in the police court were called up at the specified times, and lastly, but not least, in contending with the opposition that I was compelled to encounter. I made up my mind that the spirit of the opposition sprung from envy, hatred, ill-will and strife, and must therefore, be overcome with good. I had marked well the shoals and rocks, and could guide my bark successfully and in tolerable safety over this somewhat dangerous sea.

I found that the reason for opposition in the Municipal Court was similar to that in the court below, their fees for serving a mittimus [a warrant to imprison a person] to jail were sixty-two cents, and every person whom I bailed required no mittimus, and thus, of course, in such cases there was no opportunity for earning the fee.

It became pretty generally known that my labors were upon the ground of reform, that I confined my efforts mainly to those who were indicted for their first offence, and whose hearts were not wholly depraved, but gave promise of better things; it was also known that I received no compensation for so doing, and it early appeared that the judges were favorably disposed toward my plan of operation. That year I bailed one hundred and forty-eight persons, one hundred and ten of whom were in the Police Court, and the remainder in the Municipal Court; of this number forty-five were women and girls.

I need not weary the patience of my friends by a detailed account of the proceedings in this court or in the mention of the too frequent scenes of opposition. My path was strewed with obstacles which required both patience and perseverance to remove.

As illustrative of some of the lesser obstacles which I was sometimes called upon to overcome, I will extract a brief notice from the *Morning Post*, which was published about the time I first began my labors in the Municipal Court:

Ann—was called for sentence, convicted of petty larceny, which brought Mr. John Augustus to his feet, and the following is the substance of what occurred:

Mr. Augustus. I thought, your Honor, that Ann was not to be sentenced till next term?

Mr. Parker—(county attorney) Why not? I know no reason why she should not be sentenced now; nothing has been said to me about postponing it.

Mr. Augustus. Yes there has. I said something about it myself—and I understood his Honor that the sentence was put off.

Mr. Parker. You may have expressed yourself to that effect, but not in my presence. Perhaps the gentleman will seat himself on the *Bench* sometime!

Mr. Augustus. Perhaps I shall (a laugh), or *under* the bench. I'll try to speak so as to be understood. Ann's mother is away now out of the city and the girl is in a good place, out of the way of bad example; and I think we shall be able to make a reformed woman of her—if your Honor will give us time. What's the use of being in a hurry to punish the girl when kindness may save her?

Mr. Parker. We do not wish to punish, except for a purpose of warning others. I will not urge a sentence now, if it interferes with any plan for the reformation of the girl; but that cannot be brought about by sending her to her mother.

Mr. Augustus. We do not propose to send Ann to her mother; I think myself it would do her no good. She is but sixteen years old, and she possesses a good heart, amiable and kind feelings, and though she has been guilty of stealing some small articles, yet she is too young to be very wicked; and I am confident that if she can remain in the excellent place where she is now, for a time, she will be a good girl hereafter. I am her bail and I want your Honor to postpone her sentence till next term (and I thought it was so understood) to give us an opportunity of saving her—leading her in a new course, and making her live a better life—which I believe can be done.

His Honor listened attentively to the remarks of the worthy philanthropist, and granted the request.

The Imbroglio of the House of Ill-fame:
A Plot to Imprison Augustus and a Dispute about Justice

In 1845, I continued my labors in both courts as in former years. In the early part of this year, a woman was indicted for keeping a house of ill-fame in the south part of the city; her purlieu of vice was in one of our fashionable streets, and was a constant source of annoyance to the citizens in the neighborhood, and at length she was called to answer for the violation of the law. She was required to give bail for her appearance for trial, and importuned me to become her surety, giving me her promise that if I would do so, she would leave the city, abandon her career of vice, and return to her friends in the State of New York. I thought her removal from the city would not cause much grief, or her absence prove detrimental to the morals of that part of the city, and having confidence in her promise, I bailed her, and in a fortnight she removed to S., in the State of New York, the home of her friends. As the court was not in session at that time, of course the case could not be disposed of. I had informed her that the law allowed the Judge to impose a small fine for a first offence, and that this course had generally been pursued, and thus obtained her promise to return to Boston at such time as her case might be called for trial. At the opening of the next term, I requested a continuance of the case till another term, which was granted. I wrote to the woman, advising her of the assigned time, and stated that the case could probably be settled for thirty dollars. She came back to this city, but unfortunately I was absent. She applied to a lawyer, and was in high hopes of having the matter settled on the following day. The next morning I went into court, intending to pay the fine, but was informed that the defendant must be present, and unfortunately I had forgotten her place of temporary residence, nor did her counsel remember; here then was a dilemma; the woman was ignorant of the requirement and I ignorant of her whereabouts, and of course I was defaulted. The woman learned the fact, and being informed that she would be sent to the House of Correction, she became alarmed and immediately returned to New York without seeing me.

The County Attorney sued me forthwith, and Sheriff Eveleth called upon me and said that his duty was to attach my goods and chattels, if he could find any, and if not to take my body [Note: the legal term is, *habeas corpus*], and it (my body) must in that case be kept safe, so that no one else could take it, before the next term of the Municipal Court; at that time it would probably be made to appear that I had designedly committed a violation of the law. I recollected that I had caused one house in Shawmut to become desolate, and there was but one other house upon that street, similar in character to the one now deserted.

I asked how much time would be allowed me to find security, and was informed until three o'clock of that day. I complied with his demands, placed two hundred dollars [Note: adjusted for inflation, this was equivalent to about $3,700 today] in his hands, and was permitted to enjoy my liberty, and to continue my labors, from the prosecution of which I was by no means discouraged. I did not run away, but made my appearance every day during the session of the Court for the next term, and continued my efforts as before. That term the noble hearted Judge, Luther S. Cushing, presided. When my case was called, I pleaded guilty to the forfeiture of the bond, but asked a remission of the penalty. One half of the sum paid was immediately remitted; so that I had actually paid one hundred dollars for breaking up a den of vice, and making an effort to reform the abandoned, by which in various ways, I had saved the county and the Commonwealth at least two or three thousand dollars, to say nothing of the removal of bad influences. I then became aware that it was useless to attempt to break up a den of vice of this kind, as the strong arm of the law was averse to such an act.

I was advised to petition the Legislature for a remission of the money paid, and I determined to appeal to the State's paternal ear. Judge Cushing signed a petition to this effect, and stated that from a careful investigation into the circumstances of the case, I ought to receive back the money. The petition was referred to a Committee of the Legislature.

I went before the Committee and made a full statement of the case; I explained to them that I was instrumental in saving the Commonwealth a large sum annually, and also stated my relation to the unfortunate, but those men after much deliberation, decided that the ends of justice had been thwarted, and that the petition should not be granted; they thought justice could only be answered by sending such persons to the House of Correction for punishment, and this I had prevented.

That Committee perhaps were not aware of the fact that almost invariably all who are sent to the House of Correction, for such offences, at the expiration of their term of imprisonment, return to their former mode of life; there may be instances where such is not the case, but I know of none.

According to the decision of this Committee, punishment must be administered upon those who abandon their course of vice as upon those who do not. The object of the law is to reform criminals, and to prevent crime and not to punish maliciously, or from a spirit of revenge. Acting upon that principle which actuated the Committee in the case before them, what would they do if the keepers of every den of vice in Boston, upon being indicted, should forfeit their bonds by removing into the country, and becoming good members of society? It was to effect this object as far as possible,—the removal of such persons from the city, that I adopted the course which I did, and I think if any money should have been paid at all, the operation should have been reversed and the money paid to those who labored to accomplish the end of the law, and the benefit of society; I think the reader will admit that such a course would have been more in accordance with justice.

Would it not be more in consonance with the desires of the thinking part of society, and more productive of good, to allow such persons and those who sell spirituous liquors to be bailed, on a plea of guilty, on the ground of their renouncing their business, and to discharge the bail by laying the indictment on file when such places shall have been thus broken up? Such a course would be perfectly safe, for if the party should again be guilty of a violation of the law, the indictment can be taken from file, and upon it the party can be brought in for sentence; with this indictment hanging over them, there is little danger of a new offence of similar character. Of course this rule would not be applicable to the cases of those indicted as common thieves, robbers, or for the commission of many other kinds of felony, but may safely be used in the cases above mentioned. But enough upon this point.

Bail for Young Females and Boys: Ways of Choosing and Handling These Cases

During the year I bailed a number of young females, who were destitute of a home, and for whom I was obliged to find a temporary abode; I had so many calls of this kind that I was brought in contact with all sorts of people, and every grade of society, and thus my labors became extremely arduous. I was frequently obliged to incur the expense of carriage hire, and as a matter of economy and convenience, I resolved to adopt a new mode of traveling, and therefore bought a horse and chaise. I employed him a large portion of every day; I have used the same animal to the present time, and he appears to be pretty familiar with every part of the city; the Jail and the Court House have been his usual stopping places; one chaise after another has done excellent service, and become worthless; three have already been worn out, and the fourth is now in requisition. I have traveled 16,000 miles within the limits of the city; 4,000 women have been conveyed in my carriages to and from various parts of the city.

That year I made 1,500 calls and received more than this number at my house. I bailed in both courts, one hundred and thirty-three, forty-five of whom were females. The amount of my bonds was $13,020....

During the year 1846 I became bail to the amount of about $3000, in the Police Court, having bailed between sixty and seventy persons. That year I became surety for eleven boys, who were arrested for larceny; they were young, being from nine to thirteen years old. I also bailed ten other boys, from thirteen to sixteen years of age, and also nine girls, from fourteen to eighteen years old, who were arraigned for various offences, chiefly for larceny. By a decision of the Court upon my motion, the cases of these children were to be continued, but the question of the term of continuance caused considerable discussion. I always urged a protracted continuance, but Mr. Parker was extremely anxious to have the cases disposed of as early as possible. I wished ample time to test the promises of these youth to behave well in future. Judge Cushing was disposed to allow such cases to stand continued from term to term, and if at the expiration of a certain period, a good report was given of their behavior during the time they had been on probation, their sentences were very light....

Great care was observed of course, to ascertain whether the prisoners were promising subjects for probation, and to this end it was necessary to take into consideration the previous character of the person, his age and the influences by which he would in future be likely to be surrounded, and although these points were not rigidly adhered to, still they were the circumstances which usually determined my action. In such cases of probation it was agreed on my part, that I would note their general conduct, see that they were sent to school or supplied with some honest employment, and that I should make an impartial report to the court, whenever they should desire it.

This course adopted by the court I hailed as one extremely favorable to the success of my efforts, and I soon found, that it spared me an immense amount of labor which I should otherwise have been compelled to perform; I was pleased too, to observe that the opposition on the part of the District Attorney was gradually and rapidly giving way. But the toil thus saved was required in another manner, for I had frequent occasion to provide indigent girls with suitable places, and often young females were brought to my house, sometimes late at night, who required a shelter, and frequently these cases were extremely urgent; although by no means situated in a manner suited to open an asylum of this kind, I accommodated them as well as my humble means would allow....

Labors Curtailed:
Withdrawing from the Police Court and New Bail Rules

In the years 1849 and 1850, I frequently resolved to leave the Police Court, and confine my labors exclusively to the Municipal Court, believing I could thereby accomplish a greater amount of good; the cause of this state of feeling was the continued opposition and hostility which was evinced toward my efforts on every occasion, by the officers of the court. Every time in which I here attempted to aid the prisoner in any way, a storm burst upon my head in all its fury. Among the officers most vindictive, was one Mr. Stratton, who might have been indicted for assault and battery, so great was his rudeness and violence toward me on numerous occasions; but I regarded him more as an object of pity than of anger or of punishment. He had power to allow me access to the lock-up, and whenever I had occasion to request permission to thus enter for the purpose of conversing for a few moments with prisoners who had been required ... to appear before the grand jury, he always took great delight in peremptorily refusing me. I would at times endeavor to expostulate with him. I would perhaps, tell him frankly, that the prisoner's counsel, Mr. B., or the mother of the prisoner had requested me to make the visit; but I would be told that I had better mind my own business, and his tone and manner would excite the attention of the clerk—another 'allied power,' who would pettishly exclaim, "Mr. Stratton, shut that door," and turning contemptuously toward me, ask, "What does Mr. Augustus want?" Mr. S. would then order me away, saying that he wished to close the doors. Mr. T. would then come to the rescue, to see that the orders of his brother officer were complied with, well knowing that if I succeeded in becoming bail for the prisoner, Stratton would lose the job of taking him to jail, the fee for which was sixty-two cents, the clerk would lose twenty-five cents, and the turnkey forty more, which he believed would be an unprofitable operation. The poor woman who was a prisoner, doubtless knew that some of the constables and officers of the court were temperate drinkers, and might be supposed to have written an inscription appropriate to be placed over the desks of the officers of the Police Court.

"As you are now (temperate drinkers) so once was I,—
As I am now (common drunkard) so you may be:
Prepare for prison and follow me."

But I need not here say more of the corruption of this miscalled "temple of justice." No institution in the State calls louder for reform; and we are glad to see that the press are holding up its hideous deformities and evils to the public gaze,—and we have reason to hope that the time is near when this court shall receive attention, and have its evils eradicated. For the reasons above briefly alluded to, my efforts have of late been limited here. Another reason, however, that has prevented more extended effort on my part is, that a rule has recently been adopted here, that the person who offers himself as surety must subscribe and swear to certain documents respecting the amount of property which they may possess. I could not consistently comply with this requirement....

Here I began to abate my labors in the Police Court, as I was able to accomplish an equal amount of good, without being brought in daily contact with so much that was disagreeable. In the year 1849, I bailed, in the Police Court, forty-one persons, and in the ensuing year, but twenty; but in the Municipal Court, during this period, I bailed one hundred and twenty-six persons. In 1851, I bailed fifteen in the Police Court, while in the Municipal Court, about six times that number. By the statistical tables on the following pages, the reader will readily see in brief, a synopsis of my labors in the courts for the ten years.

Introduction to
Donald Clemmer

Donald Clemmer was born in Morgan Park, Illinois, a suburb of Chicago, on October 1, 1903. He attended Morgan Park Military Academy. After graduating from Cornell University, he returned to teach at Morgan Park Military Academy. Here he first became interested in criminology because the students included sons of some of Chicago's most notorious hoodlums. He earned a Master of Arts degree in sociology at the University of Chicago in 1931. Until 1942 he worked at three Illinois prisons. He then worked for two years as personnel manager at Republic Steel and Tool Co. in Chicago. He moved to Washington, D.C. in 1944 to set up an in-service training program for personnel of the Federal Bureau of Prisons. After that he was Associate Warden of the federal penitentiary in Atlanta, Georgia. In 1946 he moved back to Washington, D.C. as the Director of Corrections for the District of Columbia. For nineteen years he served in that position, overseeing the operations of the District Jail and various facilities for adult offenders, for juveniles, and for women. He was known personally for his humanity and progressiveness. He was also an ardent social scientist, constantly using his positions to seek a deeper understanding of the causes of criminal behavior and the means of reforming offenders. He believed that human nature included the potential for reform and that prisoners were people with potential to change themselves, not hopeless criminals. He pioneered new methods of correctional treatment, and he furthered the professionalization of prison personnel. He died suddenly from a stroke in 1965.

Clemmer's approach to understanding crime and reforming offenders reflected the basic beliefs of the University of Chicago sociologists who took the lead in developing American criminology in the first decades of the 1900s. Like Shaw and McKay, Clemmer believed that the explanation for most behavior was a person's social environment. Human beings were viewed as primarily social beings, not simply individuals. It was not the physical environment but the people environment that shaped an individual's behavior. Still, not everyone in the social environment was equally influential in molding an individual. The important people in shaping an individual's behavior were the people with whom the individual had close personal ties based on liking one another. People who were accidentally thrown together or who were together for some reason other than personal attractions were not so influential. In sociology the terms "primary group" and "secondary group" had been coined to distinguish groups of different kinds. Groups based on mutual liking were called "primary groups"; groups brought together for some purpose or accidentally thrown together were called "secondary groups." Primary groups were the social force which had the strongest impact on shaping an individual.

Clemmer was also strongly influenced by the psychology of "adjustment" of the early 1900s. At that time psychologists defined mental health in terms of "adjustment." A well adjusted individual was one who fit in well with others. People who did not fit in were "deviant," which might include such deviants as eccentric geniuses. But, generally, deviance was seen as a mentally and socially undesirable state. Maladjusted people were likely to be problems to themselves and to cause problems for others. Child rearing practices in homes and in schools emphasized the need for children to fit in with others and obey their elders. In work and social settings, too, people were expected to fit in and be deferential to their seniors. A "good" person was one who fit in with neighbors or associates. Psychotherapists as well as other reformers of people made it their goal to help individuals adjust to their roles and places in society.

In the early 1900s the northeast and north central parts of America experienced a great influx of immigrants from Europe. The United States was viewed as a "melting pot" in which people from different lands and cultures could be melted into the existing American culture. The goal of various social organizations, especially schools, was to take the children of immigrants and homogenize them into Americans. Whatever remnants of a foreign culture might survive the process could be seen as attractive fragments of their ethnic origins but had to be small and marginal enough not to interfere with the basic process of making the new citizens fit in with the existing society. The theory of adjustment applied to whole groups of people as well as to individuals. In the field of anthropology this was expressed by theories of "assimilation," which was a way of describing one culture being absorbed by another. Ordinarily assimilation referred to one culture absorbing a very different foreign culture. Clemmer adapted the term "assimilation" to describe the process of a somewhat distinct group of people, i.e., prisoners, absorbing newcomers from the same society.

Some Chicago criminologists had explained crime in terms of "culture conflict." They were not particularly interested in conflicts between foreign cultures and mainstream American culture. The notion of smaller cultures within cultures had already been developed by anthropologists. These small cultures within larger cultures were called "subcultures." Chicago criminologists regarded juvenile gangs and adult criminal organizations as social groups with their own cultures. They regarded them as cultures because these groups, to a certain extent, had a distinguishable set of beliefs, attitudes, behaviors, rituals, organization, and even some language of their own. These were deviant or criminal cultures in contrast to the dominant American culture. Clemmer carried the idea one step further by describing the prison in terms of a culture. Hence, Clemmer constructed an anthropology of prisons as well as a sociology of prisons.

Prisons during the career of Donald Clemmer were just beginning the transition from the model of "the industrial prison" to the prison as a place of confinement. The ideal of reforming prisoners always remained a small current in penal thought and practice but was largely abandoned after 1900, if not before. The industrial prison was a large penal complex devoted to producing goods of some kind. Although there was some consideration that these factory prisons might teach inmates useful job skills, the emphasis was on producing goods which could defray the costs of operating the prison itself. The prisoners were subject to a system of discipline which facilitated productivity. Contact with the outside world was limited, all prisoners worked, prisoners were marched from one place to another in lock step, prisoners were required to keep their eyes down at all times, prison clothing consisted of black and white striped baggy clothes or some other distinctive garb, silence was maintained in most situations, but there were daily periods of talk and recreation, usually in the prison yard. Reforming prisoners was left mostly to chaplains who conducted services on Sundays, counseled prisoners, and often taught reading and writing to illiterate prisoners in classes on Sundays. Although the modern prisons at that time employed such professionals as psychologists and occasionally teachers, the psychologists were mostly limited to testing inmates at time of entry into the prison, and the teachers worked with only a few prisoners to provide some general education or vocational training.

However, the 1930s saw the demise of the industrial prison. After the stock market crash of 1929 came the Great Depression with millions of people thrown out of work. States and even the federal government quickly passed laws which curtailed the production of goods in prisons. They did not want the penal labor force to take jobs from people on the outside. Soon prisons were limited to producing goods for their own use or providing some limited goods for use by other government agencies, such as the production of automobile license plates. Laws generally prohibited prisons from giving prisoners training in skilled occupations which might enable them later to earn a good living.

At the end of the 1930s most prisons still maintained the regimens of the earlier age of the industrial prison although there was little work to be done by prisoners. It was only a matter of time before the system of prison discipline broke down. Many prisons were run on a day by day basis by inmates who had been put in charge by the prison administrators. These "prisoner trusties" were sometimes effective in running the prisons but often brutal and corrupt. In the 1950s, starting with the prisons in California then spreading to Texas and after that across the nation, prison gangs developed. The prison gangs were based largely on ethnic group membership. Members of each ethnic group banded together, took their own area in the mess hall and the cell blocks and in the prison yard, and gained control over various work assignments in the prison. The gangs became the new social organization of the prison. Court decisions forced the end of the trusty system, but the gang system persists. Today's prisons are characterized mostly by noise, disorder, idleness, and conflict. Penal theory and practice emphasize that the prison is a place of detention where offenders are kept away from society so that they cannot prey on other people.

A change of ideas also contributed to the aimlessness of prisons. Some fundamental ideas about molding people were abandoned in the second half of the twentieth century. In the late 1930s the Nazi phenomenon in Germany, and the World War which it led to, provoked strong reactions against the ideas of "adjustment" and "assimilation." Clemmer's book, *The Prison Community,* was based on the American social sciences of the 1930s. But World War II was breaking out as Clemmer was finishing the book, and he, like others, was beginning to have doubts about very basic beliefs. As for adjustment, people first wondered then were distressed at the fact that a rather small political party under the leadership of Adolph Hitler was able to take control of the German government and lead the nation into a disastrous war. The explanation seemed to lie in the German culture's strong emphasis on obedience and conformity. Children were brought up to obey their elders and conform to society's rules and expectations. In short, the German people were well adjusted. This made it easy for a small political faction to come to power and to impose its will on the nation. With regard to "assimilation, the Nazi emphasis on racial purity and its policy of eradicating groups which did not fit the national stereotype prompted people in other places to question the desirability of eradicating the differences between people. In reaction to the Nazi phenomenon, Americans discovered the values of individuality, nonconformity, and pride in cultural differences. After World War II the new America was a land of protest rather than conformity. The new psychology was a psychology of individual differences and self-actualization instead of adjustment. And America became the "stew pot" with a mix of distinctive ingredients instead of the melting pot for blending away differences through assimilation. In this light one can understand the confusion and disillusionment expressed by Clemmer at the end of *The Prison Community.*

Clemmer gave a fairly complete description of his research methods. They are the standard methods of sociologists and cultural anthropologists: observations, interviews, written reports, and even a focus group of some prisoners to judge the extent of prisonization experienced by others. Although he did not use the method of "participant observation," which would have required him to be incarcerated like a prisoner to see things as they did, he made sustained and deliberate efforts to grasp a prisoner's point of view. Cultural anthropologists are aware of the danger that a researcher may become so immersed in a group being studied that the researcher can lose objectivity. One may ask whether this seemed to happen with Clemmer and to what extent he may have projected his own thoughts and feelings onto the prisoners. For example, he stated that for a prisoner "a number replaces a name," which may have been more a statement of feelings than a fact. For even in prison people are known and called by their names, not by their administrative record numbers; prisoners and correction officers rarely even know the numbers of prisoners.

The Prison Community provides a platform for reexamining the role of prisons, the management or rehabilitation of offenders in prisons, and the goals of a criminal justice system. One may ask to what extent the late nineteenth century ideal of a prison in which prisoners might acquire the skills and habits of laborers is still feasible or desirable. Clemmer's profiles of prisoners raise questions about what sorts of persons are in today's prisons and whether they are likely to benefit from rehabilitation programs. Some of Clemmer's assumptions could also be examined. For example, Clemmer made certain assumptions about prisoners' families and the relationships between prisoners and their families. He did not consider that some prisoners' families may have a history or a concentration of habitual offenders, or that some families might deliberately avoid contact with a prisoner to reduce the prisoner's influence on younger family members. Also, Clemmer assumed that prisoners had to adapt from general American culture to a prison subculture rather than from a criminal subculture on the outside to a prison subculture on the inside. Although American prisons no longer resemble the prison described by Clemmer, the fundamental questions about what effects prisons actually have on prisoners, about the goals of prisons, and about the possibilities for rehabilitation of offenders remain the same.

Donald Clemmer, *The Prison Community.* (1958). New York: Holt, Rinehart and Winston. The following selection is taken from an appendix on methodology and from Chapter 12, the concluding chapter. Some section titles have been added. Footnotes have been renumbered and put at the end of the selection. Some notes have been inserted in the text in square brackets.

Donald Clemmer

The Prison Community

A Methodological Note

This volume, intended as a contribution to the literature of penology, would be incomplete without mention of the methodological frame of reference. To be sure, the methods used have become largely self-evident, but a few additional explanations may prove helpful. Subsequent studies of the prison community should refine the exploratory and oftentimes hypothetical problems brought forth here. No one can be more aware of the limitations of the studies than the writer.

Most important, perhaps, as a phase of method, has been the writer's routine, daily, service work. In the prison which this study describes, he has examined sociologically over 2,500 men and has learned in greater or less detail the themes and activities of the 2,500 lives. Substituting for the psychologist the writer (has conducted over a thousand intelligence test routines) and has administered several hundred individual psychometric examinations. As colleague and friend of physicians and psychiatrists, he has assisted with medical treatment, with surgery, with spinal punctures, with the care of the violently insane and the mildly neurotic. He has seen prisoners work, sleep, eat, fight, play and die. He has purposefully affiliated himself with officials and guards in order to understand their point of view. In short, the experiences and observations brought about through the writer's job are important aspects of the method. Additional years of experience in two other penitentiaries of the same state have added maturity to his experience and thousands of sociological examinations and interviews to his general knowledge. Investigations of prisoners' homes, communities and hangouts have furthered integrative speculation concerning the problem of the prison community. Continued contact of long standing with inmates who have been discharged from the prison has provided additional insight. Particularism has been avoided by the writer's interest and deep concern with human activities divorced from the prison world. National and international affairs, civil liberties, music and athletics have served to aid him in avoiding a too heavy specialization, and these facts are mentioned here only because portions of the study are interpretative, and the reader has the right to know something of the interpreter's orientation.

To return to the more concrete problem of method, the purpose of this volume must be appraised. Purpose and method go hand in hand. Had we been attempting to prove or disprove an exactly phrased hypothesis, the methods would necessarily have been different. But our purpose has not been specific, but general. It has been to show in sociological form all the important phases in the social life of the prison. Not intended as an objective or hypothesis, however, there has nevertheless evolved from the data, long after the observations for the study began, a somewhat specific hypothesis. And this hypothesis refers to the degree and extent of consensus among prisoners. Contrary to impressions and writings of other investigators, this study has found and reported considerable evidence to indicate that consensus, solidarity, we-feeling among prisoners has been previously exaggerated. Important as this fact is (it might well form one basis of new penological treatment), it was not sought for but arose out of the more general purpose of presenting for the first time a sociological study of the prison community. In terms of purpose and method, then, our studies most closely approach the method of cultural analysis, or in another sense, the method may be thought of as the case method, in which the *case* is the prison community....

It is evident that much of our material has resulted from interviews with inmates. Space need not be taken here to describe the intricate aspects of the sociological interview.[1] It is sufficient to state that the goal of the interview is to break down distrust and build up rapport. Numerous means and techniques are employed to this end, but fundamental to all is a condition of empathy on the part of the interviewer. In over 30,000 various conversations with inmates, only three have flatly refused to cooperate, and only a dozen or so have shown an unfriendly attitude. It has been possible to develop positive friendly relationships of long standing with a large number of men. The social warmth of such relationships has been the entree to the material for our studies. When close rapport is gained with men in prison and when one understands the conditions which has made them what they are, it is no easy matter to keep a calm, impartial perspective. Thus, though the writer as a human being has developed sympathy and understanding, he has made every effort, as the pages of the book will show, to keep an objective, dispassionate viewpoint.

As one result of the rapport developed through interviews, it has been possible to have the men write their experiences and attitudes on a wide variety of subjects. Over fifty lengthy autobiographies have been prepared, some of which refer primarily to prison life. Over two hundred various descriptions, character sketches, and expoundings upon conditions have been collected over the years. Such materials have legitimate research value if the atypical and sensational is avoided, and if the statements are fairly representative of the population in general. The point should be made here that the written materials of prisoners which have been shown in the volume are fairly representative of all aspects of the prison population, except that inmates of low intelligence have been unable to produce written materials. This seems to be an unavoidable difficulty although the writer has attempted through his own words to show the ideations and activities of inmates, who, because of a (low I.Q., are unable to express themselves in the written word....)

Culture and Structure of the Prison Community

In the foregoing chapters we have been dealing with numerous items, traits, and levels of culture. We have shown to some extent how these various aspects of culture influence relationships and shape the attitudes of the men. We have broken the social life into segments in order that study might be easier, but we must be careful not to over-simplify. The interdependence and interrelationships of these segments which we have observed weld themselves together and make of penal life a continual ongoing process. In this final chapter we wish to summarize and categorize, if possible, the manner in which attitudes of prisoners are modified as the men spend month after month in the penal milieu. The inmates are adults before they come to prison. There is much behind them. Attitudes and philosophy of life may or may not be developed. Regardless which of many conditions exist, the detection, detention, and trial procedures tend to raise questions and to disrupt philosophic equanimity. No matter the state of mind, men who enter prison are subject to the pressures of the environment. There can be no accounting for the miniscule differences in the assimilation process, and we must be satisfied, at the present stage of social science, to learn of the major trends. We will first try to weave together the predominant factors which make up the prison culture as viewed in a structural sense, then to point out the possible extremes of assimilation which may take place, and finally, to illustrate the relationship existing between various stages or degrees of assimilation and the possession of certain attitudes.

What do we mean by the totality of the prison culture? In the most complete sense the prison culture is the social organization of the penitentiary, both formal and informal, plus the interactions among the (2,300 men and 200 officers living in the prison's thirteen acres.) The culture consists of the habits, behavior systems, traditions, history, customs, folkways, codes, the laws and rules which guide the inmates, and their ideas, opinions and attitudes toward or against homes, family, education, work, recreation, government, prisons, police, judges, other inmates, wardens, ministers, doctors, guards, ball-players, clubs, guns, cells, buckets, gravy, beans, walls, lamps, rain, clouds, clothes, machinery, hammers, rocks, caps, bibles, books, radio, monies, stealing, murder, rape, sex, love, honesty, martyrdom, and so on. Such an answer does not tell us exactly what the prison culture is, but it does suggest its extreme complexity, especially when one considers the multitudinous shades of attitude and opinion which may exist. As a matter of fact, throughout this book we have been delineating phases of the prison culture, and at this point we wish to integrate our previous findings and to suggest the significance of them in the determination of attitudes.

In attempting to answer the question, "What is the prison culture?" it will be helpful to think of the social structure and of the social processes operating reciprocally as a force in the formation of attitudes in individuals.

If we may accept as reliable the data presented in Chapter V (they would seem reliable because two distinct samples yielded essentially the same results), we can extend the findings for the entire population. We learned that about 18 per cent of the inmates were affiliated with what was called prison-primary groups, and that each group had about four members. [A "primary group" is one with no purpose other than friendship.] From this finding we are able to compute that about 400 of all our prisoners are rather intimately associated in some 103 different informal groups. The interaction in and about these groups, and the social life that exists is part of the "unseen environment" and has much greater influence on individual personalities, we are inclined to believe, than all the rules, official admonishments, sermons, or other factors intended to guide lives. In Chapter V we also learned that 40 percent of the men were affiliated to some extent with larger collectivities which we called semi-primary groups. The average size of these was eight members, and from this we are able to compute that some 920 of the total inmates are loosely affiliated in about 115 different groups. Slightly over 40 per cent of the sample, as shown in Chapter V, were found to be more or less "ungrouped." If this is so, about 960 men in our prison have no definite or intimate social relationships with other prisoners. Such data as these are important in comprehending the structure of the prison society.

The structure may be viewed in other ways. First, of the 2,500 men in the community the 200 officers are dominant and the 2,300 inmates subordinate, and this stratification tends to be rigid. Secondly, there seems to be a distinction between the elite class, the middle class, and the "hoosiers," and while this demarcation is not strictly rigid, the members of the elite class seem also to be those men affiliated with primary groups. A third view of the social structure refers to the various work gangs and cellhouse groups, but these stratifications are administrative and not spontaneous, though they are important because they cause isolation and preclude to some degree spontaneity in the development of social relations. A fourth structural factor refers to Negro and white aggregations. A fifth point of view will interpret the social structure according to similarity of criminal types: the confidence men and embezzlers constitute one class of the total structure; the bank robbers and advanced thieves comprise another segment; the abnormal sex offenders are a type; the aggravated assaulters are another, and so on. Sixth, the "politicians" and trusties compose a part of the structure, while the ordinary working convicts comprise another segment. A seventh viewpoint might structurally categorize the population according to those whose sex behavior in prison is normal, quasi-abnormal, or abnormal. Yet another categorization might place recidivists in one stratum and the non-criminalistic offenders in another. And still another structural delineation might refer to the personality differences resulting from the regional influences of pre-penal conditioning.

To view the prison population in this structural sense is important because the framework of a society sets up and limits the social processes. "What distinguishes societies and individuals is the predominance of certain attitudes over others, and this predominance depends ... on the type of organization which the group has developed to regulate the expression of the wishes of its members."[2] "In other words, attitudes correspond in the main to the established social structure. The lines of cleavage among groups, whether of superordination or subordination or of amity, hostility, etc., are marked by distinctive attitudes; and this is true also of the relations between the members within each group."[3]

Of the nine structural aspects of the prison community two seem to be of outstanding importance in the determination of attitudes. Greatest is the fairly definite cleavage between officials and inmates. This structural stratification gives rise to conflict (a function or social process) which is of great importance in developing attitudes. Next in importance in a structural sense is the existence of spontaneously formed primary and semi-primary groups, which, as structures, provide an opportunity for the operation of social processes. The processes in operation for group members and the unaffiliated as well, as detailed in previous chapters, are competition for inclusion in the group, occasional conflict, followed by accommodation and assimilation, and, in some cases, a subsequent connect and a new accommodation to another primary or semi-primary group. Thus, the existence of groups is an occasion for social processes. Social processes are an occasion for attitudes which result from values which make for positive or negative personal relations and cause associations or disassociations.

Our problem of determining the origin, development, and type of attitudes which exist would be relatively simple if in the prison community we had an *established social structure,* because then the attitudes which develop would in the main correspond to it. But as has been shown throughout the study, cleavages are by no means absolute. Even the stratification between officialdom and inmates is not definite, as witness the "stool pigeons," the prisoners who identify themselves with the officials, or even the occasional official who identifies himself with the prisoners, as well as the "marginal men" who are "two ways," and the "social strangers" who are of no strata. While the primary groups tend to set up cleavages, there are no definite or absolute structural demarcations. Disassociation abounds in the population in general, and only less so in the spontaneous groups. There is no absolute definition of situations nor is there, except in a few instances, even a majority of the men who agree as to a common definition of a situation. Our discussion of group life, leadership, and the mores indicates this. Yet in spite of the opposition, conflict, and disassociation which comprise a goodly portion of the personal relationships within the prison world, the men tend to adjust among one another even though sympathy and other-regarding attitudes may be more the exception than the rule. Such adaptation can be explained by the relation known as symbiosis, by which is meant a living together so that a benefit exists which is mutual for the parties involved. This occurs in spite of the ruggedness of individualism among the inmates, and, while symbiosis does not rule out impersonalization, the need for a degree of cooperation in coping with an unfriendly environment keeps individualism from becoming too rampant. Let us now try to characterize the social world of the prison.

The prisoner's world is an atomized world. Its people are atoms interacting in confusion. It is dominated and it submits. Its own community is without a well-established social structure. Recognized values produce a myriad of conflicting attitudes. There are no definite communal objectives. There is no consensus for a common goal. The inmates' conflict with officialdom and opposition toward society is only slightly greater in degree than conflict and opposition among themselves. Trickery and dishonesty overshadow sympathy and cooperation. Such cooperation as exists is largely symbiotic in nature. Social controls are only partially effective. It is a world of individuals whose daily relationships are impersonalized. It is a world of "I," "me," and "mine," rather than "ours," "theirs," and "his." Its people are thwarted, unhappy, yearning, resigned, bitter, hating, revengeful. Its people are improvident, inefficient, and socially illiterate. The prison world is a graceless world. There is filth, stink, and drabness; there is monotony and stupor. There is disinterest in work. There is desire for love and hunger for sex. There is pain in punishment. Except for the few, there is bewilderment. No one knows, the dogmas and codes notwithstanding, exactly what is important....

It is into this complex maze of the prison world that the newly-committed inmate comes. Most all of the men who enter prison are confused and uncertain about the social world they have left. They are preoccupied with self and their philosophies are frequently in a state of flux. They have anxiety over the future. What the prison does to them depends upon the degree to which they become assimilated.

Assimilation or Prisonization

When a person or group of ingress penetrates and fuses with another group, assimilation may be said to have taken place. The concept is most profitably applied to immigrant groups and perhaps it is not the best term by which to designate similar processes which occur in prison. Assimilation implies that a process of acculturation occurs in one group whose members originally were quite different from those of the group with whom they mix. It implies that the assimilated come to share the sentiments, memories, and traditions of the static group. It is evident that the men who come to prison are not greatly different from the ones already there so far as broad culture influences are concerned: All speak the same language, all have a similar national heritage, all have been stigmatized, and so on. While the differences of regional conditioning are not to be overlooked, it is doubtful if the interactions which lead the professional offender to have a "we-feeling" with the naïve offender from Coalville can be referred to as assimilation—although the processes furnishing the development of such an understanding are similar to it. As briefly defined in Chapter IV, the term assimilation describes a slow, gradual, more or less unconscious process during which a person learns enough of the culture of a social unit into which he is placed to make him characteristic of it. While we shall continue to use this general meaning, we recognize that in the strictest sense assimilation is not the correct term. So as we use the term Americanization to describe a greater or less degree of the immigrant's integration into the American scheme of life, we may use the term _prisonization_ to indicate the taking-on in greater or less degree of the folkways, mores, customs, and general culture of the penitentiary. Prisonization is similar to assimilation, and its meaning will become clearer as we proceed.

Every man who enters the penitentiary undergoes prisonization to some extent. The first and most obvious integrative step concerns his status. He becomes at once an anonymous figure in a subordinate group. A number replaces a name. He wears the clothes of the other members of the subordinate group. He is questioned and admonished. He soon learns that the warden is all-powerful. He soon learns the ranks, titles, and authority of various officials. And whether he uses the prison slang and argot or not, he comes to know its meanings. Even though a new man may hold himself aloof from other inmates and remain a solitary figure, he finds himself within a few months referring to or thinking of keepers as "screws," the physician as the "croaker," and using the local nicknames to designate persons. He follows the examples already set in wearing his cap. He learns to eat in haste and in obtaining food he imitates the tricks of those near him.

After the new arrival recovers from the effects of the swallowing-up process, he assigns a new meaning to conditions he had previously taken for granted. The fact that food, shelter, clothing, and a work activity had been given him originally made no especial impression. It is only after some weeks or months that there comes to him a new interpretation of these necessities of life. This new conception results from mingling with other men and it places emphasis on the fact that the environment should administer to him. This point is intangible and difficult to describe in so far as it is only a subtle and minute change in attitude from the taken-for-granted perception. Exhaustive questioning of hundreds of men reveals that this slight change in attitude is a fundamental step in the process we are calling prisonization. Supplemental to it is the almost universal desire on the part of the man, after a period of some months, to get a good job so, as he says, "I can do my time without any trouble and get out of here." A good job usually means a comfortable job of a more or less isolated kind in which conflicts with other men are not likely to develop. The desire for a comfortable job is not peculiar to the prison community, to be sure, but it seems to be a phase of prisonization in the following way. When men have served time before entering the penitentiary they look the situation over and almost immediately express a desire for a certain kind of work. When strictly first offenders come to prison, however, they seldom express a desire for a particular kind of work, but are willing to do anything and frequently say, "I'll do any kind of work they put me at and you won't have any trouble from me." Within a period of a few months, however, these same men, who had no choice of work, develop preferences and make their desires known. They "wise up," as the inmates say, or in other words, by association they become prisonized.

In various other ways men new to prison slip into the existing patterns. They learn to gamble or learn new ways to gamble. Some, for the first time in their lives, take to abnormal sex behavior. Many of them learn to distrust and hate the officers, the parole board, and sometimes each other, and they become acquainted with the dogmas and mores existing in the community. But these changes do not occur in every man. However, every man is subject to certain influences which we may call the *universal factors of prisonization.*

Acceptance of an inferior role, accumulation of facts concerning the organization of the prison, the development of somewhat new habits of eating, dressing, working, sleeping, the adoption of local language, the recognition that nothing is owed to the environment for the supplying of needs, and the eventual desire for a good job are aspects of prisonization which are operative for all inmates. It is not these aspects, however, which concern us most but they are important because of their universality, especially among men who have served many years. That is, even if no other factor of the prison culture touches the personality of an inmate of many years residence, the influences of these universal factors are sufficient to make a man characteristic of the penal community and probably so disrupt his personality that a happy adjustment in any community becomes next to impossible. On the other hand, if inmates who are incarcerated for only short periods, such as a year or so, do not become integrated into the culture except in so far as these universal factors of prisonization are concerned, they do not seem to be so characteristic of the penal community and are able when released to take up a new mode of life without much difficulty.

Factors Which Affect the Rate and Extent of Prisonization

The phases of prisonization which concern us most are the influences which breed or deepen criminality and antisociality and make the inmate characteristic of the criminalistic ideology in the prison community. As has been said, every man feels the influences of what we have called the universal factors, but not every man becomes prisonized in and by other phases of the culture. Whether or not complete prisonization takes place depends first on the man himself, that is, his susceptibility to a culture which depends, we think, primarily on the type of relationships he had before imprisonment, i.e., his personality. A second determinant affecting complete prisonization refers to the kind and extent of relationships which an inmate has with persons outside the walls. A third determinant refers to whether or not a man becomes affiliated in prison primary or semi-primary groups and this is related to the two points already mentioned. Yet a fourth determinant depends simply on chance, a chance placement in work gang, cellhouse, and with cellmate. A fifth determinant pertains to whether or not a man accepts the dogmas or codes of the prison culture. Other determinants depend on age, criminality, nationality, race, regional conditioning, and every determinant is more or less interrelated with every other one.

With knowledge of these determinants we can hypothetically construct schemata of prisonization which may serve to illustrate its extremes. In the least or lowest degree of prisonization the following factors may be enumerated:

1. A short sentence, thus a brief subjection to the universal factors of prisonization.
2. A fairly stable personality made stable by an adequacy of positive and "socialized" relationships during pre-penal life.
3. The continuance of positive relationships with persons outside the walls.
4. Refusal or inability to integrate into a prison primary group or semi-primary group, while yet maintaining a symbiotic balance in relations with other men.
5. Refusal to accept blindly the dogmas and codes of the population, and a willingness, under certain situations, to aid officials, thus making for identification with the free community.
6. A chance placement with a cellmate and workmates who do not possess leadership qualities and who are also not completely integrated into the prison culture.
7. Refraining from abnormal sex behavior, and excessive gambling, and a ready willingness to engage seriously in work and recreative activities.

Other factors no doubt have an influencing force in obstructing the process of prisonization, but the seven points mentioned seem outstanding.

In the highest or greatest degree of prisonization the following factors may be enumerated:

1. A sentence of many years, thus a long subjection to the universal factors of prisonization.
2. A somewhat unstable personality made unstable by an inadequacy of "socialized" relations before commitment, but possessing, none the less, a capacity for strong convictions and a particular kind of loyalty.
3. A dearth of positive relations with persons outside the walls.
4. A readiness and a capacity for integration into a prison primary group.
5. A blind, or almost blind, acceptance of the dogmas and mores of the primary group and the general penal population.

6. A chance placement with other persons of a similar orientation.
7. A readiness to participate in gambling and abnormal sex behavior.

We can see in these two extremes the degrees with which the prisonization process operates. No suggestion is intended that a high correlation exists between either extreme of prisonization and criminality. It is quite possible that the inmate who fails to integrate in the prison culture may be and may continue to be much more criminalistic than the inmate who becomes completely prisonized. The trends are probably otherwise, however, as our study of group life suggests. To determine prisonization, every case must be appraised for itself. Of the two degrees presented in the schemas it is probable that more men approach the complete degree than the least degree of prisonization, but it is also probable that the majority of inmates become prisonized in some respects and not in others. It is the varying degrees of prisonization among the 2,300 men that contribute to the disassociation which is so common. The culture is made complex, not only by the constantly changing population, but by these differences in the tempo and degree of prisonization.

Assimilation, as the concept is customarily applied, is always a slow, gradual process, but prisonization, as we use the term here, is usually slow, but not necessarily so. The speed with which prisonization occurs depends on the personality of the man involved, his crime, age, home neighborhood, intelligence, the situation into which he is placed in prison and other less obvious influences. The process does not necessarily proceed in an orderly or measured fashion but tends to be irregular. In some cases we have found the process working in a cycle. The amount and speed of prisonization can be judged only by the behavior and attitudes of the men, and these vary from man to man and in the same man from time to time. It is the excessive number of changes in orientation which the men undergo which makes generalizations about the process so difficult.

In the free communities where the daily life of the inhabitants is not controlled in every detail, some authors have reported a natural gravitation to social levels. The matter of chance still remains a factor, of course, in open society but not nearly so much so as in the prison. For example, two associates in a particular crime may enter the prison at the same time. Let us say that their criminality, their intelligence, and their background are more or less the same. Each is interviewed by the deputy warden and assigned to a job. It so happens that a certain office is in need of a porter. Of the two associates the man whom the deputy warden happens to see first may be assigned to that job while the one he interviews last is assigned to the quarry. The inmate who becomes the office porter associates with but four or five other men, none of whom, let us suppose, are basically prisonized. The new porter adapts himself to them and takes up their interests. His speed of prisonization will be slow and he may never become completely integrated into the prison culture. His associate, on the other hand, works in the quarry and mingles with a hundred men. The odds are three to five that he will become integrated into a primary or semi-primary group. When he is admitted into the competitive and personal relationships of informal group life we can be sure that, in spite of some disassociation, he is becoming prisonized and will approach the complete degree.

Even if the two associates were assigned to the same work unit, differences in the tempo of prisonization might result if one, for example, worked shoulder to shoulder with a "complete solitary man," or a "booster." Whatever else may be said of the tempo of the process, it is always faster when the contacts are primary, providing the persons contacted in a primary way are themselves integrated beyond the minimal into the prison culture. Other factors, of course, influence the speed of integration. The inmate whose wife divorces him may turn for response and recognition to his immediate associates. When the memories of pre-penal experience cease to be satisfying or practically useful, a barrier to prisonization has been removed.

Some men become prisonized to the highest degree, or to a degree approaching it, but then reject their entire orientation and show, neither by behavior nor attitudes, that any sort of integration has taken place. They slip out of group life. They ignore the codes and dogmas and they fall into a reverie or stupor or become "solitary men." After some months or even years of playing this role they may again affiliate with a group and behave as other prisonized inmates do....

For the present it is of some value to recognize that prison life affects the attitudes of men in varying ways depending on the many factors already set forth, and we will give closer attention to the prisonization process now.

Attitudes and Adjustment Reflecting Prisonization

The study of individual cases is probably the most fruitful source of information concerning the relationship between prisonization and the determination of attitudes. In the last chapter brief character sketches were presented of "Seven Daily Workers," in which occupational adjustment was emphasized. As a first step in making specific the meaning of the concept of prisonization, we will take these same seven men and interpret their roles as inmates in terms of the prisonization process. [Note: Only three of the cases are included in this selection.]

1. Guzumback has worked in the quarry for five years. He had been in prison before and when he first came to us he was already "prison wise." His reputation as a good thief preceded him and gave him an entree into personal relationships with the prisoners, but it also made him a marked man with the officials. He was assigned to the quarry and was satisfied to be there for the first year or two. He did not at once "group up" but after a few months he became integrated with three other men and they formed a clique. Guzumback shared his past experiences with these men telling them in detail of his thefts and encounters with the law. In turn he learned of his associates' experiences and in time they all came to think of each other as "right guys." All four of the group hated the officials and the parole board, and despised stool-pigeons. For the "hoosiers" they felt a pitying contempt, but they mingled with other convicts in a friendly and congenial way. They had some strife among themselves but it was always patched up until a day came when X, who was more or less the leader, was suspicioned of talking too much in the wrong places, that is, where stool-pigeons could hear him. Gradually X was excluded and Guzumback became more or less the leader. He gambled occasionally, made some plays for "kids," told endless yarns and continued to express his hate for officialdom. He kept his clothes as clean as he could, "made connections" for food which he cooked in his cell, wore his cap at the correct angle, and conducted himself as a right guy should. He boasted a little, but in a tactful way, and not too frequently. He was sent to solitary a time or two for insolence and when he returned to the gang his prestige rose. His few contacts with persons outside dwindled until he received not more than one letter a month and very infrequent visits.

By the end of the first year Guzumback was prisonized to a high degree. He saw the parole committee and got his set, a fifteen-year final. He became hypomanic [hyperactive] when he learned of the long time the board had given him; he became completely prisonized. He soon started plans to escape but his attempt was discovered and he was sent to solitary for twenty-one days. As the second and third year passed Guzumback remained more or less a primary-group man, but with his unending days of labor in the quarry he became more and more self-centered and less interested in those about him. Finally one of his associates developed a cough which was soon diagnosed as due to tuberculosis. The friend was sent to the hospital and stories leaked out that he was having hemorrhages. This frightened Guzumback. Some inmates say that he was so frightened at the possibility of his contracting the disease that he turned "rat" to his keeper hoping to get transferred to another job. True or false, his prestige ebbed, but Guzumback did not care a great deal. Though frightened about his health he was physically strong and could take care of himself. He fell silent and for days at a time would talk very little. Reverie-plus controlled him. In the early part of his fifth year he was transferred to another quarry gang. There were new faces and he made new friends, eventually becoming integrated into another primary group. He took up his old denouncements of officialdom. He was insolent and threatening to his keeper. Again he gave indication of a high degree of prisonization.

In Guzumback we see the cycle of prisonization. In the later part of his first year and in the two succeeding years he was probably completely prisonized, but in his fourth and early in his fifth year his behavior gave less evidence of prisonization as he became more introverted. He violated the mores for his own gain and was indifferent to his loss of prestige. During the later part of the fifth year, through an assignment to a different work gang he again demonstrated a fairly complete degree of integration.

2. While Guzumback represents one of the higher degrees of prisonization, Penrose, the clerk, represents the least. Penrose entered prison in late middle life, dignified, polite, and outwardly calm. A small bank of which he was cashier was eleven thousand dollars short when the examiner came. In terms of social consequence his crime may have been much worse, for example, than of a man who held up a filling station, but at any rate the officials liked him. Penrose was capable, too. He was a good bookkeeper and was assigned to an office at once. The officers felt sure he would never escape and he was made a trustie [trusty]. He got to wear a white shirt and to eat with the other inmate "politicians." While he had to sleep in a cell, his cellmate was also an older man and both were new to prison. He was friendly with all inmates in a quiet way and listened to their stories with astonishment. His wife wrote him a letter every day and his daughters at least once a week. He heard about stool-pigeons and abnormal sex behavior. He heard typical rumors of graft and that the parole board could be bought but none of these things penetrated deeply into his inner thinking.

Penrose served about two years. When he left he knew but little more of the unseen environment in prison, than when he came. He was first of all not susceptible to acculturation. He was isolated from the penal community proper by his trustie job as a clerk; most of his daily associates were either people like himself, and those who were integrated in the culture did not attempt to include him in their circles. His cellmate was as isolated as he. While he learned about some phases of prison life and found them interesting, they did not seem important as compared with his daughter's baby, his wife's health, and his own fallen prestige in the home town.

3. After a few months in the quarry Durken was assigned to the carpenter shop where he did reasonably good work if the instructions were clear. He

had been married at the age of nineteen and by the time he was twenty-eight, at the time he was incarcerated, he had three children. Before marriage he had done some petty stealing without being detected, but never stole again until a few months before he came to prison. "Christ, almighty," he would say, "a man can't go on and on and on and never have nothing." Durken is extraverted and makes friends easily. After the swallowing-up process, during which he was glum, and after he got a good job in the carpenter shop, he began to blossom out and to find the penitentiary life quite interesting. Due to his job he had considerable freedom of movement and more or less freedom in his selection of associates. He finally fell in with seven or eight other fellows who worked next door to the carpenter shop and spent such time as he could with them. They were a good mob, he said, and were always finding something funny in a bad world. All of his relationships were not jocular, however, and he learned about "rats," "punks," escapes, and stealing methods. He also liked to listen to the real big-shots talk and felt quite flattered when Blatoni once called him by name. Durken never squealed on anyone and had only contempt for anyone who would. He didn't hate the officials or the parole board because they had treated him very well. He gambled occasionally on the ball games, and for the first time in his life he learned why, in some cigar stores he had seen, there was always a big crowd hanging around the back door. He learned that such places were "bookies" and if you were lucky you could make lots of money there, and he kept this in mind. He bet a few sacks of tobacco on the horses and learned how to read the entry lists. Durken has never engaged in abnormal sex behavior, but he has heard quite a bit about it and it has set him wondering sometimes.

We see in Durken an inmate who is prisonized in some respects and not in others. His boyhood delinquencies, his early marriage causing some lack of freedom, his extraverted personality, and similar factors make him susceptible to acculturation. Combining to aid these factors are the type of work given him, the slow but distinct integration into a loosely organized semi-primary group, his aptitude for remembering devices for making easy money, and his amused respect for big-shots, all of which indicates that he is prisonized to some extent. Had it not been for the short time the parole board gave him and the fact that his wife writes frequently telling him in great detail of his children, Durken might have become affiliated in a primary group and more completely prisonized....

Degrees of Prisonization

With the exception of Penrose, the clerk, prisonization has advanced to a fairly high degree in the seven cases just sketched. While complete data are not shown here, success on parole would be considered unlikely for Guzumback, the quarryman, Sam, the laundry worker, Curly, the shop boy, and Blatoni, the gangster. Durken, the carpenter, and Joe, the runner, would seem somewhat better risks on parole, but their adjustment in the free community would have to be considered as questionable. While no one criterion can be an adequate determinant for predicting parole success, the degree of prisonization must always be given the attention of a major determining factor by parole authorities. Other things being equal, the inmate who has become prisonized to advanced degrees would be a poorer risk on parole than others who had not. This would seem so because a high degree of prisonization involves so many "unfavorable" factors. The most important of these, we think, is affiliation with a prison primary group. It has been shown that forty per cent of the inmates belong to primary or semi-primary groups. From studies made quite independently of this present investigation we know that about 17 per cent of the men violate parole. (This figure is the ratio of men violating parole in a selected year considering all men on parole, and is the most common measure of violation.) Who knows but what the 17 per cent of men who become parole violators are the same men who in prison were affiliated with primary groups? It is an interesting speculation and mentioned here simply as hypothesis.

As a further effort to understand the workings of the prisonization process, and to illustrate the relationships existing between its various degrees and the possession of certain attitudes, the considered judgement of ten inmate advisors was obtained. These advisors were given detailed explanation of the prisonization concept, and were then queried, not concerning their own status of prisonization, but of the population in general, and then of their four closest associates. Obviously, data so subjective are difficult to tabulate and analyze, but the impressions and comments of these men are suggestive.

All ten advisors agreed that a process which might well be called "prisonization" existed. They were in essential agreement that the writer's hypothetical schema, showing the lowest and highest degree of prisonization, was as suitable and practical a measuring rod as could be devised but they frankly admitted that their judgements were impressionistic to a large extent.

Concerning the inmate population in general, the ten inmates offer the following judgements in regard to prisonization. First, more of the 2,300 inmates approach the higher degrees of prisonization than the lower. Second, averaging the ten answers to the question, "What per cent of all the inmates are completely prisonized?" the result was 20 per cent, and the respective answers, in terms of per cent, were: 40, 10, 15, 5, 30, 25, 5, 45, 5, 25. The reader can see the wide divergence in opinion, and we can come to no definite conclusion but it is interesting to note that none of the ten advisors considered that a full half of the penitentiary population to be completely prisonized. Third, it was the collective judgement of the advisors that those inmates who became prisonized to high degrees were much more likely to return to crime upon release than those whose prisonization did not advance, but that there were exceptions. Fourth, of the seven factors in the writer's hypothetical schema to show the most extreme degree of prisonization, eight of the ten advisors agreed that the strongest determinant making for a high degree of prisonization was a long sentence, but the judgements on this topic were not clear cut due to the inter-dependence of the six other factors.

When the ten advisors were questioned about their four closest associates in regard to prisonization the following impressions resulted. Of the 40 men under appraisal by the ten advisors, 11 were considered completely prisonized and only 2 were thought to be prisonized in the least degree. Of the remaining 27, the degree of prisonization varied but the judgement of the advisors was to the effect that of the respective men whom they were evaluating, more approached the higher degrees than the lower degrees. Other questions put to the advisors about their four closest associates yielded such a jumble of opinions, that analysis is almost impossible.

From the case sketches illustrating the various ways in which prisonization occurs and from the judgments of the ten inmate advisors, we have enough knowledge, imperfect and inexact as it is, to suggest that most men in penitentiaries have no chance of being salvaged if they become prisonized to any appreciable extent.

The apparent rehabilitating effect which prison life has on some men occurs in spite of the harmful influences of the prison culture. Among the writer's wide acquaintanceship with hundreds of inmates those who were improved or rehabilitated were men who, in the first place, should never have been committed to prison at all, and who, in the second place, were engulfed by the culture, or prisonized, in only the slightest degree. While sometimes the so-called real criminals are rehabilitated, the occasions are so rare that the total effect is negligible. Such "rehabilitation" as occurs with the actual criminals refers to the type of "treatment" which keeps them in prison until they reach such an age that they no longer have sufficient physical nor mental vigor to commit further crimes. In a cold, objective sense this means of "rehabilitation" has some societal utility, but, at the same time if other methods had been used the waste of human resources might have been avoided and the dignity of human personalities maintained.

To a few men the pressure and unpleasantness of prison life is such a shock that they are literally "scared out of" further adventures in crime and thus become prisonized to a lesser degree. The same fright phenomena are frequently found in persons who at one time became highly prisonized but who later rejected the influences of the prison culture and remained at a low level of prisonization. "I don't want any part of it," such men say, "this is the low spot in my life and I'm all done with it—I'm all washed up." Their sincerity is demonstrated by their behavior as shown when they slip out of group life, avoid close contacts with other men, take up new studies, and lay plans for a legitimate life when released....

Conclusion: Prisons and Society

We have looked into the unseen environment in the penal community. We have weighed data impartially and with objectivity. Where data were inconclusive, we have not hesitated to say how little understood are some of the processes and problems. We conclude our studies by presenting some observations and comments, comments which are not based on specific data, but which are intended to reflect one investigator's speculation on the problem of prison as related to the totality of society....

In twelve chapters we have painted a sorry picture of the prison community. It is what it is, because of what it has been in the past. It is what it is because of the influences which have played upon the men who make it up. It has been a commonplace to say that prisons are behind the times, decadent, and that they have not kept step with advances on other frontiers. But we wonder if this is actually true. Now, in 1940, international murders are raging on two continents. A brown shirted fanatic is menacing the peace of the world! Mighty nations build mighty guns. Diplomacy among nations is largely the same class conscious maneuvering it always has been. In our own country there is scarcity in the face of plenty; there is unemployment by millions; there is strife and conflict. Can we say that the prisons are far behind the times when conditions in more important world sectors, are what they are? Probably not. In fact some few prisons are ahead of the times when we give attention to the present plight of the world. This does not mean that our total system of criminal justice is not decadent, to be sure, and its faults and the faulty assumptions on which it is based have been well set forth.[4] The point we are attempting to make is that the better prisons with their libraries, vocational training, payment for labor and so on, are, even though a part of a decadent system of criminal justice, in and of themselves, no less progressive than the rest of a disorganized world. For example, the prejudice against race, so prominent in some nations, exists in only the mildest form in most of our prisons. Freedom of speech, though restricted in prison, is curtailed even more so in some supposedly free countries. If graft and swindle exist in some criminal agencies, so do they also exist in many cities. The prisons do not let their men go hungry; they do not let disease go unchecked as many free communities do. It is in this sense, we say, that the prisons are no more decadent than other institutions in society....

Within the framework of the present developing social organization, improvement can be made. The principles as shown in resolutions developed through many years by the American Prison Association, can be applied to our prisons in greater or less degree with beneficial results. As for the more pressing aspects of the criminal problem, let every dollar spent for improvement of prisons, be increased three fold for the development of Probation systems, and increased five fold for study and an integrated service in the communities from which the heavy majority of our inmates come.

Footnotes

1. Pauline V. Young. *Interviewing in Social Work*, McGraw-Hill Book Co., New York, 1937, pp. 282–292. See also, Saul D. Alinsky, *A Sociological Technique in Clinical Criminology*, Proceedings of the Sixty-Fourth Annual Congress of the American Prison Association, 1934.
2. Robert E. Park and Herbert A. Miller. *Old World Traits Transplanted,* Harper and Brothers, New York, 1921, p. 25.
3. E. T. Hiller, *op. cit.,* pp. 70, 71. [*The Strike,* University of Chicago Press, Chicago, 1928.]
4. Frank Tannenbaum, *op. cit.,* pp. 474–478. [*Crime and the Community*, Ginn and Co., New York, 1938.]

Index